ADAM, NOAH, ABRAHAM

Genesis Volume One

ADAM, NOAH, ABRAHAM

Father, Son, Spirit

Rex Frost

Copyright © 2011, 2017 by Rex K. Frost.
All rights reserved. Fair use copyright law will be respected.
Genesis two-volume edition.

Published in the United States by **Josiah ben David:**

JOSIAH BEN DAVID
1111 JOHN ST
BROOKVILLE IN 47012-1041

http://www.josiahbendavid.com/

Editorial comments may be directed to admin@josiahbendavid.com. Theological questions may be directed to info@rexfrost.com.

Bible verses are taken from the King James Version standard English text printed by Holman Bible Publishers (originally published in 1611, with major editorial tuning completed by 1769). The King James Bible text is in the public domain.

Biblical word studies are derived from the *Brown-Driver-Briggs Hebrew and English Lexicon* (reprinted from the 1906 edition published by Houghton, Mifflin & Company), *Thayer's Greek-English Lexicon of the New Testament* (reprinted from the 1896 fourth edition published by T&T Clark), and *Strong's Exhaustive Concordance of the Bible . . . with . . . Brief Dictionaries of the Hebrew and Greek Words* (copyrighted 1890 by James Strong, thirty-eighth printing). These original source materials are also in the public domain.

Brief quotations from diverse commentaries and other source materials are footnoted, with annotations, for the purpose of critically analyzing the major hermeneutical traditions. All such materials are used in accordance with fair use copyright law and well within the widely accepted guidelines developed by the University of Chicago Press.

ISBN-13: 978-0-9834040-1-9
ISBN-10: 0-9834040-1-1

The title page illustration is a juxtaposition taken from the Bible moralisée Codex Vindobonensis 2554. The cover design and interior headers show details adapted from the 1611 King James Bible. The end page, connected with the author biographical sketch, shows a Fibonacci spiral. All employed images are in the public domain.

The JbD Publishing House medallion is taken from *Promptuarii iconum insigniorum* by Guillaume Rouille, also in the public domain.

All proceeds from the original purchase price of this book are donated to Christian charities and missions. Visit RexFrost.com for more information.

IN MEMORY OF the unnamed wife of Noah, who was with Noah in the antediluvian world, went with him into the ark, and became the new Eve, the new mother of all humanity. And so did Noah's wife silently testify to the rebirth through the baptism in the floodwaters. The subtlety of her presence in the narrative is a reflection of the ethereal nature of the Holy Spirit.

ΑΩ

PREFACE

This work is a study of the first twenty-five chapters of the book of Genesis. The focus is the Biblical text itself, expanded by concordance and lexicon studies. The reading of the Old Testament text is Christological, guided by New Testament precedents. The Old and New Testaments together are understood to be a coherent and perfect whole inspired by the one Holy Spirit, the person of God the Spirit. The distinguishing characteristic of this study is an emphasis on elements, patterns, and motifs, not merely as literary elements, but as unique representations of the Trinity. Additionally, a sampling of Rabbinic, Orthodox, Roman Catholic, Protestant, and so forth, and also literary commentaries is surveyed in the footnotes in order to compare and contrast the present work with the ancillary context established by the many and varied traditional and prevalent schools of thought.

The intended audience is the believer who is already familiar with at least the New Testament. The person seeking a first understanding of Christianity is advised not to start with this commentary but rather to go directly to the New Testament itself, in which is found the clearest call of the faithful to life and truth, namely, the life of Jesus Christ followed by the acts of his followers. The child of God should feel a kinship with Christ when confronted with his good news, even if the nature of the kinship at first seems impossible (Matt 19:26). After the Gospels ("Good News") and the Acts of the Apostles, one should next proceed through the Epistles ("Letters") for the most explicit explanation of the meaning of the incarnation. The faithful should guard against substituting any popular-culture beliefs or even church traditions for an honest and humble reading of the Holy Scriptures.

The New Testament is the correct focus of Christian study, but ultimately the Bible must be read from cover to cover because the meaning of Christ is immersed, baptized, in the precepts of the Old Testament. Jesus Christ presents himself as the fulfillment of the law and the prophets, and thus to understand the meaning of the incarnation, the believer necessarily seeks a fluency in the Old Testament in general and the Covenant of Law in particular (Matt 5:17). Christ quoted the law of Moses each time he was tempted in the wilderness, whereby the believer now tempted in the world, in imitation of Christ, naturally seeks to understand, again in imitation of Christ, the law and the prophets of the law (Matt 4:1–11). One should be aware, however, that a palpable tension between law and grace is manifested in the contrast between the Old and New

PREFACE

Testaments ("Covenants"). The carnal desire to dismiss the realities of law and justice must be resisted since the resolution of the tension between justice and mercy is our vision of God and likewise our way in the will of God, namely, our redemption in Christ. Several readings of the Bible in its entirety may be necessary to appreciate this fundamental paradox, but the child of God should feel impelled to the Word (John 10:27). The tension between law and grace is the universal conflict between flesh and spirit that is ultimately resolved on the cross and only on the cross (Mark 10:21).

The author finally wishes to express his thankfulness for the selfless support and painstaking proofreading of his wife, Jennifer, and mother, Marlene. And for the abiding reader, a final word of counsel is to learn the lay of the land before delving into the focused analyses of local contexts. Read through the overview materials first, beginning with the introduction, prologue, and afterword. Next read together as a group the introduction and conclusion sections from each of the six main commentary chapters, followed only then by the bodies of the six commentary chapters. The epilogue can be read last of all since it is principally forward looking.

Rex Frost
June 21, 2011

PROLOGUE

The original six days of creation recorded in the first chapter of the book of Genesis foreshadows the totality of the six millennia of creation, spanning the first histories of the book of Genesis through the final apocalyptic visions of the book of Revelation. Foremost, a *serial*, or simple repeating, 1-2-3 pattern is evident in both the six days and also the six millennia. In the original creation account, days 1, 2, and 3 can be compared, respectively, to days 4, 5, and 6. In the Biblical timeline—that is, the historical timeline following the Messianic bloodline—counting from the creation of Adam, millennia 1, 2, and 3 can be compared, respectively, to millennia 4, 5, and 6. The images demarcating the repeating 1-2-3 pattern in the six days parallel corresponding images demarcating the repeating 1-2-3 pattern in the six millennia. These primal 1-2-3 images are, respectively, light, water, and life. The extreme brevity of the prologue, which is related by the creation account in the first chapter of Genesis, reflects the essential nature of prophecy being a mere foreshadowing of the fullness of a reality yet to be experienced.[1]

The first and fourth days of creation are both marked by the sign of light. The first light, the light of the first day, is the primordial light of creation heralding the first millennium and, thereby, also heralding each subsequent millennium, that is, creation as a whole.[2] The second light, the light of the fourth day, represents the promised light of redemption, a light of promise first announced in the opening of the fourth millennium by the kingship of David and finally realized at the end of the fourth millennium in the kingship manifested perfectly in the birth of Jesus Christ. The progression of the second light is like that of the rising sun, wherein David is the antecedent of Christ just as the night is prelude to the day. The first day is the light of the Father, the creator, while the fourth day is the light of the Son, the redeemer. The light of the first day is fulfilled in the light of the fourth day just as the Son proceeds from the Father as the visible image of the Father (Col 1:15). The first and second lights, the lights of creation and redemption, point to the third light, the light of the Holy Spirit, the light of sanctification, to be fully revealed in the resurrection of the dead in the last days. The image of light being shared between the Father and the Son reflects the unity of the Holy Spirit. The

---

[1] See Sarna's six days of creation (Sarna 4; Gen 1:1–2:3).
[2] The promised new creation will likewise have no need of the sun or moon, Rev 21:23.

PROLOGUE

singular light of the first day is the oneness of God, while the two lights of the fourth day, the sun and the moon, are the twofold natures of the one Son, being true God and true man. The stars are specifically the angelic host but generally all the faithful.[3]

The second and fifth days are both marked by the sign of water. The division of the waters under the firmament from the waters above the firmament on the second day foreshadows the separation of the sons of God from the daughters of men by the floodwaters in the second millennium (Gen 6:1–7). The separation of the sons of God and the daughters of men is seen in the floodwaters finally receding, at least nominally, back from whence they came, retreating behind the windows, or floodgates, above and the fountains below (Gen 7:11). The bringing forth of fish into the waters and fowl into the open firmament on the fifth day foreshadows, respectively, the call of Jews and Gentiles in the fifth millennium. Water is a symbol of flesh and likewise the law that governs flesh, whereby fish dwelling in the waters represents the natural body under the law, generally Adam, or mankind, under natural law but specifically the Israelites under Moses. The firmament, or sky, is a symbol of spirit and likewise the grace that governs spirit, whereby fowl flying above the earth, toward the waters above the firmament, represents the spiritual, or glorified, body in grace, generally the visible church but specifically the resurrected faithful in the ascendant Body of Christ.[4] The call of the second millennium to repentance from profaning the name of God, a call signified by the wooden ark, foreshadows the call of the fifth millennium to repentance from profaning the person of Christ, a call signified by the wooden cross (Gen 4:26). The baptism in the floodwaters of the second millennium foreshadows the baptism in water of the fifth millennium (1 Pet 3:20–21). The bringing forth of life into the waters and above the earth on the fifth day is a fulfillment of the separation of the waters on the second day just as the call to repentance in the fifth millennium is a fulfillment of the call to repentance in the second millennium. The first water of creation followed by the second water of repentance points to the third and final water of redemption (Rev 22:17).

---

[3] The names *Father*, *Son*, and *Spirit* represent not only Trinitarian relationships within the Godhead but also Trinitarian relationships and attributes with respect to creation and new creation. The movements of God in the acts of creation, redemption, and sanctification—identified, respectively, with the Father, Son, and Spirit—are all three movements of creation and, thereby, testify to the oneness of God, the fullness of divinity, existing in each person of the Trinity. Nevertheless, the Father is uniquely the father, or spiritual progenitor, of creation. The Son is uniquely our redeemer as the one who suffered and died in the flesh for our sins. And the Holy Spirit is uniquely our sanctifier through the agency of indwelling the faithful in the Body of Christ.

[4] The distinction between the spiritual, or glorified, resurrection body and the present natural body is not based on corporeality, for both the spiritual and natural bodies are true physical bodies; rather, the distinction is based on nature, that is, the sinful nature of the natural body being governed by the law of flesh in contrast to the glorified nature of the spiritual body being governed in the grace of the Holy Spirit.

PROLOGUE

The third and sixth days are both marked by the sign of life. The first sign of life on the third day in the form of simple plant life foreshadows the preservation of life formally established in the third millennium in the form of simple obedience to the law. The sign of life in the form of simple plant life, which is not conscious and therefore not fully alive, foreshadows the preservation of life in the form of simple obedience to the law, which is not complete and therefore does not yield eternal life (Gal 3:21). The formal law begins with the sign of circumcision in the flesh given to Abraham in the beginning of the third millennium (Gen 17:10) and is codified with the tables (tablets) of stone given to Moses in the midst of the third millennium (Exod 24:12). The connection between the law and life is clear in the call to obey the law and live long in the land (Deut 4:40). The first appearance of dry land on the third day is the herald of life and foreshadows the first promise of an eternal inheritance of the promised land in the third millennium (Gen 12:7). The promise of the land in the third millennium from the formation of Adam points, in turn, to the resurrection of the body in the third millennium from the birth of Christ. The bringing forth of the higher forms of life and finally man in the very image of God, concluding the work of the six days of creation, prefigures our promised rebirth in the very Body of Christ as being the culmination of the six millennia of creation. The simple plant life of the third day foreshadows the final revelation of the higher forms of life of the sixth day just as the law foreshadows grace just as the natural body foreshadows the spiritual, or glorified, resurrection body. The original life proceeding from God in the act of creation followed by the second life proceeding from God in the call to obedience under the law points to the third and final life that proceeds from God by grace through faith.

1	2	3	4	5	6
LIGHT	WATER	LIFE	LIGHT	WATER	LIFE
1	2	3	1	2	3

The Lord God finally resting on the seventh day prefigures the foretold thousand-year kingdom of Jesus Christ in the seventh millennium (Rev 20:6). The parallel between days and millennia evident in the comparison between the original creation account and the Biblical timeline, or overall historical timeline, testifies to the universal will of God being manifest on all levels of reality. One day is with the Lord as a thousand years, and a thousand years as one day (2 Pet 3:8). The three serial images of light, water, and life demarcating the 1-2-3 pattern of creation signify, respectively, the promise of God, the death and resurrection of the Son, and the sanctification of the faithful by the Holy Spirit. The threefold symbols light, water, and life thereby reflect the triune God the Father, God the Son, and God the Holy Spirit. The promise of the Father, the spiritual progenitor of all creation, is implicit in the original consummation of creation, specifically as marked by the light of God appearing in the darkness. Our participation in the death and resurrection of the Son is represented by the baptism in water, that is, the baptism of repentance while still in the flesh. Our sanctification by the Holy Spirit is our eternal life by the agency of the

PROLOGUE

indwelling Holy Spirit received only by grace through faith, the fullness of which will not be revealed until the last days in the resurrection of the body. The repetition of threefold images of the Godhead, all pointing to the last days, foreshadows the fulfillment of the Trinity in the culmination of creation, namely, the Father receiving the faithful in the Son through the power of the Holy Spirit. The preordained will of God evident in the primordial creation account reflects the inexorable nature of the love of God for his children. The counsel of God shall stand and he will do all his pleasure, declaring the end from the beginning, from ancient times the things that are not yet done (Isa 46:10).[5]

1	2	3
LIGHT	WATER	LIFE
PROMISE	REPENTANCE	REDEMPTION
GOD THE FATHER	GOD THE SON	GOD THE HOLY SPIRIT

The 1-2-3-4-5-6-7 days of creation and likewise the 1-2-3-4-5-6-7 millennia of the Biblical timeline also show a *chiastic*, or mirrored, structure A-B-C-D-C'-B'-A' with day 4 and the corresponding millennium 4 as the pivot. The A, B, and C positions reflect, respectively, the A', B', and C' positions, while the pivotal D position is unique. Days 1 and 7 are both marked by the sign of peace. Day 1 is the peace of God inherent in the certainty of the promise of God as represented by the very act of creation, while day 7 is the peace of God, resting after the act of creation, in assurance of the inevitable fulfillment of the promise embodied by creation. The peace of the first millennium is the preservation of Adam, while the peace of the seventh millennium is the promised end of all suffering. Days 2 and 6 are both marked by the sign of division. Day 2 is the division of the waters, representing the distinction between earth and heaven, while day 6 is the division of dominions, representing the distinction between natural creation and man formed in the very image of God. The division of the second millennium is the Flood, while the division of the sixth millennium is the schism of the visible church. Days 3 and 5 are both marked by the sign of life. Day 3 is the first sign of life, represented by simple plant life, while day 5 is the first sign of life animated by blood, represented by animal life. The life of the third millennium is the law, while the life of the fifth millennium is the fulfillment of the law in Christ.

The pivotal fourth day is the separation of day and night, representing the separation of good and evil, a governance of day and night appointed on the fourth day, which points to the establishment of the kingdom in the fourth

---

[5] If the rest and peace of God on day 7 is identified with the light of God marking the millennial reign, also on day 7, Rev 21:23, and day 4 is understood to be a type of the millennial kingdom of Christ, then the serial 1-2-3, 1-2-3 six-day pattern can be viewed alternatively as an overlapping 1-2-3-4, 1-2-3-4 seven-day pattern with day 4 being simultaneously the first 4-position and the second 1-position. But this alternative organization is complementary, not technically unique, since the repeating 1-2-3, 1-2-3 core pattern remains unchanged.

PROLOGUE

millennium, a kingdom first announced by David but ultimately revealed in the birth of Jesus Christ, the Son of David (Matt 22:42–45). The fourth day being the pivot represents the central importance of the separation of good and evil as embodied by the establishment of the kingdom of God. The mirroring of the threefold ABC | C'B'A' chiastic pattern of peace, division, and life represents the threefold promise, death, and rebirth proclaimed by the three persons of the Trinity. Whether looking forward or backward, the Trinity points to the formation of the kingdom as being the very apex of the one will of the one Godhead. The kingdom would not be explicitly announced either before or after the time of the present world but rather in the very midst of it, which itself reflects the incarnation of God as a true man.[6]

1	2	3	4	5	6	7
				LIFE	DIVISION	PEACE
				∧	∧	∧
A	B	C	D	C'	B'	A'
∨	∨	∨				
PEACE	DIVISION	LIFE				

The 1-2-3-4-5-6-7 days of creation and likewise the 1-2-3-4-5-6-7 millennia of the Biblical timeline show yet a third pattern type, a *staircase* 1-2-3, 1-2-3, 1-2-3 pattern with the first 3-position overlapping the second 1-position, and the second 3-position overlapping the third 1-position. The core 1-2-3 pattern again reflects the Trinity, respectively, the promise of the Father, the death and resurrection of the Son, and the sanctification of the faithful by the Holy Spirit. Days 1, 3, 5 and the corresponding millennia are all three 1-positions in the repeating staircase pattern, with all three marked by the sign of promise as embodied by creation, specifically the creation of life. The first day and likewise the first millennium mark the original act of creation as the primordial manifestation of the promise of life, the original movement of the Spirit that is the breath of life (Gen 1:2). The third day is the first sign of life, in the form of simple plant life, while the third millennium is the promise of life through simple obedience to the first covenant, the Covenant of Law. The fifth day is the first manifestation of life animated by blood, while the fifth millennium is the first revelation of eternal life through the blood of Jesus Christ.

Days 2, 4, and 6 and the corresponding millennia are all three 2-positions in the repeating staircase pattern, with all three marked by the sign of division. The second day is the division of the waters below and above the firmament, while

---

[6] "The number three had obvious importance to Christians in representing the triune nature of God . . . . In most ancient cultures, including ancient Jewish culture, the number four was a universal symbol (an archetype) representing the earth. . . . The sum of three and four [seven] represents the union of the divine and holy one with earth and nature" (Haggith 124–26). Further, the seven millennia of creation, viewed as the four millennia before the cross plus the three millennia after the cross, reflect the union of law and grace as embodied by Christ, but the representation 7 = 4+3 does not preclude other simultaneous or parallel significations, particularly since numbers inherently allow multiple organizations.

PROLOGUE

the second millennium is the division of the floodwaters. The fourth day is the division of night and day, while the fourth millennium is the separation of the one kingdom of Israel from all the other kingdoms of the world. The sixth day is the division between lower creation and man formed in the very image of God, while the sixth millennium is the separation of the faithless from the faithful, represented by the schism of the visible church. Each division reflects the distinction between flesh and spirit, between death and life, which is ultimately embodied by the death and resurrection of the Son.

Days 3, 5, and 7 and the corresponding millennia are all three 3-positions in the repeating staircase pattern, with all three marked by the sign of the fulfillment of the promise of life. The third day is the first fulfillment of the promise of life as represented by simple plant life, while the third millennium is the fulfillment of the promise of the preservation of life under the law. The fifth day is the fulfillment of the promise of life as represented by life animated by blood, while the fifth millennium is the fulfillment of the promise of life as embodied by the blood of Christ. The seventh day is the fulfillment of the promise of life as represented by the rest and peace of the Sabbath, while the seventh millennium is the fulfillment of the promise of life as represented by the rest and peace of the foretold millennial kingdom. The 1-2-3, 1-2-3, 1-2-3 repeating staircase pattern leads inexorably, like a stairway, to the last days and the fulfillment of our promised inheritance in the peace of God.[7]

1	2	3	4	5	6	7
LIGHT	WATER	LIFE	LIGHT	WATER	LIFE	REST
				1	2	3
				FIRST SIGN OF LIFE BLOOD	DIVISION OF DOMINION	PROMISE OF LIFE FULFILLED
		1	2	3		
		FIRST SIGN OF (NEW) LIFE	DIVISION OF DAY & NIGHT	PROMISE OF LIFE FULFILLED		
1	2	3				
FIRST ACT OF CREATION	DIVISION OF THE WATERS	PROMISE OF LIFE FULFILLED				

The three organizational patterns *serial*, *chiastic*, and *staircase*, evident in the accounting of creation, themselves reflect the triune Father, Son, and Holy Spirit. The first pattern, the relatively simple serial, or repeating, pattern, which focuses on the first six days of creation, represents an emphasis on creation and, therefore, an emphasis on God the Father, from whom creation proceeds like an offspring. The emphasis on original creation, also the relative simplicity of the serial pattern, represents a kind of infancy. The second pattern, the chiastic, or mirrored, pattern, which focuses on the fourth day, represents the pivotal

---

[7] " '... The world will endure six thousand years—two thousand years in chaos, two thousand with Torah, and two thousand years will be the days of the Messiah' [*Sanhedrin*]" (Cohen, *Rabbinic Sages* 356). Surely, since the time of the first Adam, at least a remnant has always anticipated the Sabbath millennium.

PROLOGUE

importance of the incarnation of God the Son, as manifested in the fourth millennium from Adam. This is the essential epiphany of puberty, or the age of accountability, that is the recognition of the face of God. The third pattern, the repeating and overlapping staircase pattern, which points inexorably to the fulfillment of the promise of life in the last days, represents an emphasis on God the Holy Spirit and, therefore, the movement of the Spirit. The Spirit of God, God the Spirit, is the original breath of life animating natural man and, therein, pointing to the fullness of the indwelling Holy Spirit, which will animate the promised new man. This is like a child growing into maturity. All three patterns showing the same fundamental 1-2-3 elements testifies to the one will of the three persons of the Trinity that is the essential oneness of God. The layering of simultaneous patterns, all reflecting the Trinity in creation, reflects the undeniable and unassailable nature of the will of God for the sanctification of the faithful. The increasing complexity of basic elements and patterns building successively more complicated patterns and motifs reflects the character of progressive revelation, moving from an emphasis on the revelation of the one God to the incarnation of the one Son to the promise of the indwelling of the one Holy Spirit. The analogy between the maturation of the individual and the overarching progressive revelation of God is itself a testimony that man is truly made in the very image of God.[8]

---

[8] "... 'The Old Testament proclaimed the Father clearly, but the Son more obscurely. The New Testament revealed the Son and gave us a glimpse of the divinity of the Spirit. Now the Spirit dwells among us and grants us a clearer vision of himself....' [Gregory of Nazianzus, *Orations*]" (Rom. Catholic Church, *Catechism* 196–97). God the Father, God the Son, God the Holy Spirit. First, second, third.

TABLE OF CONTENTS

PREFACE vii

PROLOGUE ix

INTRODUCTION xviii

PART I: ADAM

CHAPTER 1: ADAM AND EVE 3
    THE GARDEN OF EDEN 1:1–2:15 4
    THE FIRST LAW 2:16–17 12
    MALE AND FEMALE 2:18–25 15
    NAKED 3:1–13 21
    THREE CURSES 3:14–19 27
    EXILE 3:20–24 36

CHAPTER 2: CAIN, ABEL, SETH 47
    FIRSTBORN 4:1 48
    TWO SONS 4:2 51
    TWO SACRIFICES 4:3–9 53
    JUDGMENT 4:10–24 58
    NEW LIFE 4:25–26 65

PART II: NOAH

CHAPTER 3: NOAH 75
    PROMISE 5:1–32 76
    JUSTICE AND MERCY 6:1–10 80
    THE ARK 6:11–7:6 88
    RENEWAL 7:7–8:14 96
    COVENANT 8:15–9:17 106

CHAPTER 4: HAM, SHEM, JAPHETH 125

- The Vineyard 9:18–21 126
- Nakedness 9:22–23 129
- Curse and Blessing 9:24–29 131
- Three Sons 10:1–32 133
- Oneness 11:1–2 137
- The Name 11:3–4 139
- Son of Man 11:5–6 143
- Son of God 11:7–8 146
- Babel 11:9–25 148

PART III: ABRAHAM

CHAPTER 5: ABRAHAM AND SARAH 157

- The Call 11:26–12:5 158
- Two Altars 12:6–8 166
- Famine 12:9–13:4 169
- Division 13:5–13:17 173
- Melchizedek 13:18–14:24 177
- Firstborn 15:1–17:27 186
- Mystery 18:1–19:38 203
- Abimelech 20:1–18 220

CHAPTER 6: ISHMAEL, ISAAC, KETURAH'S SONS 232

- Promise 21:1–21 233
- Two Treaties 21:22–34 245
- Blood Sacrifice 22:1–24 250
- The Death of Sarah 23:1–20 260
- The Eldest Servant 24:1–9 264
- The Call of the Bride 24:10–67 268
- East Country 25:1–11 280
- Twelve Princes 25:12–18 284

AFTERWORD 293

EPILOGUE 296

SELECTED BIBLIOGRAPHY 299

AUTHOR 307

INTRODUCTION

This commentary is organized around the King James Version standard English text, with Biblical text and commentary text alternating in the minimum practical units that allow the development of complete thoughts. Strong's numbers are used to connect the Biblical text to word studies in the commentary text. Chapter introductions preview key chapter images, while chapter conclusions set the major chapter types and themes in the broader Biblical context of progressive revelation. Outlines of key chapter images and verse-by-verse interpretations follow each chapter conclusion. Additionally, a sampling of Rabbinic, Orthodox, Roman Catholic, Protestant, and so forth, and also literary commentaries is surveyed in the footnotes. The precedents and anti-precedents detailed in the footnotes provide a critical comparison with traditional and prevalent worldviews.

KING JAMES VERSION (1611)

Bible excerpts are taken from the King James Version standard English text, specifically the 2014 text printed by Holman Bible Publishers, which is, as is normally the case with modern King James Bibles, tantamount to the 1769 edition completed under Benjamin Blayney. The 1769 edition does not, however, represent a new translation or a new version compared with the original 1611 text, for the majority of the differences are minor matters of spelling, that is, matters of presentation, not actual content.[1]

Why the King James Bible? The historical predominance of the King James Version is derived from a convergence of form and function. The Bible of the Pilgrims on the *Mayflower* was almost exclusively the Geneva Bible, but this notably Calvinist Bible would ultimately be displaced by the King James Version, which itself is an ironic testimony to the transcendent nature of the King James Bible, considering the original Pilgrims were Separatists fleeing the Jacobean crown and church, both closely identified with the so-called Authorized Version.[2] The King James Version is characterized by a sublime union of the plain and the majestic, which reflects the surprising juxtaposition of Puritan and Episcopal interests within the King James translation

---

[1] Norton 3, 113–14.
[2] Nicolson 228–30.

INTRODUCTION

committees.³ The King James Version embodies the intensity of the original Hebrew and Greek by embracing the literary ambiguities intended by the original inspired writers.⁴ The essential ambiguity of the text reflects, not an uncertainty or arbitrariness of meaning, but rather the fundamental universality of the image of the Lord God being manifest, necessarily, on all levels of reality. The Scriptures are characterized by levels of meaning just as everything in life is characterized by levels of meaning.⁵ Additionally, the King James Version has been usefully organized in *Strong's Exhaustive Concordance*, an indexing expedited, not coincidentally, by the approximately word-for-word quality of the King James translation.⁶

The King James Version should not, however, be considered as exactly identical with the *textus receptus*, or "received text." Technically, the term *textus receptus* refers to the traditional Greek text and corresponding manuscripts underlying the King James New Testament and only those specific Greek source materials, but neither does this relate an appropriate worldview given the supernatural significance of receiving the written Word. A more complete understanding of the received text would be the entire inspired corpus of Biblical texts received as a unified whole from God, not simply in the original Hebrew and Greek, but in all languages throughout all creation, in all tongues, or translations.⁷ Additionally, the King James Version is written in a form of

---

³ "The book [KJV] they created was consciously poised in its rhetoric between vigour and elegance, plainness and power. . . . It aimed to step beyond those categories [related to Puritans and Episcopalians] to embrace the universality of its subject" (Nicolson xii). The paradoxical juxtaposition of vigor and elegance, likewise plainness and power, that characterizes the coming together of the KJV, reflects the dichotomy of flesh and spirit, likewise law and grace, characterizing all creation.

⁴ The central but very subtle method of the King James translators was the selection of words not for their crispness of meaning but for their nuanced facets. The Tyndale Bible and the Geneva Bible translations had previously striven for a rigid clarity, while the King James translation intentionally sought a beautiful kind of shimmering connotation, which would allow more than one meaning of the text, not bound to any one system of doctrinal thought (Nicolson 77–78). Even secular scholars have a tendency to speak of the King James Bible in otherworldly terms.

⁵ "Poetry is as universal as language and almost as ancient. . . . Initially, poetry might be defined as a kind of language that says *more* and says it *more intensely* than does ordinary language" (Perrine 553). The Word is the primordial poetry of creation.

⁶ "Tyndale was indebted to Luther's translation, which to a large extent he copied, and this first modern English version [Tyndale Bible] is an extremely Protestant one, accessible, useful, clarifying, less interested in the grandeur of its music than the light it brings. . . . The Geneva Bible, a far more sophisticated and professional job, performed by a small team of English Calvinists in Geneva in the late 1550s, had taken Tyndale's bare bones and made something a little more fluent of them: . . ." (Nicolson 193). The progression of the written Word from the original languages into all languages reflects the progressive revelation of God, likewise creation simultaneously being formed in and being conformed to the image of God.

⁷ "[L]inguistic hierarchy is also one of the sources of the King James style. This English is there to serve the original not to replace it. It speaks in its master's voice and is not the English you would have heard on the street, then or ever. It took up its life in a new

archaic English, and thus it is completely normal to have other translations, English or otherwise, available to serve as a form of commentary. And comparative translations would actually be valuable tools for bringing out nuanced and layered meanings even if the King James Version did exist in modern English. The Amplified Bible, for example, is more accessible in modern English, and it also inserts expanded definitions and clarifications, striving to convey a more holistic expression of the underlying languages. The New International Version, as another example, purposefully deviates from a word-for-word translation in an attempt to compensate for differences in thought patterns, syntax, and so forth.[8]

The written Word was always intended to exist in multiple translations and, finally, to be translated into all languages. The providential progression of the Word is evident in the apostles speaking in all tongues on the first Pentecost following the ascension of Jesus Christ (Acts 2:4) and also in the call to take the Gospel unto all nations and therefore into all languages (Matt 28:18–20). And the absolute necessity of this reality is affirmed in the original confounding of languages at the tower of Babel (Gen 11:9). The differences between different extant manuscripts and also different translations are grossly exaggerated by religious schismatics and academic atheists in accordance with their personal biases and agendas. The common statement in this area, attributed to Jerome, is that there are almost as many versions of the Gospels as there are manuscripts; but any such sentiment expressed by Jerome should be attributed to the normal hyperbole of an editor fixated on the minutiae of his endeavor, since the majority of the differences between Gospel manuscripts were no doubt very minor.[9] The simple truth is that the Jewish, Orthodox, Roman Catholic, and Protestant translations are equivalent for all practical purposes. And for anyone who has a heart to perceive, this simple fact alone is startling evidence of the providential movement of God in the world. The largest difference between

---

and distinct dimension of linguistic space, somewhere between English and Greek (or, for the Old Testament, between English and Hebrew). These scholars were not pulling the language of the scriptures into the English they knew and used at home. The words of the King James Bible are just as much English pushed towards the condition of a foreign language as a foreign language translated into English. It was, in other words, more important to make English godly than to make the words of God into the sort of prose that any Englishmen would have written, and that secretarial relationship to the original languages of the scriptures shaped the translation" (Nicolson 210–11). The unique nature of the King James Bible testifies to its unique authority.

[8] A word of caution, particularly when referencing modern Bible versions, is that humanist scholarship has introduced into different translations various, often-subtle Alexandrian corruptions as well as anti-supernatural biases. But it should also be understood that all known extant Bible manuscripts do show some deviations from the overall pure stream of transmission. So where exactly is the one true Bible? The Holy Bible is simultaneously everywhere and nowhere just as the Holy Spirit is simultaneously everywhere and nowhere, visible and invisible, leading the faithful while never violating freewill. The written Word of God is conceived of and inspired by the Holy Spirit just as the incarnate Word is conceived of and guided by the Holy Spirit.

[9] De Hamel 15.

INTRODUCTION

religious groups concerning the sacred texts is, by far, the canon itself and not translations or the texts per se. And disagreements over the canon are primarily issues of worldview, not questions of textual corruption.[10]

Since the time of the Enlightenment, Biblical scholarship has become dominated by systems of literary criticism, or analysis, commonly termed the historical-critical method or historical criticism, presupposing that the Biblical texts are innately inconsistent, historically inaccurate, and have been additionally corrupted over time by copying errors and translating errors as well as blatant manipulations.[11] Nevertheless, the most extreme academic positions—asserting, for example, that Biblical personages and places never existed—have become increasingly disputed by archaeology and also by manuscript evidence.[12] And some modern scholarship is also admitting a purposeful structure in the Scriptures, though it is being incorrectly attributed to hypothetical redactors manipulating the texts.[13] And although the antiquity, or theoretical antiquity, of a discovered manuscript in no way ensures its authenticity, a survey of modern scholarship further testifies that the received Biblical texts are, even in the eyes of the world, extremely accurate compared with the oldest extant copies and absolutely superior compared with extra-Biblical texts of similar antiquity.[14] And yet despite the highly speculative nature of historical criticism, also despite its many failures, increasing numbers of churches and seminaries have explicitly or implicitly accepted the secular dogma that the Scriptures are hopelessly corrupted and, by implication, cannot be inerrant, or divinely inspired, at least not in their modern forms.[15] Legitimate lexicon and translation questions do exist, but the faithful should know that the technical questions concerning the received text are completely insignificant compared with the confusion caused by the traditions of men. The true believer should understand that the written

---

[10] Judaism rejects the New Testament books, while Roman Catholicism and other non-Protestant faiths accept apocryphal books and additions (Ramm 7). Adding to the Word of God and subtracting from the Word are two sides of the same coin.

[11] Alter and Kermode 3–4, 605–6.

[12] McDowell, *Evidence* 43–76; McDowell, *More Evidence* 17–22.

[13] Alter and Kermode 24–26.

[14] "Although the biblical texts among the Dead Sea Scrolls are a thousand years older than the oldest extant Hebrew Bible, they indicate that, all in all, modern copies are amazingly accurate" (Shanks 142); "The Bible exists simultaneously in many languages (in this it differs from many holy texts of other religions) but its actual text has hardly changed at all in thousands of years, except for the occasional disputed phrase here or there, or a delicate realignment of emphasis" (De Hamel viii); "After the most careful scrutiny by scholars of the Old and New Testament texts, it is now evident that the Old and New Testaments are the best preserved texts from antiquity" (Ramm 8).

[15] "Rationalism in Biblical studies boils down to the fundamental assertion that whatever is not in harmony with *educated* mentality is to be rejected. . . . The rationalistic premise has led to radical criticism of the Scriptures. . . . This radical treatment of Scriptures reached its full tide in the nineteenth century . . . [B]y the middle of the twentieth century most theological seminaries have accepted the basic theses of radical criticism, and many of its conclusions" (Ramm 63). The final end of human rationalism is, ironically, irrationalism and paganism.

ADAM, NOAH, ABRAHAM

Word of God and the incarnate Word of God are, though on different levels of reality, both perfect in exactly the same sense.[16]

STRONG'S CONCORDANCE (1890)

The primary concordance used in this commentary is *Strong's Exhaustive Concordance of the Bible*, copyrighted in 1890 by the American Methodist James Strong. *Strong's Exhaustive Concordance* is an alphabetical index of the English words used in the King James Bible,[17] cataloging every occurrence of each indexed word form with brief excerpts.[18] Strong also published brief and simple Old Testament Hebrew and Aramaic (Hebrew and Chaldee) and New Testament Greek dictionaries, titled *Concise Dictionaries of the Hebrew Bible and Greek Testament*, together with his *Exhaustive Concordance of the Bible*. Strong assigned a number, subsequently called a Strong's number, to each Hebrew, Aramaic, and Greek word underlying the English text. And the use of Strong's numbers has also been incorporated into the *Brown-Driver-Briggs Hebrew Lexicon* and *Thayer's Greek Lexicon* and also many other reference works. *Strong's Exhaustive Concordance* summarizes where and therefore how often a particular English word is used, while the accompanying *Strong's Concise Dictionaries* summarize the common meanings of words and also the ranges of translation of words from the underlying languages into the English.[19] In the present commentary series, Strong's numbers corresponding to Hebrew or Aramaic words (of the Hebrew Bible) are marked by a letter *H* prefix while Strong's numbers corresponding to Greek words (of the Greek Testament) are marked by a letter *G* prefix.

Strong's Exhaustive Concordance and the accompanying *Concise Dictionaries* are primarily works of reference, not exegesis, but nonetheless the signification of words, usage commonalities, and so forth, as well as etymological relationships are all inextricably linked to the interpretation of the Biblical narratives.[20] The Strong's numbering system for the Hebrew, Aramaic, and Greek specifically organizes ground forms of words,[21] though the overall Biblical translation does,

---

[16] See Screwtape's praise of the "historical point of view" (Lewis, *Screwtape* 128–29). In a dark imitation of the faithful in Christ being conceived of the Spirit, there is a collusion between the faithless and the devil that characterizes the spirit of disobedience.

[17] The King James Version spelling, capitalization, and so forth, used in *Strong's Concordance* are taken from the Parallel Bible, 8-volume minion edition, produced by Oxford Press in 1886 (Strong 4).

[18] The occurrences of forty-seven "unimportant" words of very frequent usage are cataloged, by chapter and verse only, in the *Strong's Concordance* appendix.

[19] Actually tracing a given Hebrew, Aramaic, or Greek word through its different verses is, of course, cumbersome without the aid of digital resources.

[20] Lexicons and dictionaries are not inspired per se, and therefore the exact meanings of words, also etymological relationships, are open to debate.

[21] "[*Ground form*:] (Grammar), the stem or basis of a word, to which the other parts are added in declension or conjugation. It is sometimes, but not always, the same as the root" (*Webster's Revised Unabridged Dictionary*, 1913 ed., s.v. "ground form").

INTRODUCTION

of course, comprehend local nuanced meanings. *Strong's Concise Dictionaries* present common meanings and the ranges of translation in the King James Version but not detailed nuanced meanings in local contexts. Strong's concordance is therefore normally used in conjunction with more elaborate Hebrew and Greek lexicons. Also note that the ground-form words organized by Strong's numbers are referred to in the present work simply as "words," while the proposed etymological roots of words are referred to as "roots." Some etymological roots are themselves ground forms and therefore have unique Strong's numbers, whereby such forms are called either "words" or "roots," depending upon the exact context. Etymological roots not used in the Biblical text have no assigned Strong's number and, accordingly, are referred to as "unused roots."

BROWN-DRIVER-BRIGGS LEXICON (1906)

The primary lexicon used in this commentary is the *Brown-Driver-Briggs Hebrew and English Lexicon* founded upon the lexicon of William Gesenius as translated by Edward Robinson. The specific *Brown-Driver-Briggs* volume used is a reprinting of the 1906 American edition, coded with Strong's numbers and corrected for errors and misprints. Etymological relationships and definition wordings are taken primarily from the *Brown-Driver-Briggs Lexicon*, but a basic agreement is maintained with *Strong's Concise Dictionary of the Hebrew Bible* (published as a companion to *Strong's Exhaustive Concordance*). The standard King James Version English text is also specifically consulted in each word study, with King James wordings occasionally substituted for those of *Brown-Driver-Briggs*. Any significant deviations from the wordings or etymologies in *Brown-Driver-Briggs* are footnoted. For the relatively small number of New Testament word studies developed in the present commentary, *Thayer's Greek-English Lexicon of the New Testament* is used primarily but likewise in conjunction with *Strong's Concise Dictionary of the Greek Testament* (also published with *Strong's Exhaustive Concordance*). Any significant deviations from the wordings or etymologies in *Thayer's* are footnoted. The specific *Thayer's* volume used is a reprinting of the 1896 fourth edition, coded with Strong's numbers and corrected for errors and misprints. Other translations of the Scriptures are also variously considered for overall perspectives, including but not limited to the Amplified Bible, the New International Version, the New American Bible, and the Jewish Publication Society Tanakh.[22]

The organization of *Brown-Driver-Briggs* is not simply alphabetical but rather alphabetical by etymological roots, with related words collected under their roots. Words that are difficult to locate by root are, however, set a second time

---

[22] The supposed inadequacy of Biblical lexicons predating the modern-day rediscovery of manuscripts from antiquity, such as the Dead Sea Scrolls, is part of the myth that the Bible has been corrupted. And since uncovering manuscripts is an open-ended process, no Biblical lexicon and actually no Bible translation could ever be considered completely trustworthy according to such a worldview.

in their alphabetical place, with cross-reference to their primary position within the etymological system. Hebrew and Aramaic words are grouped separately. In contrast, *Strong's Concise Dictionary of the Hebrew Bible* is purely alphabetical, with Hebrew and Aramaic words grouped together and with etymology notes and cross-references included within the individual Hebrew and Aramaic entries. In *Brown-Driver-Briggs*, a lexicon entry begins with the common meanings, followed by nuanced meanings connected to specific Biblical passages. Information from other sources and scholars has also been added, including notes on cognate languages. For word studies in the present commentary, complete lexicon common meanings are not always quoted, rather only the aspects most relevant to the immediate discussion. The myriad of nuanced meanings are, as a practical matter, never quoted in their entirety, again only the relevant aspects. *Connotations*, as termed in the present work, are nuances derivative of different usages in parallel passages, that is, different usages in different contexts connected by common ground forms. In contrast, *associations*, here termed, are relationships founded upon etymological root commonalities, including root homonym constructions. Detailed etymologies are not reproduced in the present work, because they are readily available in the cited lexicons.

The primary guide for selecting and shaping word studies is the Bible itself, specifically the defining Christological themes evident throughout the Bible. In principle any arbitrary word study plays into Christology, but in practice some word studies are more obvious and therefore more practical. The meaning of a word or phrase is shaded by its different Biblical usages and also by underlying etymological relationships. A number of relationships also arise simply because of the sounds of words. The network of connotations and associations and wordplays narrowly defined by the Biblical Hebrew, Aramaic, and Greek should be emphasized since the Bible is directly conceived of and inspired by God the Holy Spirit. The wider Middle Eastern, Mediterranean, and so forth, linguistic traditions are not directly, or overtly, inspired by the Holy Spirit and, therefore, should be de-emphasized. Neither should word studies emphasize any inferences presumably drawn by the original native audiences, who would have had an imperfect and biased understanding of their specific time; rather, the focus must be the implications intended by God the Holy Spirit, who always has a perfect understanding of all times. Selected word studies are technically also limited to cases with better agreement between *Brown-Driver-Briggs* and *Strong's*, but more disputed word studies can usually be excluded entirely or replaced by less controversial cases, without significantly altering any interpretation, because of the high level of redundancy in the Scriptures. Any significant differences between *Brown-Driver-Briggs* and *Strong's* with regard to employed wordings or etymologies are footnoted. However, when exact etymological relationships do differ between *Brown-Driver-Briggs* and *Strong's*, close relationships are still normally evident in both sources. And when exact definitions differ between *Brown-Driver-Briggs* and *Strong's*, clear analogies are still normally evident.[23]

---

[23] "The first problem in reading poetry, therefore, or in reading any kind of literature, is to develop a sense of language, a feeling for words. One needs to become acquainted

INTRODUCTION

HERMENEUTICS AND EXEGESIS

Hermeneutics is the science and art of interpretation, while exegesis refers to specific interpretations. The hermeneutics of the present work is Christological, while the exegesis is the Body of Christ.[24] The progression from the theoretical to the actual reflects the movement from the promise to the fulfillment of the promise, embodied foremost by our original creation through Christ (John 1:3) pointing to our promised new creation in Christ (2 Cor 5:17). The mark of faith likewise proceeds from God the Spirit and also points to God the Spirit. The children of God receive the Spirit by faith (Gal 3:2), while faith itself is simultaneously the fruit of the Spirit (Gal 5:22). Further, the beginning of the true and perfect knowledge of God is the recognition of an innate ambiguity marking the dual nature of Jesus Christ, being simultaneously the Son of man and the Son of God.[25] This ambiguity elicits a universal question. Christ asks not only his original disciples but ultimately all of us, "But whom say ye that I am?" (Matt 16:15), to which we must answer, "Thou art the Christ, the [unique] Son of the living God" (Matt 16:16). And the wisdom in Christ is finally complete with the recognition that the Son of God is the incarnation of God. "Have I been so long time with you, and yet hast thou not known me . . . he that hath seen me hath seen the Father; and how sayest thou then, Show us the Father?" (John 14:9). Like begets like, thus the only begotten Son must truly be God, for God is one (Deut 6:4).[26]

---

with their shape, their color, and their flavor. There are two ways of doing this: extensive use of the dictionary and extensive reading" (Perrine 591). The Body of Christ, of the incarnate Word, is likewise called to be a people of the written Word.

[24] "The finest statement of the Christological principle in Old Testament interpretation is that of Francis Roberts who lived in the seventeenth century: '. . . (1) Christ is the truth and substance of all types and shadows. (2) Christ is the matter and substance of the Covenant of Grace under all administrations thereof; under the Old Testament Christ is *veyled* [veiled], under the New Covenant *revealed*. (3) Christ is the centre and meetingplace of all the promises, for in him all the promises of God are yea, and they are Amen. (4) Christ is the thing signified, sealed, and exhibited in all the sacraments of the Old and New Testaments, whether ordinary or extraordinary. . . .'" (Ramm 267–68). And who is the Christ, God the Son, except the only begotten of God the Father, conceived of God the Holy Spirit?

[25] "The ambiguity and multiplicity of meanings that words have, then, are an obstacle to the scientist but a resource to the poet" (Perrine 590). The true scientist is a seeker who, in the fullness of understanding, becomes a poet in addition to a scientist.

[26] "It [Jewish exegesis] is a complex system contained in a voluminous corpus . . . . The major weakness of their [Rabbinical] system was the development of a hyperliteralism or a *letterism*. . . . The errors were then compounded by the enormous authority given to tradition" (Ramm 46–47); The works of the two [often-regarded] greatest minds of the early church, Origen and Augustine, are marked by a distinct tendency to allegory (Ramm 33–35, 173); "The Fathers did it [make the entire Bible a Christian book] with their allegorical method. Luther does it with his Christological principle" (Ramm 56); Luther founded Protestant hermeneutics, but Calvin exemplified it (Ramm 57). The way

ADAM, NOAH, ABRAHAM

Christology is the study of Jesus Christ, who is the visible image of the invisible God (Col 1:15). The essence of Christology as applied to the Old Testament is the study of the image of God as reflected in signs, types, and motifs. Jesus Christ can be properly understood only in the context of the Trinity, while the different aspects of the Trinity, likewise Christ, can be perceived in the different levels of reality (Rom 1:20). *Prime*, or singular, images reflect the oneness of God; *twofold* images reflect the twofold natures of Jesus Christ; *threefold* images reflect the dynamic of the Trinity. The image of God is evident on all levels of reality just as the will of God is universal. The image of God is evident despite the defilement of creation just as the will of God is undeniable, or relentless, despite the disobedience of man. The image of God is evident not only in the Scriptures but also in creation, physical and spiritual, because the Lord God is the one story, as well as the one author, of both the Scriptures and creation as a whole. And the image of God is uniquely manifest in the intellect and conscience of humanity because living man is made in the image of the living God. Any disagreement between Biblical interpretation, the human faculties, and the realities of the world is wholly inconsistent with the unity of the Holy Spirit and, therefore, indicates some human misunderstanding somewhere. Further, the three witnesses represented by the Scriptures, the human condition, and creation as a whole can themselves be compared to the Father, Son, and Holy Spirit. The abstract nature of the Scriptures reflects the invisible God the Father; the human condition reflects God the Son; the transcendent nature of creation as a whole reflects God the Spirit as the breath of life animating all creation.[27]

The motif emphasized in the Scriptures is, surprisingly, not singular or threefold but rather twofold. The basic literary building block constructing the Scriptures is twofold, reflecting the centrality of the twofold natures of Christ in both our original creation and also our promised new creation. The incarnation of the Son represents the essential condescension of God in the act of creation. The twofold natures of the Son are manifest throughout the Scriptures and likewise creation because all creation proceeds through the Son (John 1:3). Adam being formed from the dust of the ground and quickened by the breath of God (Gen 2:7) prefigures the essential union of flesh and spirit ultimately established in the person of Jesus Christ, whereby the Scriptures boldly identify Adam with the very image of God (Gen 1:27). All levels of reality reflect the same fundamental tension between flesh and spirit embodied by the paradox of the incarnation of the infinite God. The dichotomy of flesh and spirit is affirmed in the contrast between the law that governs flesh and the grace that proceeds from the Spirit. The natural precedes the spiritual just as law precedes

---

of Christology is not simply allegorizing any given text but rightly connecting the spiritual to the natural in complete accordance with the image of God.

[27] "We do not confess three Gods, but one God in three persons . . . The divine persons do not share the one divinity among themselves but each of them is God whole and entire . . . ." (Rom. Catholic Church, *Catechism* 75). The seeming paradox of the oneness of the Trinity is impressed upon all creation and, thereby, affirmed by all of creation.

INTRODUCTION

grace just as the first man Adam precedes the second man Christ just as the incarnation of Christ at the First Advent precedes the glorification of the Body of Christ in the Second Advent (1 Cor 15:46). The resolution of the tension between flesh and spirit, likewise between law and grace, in the person of Jesus Christ is the universal theme of the Scriptures, to be finally completed, or revealed, in the promised perfection of the faithful in Christ.[28]

Satanic images and motifs do also exist in the Scriptures and throughout creation but not independently of the one true God of creation. Images of the devil are understood not in isolation but rather as corruptions of the image of the Lord God just as the devil is not an eternal being in any way equal to God but rather a being created by God, with absolutely no power over God or apart from God (Ezek 28:15). Neither is sin something of itself but rather a corruption of goodness. The devil was originally formed without corruption just as creation as a whole was originally formed without corruption (Gen 1:31). Attempting to understand the devil independently of God implies a false equality between the devil and God, and just such an insidious equality even now pervades popular conceptions.[29]

The exegesis developed in the present commentary is derived specifically from Biblical precedents, literal imagery, lexical shading of words, and implicit contextual relationships. The meaning of any specific word or passage can always be debated, but the layered motifs in the Scriptures provide liberal redundancy ensuring internal consistency.[30] Further, following New Testament precedents, the fullness of interpretation is achieved by completing literal meaning with figurative, or spiritual, meaning (Gal 4:24). But the figurative is never arbitrary, always derived from the literal, and always complements the literal.[31] The relationship between literal and figurative meanings can be compared to the relationship between the material and the spiritual or, more abstractly, the relationship between flesh and spirit. The same fundamental dichotomy is evident from all perspectives. The Scriptures are a union of the literal and figurative just as creation is a union of the physical and spiritual. The completion of the literal with the spiritual is epitomized in the Old Testament through the expression of latent images of Jesus Christ.[32] And the spiritual is ironically more real, or relevant, than the material just as the spiritual man Jesus transcends the natural man Adam. The progression of the Scriptures, moving from images of Christ to the reality of Christ, reflects the progression of creation, epitomized by a child growing into the maturity of faith (1 Cor 13:11).

---

[28] The pressure to dismiss the spiritual interpretation of the Holy Scriptures as arbitrary or even self-serving is part of a larger movement to persuade the earthly church, the carnal church, to put away their Bibles altogether.

[29] See C. S. Lewis's discussion of goodness and badness (Lewis, *Mere Christianity* 49–50).

[30] From DNA replication to the Apollo moon missions, the stability of all functioning systems—that is, real systems—is necessarily founded upon redundancy.

[31] "All secondary meanings of documents depend upon the literal stratum of language. . . . Only in the priority of literal exegesis is there control on the exegetical abuse of Scripture" (Ramm 124). The literal and the spiritual are one unified reality.

[32] As defined by Ramm, not allegorically, but rather typologically (Ramm 223).

The progression from mere images to concrete reality reflects the progression from the promise to the fulfillment of the promise.[33]

The Old Testament emphasizes law, while the New Testament emphasizes grace. And yet the Old and New Testaments do form a unified whole. The emphasis in the Bible progresses from law to grace, but the underlying twofold motifs of flesh and spirit, justice and mercy, and law and grace can always be discerned. The Old and New Testaments, individually and juxtaposed, represent the union of law and grace. The fabric of reality is so tightly woven that one actually cannot speak about law or grace without at least implying something about the other.[34] The traditions of men concerning the Old Testament emphasize the oneness of God, but the Old Testament itself emphasizes the relationship between the Creator and the creation, which is not fundamentally singular but twofold. And the immediate separation, or bifurcation, of man and God because of sin affirms that the essential condescension of God in the act of creation is innately twofold. Nevertheless, an overarching threefold reality reflecting the Trinity is still evident, as is an underlying unity reflecting the oneness of God. The twofold is forefront, reflecting the present human condition, while the singular and the threefold, specifically the progression from the singular to the twofold to the threefold, is recessed, reflecting the promised new creation not yet being realized. The progressive revelation of the Scriptures is a movement from the oneness of God the Father, the God of creation, to the twofold natures of God the Son to the threefold dynamic of God the Son anointing the faithful by the indwelling of God the Holy Spirit in accordance with the will of God the Father. And the progressive revelation of creation likewise reflects the threefold movement from the original creation before the Fall of Man to the present corrupted creation to the promised new creation. The natural body is fixated on the twofold, but the distinctions between the prime, twofold, and threefold will fade in the spiritual, or glorified, resurrection body in the fulfillment of the promised unity of the Spirit.[35]

---

[33] For one example of dealing with abstract, or spiritual, reality as part and parcel of a comprehensive understanding, see Perrine's rules for identifying and interpreting symbols (Perrine 214–15). Secular literary methods normally assume that a single, coherent author exists, and therefore such methods can often be related to Christology, which similarly assumes one Author.

[34] One could argue that anything can be parsed into a dichotomy of flesh and spirit, but this is an argument for the sovereignty of the Lord God over all reality, not against the manifest structure of the Scriptures.

[35] "[T]he early church accepted the conviction that God [Father], the maker of heaven and earth, is one. . . . The binitarian formulas [Father, Son] are found in . . . [Gal 1:1, 1 Tim 1:2, etc.] . . . The triadic schema [Father, Son, Spirit] is discovered in [Matt 28:19, 1 Pet 1:2, etc.] . . . . However, the threefold pattern [Father, Son, Spirit] is evident throughout [the New Testament], in spite of the fact that there is usually nothing in the context to demand it" (Rusch 2). The Trinity is the paradigm of creation, the shape of our salvation, and the mode of our prayer, and as such, the Trinity is our one and only proper hermeneutics for reading the Bible, likewise perceiving reality as a whole, and therein relating to God.

INTRODUCTION

Complex Pattern Types

The three pattern types serial, chiastic, and staircase, developed in the prologue, are all based on the uniformly repeating time intervals of days and millennia. These uniform pattern types show exactly repeating days paralleling exactly repeating millennia, which reflects the infallible and unmovable nature of God Almighty. A complementary set of three pattern types, here introduced, are based on nonuniform time intervals, which reflects the universality of the Lord of lords, transcending simple linear time. Further, an abstract set of three elements—representing the oneness of the Father, the twofold natures of the Son, and the threefold movement of the Spirit—underlies all patterns types, as is discussed in detail in the afterword. The innate rigidity of temporally uniform pattern types, strictly ordering creation, reflects the absolute nature of the law, while the transcendence of nonuniform types, filling and encompassing all creation, reflects the humbly condescending nature of grace. The more complex nonuniform reality transcends the uniform just as grace transcends the law. Further, the movement from abstract elements to temporal patterns reflects the same movement from law unto grace. And all pattern types being characterized by the concrete and the ethereal reflects the essential union of law and grace, likewise flesh and spirit, embodied by God the Son. The movement from the elemental and abstract to the more complex and transcendent reflects the natural being subsumed by the spiritual. The transcendent subsuming the immanent and thereby being actualized is the same paradox of the spiritual being more real than the natural, likewise faith being accounted as righteousness, likewise eternal life being more sure than mortal life, likewise the Creator being realized in the creation.

The discussion of temporally nonuniform patterns involves the entirety of the Biblical timeline of human history and, therefore, is the natural purview of the main commentary, in concert with an ongoing development of their temporally uniform and nontemporal counterparts, but a brief outline is useful as an introductory overview. The basic structuring concepts applicable to nonuniform time are the same as those for uniform time, in that the three fundamental Trinitarian elements—(1) *prime*, (2) *twofold*, and (3) *threefold*—build three distinct pattern types, themselves being individually related to the three persons of the Trinity—(1) Father, (2) Son, and (3) Spirit. The three distinct temporally nonuniform pattern types, or spheres of operation, entail (1) the natural history of creation as a whole, (2) the individual as a microcosm of all creation, and (3) the progression of the generations of the chosen people. And these three nonuniform pattern types—denoted in the present commentary as (1) *historical*, (2) *individual*, and (3) *generational*—are the analogues, respectively, of the previously discussed uniform pattern types—(1) *serial*, (2) *chiastic*, and (3) *staircase*. The nontemporal Trinitarian elements represent the image of God being the paradigm of all creation. The threefold pattern organization founded upon uniform time represents an emphasis on the tangible clockwork creation, which is an emphasis on the natural. In contrast, the threefold nonuniform pattern organization transcending uniform time represents an emphasis on the intangible, which is an emphasis on the spiritual. And the more complex nonuniform organization necessarily incorporates aspects of both nonuniform and uniform time, which reflects grace not replacing the law but rather completing the law, likewise the spiritual subsuming the natural. The spiritual, or glorified, resurrection body is a true flesh-and-blood physical body.[36]

The identification of signs and types and motifs is necessary to establish the fullness of context in the exegetical process, but the overarching structuring of reality in and of itself is distant and detached from the essentially personal experience that is the Good News of Jesus Christ. The demarcation of patterns represents foremost a top-down view, focusing on the organizational system itself and understanding the Biblical text from a global perspective, whereas the present commentary consciously emphasizes a bottom-up view, beginning with word studies and literal imagery and only then considering the overarching patterns from a local perspective. Accordingly, the present commentary is structured around the flow of the received text, the written Word, following the path of progressive revelation established by God the Holy Spirit and, thereby, conforming to the purposeful structures of special revelation, which ultimately point to Jesus Christ, the incarnate Word, and finally to the Body of Christ. From either the bottom-up or top-down perspective, however, it should be recognized that the bottom-up and the top-down are innately interwoven complements. The top-down view can be compared to the heavenly, while the bottom-up view can be compared to the earthly. And the earthly bottom-up view reflects the heavenly top-down view just as the written Word reflects the incarnate Word just as Jesus Christ reflects the Trinity.

The outlining of complex patterns is expanded in chapter conclusion sections, with the goal of facilitating a proper understanding of creation in the context of the Trinity, wherein the Trinity is recognized as the only way to comprehend the fullness of the promise embodied by creation and the corresponding incarnation of Christ. As created beings, our primal experience of God is necessarily through creation, or the natural, expressly the tree of the (experiential) knowledge of good and evil. And since all creation proceeds through the Son—who would be nailed to the tree of the cross, spiritually the tree of knowledge—an instinctive, or intuitive, hermeneutics begins with the twofold natures of the Son, who is simultaneously fully man and fully God, that is impressed upon all creation. The way of the Spirit leads the faithful in the Son to an understanding of the Trinity just as all things proceed through the Son. Jesus Christ points to the Trinity just as the earthly bottom-up perspective points to the heavenly top-down perspective. As created beings, we necessarily seek the invisible things through the visible and not vice versa, and it is the Son

---

[36] "Reading the [Biblical] prophecies in this book, one should expect questions too great to be answered, words that push forward through time like a shock wave, turning over everything in their path. . . . Fractal-like patterns recycling through time, instead of straight lines to the truth" (Haggith 7). Language always operates on multiple levels and, thereby, transcends the merely literal, or natural.

INTRODUCTION

who is the perfect visible image of God (Col 1:15). The complex, inherently global top-down nature of threefold patterns is most closely identified with the Trinity, reflecting the infinite nature of God, while our principally twofold, local bottom-up experience of reality is most closely identified with the Son, reflecting the humble condescension of God.[37]

The myriad undertones and overtones manifest in the layering of reality reflect the divers existential themes of creation that will finally come together to form a single, uncorrupted harmony, or image, of the true and full reality relating the Lord God, the self-existent one. The study of the relationship between the macrocosm and the microcosm is the study of the relationship between the infinite God, the creator, and finite created man formed in the very image of God. And the image of God in which creation is formed has always been perceivable despite the defilement of creation just as the will of God has always been inevitable despite the disobedience of man (Rom 1:20). The ironic resolution of the image of the one true God through a multitude of variations reflects the surprising promise of a multitude of faithful composing the one Body of Christ. And the providential self-assembling of fractured images in progressive revelation points to a corresponding fullness of understanding. The fundamental parallels between the different layers of reality show a pattern complementarity that reflects the infinite nature of God and likewise the universality of God. The parallels between different epochs represent a new telling of history, spiritually a folding of time, which reflects the recapitulation of all creation in the person of Christ. Pattern complementarity and pattern recapitulation are prophetic constructions reflecting and foretelling the unification and sanctification of all creation. Pattern complementarity is a nontemporal vertical stacking of patterns that points to the heavenly, while pattern recapitulation is a horizontal construction, or reconstruction, in time and space that is most closely connected with the earthly. And the basic mechanics of interpretation is necessarily founded upon a recognition of the essential alignment of what are fundamentally triune elements throughout all creation, the earthly and the heavenly domains.[38]

ORGANIZATION PRINCIPLES

Chapter introductions preview key images, or elements, beginning with prime, or singular, and followed by twofold and lastly threefold. Prime images

---

[37] "[I]t is not primarily to communicate information that novels and short stories and plays and poems are written. These exist to bring us a sense and a perception of life, to widen and sharpen our contacts with existence. Their concern is with experience. We all have an inner need to live more deeply and fully and with greater awareness . . . ."
(Perrine 554). The Bible, the Holy Bible, is concerned with experiential knowledge as identified with the tree of the knowledge of good and evil, but expressly for the sake of making us increasingly holy, that is, increasingly aware of God in whose sinless image we are created.

[38] "The poet, we may say, plays on a many-stringed instrument. And he sounds more than one note at a time" (Perrine 591). The harmony of creation is a kind of poetry.

reflect the oneness of God, ultimately God the Father. Twofold images reflect the twofold natures of Jesus Christ, God the Son, who is simultaneously and without contradiction fully man and fully God. Threefold images are most closely identified with God the Holy Spirit, expressly the threefold movement of the Holy Spirit leading the faithful in the Son unto the Father. Chapter conclusions set major themes in the global context of the overall Biblical progression. After each chapter conclusion, outlines of key images and verse-by-verse interpretations are presented, using a format that emphasizes the parallel between natural and spiritual meaning. In the body of each chapter, the Biblical text and commentary text alternate in the minimum practical units that allow the development of complete thoughts. The commentary text is formally constructed around the subtleties of word studies, but the overarching organization is based on the motifs apparent in the plain-sense flow of the Bible. Detailed word studies are not primarily used to identify motifs but rather corroborate and elaborate motifs. The reproduction of the King James standard English text in its entirety represents an emphasis on the central importance of the received text and also expedites, via Strong's numbers, the essential connection between the Biblical text and commentary word studies. Further, Biblical verses are presented consecutively in order to avoid skewing the inspired progressive development of the sacred text.[39]

The main commentary chapters developed in the present volume are demarcated by Biblical personages, reflecting a purposeful centrality of the individual in progressive revelation. The first three major patriarchs, or fathers, emphasized in Bible are Adam, Noah, and Abraham. Adam is the father of all mankind; Noah is the father of all postdiluvian mankind; and Abraham is the father of all the faithful (Rom 4:16). Successive chapters in the present volume form an alternating chorus and refrain structure, following the natural rhythm of parents being succeeded by their offspring. The basic structuring of the commentary text stresses twofold images, reflecting the vital relationship between the Creator and the creation, but prime and threefold images, particularly as related to twofold reality, are also developed, affirming an underlying unity of creation and Creator and an overarching progression unto the promised new creation. A spiraling, inward and outward, relationship between man and God is evident in the dichotomy of flesh and spirit that is embodied by man, being formed in the very image of God. And an ever-expanding triunity—prime, twofold, and threefold—marks the sweeping events of natural history, the personal lives of individuals, and also the progression of chronology and genealogy. The layering of motifs testifies to the universality of the Lord God and finally the undeniable and unassailable will of God for the welfare of his children, the faithful.[40]

---

[39] A distortion of the Biblical texts can be achieved through religious liberalism either by picking and choosing verses to taste or by reading liberal views into the texts, effectively allegorizing them (Ramm 176). The full counsel of God is the whole Word of God founded upon the literal, or natural, plain-sense meaning.

[40] "Apocalyptic writing is highly poetic. In fact, prophets and poets were once regarded as the same breed. Poets will load as many meanings upon a single phrase as they wish

INTRODUCTION

Additionally, a sampling of Rabbinic, Orthodox, Roman Catholic, Protestant, and so forth, and also literary commentaries is surveyed in the footnotes. Any clarifications added within direct quotations are delimited by brackets. The careful study of extant commentaries throughout time and across traditions is itself a microcosm of the human condition, notably reflecting the commandment to honor our parents and, by extension, our forefathers as well as our contemporaries (Eph 6:2). And maintaining such a context is essential for understanding the subtle but critical implications of diverging methodologies. Nonetheless, the establishment of religious precedents should not be considered legally, intellectually, or morally binding, that is, apart from the perfect and complete will of God. And neither is the goal simply a review of the representative thought of the cited sources, rather a study of the different traditional and prevalent interpretation styles and conceptions as directly related to Christological hermeneutics. Footnoted source materials may represent a complement or contrast as compared with the main commentary. In either case, the relationships are commonly abstract, requiring an annotation to be added following the footnote citation. A minority of footnotes are simple citations, author's comments, and etymology notes.[41]

---

to—and often a few meanings they didn't foresee but would agree with if they were pointed out. . . . Narrowly insisting that prophets speak only to the events of their own times, or only to one particular future event, places a constraint on apocalyptic writing that no literate reader would place on other poetic writings" (Haggith 7–8). The Lord God declares the end from the beginning, Isa 46:10.

[41] "The primal artistic act was God's creation of the universe out of chaos . . . and every artist since, on a lesser scale, has sought to imitate Him . . . ." (Perrine 771). It is our essential nature to be creative because we are created in the image of the Creator. But given the reality of freewill, the question is always whether our acts of creation are in imitation of God, reflecting the true image of God, or in opposition to God, corrupting the image of God.

ADAM

יהוה

CHAPTER ONE

Adam and Eve

The one man Adam reflecting the one God is the prime image emphasized in the account of our genesis. The formation of the one man Adam in the image of the one God attests to the oneness of God, while all humanity proceeding from the one man Adam represents all creation proceeding from the one God (Gen 1:27). The ubiquitous emphasis in the Scriptures on the individual reflects the immeasurable value of the individual to God, while our immeasurable value to God reflects the infinite nature of God. The progressive nature of revelation in the Scriptures, moving from images of Christ to the reality of Christ, is a reflection of the singular will of God to fulfill the promise of life in the fullness of the Holy Spirit (Col 2:17). The promise points to the reality just as mortal life points to immortal life just as the one man Adam points to the one man Jesus the Christ. The same images repeat on all levels of reality. Our physical reality is like a shadow of spiritual reality (Heb 8:4–5) such that the one creation reveals the one Creator (Rom 1:20). The one garden made for the one man reflects the one will of the one God. And our preservation even after the Fall of Man affirms that the will of God for his children is undeniable, that is, relentless.

The twofold images emphasized in the account of our genesis are the two names of God, the two natures of flesh and spirit, the two sexes, and the two trees. Each pair on each level of reality reflects the same essential tension between flesh and spirit, likewise between justice and mercy, and likewise between law and grace. The resolution of the tension between justice and mercy is the universal theme of the Scriptures—namely, our singular redemption revealed as the image of the one God, ultimately in the person of Christ and finally in the Body of Christ. God the Father is the perfect union of justice and mercy just as God the Son is the perfect union of flesh and spirit just as God the Holy Spirit is the perfect union of, or unifies perfectly, the breath of man and the breath of God. The one man Adam prefigures the one man Jesus the Christ (Rom 5:19) just as this world prefigures the next just as the natural body prefigures the spiritual, or glorified, body (1 Cor 15:44–45). This is the child that becomes an adult, the blurred reflection that becomes clear, the partial knowledge that becomes a full knowledge (1 Cor 13:11–12). The former foreshadows the latter while the latter fulfills the former, such that the two are one. The two trees evoke an image of the one garden just as the two sexes evoke an image of one flesh just as the two natures of flesh and spirit evoke an image of individual man just as the two fundamental names *God* (Elohim) and *Lord* (YHWH) evoke an image of the one God.

The threefold Father, Son, and Holy Spirit are manifest in the threefold man, woman, and the implied progeny of man and woman. Man was formed in the image of God—namely, the Father—while woman and the progeny embodied by woman originally proceeded from man just as the Holy Spirit and the Son eternally proceed from the Father. The original unity in man of the threefold man, woman, and child, before woman was taken from man, represents the oneness of the Godhead (Gen 2:20–22). In contrast, man separated from woman embodies justice while woman separated from man embodies mercy. And the offspring of man and woman represents the union of justice and mercy. God the Father likewise formed creation under law (justice), while our redemption in the Son is conceived through the Holy Spirit by grace (mercy). And the indwelling Holy Spirit animates and sanctifies our new creation in the Son (the union of justice and mercy). The image of the Godhead impressed upon all creation testifies that all creation proceeds from the one God, while the unity of creation testifies to the oneness of God.

The Garden of Eden

Genesis 1:1 In the beginning God [H430] created the heaven [H8064] and the earth [H776].

The title *God* [H430] (God created) is *Elohim* in the Hebrew, connoting "rulers" and "judges," which is an emphasis on authority and power and righteousness in contrast to condescension and obedience and faithfulness. The revelation of the first name of God, *Elohim*, in the context of the original act of creation therefore most closely identifies our original creation with justice in contrast to mercy. Our original creation is an act of power and authority by a sovereign and righteous God. Accordingly, our genesis is like a birthright that proceeds from the perfect justice of God while our promised new creation in the Body of Christ is like a blessing that proceeds from the perfect mercy of God as the fulfillment of justice in mercy. Authority is completed by humility just as justice is completed by mercy just as righteousness is completed by faithfulness. The words *heaven* [H8064] and *earth* [H776] (God created) literally refer to "sky" and "land" and together represent the whole of material creation, but heaven and earth, as the foremost abodes of spirit and flesh, figuratively reflect the union of spirit and flesh embodied by all creation. Flesh is completed by spirit just as justice is completed by mercy. Justice compared with mercy is the contrast between God the Father and (collectively) God the Spirit and God the Son proceeding from God the Father, while the union of justice and mercy is the oneness of the Trinity finally affirmed by the unity of the Holy Spirit indwelling the Body of Christ.[1]

Genesis 2:4 These [are] the generations of the heavens and of the earth when they were created, in the day that the LORD [H3068] God [H430] made the earth and the heavens,

The name *God* [H430] in the compound name *Lord* [H3068] *God* [H430] is the first name of God, *Elohim*, originally identified with the original creation, and thus the emphasized new quality is the name *Lord* [H3068], traditionally denoted *Jehovah* or *Yahweh* or by the tetragrammaton, *YHWH* (Gen 1:1).[2] The name *Lord* (YHWH) [H3068] is derived from the root "to become, be" [H1961], evoking an image of God as "the Self-Existent," while the root "to become, be" [H1961] is itself used as the name of God *I AM* [H1961] (Exod 3:14).[3] The names *Lord* (YHWH) [H3068] and *I AM* [H1961] are both explicitly identified with mercy via the redemption of Israel out of slavery just as the promise of life evoked by the image, or concept, "the Self-Existent" is fulfilled in the perfect mercy of the redemption of the faithful out of sin (Exod 6:3). The first name *God* (Elohim) [H430] is identified with physical creation, likewise flesh, and likewise the law that governs flesh, while the second name *Lord* (YHWH) [H3068] is identified with our new creation, likewise spirit, and likewise the grace that governs spirit. The first revelation of the name *Lord* [H3068] *God* [H430] follows the account of the original blessing of the seventh day just as our new creation in eternity is figuratively the eighth day and the eighth millennium (Gen 2:3).[4]

The revelation of the name *God* [H430] followed by the revelation of the name *Lord* [H3068] *God* [H430] is an affirmation that justice is followed by mercy. Our original creation is likewise followed by our new creation just as the natural body is followed by the spiritual, or glorified, body just as the Covenant of Law is followed by the Covenant of Grace (1 Cor 15:44). The unity implied

---

[1] Some commentators put a long expanse of time between Gen 1:1 and 1:2, commonly called a "gap," during which the world at some point *became* without form and void through a corruptive work of lucifer (Guzik 12; Gen 1:2). Gap theory, also known as ruin-reconstruction theory or gap creationism, requires a twisting of the traditional understanding of key verb tenses in Gen 1:2, and it is also normally connected with a misguided desire to conform the Bible to the fossil "records," radiometric "dating," and so forth. Further, the assertion of a pre-Adamic creation within gap theory is antithetical to the unity and oneness of creation and likewise the unity and oneness of the Creator.
[2] H3068 is translated *Lord* the vast majority of the time in the King James Bible but is also translated *God* and *Jehovah*.
[3] *Lord* (YHWH) [H3068] = "(the) self-Existent" and corresponding etymology per *Strong's*, but an equivalent meaning is inferred from *Brown-Driver-Briggs*. The exact construction "to become, be" [H1961] = *I AM* is found in *Green's Interlinear*, Exod 3:14.
[4] The name of God *Elohim* connotes "judgment," while the name of God *YHWH* connotes "mercy," *Genesis Rabbah* (Cohen, *Rabbinic Sages* 17). The Old Testament, or Old Covenant, is the law pointing to grace, not the law in isolation.

by the compound construction *Lord* [H3068] *God* [H430] is not a vision of mercy supplanting justice but rather the fulfillment of justice in mercy in the perfect union of justice and mercy. The construction *Lord* [H3068] *God* [H430] is an edifying image, but the unified wholeness of God is ultimately represented simply as *Lord* [H3068] because the singular image of God as "the Self-Existent" projects the literal and perfect union of justice and mercy. The perfect union of justice and mercy is life—that is, the wholeness of God transcends the simple sum of justice and mercy just as the name of God transcends a simple compound construction.[5]

The variegated names of God revealed in the Scriptures affirm the universal dominion of God, but ultimately the many names of God reflect only the two essential images represented by the names *God* (Elohim) [H430] and *Lord* (YHWH) [H3068]. The former foreshadows the latter, while the latter fulfills the former. The name *Lord* [H3068], the singular proper name of God, being used in the construction *Lord* [H3068] *God* [H430] additionally represents a procession of the name *God* [H430] from the name *Lord* [H3068]—reflecting the Son, expressly in fulfillment of the law, (eternally) proceeding from the oneness of the Trinity. The name *God* [H430], in contrast to the name *Lord* [H3068], appearing first in the Scriptures represents the perspective of creation looking back at God, seeing first the procession from the Godhead before realizing the fullness of the Godhead. The reduction of the many names of God to only two essential images of justice and mercy and finally to the one name *Lord* [H3068], signifying life, reflects the genesis of all creation proceeding from the one God. Two names of God, two covenants, two creations. One God, one promise, one salvation in the one man Jesus the Christ.[6]

Genesis 2:5–6 And every plant of the field before it was in the earth, and every herb of the field before it grew: for the LORD God had not caused it to rain upon the earth, and [there was] not a man to till the ground. 6 But there went up a mist from the earth, and watered the whole face of the ground.

The sign of rain, water from heaven, represents the baptism of the flesh under the law, signifying death and resurrection, and is therefore identified with, not the time of the First Creation before the Fall of Man, but the time of the Flood and the corresponding death and resurrection of the world.[7]

---

[5] The compound name *Lord God* (YHWH + Elohim) is understood to reflect a mixture of the divine characteristics of mercy and justice, particularly as related to the same two fundamental traits of creation, *Genesis Rabbah* (Cohen, *Rabbinic Sages* 17). The nature of the Creator is manifest in creation.

[6] "You [Lord] made it [creation] not because you needed it, but from the fullness of your goodness. . . ." (Augustine, *Confessions* 275). The fullness of goodness is the union of justice and mercy.

[7] "[W]e agree with [K. F.] Keil and [F.] Delitzsch . . . that 'the establishment of the rainbow as a covenant sign of the promise that there should be no flood again, presupposes that it appears then for the first time in the vault and clouds of heaven.

ADAM AND EVE

Genesis 2:7 And the LORD [H3068] God [H430] formed man [H120] [of] the dust of the ground [H127], and breathed [H5301] into his nostrils [H639] the breath [H5397] of life; and man became a living soul [H5315].

The primordial image of Adam being formed from the dust of the ground specifically by the *Lord* (YHWH) [H3068] *God* (Elohim) [H430], in contrast to simply by the *Lord* [H3068], emphasizes justice via the name *God* [H430] and establishes a context for the original commandment given to man. The natural body, figuratively flesh, is the preordained dominion of the law, as exemplified by the original commandment being administered even before the Fall of Adam (Gen 2:17). Man is not merely dust, however, but rather the union of the dust of the ground and the breath of God, that is, we are born of flesh and spirit, likewise justice and mercy, and likewise law and grace. The dichotomy of flesh and spirit is the fundamental duality of both the natural world and likewise the Scriptures. Man, formed in the image of God, is the embodiment of flesh and spirit just as God is the perfect union of justice and mercy. Jesus Christ, the invisible God made visible, would likewise be conceived in the flesh through the power of the Holy Spirit (Col 1:15). Adam and Jesus Christ both embody the union of flesh and spirit. But Adam is governed by the flesh (law) while Jesus Christ is governed by the Spirit (grace). We are born of justice through our inheritance in the flesh from Adam (birthright), but we are reborn of mercy through our inheritance of the Holy Spirit in Christ (blessing).[8]

The image of God breathing the breath of life into Adam testifies to our life proceeding from God and also prefigures the promised fullness of communion with God. The breath of God is not, however, the same as the breath of Adam. The former *breathed* [H5301] (by God) is a primitive root "to breathe, blow," which reflects God as the font of life, while the latter *breath* [H5397] (of Adam) is derived from the root "to pant (as a woman in travail)" [H5395], which reflects our uneasy breath, our uncertain hold on life, in stark contrast to the utter certainty of God and the certitude that proceeds from God. The word *nostrils* [H639] (Adam's nostrils) is derived from the root "to be angry (snort)" [H599], which is another negative undertone identified with the natural body. But the breath of life foreshadows eternal life just as the natural body foreshadows the spiritual, or glorified, body (1 Cor 15:44) just as the garden foreshadows the kingdom just as the formation of Adam foreshadows the incarnation of Jesus Christ (Rom 5:14) just as the deposit of the Holy Spirit in this life foreshadows the promised fullness of the Holy Spirit in the next life (2 Cor 5:5). The uncertain breath of man presaged the Fall of Man and affirms the foreknowledge of God, but our life proceeding directly from God prefigures

---

From this it may be inferred, not that it did not rain before the flood [see Gen 2:5–6], but that the atmosphere was differently constituted' " (*New Unger's Bible Dictionary*, s.v. "rainbow"). Regardless, rain is identified with the time of the Flood, not the Creation before the Fall of Man.

[8] Anthropomorphisms, such as God breathing [acting in time and space], point to the incarnation of Christ (Coffman 47; Gen 2:7). The whole of the Bible is prophetic.

our final destiny and affirms the undeniable and unassailable will of God, which is not our death in Adam but rather our eternal life in Christ.⁹

The words *man* [H120] and *ground* [H127] (God formed) both have an association in the Hebrew "to be red" [H119], whereby a ruddy appearance is probably implied for both man and earth. But regardless of the exact etymology, man is intimately linked with the earth in that the literal origin of our physical body proceeds from the dust of the ground. The image of redness associated with both man and the ground signifies blood and likewise the life represented by blood, but the red earth is not alive in the sense that man is alive (Lev 17:11). Conscious existence proceeds from the breath of God separately from the dust of the ground, as evident in the spirit of man enduring between physical death and the resurrection of the body (Luke 16:22). The red earth and ruddy man share a common life only in the sense that the physical world is an extension of the physical body as the natural habitat of the physical body. Physical creation, the red earth, specifically signifies flesh separately from spirit and, thereby, presages, even before the Fall of Man, the blood of Abel being spilled on the earth (Gen 4:10) and likewise the blood of Jesus Christ spilled for the sins of the world (Matt 26:28). The brotherhood, or blood kinship, of dust and flesh portends the condemnation of all flesh under the law.¹⁰

In accordance with the perfect foreknowledge of God, our original kinship with the dust of the ground before the Fall of Man foreshadows our degraded state after our rejection of the garden. But flesh is not innately evil, for otherwise Jesus Christ could not be both incarnate and sinless (1 Pet 2:22). Our kinship with the red earth reflects our preference for flesh over spirit, that is, our preference for the dominion of the spirit of disobedience in conflict with the Holy Spirit (Eph 2:2). Flesh embodies disobedience because of our freewill choice to be enslaved to sin, a choice first made by Adam and universally affirmed through the sins of all subsequent men—all men, of course, except Jesus Christ. Creation is very good (Gen 1:31)—that is, freewill is very good—but choosing the bad is evil (Gen 4:6–7). The idea that creation is very good but not perfect in the sense that God is perfect is a paradoxical but inevitable consequence of the peerless perfection of God. A lack of perfection is not, however, the same as corruption. A newborn infant, for example, does not possess the wholeness of maturity and, therefore, is not complete, or perfect, in this sense; nonetheless, an infant would not be considered culpable for not having been born an adult. The primordial condescension of God creating in his own image lowly Adam is the essential condescension of the incarnation of

---

⁹ "The Spirit of God is the source of natural life [Ps 104:29–30]" (Waltke 117). God the Holy Spirit sustains the whole of creation, including every subatomic particle spinning on its quantum mechanical top.

¹⁰ "He sheweth whereof man's body was created [of the dust], to the intent that man should not glory in the excellency of his own nature [script updated]" (Whittingham et al., *Geneva Bible* 2L n. e [leaf 2, left-hand, note e]; Gen 2:7). The physical body is humble but not innately evil, for otherwise the incarnation of the Lord could not be real.

Jesus Christ (Heb 2:9), while God humbly suffering the Fall of Man is the essential humiliation of the Passion of Christ (Gal 3:13).[11]

The word *soul* [H5315] (the soul of man) has connotations of "appetite" and "desire" and "emotion" and "passion" and evokes an image of "that which breathes." Taking breath, not once and for all, but rather taking breath again and again forevermore is an image of our continuous reliance upon the Holy Spirit and likewise the continuous mediation of Jesus Christ (Heb 7:25), while our appetites, in the purest sense, are the embodiment of our freewill inherited from God, that is, our creation in the image of God (Gen 1:26). Man becoming a living soul implies receiving the dominion of freewill. Lower forms of life can only follow their base instincts and, therefore, do not possess true freewill. The sanctity of freewill is ultimately affirmed in the incarnation of God as a true man. The Son of man is the visible image of God, wherein the qualities of freewill and likewise individuality marking the incarnation are a reflection of the oneness of God (Col 1:15). The original creation of ruddy man and the red earth through the Son (John 1:3) foreshadows our new creation in the Son (2 Cor 5:17) just as the original breath of life proceeding from the Spirit of God prefigures our promised eternal life in the fullness of the indwelling of the Holy Spirit (1 Cor 15:45). The promised new life and new creation is an elevation to the fullness of communion with God and, therefore, represents a clarification of our inherited image of God, not a degradation of that image and likewise not an annihilation of freewill.[12]

Genesis 2:8–9 And the LORD God planted a garden eastward in Eden; and there he put the man whom he had formed. 9 And out of the ground made the LORD God to grow every tree that is pleasant to the sight, and good for food; the tree of life also in the midst of the garden, and the tree of knowledge of good and evil.

---

[11] That the Messiah would be only human and not superhuman is a rare case where the rabbis have spoken with one voice (Cohen, *Rabbinic Sages* 347). Confusion naturally arises because the Lord is simultaneously immanent and transcendent, fully man and fully God, but nonetheless the one voice opposing Jesus Christ should be recognized as the one voice opposing God at the tower of Babel, Gen 11:1, 11:4.

[12] The oneness of Adam becomes the twofold Adam and Eve and finally the threefold Adam, Eve, and their offspring. Likewise, the oneness of man is perceived foremost as a twofold flesh and spirit, or body and spirit, Matt 26:41, but is finally understood to be a threefold *body* [G4983], *spirit* [G4151], and *soul* [G5590], 1 Thess 5:23. And the distinction between soul and spirit should be recognized as a testimony to our essential nature being characterized by freewill, not simply the indwelling Holy Spirit expressing the divine will. This is man, who is triune, formed in the very image of God, who is triune. In the present commentary, as in the Scriptures, the twofold is emphasized, reflecting the perspective of fallen man exiled from the presence of God, whereby the words *spirit* and *soul* are both individually used to denote the intangible aspect of life, or spirit and soul collectively. And this usage is purposefully reflective of our breath, or life, now being separated from the fullness of the Holy Spirit.

ADAM, NOAH, ABRAHAM

Creation, or reality as a whole, is an extension of mankind, in accordance with the nature of freewill, which necessarily operates in space and time. The garden—representing the creation of God, likewise the will of God—is connected to mankind by the two trees, which signify the dominion of freewill as created in the image of God. The garden, or original creation, represents the will of God, specifically the will of God the Father. The first tree to be taken by mankind, the tree of the knowledge of good and evil, is twofold, reflecting the spiritual and the natural and ultimately Jesus Christ, God the Son—who is fully God and fully man, embodying on the tree of the cross both the good blessing of God and the evil curse upon mankind (Gen 3:22–24). The second, yet future tree to be partaken of by mankind, the tree of life, is something new, relating the promised new creation that will be animated by the fullness of the indwelling of God the Holy Spirit.

Genesis 2:10–14 And a river went out of Eden to water the garden; and from thence it was parted, and became into four heads. 11 The name of the first [is] Pison: that [is] it which compasseth the whole land of Havilah, where [there is] gold; 12 And the gold of that land [is] good: there [is] bdellium and the onyx stone. 13 And the name of the second river [is] Gihon: the same [is] it that compasseth the whole land of Ethiopia. 14 And the name of the third river [is] Hiddekel: that [is] it which goeth toward the east of Assyria. And the fourth river [is] Euphrates.

The four rivers flowing from the one garden, representing the original creation, point to the conception of Jesus as king of kings, embodying the promised kingdom of God, at the end of the fourth millennium from Adam.

Genesis 2:15 And the LORD God took the man, and put [H3240] him into the garden [H1588] of Eden [H5731] to dress [H5647] it and to keep [H8104] it.

The name *Eden* [H5731] (the garden of Eden) has a connotation of "luxury, dainty, delight" [H5730], while the word *put* [H3240] (God put Adam) has a connotation "to rest" [H5117]. Images of working in paradise, keeping the garden, are not incongruous. Work, or activity, is not inherently bad just as the flesh is not innately evil. Our freewill as expressed in the flesh is neither synonymous with sin. Work has negative connotations because of the curse incurred by Adam, making work in this life literally oppressive and figuratively vain, but the image of work recast in terms of dominion and growth is more recognizable as a positive manifestation of freewill. Man cannot fully comprehend paradise, but feckless luxury is a pagan ideal that clearly should not be connected with either the garden or eternity.[13]

---

[13] "Because Gen 1 is a portrait of what God intends, it is also an eschatological statement. This serene, beautiful world, in which all is ordered to humans, and humans

ADAM AND EVE

The word *dress* [H5647] (Adam to dress the garden) means "to work" and "to serve," which emphasizes Adam as the vassal of God, not as the friend of God, while the implicit subjection of Adam is also consistent with the prevailing themes of power and authority and justice identified with the original creation. Adam is a spiritual child, not a spiritual adult, whereby Adam and likewise all mankind in Adam are restrained and disciplined not simply as a servant but as a child. The word *keep* [H8104] (Adam to keep the garden) means "to keep" and "to watch" and "to preserve," while the word *garden* [H1588] (the garden of Eden) means "enclosure, garden" and is derived from the root "to defend" [H1598]. And these are all images of guardianship, implying a relationship between the explicit guardianship of the garden and the implicit growth of the garden. The first man Adam being formed to protect the garden of God is a vision of mankind called to keep the ways of God. The image of an enclosed (hedged) garden finally prefigures the enclosed (walled) kingdom where no evildoer will enter (Luke 13:28). The implicit growth of the garden reflects the implicit promise of the growth of mankind, both in number and also in spiritual character, elevated from the adolescent servants of God to be the mature friends of God (John 15:15).[14]

The preordained occupation of man, or Adam-kind, even before the original sin, is to grow in communion with the Spirit of God and to guard against the spirit of disobedience. The universality of our preordained occupation, whether in the garden or outside the garden, is a testament to the undeniable nature of the will of God. The calling of Adam to keep the garden is the call of all mankind to faith, while the sanctity of our freewill is an affirmation of our creation in the image of God and likewise our inherited dominion, which is also from God. Freewill implies a real choice, which implies good and bad, which implies a separation of good and bad. The existence of freewill thereby affirms the primordial image of an enclosed garden, separate from an outer realm even before the Fall of Adam. The calling of the first man Adam to keep the garden of God from evil affirms that the spirit of disobedience preexisted the original fall of mankind in Adam just as the blood kinship of ruddy man with the red earth preexisted the original rejection of God. Disobedience is not something of itself but rather is a corruption of obedience and, therefore, is always waiting at the door (Gen 4:7).[15]

The garden of Eden foreshadows the kingdom of God, but the foretold kingdom is not simply a return to the original garden. Man succumbed to the spirit of disobedience in the garden, but in the promised kingdom the law will

---

are ordered to God, is how it will be at the end" (Clifford, *New Jerome* 11; Gen 2:1–3). The whole of the Bible, every nuance, every jot and tittle, is sacred and therefore prophetic, and the spirit of prophecy is always poetic and fractal.

[14] "And the Lord God took the man, and made him dwell in the garden of Eden; and set him to do service in the law, and to keep it [*Jerusalem Targum*]" (Etheridge 1:163). Work precedes rest and peace just as law precedes grace and eternal life.

[15] Man was originally placed in the garden as in a school for the training of his physical powers, intellect, and moral agency (Jamieson et al. 1:36; Gen 2:8). The school of the garden is the law that governs flesh.

be written on our very hearts (Heb 10:16). Adam embracing the spirit of disobedience revealed a preference of the natural body for its own flesh, but the preference of the spiritual body will be the Holy Spirit of God. And this is a progression prefigured innately by children growing into adulthood and maturity. The garden prefigures the kingdom just as the natural body prefigures the spiritual, or glorified, body just as the one man Adam prefigures the one man Jesus Christ, but the kingdom transcends the garden just as the spiritual body transcends the natural body just as Jesus Christ transcends Adam.[16]

Man was predestined for full communion with the Lord even before our creation just as good parents plan for the elevation of their children into maturity even before their conception. But the perfection of the Lord God is inconsistent with the notion that our fall in Adam—that is, our rejection of God—was somehow a prerequisite to the kingdom of God. And the completeness of the Lord God is inconsistent with the notion that evil is somehow necessary in creation. Esau could have guarded his birthright in fulfillment of the desire of his father, Isaac, just as the first man Adam could have obeyed the singular commandment in the garden and could have grown in communion with the Spirit of God without having to leave the garden (Deut 30:11). But Adam disobeyed the law of God just as Esau despised his birthright (Gen 25:34). The garden of Eden was not the beginning of human history but rather a separate path that we have rejected, a birthright that we have despised. The Fall of Man was the true beginning of human history, the history of the way of man in conflict with God. The garden was the path of God, while this world is the path of man. And yet remarkably, despite our fall, the will of God—that is, the love of God—cannot be denied.[17]

The First Law

Genesis 2:16–17 And the Lord [H3068] God [H430] commanded the man, saying, Of every tree [H6086] of the garden thou mayest freely eat: 17 But of the tree [H6086] of the knowledge [H1847] of good and evil, thou shalt not eat of it: for in the day that thou eatest thereof thou shalt surely die [H4191].

The Scriptures record many covenants just as the Scriptures record many names of God, but there are only two essential covenants in creation just as there are only two essential names of God. The first covenant, which is the Covenant of Law, governs the natural body, figuratively flesh, just as the first name of God, *Elohim* [H430], is identified with the original creation of all flesh under the law. The second covenant, which is the Covenant of Grace, governs

---

[16] In Talmudic writings, the hereafter of the righteous is called Gan Eden, "garden of Eden," but it is normally understood to be distinct from the original habitation of Adam and Eve (Cohen, *Rabbinic Sages* 383). The garden of God points to the kingdom of God, wherein the offered kingdom cannot be the same as the already rejected garden.

[17] See C. S. Lewis's discussion of freewill (Lewis, *Mere Christianity* 52).

the spiritual, or glorified, body, figuratively spirit, just as the second name of God, *Jehovah* (YHWH) [H3068], is identified with our new creation by grace through faith in Jesus Christ. The compound name *Lord* [H3068] *God* [H430] (commanded the man) represents an emphasis on the character of justice that also prefigures the union of justice and mercy. Likewise, the Covenant of Law emphasizes justice but is ultimately completed by the Covenant of Grace.[18]

Generally, the Old Testament represents the Covenant of Law while the New Testament represents the Covenant of Grace. Specifically, the dichotomy of law and grace is evident in both the Old and New Testaments, but the law is emphasized in the Old Testament while grace is emphasized in the New Testament. Adam and Christ are likewise both the embodiments of flesh and spirit. But Adam is governed by flesh—that is, under law—whereas Christ is governed, or led, by the Spirit—that is, by grace. Law precedes grace just as the natural body precedes the spiritual body just as this world precedes the next world. The natural man Adam (first man) likewise precedes the spiritual man Jesus Christ (second man) just as the incarnation of Jesus Christ (First Advent) prefigures the revelation of the Body of Christ (Second Advent), whereby all signs point to the fulfillment of all things in the last days.

The Biblical account begins with faithless man eating from the tree of knowledge in the book of Genesis but ends with faithful mankind eating from the tree of life in the book of Revelation. The trees of knowledge and life can be compared, respectively, to flesh and spirit, likewise to law and grace, and likewise to death and life. The word *knowledge* [H1847] (the tree of knowledge) is derived from the root "to know" [H3045], which has connotations "to discriminate, distinguish," specifically "to know by experience," reflecting the need to distinguish the evil from the good. But the natural body, figuratively flesh, is the medium of the experiential knowledge of good and evil—whereby the required judgment between good and evil is ominously consigned to the dominion of flesh and not to the Holy Spirit. This is a testimony to the sanctity of freewill that is maintained despite sin crouching at the door. Good and evil are tangible realities and not mere abstractions just as the judgment of good and evil is executed in the flesh, but the Spirit is the font of life itself, our intangible existence, and is ultimately more real than physical reality since the physical reflects the spiritual and not vice versa. The difference between the tree of knowledge and the tree of life is the difference between the first man Adam and the second man Jesus Christ. The former is governed by flesh, while the latter is governed by the Holy Spirit.

The tree of the knowledge of good and evil is the dominion of flesh and the primordial symbol of the Covenant of Law, whereby Jesus Christ would be figuratively nailed to the tree of knowledge in fulfillment of the curse incurred by Adam through that tree. But the tree of knowledge becomes the tree of life

---

[18] The name *Elohim* relates the attribute of strength, while the name *Jehovah*, YHWH, evokes an image of divine self-existence that is distinctly identified with redemption (Scofield 6 n. 2; Gen 2:4). The strength of the law that governs flesh compared with the eternal life, or existence, that comes only by grace.

in the resurrection of Jesus Christ just as the natural body becomes the spiritual, or glorified, body just as the Covenant of Law becomes the Covenant of Grace. The former foreshadows the latter while the latter completes the former, such that the two are one. The resurrection of Jesus Christ at the First Advent (as and with firstfruits) is likewise fulfilled in the resurrection of all the dead at the Second Advent (harvest) (Matt 27:52–53, Lev 23:10–12). The tree of knowledge precedes the tree of life just as the natural body precedes the spiritual body just as law precedes grace. The natural man ate from the tree of knowledge and was driven out of the garden of Eden, but the spiritual man will eat from the tree of life and enter into the kingdom of God (Rev 22:14).

The tree of knowledge and the tree of life can also be compared, respectively, to the baptism in water and the baptism of fire, that is, to the baptism of repentance and the baptism of the Holy Spirit. The tree of knowledge precedes the tree of life just as law precedes grace just as the natural body precedes the spiritual, or glorified, body just as repentance in the flesh precedes redemption in the Spirit. The baptism in water and the baptism of the Holy Spirit can be compared, respectively, to the destruction in the floodwaters and the foretold destruction by fire. The destruction in the floodwaters would be the virtual death of all flesh just as the baptism in water is the figurative death to flesh, that is, the symbolic death to sin. The foretold destruction by fire, however, will be the literal death of all flesh just as the baptism of the Holy Spirit is the literal end of the sinful nature (2 Pet 3:7). Sin would continue in the world after the floodwaters receded just as believers continue to sin after the baptism in water, but the first creation will not continue after the destruction by fire just as the sinful nature is utterly destroyed in the baptism of the Holy Spirit. Two trees, two destructions, two baptisms. One hope in the one God.

The call of the first man Adam to obedience is a prophecy of the perfect obedience of the second man Jesus Christ. The call of Adam is also the call of all men in Adam, which is in turn a prophecy of the perfect obedience of the faithful reborn in Christ. The described dominion of Adam is vast but is contingent on his obedience, whereby the singular commandment given to Adam signifies the whole of the curses and blessings of the law of Moses (Deut 11:26). The Fall of Man—that is, the death of Adam, likewise the death of all mankind in Adam—is a prophecy of the Passion of Christ for the sake of all mankind. The perfect obedience of Jesus Christ, even unto death, would fulfill the call of Adam and likewise the law of Moses. The word *die* [H4191] (man will surely die) has a connotation "to die as a penalty, be put to death" while the word *tree* [H6086] (the tree of knowledge) has a connotation "gallows," all of which reinforces the image of death under the law that would ultimately be the death of Jesus Christ for the sins of the whole world. The prophecy of death related by the tree of knowledge is not only the physical death of all flesh, which is a separation from material creation, but also the spiritual death of faithlessness, which is a separation from the Holy Spirit. The lake of fire is the

ADAM AND EVE

second death (Rev 21:8). The natural death first, the spiritual death second. The First Advent followed by the Second Advent.[19]

Male and Female

Genesis 2:18 And the LORD [H3068] God [H430] said, [It is] not good that the man should be alone; I will make him an help meet [H5828] for him.

The Hebrew word *help meet* (helper) [H5828] (God made) is derived from the root "to help, succour" [H5826], which reflects the essential complementary relationship between male and female and reinforces the image of male and female as one flesh (Gen 2:24). The nature of man personifies justice, as typified by the greater average physical strength of man relative to woman and the implied ability to administer justice by force, whereby the nature of man recalls the first name of God, *Elohim* [H430], which likewise emphasizes power and authority and justice. In contrast, the nature of woman personifies the character of mercy, as typified by the anatomical machinery for childbearing and nursing, whereby the nature of woman recalls the second name of God, *Jehovah* (YHWH) [H3068], which likewise emphasizes mercy and life. The union of male and female is thereby an image of the union of justice and mercy just as the compound name *Lord* [H3068] *God* [H430] implies the perfect union of justice and mercy, whereby male and female together are truly made in the image of God (Gen 1:27).[20]

The life of Eve proceeds from Adam just as the love of mercy proceeds from the austerity of justice. The revelation of the name *Jehovah* (YHWH) [H3068] likewise follows after the name *Elohim* [H430] just as the incarnation of the second man Jesus Christ follows after the formation of the first man Adam. The Covenant of Law prefigures the Covenant of Grace just as man (justice) prefigures woman (mercy) just as the natural man (Adam) prefigures the spiritual man (Jesus) just as the natural body (flesh) prefigures the spiritual body (spirit). But the spiritual, or glorified, body is a true body—that is, the spiritual body is a true union of flesh and spirit just as the perfection of justice is not mercy but rather the union of justice and mercy. Likewise, the perfection of man is not woman but rather the union of man and woman. The perfection of God is the perfect union of justice and mercy, together embodied by Jesus Christ (Luke 13:32). The body of Jesus Christ missing from the tomb (Luke

---

[19] Poetic exaggeration serves to create a dramatic effect, but any such overstatement may also be pointing to a more complete fulfillment of prophecy at the end of days—specifically a figurative fulfillment in the near term pointing to a literal fulfillment in the long term (Haggith 304–7). The nature of prophecy is poetic and fractal.

[20] The wisdom of man regards being an help meet as something lowly, but the wisdom of God regards being an help meet as something superior and actually the only profession worthy of his own divine status, Matt 20:25–28 (Guzik 31; Gen 2:18). The divine help meet is uniquely God the Holy Spirit, which is yet another identification of the Holy Spirit with the feminine.

24:5) and likewise the nature of the risen Christ (John 20:27) are vivid testimonies that the spiritual, or glorified, body is a true body, while the foretold marriage of the Lamb is a dramatic affirmation of the communion of creation (flesh) with God (Spirit) being the ultimate embodiment of the union of law and grace (Rev 19:7). The union of flesh and spirit in the person of Christ prefigures the union of the faithful with Jesus Christ. Likewise, the resurrection of Christ as and with the firstfruits of the grave prefigures the resurrection of all the dead in the last days (Matt 27:52–53, Lev 23:10–12).[21]

Man cannot live without woman just as perfect justice must be tempered by mercy, whereby mercy and justice are complements and not opposites just as man and woman are complements and not opposites.[22] Injustice is the opposite of justice. Cruelty is the opposite of mercy. The notion permeating popular culture that good somehow needs evil or that the Godhead is somehow a synthesis of good and evil are both the same satanic delusion. God is the perfect union of justice and mercy, without any injustice or cruelty. The progressive nature of the Scriptures moves from images of justice (in the condemnation of man) to images of mercy (in the preservation of man) to images of the synthesis of justice and mercy (in the redemption of man). This progression does not reflect an evolution of God but rather a progressive sanctification of the faithful just as our individual lives are a progressive maturation. God himself is without change, being always the perfect union of justice and mercy—as typified in Adam by the animation of the dust of the ground by the breath of God (Gen 2:7), fully revealed in the incarnation of Jesus Christ through the power of the Holy Spirit (Matt 1:20), and finally expressed in the promised resurrection of the Body of Christ (John 11:25).[23]

Genesis 2:19 And out of the ground the LORD God formed every beast of the field, and every fowl of the air; and brought [them] unto Adam to see what he would call them: and whatsoever Adam called every living creature, that [was] the name thereof.

Adam-kind, formed in the very image of God, has freewill and also dominion in accordance with freewill, the sanctity of which God—who is complete, or perfect, and therefore sinless—chooses not to violate.

---

[21] "Thus, when the Lord says of man and woman, 'Wherefore they are no longer two, but one flesh' [Matt 19:6], we may say, in accordance with the logic of union, 'They are no longer two persons but one,' even though, obviously, the natures are distinct. Just as in the example of marriage the mention of unity of flesh in not contradicted by the duality of subjects, so in the case of Christ the personal union is not destroyed by the distinction of natures [Theodore of Mopsuestia, *On the Incarnation*]" (Norris 120). Creation as a whole is formed in the very image of God.

[22] Not even the man who chooses to live alone can claim to live without woman, since he could not have lived at all apart from his mother.

[23] *Help meet* literally means "a helper fit for him," but frequently the same term is actually applied to God, Deut 33:7, Ps 33:20, Ps 70:5, etc. (Viviano, *Collegeville* 42; Gen 2:18–24). Who is God our helper, except the indwelling Holy Spirit?

ADAM AND EVE

Genesis 2:20   And Adam gave names to all cattle, and to the fowl of the air, and to every beast of the field; but for Adam there was not found an help meet for him.

The nature, or way, of flesh—representing the present fallen world—does not distinguish between man and animal. And thereby the people of the world have become like animals. But the truth is that man and woman—separated from animals, birds, and so forth—are formed in the one image of God.[24]

Genesis 2:21–22   And the LORD [H3068] God [H430] caused a deep sleep to fall upon Adam [H121], and he slept: and he took one of his ribs [H6763], and closed up the flesh instead thereof; 22 And the rib [H6763], which the LORD [H3068] God [H430] had taken from man, made he a woman, and brought her unto the man.

The name *Adam* [H121] and the words *man* [H120] and *ground* [H127] all have an association in the Hebrew "to be red" [H119]. The implied kinship between man and earth, in contrast to between man and heaven, is an emphasis on man as the embodiment of carnal nature, flesh governed by law. Adam being put into a deep sleep is an image of death, which is always closely identified with the natural body, while Eve proceeding from the sleeping Adam is a vision of the promised resurrection of the spiritual, or glorified, body. Eve proceeds from Adam just as the spiritual body proceeds from the natural body just as our redemption by grace proceeds from our condemnation under the law. The natural body is the image of God, through a glass darkly, while the spiritual body is the reality of the fullness of the indwelling Holy Spirit, a clear image of God, face to face, not of ourselves, but only in Christ (1 Cor 13:12). Woman is presented to man because humanity should not be bereft of companionship, while grace is bestowed on humanity because the faithful should not be bereft of the communion with God (Gen 2:18).

Eve, the mother of all the living, originating and proceeding from the *rib* (side) [H6763] of Adam prefigures all creation, represented by man and beast collectively, emerging from the side of Noah's ark after the Flood (Gen 6:16). The mother of all the living emerging from the side of Adam and also all humanity emerging from the side of the ark both point to our promised new creation, represented by the flow of water and blood, emerging from the side of Christ on the cross (John 19:34). The emergence of woman and the offspring implied by woman, being connected with the promise of redemption, closely identifies woman with spirit and likewise grace, a relationship affirmed by the prophecy that Christ would appear as the Seed of woman, in contrast to that of

---

[24] "There is, however, no doubt that the various [human] races, when carefully compared and measured, differ much from each other . . . the form and capacity of the skull, and even in the convolutions of the brain. . . . Their mental characteristics are likewise very distinct; chiefly as it would appear in their emotional, but partly in their intellectual, faculties" (Darwin, *The Descent of Man* 167). The theory of evolution leads inevitably to eugenics.

man (Gen 3:15). Christ being conceived of the Holy Spirit and simultaneously being the offspring of woman relates the twofold natures of Jesus Christ being the God-man, while the innate identification of the Spirit with the feminine relates an emphasis on grace and, thereby, identifies the incarnation of God with the grace of God. Woman and the offspring implied by woman all proceeding from man is a reflection of God the Holy Spirit and God the Son proceeding from God the Father.[25]

Genesis 2:23 And Adam said, This [is] now bone [H6106] of my bones [H6106], and flesh [H1320] of my flesh [H1320]: she shall be called Woman, because she was taken out of Man.

Flesh and bone signify, respectively, flesh and spirit. The word *flesh* [H1320] (flesh of my flesh) is derived from the root "to bear tidings" [H1319], which is an image of the body, figuratively flesh, being the medium of experience and expression, in turn recalling the tree of knowledge. The word *bone* [H6106] (bone of my bones) connotes "substance, self" and is derived from the root "to be vast, numerous" and "to be mighty" [H6105]. Our spirit is our true substance, or essence, just as our bones are our inner parts. The spirit is the life of flesh just as our bones are the foundation of our flesh.[26]

Man and woman are both individually the union of flesh and spirit just as man and woman are both individually the union of flesh and bone. The first man Adam and the second man Jesus Christ are likewise both individually the union of flesh and spirit. But the image of man emphasizes justice while the image of woman emphasizes mercy. Likewise, the first man Adam is governed by flesh while the second man Jesus Christ is governed by the Holy Spirit. Man is formed first and woman second just as the natural body precedes the spiritual body just as the Covenant of Law precedes the Covenant of Grace.

The emphasis that man and woman are the same flesh and bone forming one body is an image of the one true God as the perfect union of justice and mercy and likewise of law and grace. Man and woman and the children implied by the union of man and woman form one family just as the Father, Son, and Holy Spirit are one God. In testimony to our creation in the very image of God, the synthesis of individuality and communality is ubiquitous in all creation—as evident in the distinct parts of the body composing individuals, individuals composing families, families composing communities, communities composing regions, regions composing nations, and nations composing the world.[27] All

---

[25] "[A]nd [the Lord God] *brought her* [Eve] *unto the man* [Adam]; from the place where the rib had been carried, and she was made of it; . . . so it was a type of the marriage of Christ, the second Adam, between him and his church, which sprung from him, from his side; . . ." (Gill 1:17; Gen 2:22). Not merely the earthly church, which is transitory and corrupted, but rather the Body of Christ, which is eternal and perfected.

[26] Eve was presumably formed from both the flesh and bone of Adam's side since Adam would refer to Eve as both his flesh and bone (Clarke 1:45; Gen 2:21). Flesh and bone, representing law and grace, the union of which is a third thing, namely, life.

[27] Now ye are the body of Christ, and members in particular, 1 Cor 12:27.

levels of reality prefigure the faithful in Christ forming the Body of Christ with Christ as the Head (Eph 5:23).[28]

Genesis 2:24 Therefore shall a man leave [H5800] his father and his mother, and shall cleave unto his wife: and they shall be one flesh.

The presence of God would literally be the only parents Adam would ever know and spiritually the true parents of all mankind in Adam (Matt 23:9). The word *leave* [H5800] (man shall leave his parents) means "to leave" and "to forsake," whereby the prophecy that man would leave his parents portends Adam forsaking the presence of God, likewise all mankind in Adam forsaking the name of God (Acts 4:12). But Adam forsaking the garden ironically prefigures the Son descending from heaven, figuratively forsaking the presence of God, just as the death of Adam, likewise the death of all mankind in Adam, prefigures the death of Jesus Christ in the place of all mankind. Jesus Christ is the invisible God made visible, whereby the disfigurement of Christ on the cross embodies the corruption of the image of God in fallen Adam (Col 1:15). God forsaking Adam and exiling him from the garden foreshadows God the Father forsaking God the Son on the cross (Matt 27:46), wherein the image of the Father forsaking the Son is a graphic affirmation that Jesus Christ truly assumed our curse (Gal 3:13). The essence of the corruption of the image of God is our rejection of God, which is our corruption of our freewill.[29]

Man leaves his parents just as Adam rejected God, but the preordained marriage of man and woman is a prophecy of the reconciliation of man with God (Isa 62:5). The marriage of man and woman is an image of the perfection of flesh by spirit and likewise the perfection of justice by mercy, a perfection ultimately embodied by the marriage of the Lamb in the foretold communion of the faithful with God (Rev 19:7). The Son forsaking the Father is understood as the humble condescension of Jesus Christ, forsaking his exalted status for the sake of the faithful. The assembly of the faithful, represented by the visible church, is the bride but not directly, rather only in Christ. For the law condemns everyone, including the chosen but for Christ (Rom 3:23). Christ is not only the Lamb but is also himself closely identified with the church. The faithful are sanctified by the Holy Spirit only in the Body of Christ and, thereby, presented as a bride only through Christ. We are the Body of Christ, not merely a body of faithful as something unto ourselves. Christ is the bridegroom as the incarnation of God, but Christ also embodies the church as the substitutionary sacrifice for the church. Christ is all things in the act of offering himself (Heb 7:27). The

---

[28] "In marriage the unity of two into one makes the new unity a reflection of the unity of the Trinity, and the unity of Christ and the Church" (Hopko, *Orthodox Faith* 1:146). The progressive revelation of the Trinity is evident throughout all creation.

[29] "The image of the Father [embodied by Adam, or mankind] was left desolate. This, then, is the reason why the mystery of the Passover has been completed in the body of the Lord [Melito of Sardis, *Homily on the Passover*]" (Norris 40). God the Son is the new Adam, the new image of God, namely, the image of the Father made visible, though necessarily maintaining the eternal distinction between the Son and the Father.

unity of the Body of Christ, affirmed by the identification of Christ with both the Head and the Body, is prefigured in Adam and Eve both originally being embodied by Adam alone, before Eve was formed from Adam.[30]

The image of marriage implies offspring, but the offspring of the marriage of the Lamb and the faithful is the sanctification of the faithful themselves, reborn as new creations by the power, or new life, of the Holy Spirit. The faithful are called to Christ as a bride but are ultimately reborn in the union. The image of man leaving his father and mother is an image of the Son descending from the presence of God, specifically from the Father and the Holy Spirit, while the Son calling the faithful in him unto himself is finally fulfilled by the Son presenting the faithful to the Father through the power of the indwelling Holy Spirit. All the children of God are presented to the Father just as a patriarch claims all his descendents as his progeny. The Son prepares a place for the faithful in the Father's mansions (John 14:2).

The threefold image of man, woman, and child is ultimately a vision of the Father, Son, and Holy Spirit, wherein the image of woman is understood collectively as woman and the offspring implied by woman and, thereby, relates the Son as the perfect embodiment of the Spirit. Woman and the offspring implied by woman were originally taken from the side of man just as the Spirit and the Son proceed from the Father, while woman and the offspring of woman submit to man just as the Spirit and the Son submit to the Father. The silence of woman in the assembly of the faithful should be understood as a revelation of the subtlety of the Holy Spirit (1 Tim 2:11). To say woman is less than man would be like saying the Holy Spirit is less than the Father, which is heresy. Eve originally proceeding from the side of Adam expressly prefigures the Holy Spirit proceeding from the Father to overshadow Mary in the conception of the Son (Luke 1:35). Mary, mother of Jesus, is thereby most closely identified with the Holy Spirit in relationship to the Father, not the faithful called as the bride of the Son through the power of the Holy Spirit. The threefold man, son, and their progeny are also a vision of the Father, Son, and Holy Spirit, wherein a patriarch claiming the sons of his son reflects all creation proceeding from the Father. The image of a father's progeny proceeding through his son is a vision of the Holy Spirit proceeding from the Father through the Son to sanctify the multitudes of the faithful in Christ. The concurrent complexity and simplicity of the Godhead is the infinite nature of God revealed in the simplicity of love.[31]

---

[30] "... 'I [the Lord God] will take a righteous man from amongst them [Israel] and make him a pledge on their account, and I will atone for their iniquities' [*Exodus Rabbah*]" (Cohen, *Rabbinic Sages* 118). No man is righteous, save the Lord himself.

[31] "So if we consider in the Father and the Son the power whereby they spirate [breathe] the Holy Ghost, there is no mean [no intermediate], for this is one and the same power. But if we consider the persons themselves spirating, then, as the Holy Ghost proceeds both from the Father and from the Son, the Holy Ghost proceeds from the Father immediately, as from Him, and mediately [intervening], as from the Son; and thus He is said to proceed from the Father through the Son. So also did Abel proceed immediately from Adam, inasmuch as Adam was his father; and mediately, as Eve was his mother,

ADAM AND EVE

Genesis 2:25 And they were both naked [H6174], the man and his wife, and were not ashamed.

The word *naked* [H6174] (naked but not ashamed) has an association in the Hebrew "to be shrewd, crafty" [H6191], which reflects our kinship with the shrewd serpent. Man and woman originally being naked but not ashamed does not mean that we were in some way perfect before our fall but rather that our preference for flesh had not yet been revealed by the original commandment. A deviant nature is a prerequisite for a deviant act. Paul teaches that sin was in the world even before the law (Rom 5:13). If Adam had been perfect, he would not have been disobedient. If Adam had been perfectly innocent, he would not have been culpable. But we cannot blame God for our imperfection, because God is one and, thereby, embodies a peerless perfection. To assert our own innate perfection is to try to elevate ourselves to godhood, and that is the sin of the devil. To say we should not have been created imperfect is like saying we should not have been created at all. But neither is our imperfection compared with God an excuse for our sins. The original commandment was simple, but in Adam we have all chosen to disobey. Neither can we blame God for giving the original commandment, because the law leads us to grace, the fullness of communion with God, both in the garden and now in the present fallen world (Gal 3:24). The persistent idea among the people of the world that any command given to imperfect man is unrealistic is disputed by our observable existence under natural law.[32]

Naked

Genesis 3:1–3 Now the serpent [H5175] was more subtil [H6175] than any beast of the field which the LORD [H3068] God [H430] had made. And he said unto the woman, Yea, hath God [H430] said, Ye shall not eat of every tree of the garden? 2 And the woman said unto the serpent, We may eat of the fruit of the trees of the garden: 3 But of the fruit of the tree which [is] in the midst of the garden, God [H430] hath said, Ye shall not eat of it, neither shall ye touch it, lest ye die.

The narrator uses the name *Lord* [H3068] *God* [H430], while the serpent and the woman both use the name *God* [H430]. The narrator demonstrates a more profound understanding of the nature of God, consistent with having a transcendent perspective. The use of the name *God* (Elohim) [H430], the name closely identified with our original creation being established through the power and authority of God, reflects the perspective of the serpent and the woman,

---

who proceeded from Adam; . . ." (Aquinas, *Summa* 1:186). Confusion arises because both the 1-2-3 sequence Father, Son, and Spirit and also the 1-2-3, or 1-3-2, sequence Father, Spirit, and Son are evident in the Scriptures.

[32] The Hebrew word *Torah* means "teaching, direction," not "law" (Cohen, *Rabbinic Sages* xxxiv). The law was our schoolmaster to bring us unto Christ, that we might be justified by faith, Gal 3:24.

who are both created beings subject to divine power and authority under law (Gen 1:1). In contrast, the name *Lord* (YHWH) [H3068] is identified with our new creation proceeding from the mercy of God and being embodied by the freedom from slavery that comes only by grace (Exod 6:3).

Antediluvian mankind, spiritually Adam and Eve, could only comprehend the name *God* [H430] just as carnal man is governed by justice (law) and not by mercy (grace). Antediluvian mankind embodies a particularly close relationship between the original creation and the law since these first generations of men would fall under the condemnation of the law in the floodwaters, a condemnation of the first era of man that echoes the condemnation of the first man Adam. The life of Adam spanning almost the entire first millennium intimately connects the life and death of Adam with the life and death of antediluvian mankind, given that the overlap of the life of Adam with the generation of the Flood is so profound. However, the floodwaters are not simply equivalent to the law. The floodwaters are connected with law, likewise with death, by those condemned outside the ark, while the same floodwaters are connected with life, specifically with rebirth, by those redeemed in the ark. Accordingly, those outside the ark call upon the name *God* (Elohim) [H430] while those inside the ark call upon the name *Lord* (YHWH) [H3068]. This is the dichotomy of death and resurrection represented by the baptism in water, whereby the wooden ark foreshadows the wooden cross (1 Pet 3:21).

The word *serpent* [H5175] (spoke unto the woman) has an association "to practice divination, observe signs" [H5172], representing a primal relationship between the devil and the occult in conflict with the one true faith. The word *subtil* (subtle) [H6175] (the serpent was subtil) means "crafty, shrewd" and is related to the word *naked* [H6174] (naked but not ashamed) used to describe the nakedness of Adam and Eve, which is a relationship that implies a kinship between mankind and the serpent even before our fall (Gen 2:25). Noah or Abraham or Moses or David or Elijah or John or Peter would likewise have fallen just as Adam fell, because the root problem is not one sin or one disobedient man but rather our universal nature. All have sinned and fall short of the glory of God, not because of original sin, but in accord with original sin (Rom 3:23). The serpent did not compel Adam and Eve to disobey God, but only appealed to our universal nature of faithlessness. Every man is an Adam unto himself because every man sins in imitation of Adam, whereby no man can reject his inheritance from Adam. Only Jesus Christ, the Son of man, the God-man—because he is perfectly sinless, innately and infinitely—can reject the inheritance from the first man Adam, which is death and likewise spiritual separation from the Father.[33]

Disobedience to God, epitomized by the disobedience of Adam, is an expression of a denial of God that is the opposite of faith in God. But faith is

---

[33] "It is not stated that the serpent was more subtle than any *other* beast of the field, but that he was more subtle than *any* beast. This is an indication that he was not a beast at all; . . ." (Coffman 59; Gen 3:1). The old serpent is the physical reality, while the great dragon is the spiritual reality, Rev 12:9.

more than simple belief. Even demons believe that God literally exists, but they deny the spiritual reality of God, that is, the grace of God (Jas 2:19). The word *faith* [G4102] means "belief" and "trust" and "fidelity," not simply "belief."[34]

Genesis 3:4–6 And the serpent said unto the woman, Ye shall not surely die: 5 For God [H430] doth know that in the day ye eat thereof, then your eyes shall be opened, and ye shall be as gods [H430], knowing good [H2896] and evil [H7451]. 6 And when the woman saw that the tree [was] good for food, and that it [was] pleasant to the eyes, and a tree to be desired to make [one] wise, she took of the fruit thereof, and did eat, and gave also unto her husband with her; and he did eat.

Man is the embodiment of flesh and likewise justice, while woman is the embodiment of spirit and likewise mercy. Accordingly, the serpent deceiving Eve and not Adam—that is, Adam falling through Eve and not vice versa (1 Tim 2:14)—represents flesh being corrupted through a false spirit (2 Cor 11:3–4). A false spirit can corrupt flesh, but flesh of itself does not corrupt spirit, as affirmed by the sinless life of Jesus Christ in the flesh. The union of flesh (creation) and spirit (breath of God), in accordance with the perfect union of justice and mercy embodied by God, is life itself (a living soul), whereas the corruption of flesh by the spirit of disobedience is the antithesis of life, manifested as suffering and decay and death in both man and likewise the physical world. Adam and Eve were originally created in the image of God, and therefore the perversion of their union through their rebellion is a perversion of the image of God. Our condemnation through the one man Adam foreshadows our redemption through the one man Jesus Christ, but our fall is a reverse image of our redemption and exaltation, that is, a corrupted image (Rom 5:18). The serpent seducing Eve in the conception of sin and death (Rom 5:12) prefigures, in reverse, the Holy Spirit overshadowing the virgin Mary in the conception of the Son, who is the embodiment of life itself (Luke 1:35).[35]

The serpent's promise that mankind would become like *gods* [H430] ironically portends mankind becoming the embodiment of the justice (wrath) of God, a reality ultimately revealed in Christ being nailed to the cross as a true man. The serpent, regardless of his exact expectation, deceived Eve through a limited literal interpretation of the original commandment, a mark of spiritual ignorance always identified with the children of the serpent. The serpent did not literally lie, since Adam and Eve would not die immediately in the flesh. And

---

[34] "This is Satan's chiefest subtlety, to cause us not to fear God's threatenings" (Whittingham et al., *Geneva Bible* 2R n. d; Gen 3:4). We wrestle not against flesh and blood, Eph 6:12.

[35] "As the father of the human race according to the flesh, and the representative head of all men in the original reception and forfeiture of divine grace, Adam is a type of Christ Who is the representative head of all men in the recovery of supernatural righteousness and the spiritual father of all who are born again to the life of grace. Adam, therefore, is a type of Christ both by analogy and by contrast . . . ." (*Catholic Encyclopedia*, s.v. "Adam"). Christ is the new Adam, not simply another Adam.

ADAM, NOAH, ABRAHAM

Adam and Eve did become like gods, knowing good and evil, in the sense they became aware of the serpent, that is, aware of the evil nature of the serpent. The serpent did lie, however, in the spiritual sense relating to the ultimate truth of the original commandment, whereby the deception of Eve serves as a primordial primer, admonishing us to always seek a full understanding that complements literal meaning with spiritual meaning. The words *good* [H2896] and *evil* [H7451] (the knowledge of good and evil) have not only the meanings "good" and "bad" but also connotations of "happiness" and "misery." Personal well-being and morality—that is, the material and the spiritual—have been intimately connected from the beginning, relating the very fabric of reality, whereby both levels of reality must be understood together in order to truly understand either one. The world, originally created through the Son, embodies the union of the material and the spiritual that is the imprint of the Son—who is the perfect union of flesh and spirit and, thereby, the nexus of flesh and the Spirit (John 1:3).[36]

Genesis 3:7–8 And the eyes of them both were opened, and they knew that they [were] naked; and they sewed fig leaves together, and made themselves aprons. 8 And they heard the voice of the Lord** God walking in the garden in the cool of the day: and Adam and his wife hid themselves from the presence of the L**ord** God amongst the trees of the garden.**

The Fall of Man cannot be blamed on the devil, since the devil did not and cannot coerce our disobedience. Rather, the Fall of Man should be viewed as the material manifestation of the spiritual rebellion of lucifer just as everything in this world is a reflection of spiritual reality. The serpent tempting Eve is a vision of the spiritual translating into the material. But the spiritual compares with the material as the infinite compares with the finite. Accordingly, the eternal condemnation of fallen lucifer, the evil one, translates into only a limited condemnation of fallen Adam, specifically the condemnation of the natural body but not withholding the promise of redemption. Our experience of eternity in the mortal coil can only be through a glass darkly (1 Cor 13:12).[37]

The eyes of Adam and Eve becoming opened is not the genesis of the spirit of disobedience, for the spirit of disobedience must have preceded the original

---

[36] "The serpent, with an opening question, insinuates that God has some ulterior motive for the command . . . [T]he serpent has succeeded in attracting her attention and proceeds with three half-truths: (1) 'you will not die'; (2) 'your eyes will be opened'; (3) 'you will be like God, knowing good and evil' [Gen 3:4–5]" (Viviano, *Collegeville* 43; Gen 2:25–3:7). Even in the lies of the serpent, the faithful can still perceive the undeniable and universal will of God that is (1) the preservation of Adam, (2) the faithful seeing truly—that is, believing, trusting in, and adhering to—the incarnation, and finally (3) the faithful entering into the one Body of Christ.

[37] Proper names of the evil one are not capitalized in the present work, which is intended to relate the annihilation of freewill and individuality that inevitably occurs in the rejection of the image of God, Jesus Christ, who is the embodiment of freewill.

material act of rebellion. The physical reflects the spiritual and not vice versa; specifically, the physical is a blurred image of the spiritual reality. The opening of our eyes in the garden is an image of our receiving evil into our hearts, immediately represented by the perception of evil with our eyes but ultimately embodied by death entering the world through sin. The disobedience of Adam being magnified in his murderous offspring is an affirmation that death, as embodied by Adam's son Cain, truly did enter the world through sin, as embodied by Adam himself (Gen 4:10). Adam is the father of Cain just as disobedience is the father of death (Rom 5:12). The spirit of disobedience is the corruption of the perfect will of God. The spirit of disobedience is manifested materially as the suffering and death of the natural body. Personal sin, even hidden sin, represents a larger spiritual reality. Adam's own physical death finally prefigures all men in Adam following him in death.

The spirit of disobedience must have preexisted our fall just as God must have comprehended good and evil even before our creation. But God did not create the spirit of disobedience. God is the only creator, and God creates only good things. The devil, in contrast, can only corrupt, not create. The good creation is freewill, while the spirit of disobedience is the corruption of freewill. Freewill cannot be synonymous with corruption, for the divine freewill is uncorrupted. Accordingly, the corruption of freewill must have followed the creation of freewill. The manifestation of the spirit of disobedience is fallen man, but the spirit of disobedience is a corruption and not a creation just as fallen man is a corruption and not a creation. Corruption is not something of itself. Corruption is only a potential, not a reality, until the actual corruption occurs. The idea, or possibility, of corruption must always exist, lurking at the door, because ideas, by their nature, cannot be destroyed.

Adam and Eve hiding from the presence of God typifies the separation between mankind and God, which is caused not by God but by the sins of mankind in conflict with the will of God.[38] The nakedness of Adam and Eve foreshadows the nakedness of Jesus Christ exposed on the cross just as the fall of all mankind in Adam prefigures the death of Christ for all mankind. The symbol of nakedness is closely related to the symbol of flesh since the former is an exposure of the latter, whereby clothing is a metaphor for shame when flesh is a metaphor for sin. The nakedness of a babe signifies innocence, but the nakedness of an adult signifies the exposure of sin. The original sin of Adam and Eve making them aware of their nakedness prefigures, in reverse, Jesus Christ being exposed on the cross in order to destroy sin. The fall in Adam

---

[38] "We should assume this is God, in the Person of Jesus Christ, appearing to Adam and Eve before His incarnation and birth at Bethlehem, because of God the Father it is said, 'No one has seen God at any time. The only begotten Son, who is in the bosom of the Father, He has declared Him' (John 1:18), and no man has ever seen God in the Person of the Father [1 Tim 6:16]" (Guzik 44; Gen 3:8–9). God the Father, our spiritual progenitor, the creator of all things, visible and invisible, necessarily exists in separation from and outside of the creation proceeding from him, including space and time.

represents a corruption of the image of God just as the crucifixion would be a disfigurement of the visible image of the invisible God (Col 1:15).[39]

The knowledge of good and evil, signified by the tree of knowledge, is specifically the experiential knowledge of good and evil. God, in contrast to man, comprehends evil but does not experience evil, in that God does not in any way partake of evil. Our mortal perception of a long time delay between sin and the righteous judgment of sin is an illusion caused by our vantage point. The idea of perfection—that is, perfection without limit—is an infinite concept that only has complete meaning in the infinite domain. All time is an open book to God, who exists outside time and likewise space. The conception, birth, youth, adulthood, death, resurrection, and glorification of Jesus Christ is a recapitulation of all human existence—past, present, and future—and a corresponding sanctification of all creation—heaven and earth together. Accordingly, all time and space collapses to the singularity of the one Body of Christ. Our present experience of finite time is our fledgling freewill and in no way equates to a divine tolerance of sin or some divine participation in sin. The pain and suffering experienced in this life is beyond words, but all injustice and cruelty proceed from the hand of man, not from the hand of God. Worst of all, our contempt of self is a contempt of our creation in the image of God, a contempt made visible in the defilement of God on the cross.[40]

Genesis 3:9–10 And the LORD God called unto Adam, and said unto him, Where [art] thou? 10 And he said, I heard thy voice in the garden, and I was afraid, because I [was] naked; and I hid myself.

The nature of fallen man, figuratively the flesh, is fear, whereas the nature of the Holy Spirit is love. The opposite of fear is not courage but love, wherein courage is understood to flow from love. And it is our fear in the natural, or the flesh, embodying the corruption of love, that separates us from God and likewise from the supernatural love of God. One could similarly say that fear and also hate and avarice, and so forth, are all the offspring of pride, which is self-love, and that self-love is the opposite of true love.

Genesis 3:11–13 And he said, Who told thee that thou [wast] naked? Hast thou eaten of the tree, whereof I commanded thee that thou shouldest not eat? 12 And the man said, The woman whom thou gavest [to be] with me, she gave me of the tree, and I did eat. 13 And the LORD God said

---

[39] "We find the fig-tree cursed because it had leaves only, and not fruit. In the beginning of the human race, when Adam and Eve had sinned, they made themselves girdles of fig leaves. Fig leaves then signify sins [Augustine, *Tractates on the Gospel of John*]" (Schaff, *Nicene and Post-Nicene Fathers: First Series* 7:55). Accordingly, when you see the fig tree put forth its leaves, you will know that the end is near, Matt 24:32–33.
[40] Gen 2:4–3:24 shows a chiastic literary construction with 3:6–13 as the pivot (Waltke 81). The pivotal image of nakedness portends Christ exposed on the cross and connects the original creation of man with the final fulfillment of the curse in the last days.

unto the woman, What [is] this [that] thou hast done? And the woman said, The serpent beguiled me, and I did eat.

The serpent, woman, and man are all three found to be complicit in the rebellion against God, and neither is there any sign of true repentance. The three form an anti-trinity, standing in opposition to the Father, Spirit, and Son. The serpent, the father of lies, becomes, through the beguiling of Eve, the de facto father of Adam (John 8:44). And mankind, in choosing the promise of the serpent over the presence of God, becomes like the serpent, one with the serpent, and mankind is therefore viewed together with the serpent and judged alongside the serpent. The devil manifesting itself to be a serpent represents an embodying of the animal kingdom, signifying the nature of flesh separated from the Spirit, whereby the overt reality of an anti-trinity opposing the one true Trinity should be recognized as the ubiquitous conflict between flesh and spirit. The world seems dualistic, but it is ultimately triune.

THREE CURSES

Genesis 3:14 And the LORD [H3068] God [H430] said unto the serpent, Because thou hast done this, thou [art] cursed above all cattle, and above every beast of the field; upon thy belly [H1512] shalt thou go, and dust shalt thou eat all the days of thy life:

The serpent embodies lucifer just as the king of Babylon embodies lucifer (Isa 14:4) just as the king of Tyrus embodies lucifer (Ezek 28:12). The prevalent representation of the devil by proxy is an emphasis on our collusion with the devil, as typified by Eve obeying the serpent followed by Adam obeying Eve. Whether the serpent is the true material form of the devil is not directly relevant, although one naturally presumes that this is in fact the case. The emphasis on our collusion with the devil, rather than on the devil himself, testifies to the restraint of the devil by God and, thereby, to the inferiority of the devil as compared with the Lord God. But the persistent personification of the spirit of disobedience also testifies to the reality of the devil as a literal being, consistent with the graphic descriptions of his person, for example, in the book of Revelation. The serpent being more subtle than any beast of the field reflects the original preeminence of lucifer (Gen 3:1), but the comparison of the serpent with the beasts of the field is itself an affirmation that lucifer is merely a created being and therefore innately lower than God (Ezek 28:13). The reality of the devil, both materially and spiritually, reflects the universal dualism of flesh and spirit evident in all creation.[41]

---

[41] The individual exorcist must not confront evil spirits outside the auspices established by God, which is the visible church composed of the Eastern Orthodox, Roman Catholic, and Protestant communions (Martin 12). It is the fundamental nature of man to exist and operate within a larger family and community. Yet when a man must stand alone, he is not really alone, for God the Holy Spirit is with him. Equivalently, the visible church is real but ultimately points to the yet invisible Body of Christ.

ADAM, NOAH, ABRAHAM

The serpent tempting Eve with the idea of disobedience (Gen 3:1) is expressly a vision of the serpent as the embodiment of the spirit of disobedience proceeding from an anti-father, ever in conflict with the Holy Spirit (Eph 2:2). The devil originally being created in the angelic realm, not the human realm, reinforces the identification of the serpent with the spiritual, in contrast to the material (Isa 14:12). This does not imply that the serpent did not literally exist but merely focuses on the serpent's defining quality in the specific context, which is spiritual temptation and not physical coercion. The spirit of disobedience tempting humanity is a reverse image of the Holy Spirit encouraging humanity. The debasement of humanity through the spirit of disobedience is a reverse image of the exaltation of humanity through the Holy Spirit. The serpent originally seeking out Eve is an affirmation that the spirit of disobedience necessarily precedes the manifestation of sin. The serpent is cursed first as the most culpable, before woman and man, just as our sinful nature, not our individual sins, is the fundamental origin of our separation from God. Sin is the embodiment of evil, but the sinful nature is evil itself. The condemnation of the serpent before the condemnation of man presages the spiritual degradation of Adam in exile preceding his physical degradation in death. Spiritual reality is always the foundation of material reality and not vice versa. But material reality and spiritual reality necessarily testify to the same truth since the former is a derivative of the latter. The unity of the material and the spiritual reflects the oneness of God, while the subordination of the material to the spiritual reflects the Son proceeding from the Father and likewise fulfilling the will of the Father.

The serpent being cursed all the days of his life is an implicit affirmation that the days of evil have been limited. The days of evil are numbered just as the days of the condemnation of humanity under the law are numbered. The name *Lord* [H3068] *God* [H430] (pronouncing the curse) is an emphasis on the character of justice but also foreshadows the union of justice and mercy. The justice of God, identified with the name *God* (Elohim) [H430], is first emphasized in the creation of Adam (the embodiment of all mankind) under the law and now again in the condemnation of Adam (again all mankind) under the law. But the mercy of God, identified with the name *Lord* (YHWH) [H3068], is ultimately emphasized in the redemption of Israel out of Egypt, which represents the redemption of the faithful out of sin (Exod 6:3). The presence of evil will not persist forever, but rather justice points to mercy just as the name *God* (Elohim) [H430] points to the name *Lord* (YHWH) [H3068]. Good parents do not discipline their children for the sake of retribution but rather to point them to something better. The devil is irreconcilable, but the faithful are called to repentance and redemption (Mark 3:28–29).[42]

---

[42] "... 'Jehovah [YHWH] represents God in His special relation to the chosen people ... Elohim represents God in His relation to the world at large....' [W. H. Green]" (*New Unger's Bible Dictionary*, s.v. "Elohim"). The first man Adam, being the natural father of all mankind, represents all mankind, or the world as a whole under the law that governs flesh, while the chosen people represent the faithful from mankind that will be redeemed by the grace of the Spirit.

The serpent being cursed to move upon its *belly* [H1512] (upon the dust) represents the fruition of sin in death (Rom 5:12). The serpent desired flesh, desired to corrupt flesh, and therefore is cursed to eat flesh, as represented by the dust of the ground from which flesh proceeds (Ps 81:12). Justice seems ironic because the ways of man are not the ways of God. The serpent eating dust is ultimately an image of the devil subsisting on death itself, given that flesh returns to the dust upon death. The degradation of the serpent, moving along the ground upon its belly, parallels the degradation of man, tilling the ground in sorrow (Gen 3:19). The degradation of man and serpent both reflect the same corruption through sin just as the material and the spiritual always reflect the same reality. The magnification of evil feeding upon itself, eating dust, or figuratively eating death, is embodied in fallen creation by physical addictions of all kinds and also an ever-increasing lust for power and wealth.[43]

The serpent being consigned to eat the dust is not only the curse of the serpent but also an affirmation of the dominion of the devil in the world after the Fall of Man, which is the dominion of dust, or flesh. This dichotomy of dominion and degradation is the essence of the universal justice of God, giving sinners, even angels, over to their own desires in accordance with the sanctity of freewill (2 Chr 12:8). After our fall, the devil took possession of the dominion despised by Adam, which is the dominion of the flesh—that is, until Jesus Christ would appear in the flesh and reclaim that lost dominion. By the cross, the ultimate redemption of the faithful in the resurrection is guaranteed, but nevertheless the spirit of disobedience will continue in the flesh until the final judgment of all flesh in the end times. A final delay in a final testimony to the long-suffering of God in the call to repentance.

The curse of the serpent to become a crawling creature, close to the earth, reflects the devil being cast down to the earth (Rev 12:9) and also the final condemnation of the devil, being cast into the lake of fire (Rev 20:10). The earth is a symbol of flesh and likewise the law that governs flesh, while the heavens are a symbol of spirit and likewise the grace that governs spirit. The serpent condemned to the dust is thereby a vision of the condemnation of the devil under the law outside of grace. But the condemnation of the serpent in the garden is not the final condemnation of the devil—who is seen, for example, in the account of Job, appearing before the Lord long after the original curse (Job 1:6–7). The final judgment of the devil is delayed just as the final judgment of man is delayed. Both delays reflect the call to repentance. Likewise, the

---

[43] "I feign that devils can, in a spiritual sense, eat one another; and us. Even in human life we have seen the passion to dominate, almost to digest, one's fellow; to make his whole intellectual and emotional life merely an extension of one's own—to hate one's hatreds and resent one's grievances and indulge one's egoism through him as well as through oneself. His own little store of passion must of course be suppressed to make room for ours. If he resists this suppression he is being very selfish" (Lewis, *Screwtape* xi). Since humanity, being endued with freewill, is formed in the triune image of God, the myopic preference for mere carnality, which underlies our desire to consume one another, is in actuality a self-loathing rejection of God and a corresponding rejection, or annihilation, of freewill.

crucifixion of Christ embodies the spiritual reality of the corruption of the image of God signified by our fall in Adam, but the visible suffering of Christ would be delayed, reflecting the same call to repentance. The life of Christ is, however, more than even the call to repentance. The life of Christ is both a recapitulation of human history and a corresponding sanctification of all levels of human existence.[44]

The progressive revelation of the serpent in the Scriptures—from tempter to accuser to tormentor—parallels the progressive condemnation of the serpent. The progressive degradation of the serpent is evident in the progressive degradation of his children, of all those who embrace his false promises. This progressive degradation can be seen, for example, in the eyes of any drug addict.[45] The threefold tempting, accusing, and tormenting by an anti-spirit proceeding from an anti-father, which marks the serpent, is the vain movement of a counterfeit anti-godhead against the threefold promise, repentance, and redemption of the one true Godhead. The promise of the evil one is temptation (serpent). The repentance in the evil one is accusation (devil). The redemption by the evil one is torment (satan). The serpent was originally ranked above every beast of the field but was then debased (Gen 3:1), in converse to the Son of man, who would be ranked below the angels but would then be crowned with glory (Heb 2:9). He who exalts himself will be humbled, but he who humbles himself will be exalted (Matt 23:12). The humble condescension marking the incarnation of God as a man is the embodiment of the humble condescension of God in the original creation of man.[46]

Genesis 3:15 And I will put enmity [H342] between thee and the woman, and between thy seed [H2233] and her seed [H2233]; it shall bruise thy head [H7218], and thou shalt bruise his heel [H6119].

The word *head* [H7218] (related to the serpent) connotes "chief (man)" in the Hebrew, while the word *heel* [H6119] (related to woman) connotes "hinder-part, rear (of a troop of men)" and is associated with the word "to follow at the heel, fig. assail insidiously, circumvent, overreach" [H6117]. The seed of the serpent is collectively the unfaithful but individually the son of perdition, while the Seed of woman is collectively the faithful but uniquely the Son of man. The head related to the serpent represents the devil—the chief, or head, apostate—while

---

[44] "On what basis could we be sharers in adoption as God's sons? We had to receive, through the Son's agency, participation in him. The Word, having been made flesh, had to share himself with us. That is why he went through every stage of human life, restoring to all of them communion with God [Irenaeus of Lyon, *Against Heresies*]" (Norris 54). Christ is the new Adam.

[45] " 'The evil impulse is at first sweet; in the end it is bitter' [*Palestinian Shabbath*]" (Cohen, *Rabbinic Sages* 91). The way of all flesh, the way of all the earth.

[46] "Satan performs three functions: he seduces men, he accuses them before God, he inflicts the punishment of death [*Baba Bathra*]" (Cohen, *Rabbinic Sages* 56). Lucifer, the dragon falling from heaven, is progressively exposed as the serpent, devil, and satan, respectively, the tempter, accuser, and tormentor.

the Heel related to woman represents the faithful—the rear of the troop of Jesus Christ. And the faithful are viewed as figuratively grasping the heel of the firstborn of the grave (Hos 12:3).[47]

The word *seed* [H2233] (the Seed of woman, the seed of the serpent) is derived from the root "to sow, scatter seed" [H2232], which implies a sense of cause and effect, connected specifically with the conflict between the two seeds. One sows, one reaps. A belief in cause and effect, in contrast to fatalism, is a belief in justice, a belief that points to the undeniable and unassailable nature of the justice of God. Justice would have no meaning if actions and events were predetermined, if freewill did not prevail. The first prophecy—that the Seed of woman would bruise the head, as related to the serpent—is the victory of Christ over death and the corresponding binding of the devil through the blood of the Lamb, specifically at the First Advent (Rev 12:11). The second prophecy—that the seed of the serpent would bruise the Heel, as related to woman—is the persecution of the faithful culminating in the foretold son of perdition, who will strike humanity and herald the final judgment linked with the Second Advent (2 Thess 2:3). Two prophecies, two advents. One promise.[48]

The word *enmity* [H342] (between the two seeds) means "personal hostility." The enmity between the two seeds is the conflict between flesh and spirit in the individual, the conflict between the children of the devil and the children of God in the world, the conflict between chaos and cosmos in physical creation, and the conflict between deception and truth in the realm of the conscience. The conflict between the children of darkness and the children of the light in the present age foreshadows the final conflict between the son of perdition and the Son of man in the end times. Wars and rumors of wars foreshadow the final war just as natural disasters foreshadow the final destruction just as any blasphemy against the Son of man foreshadows the blasphemy against the Holy Spirit. Adam was hated by the serpent without reason just as Jesus Christ would be hated by the world without reason (John 15:25). There can be no fellowship between the darkness and the light (2 Cor 6:14).[49]

---

[47] That the serpent is some manifestation of satan is evident from Ezek 28:13–19, also from Job 26:13, Isa 51:9, and Rev 12:9, 20:2 (Guzik 37; Gen 3:1). The old serpent is the physical reality, while the great dragon is the parallel spiritual reality.

[48] "Christ's heel was bruised, when his feet were pierced and nailed to the cross, and His sufferings are continued in the sufferings of the saints for his name" (Henry 1:36; Gen 3:14–15); "And Satan *bruises his heel* . . . that the salvation of man could only be brought about by the *death* of Christ; and even the spiritual seed of our blessed Lord have the heel often bruised, as they suffer persecution, temptation . . . ." (Clarke 1:53; Gen 3:15).

[49] "And it shall be when the sons of the woman consider the law, and perform (its) instructions, they will be prepared to smite thee on thy head to kill thee [serpent]; and when the sons of the woman forsake the commandment of the law, and perform not (its) instructions, thou wilt be ready to wound them in their heel, and hurt them. Nevertheless there shall be a medicine for the sons of the woman, but for thee, serpent, there shall be no medicine: but it is to be that for these there shall be a remedy for the heel in the days of the king Meshiha [*Jerusalem Targum*]" (Etheridge 1:166). The medicine that will remedy sin under the law in the days of Meshiha, the Messiah or Christ, could

Genesis 3:16 Unto the woman he said, I will greatly multiply thy sorrow and thy conception; in sorrow thou shalt bring forth children [H1121]; and thy desire [shall be] to thy husband, and he shall rule over thee.

Man is most closely identified with flesh and likewise with justice, while woman is most closely identified with spirit and likewise with mercy. Accordingly, the desire of woman for man reflects the desire of spirit for flesh, or the animation of the flesh by the spirit. The desire of spirit for flesh is ultimately embodied by the desire of Jesus Christ to save the faithful. Adam (the first man) is saved through Jesus (the second man) just as man (formed first) is completed by woman (formed second). The desire of woman for man is also manifest in the desire of the faithful in Christ (bride) for Christ (bridegroom). The same truth on different levels. The faithful (the final harvest of mankind) are added to Christ (as and with the firstfruits of the grave) in the Body of Christ (Matt 27:52–53, Lev 23:10–12). Likewise, woman is added to man, with the two forming one body. Adam (the natural man) and Jesus (the spiritual man) parallel the First Advent (incarnation as a man) and the Second Advent (glorification through the Spirit). A juxtaposition that reflects the universal motif of redemption that is the call to imitate Christ.[50]

The image of man ruling woman is a testimony that justice is tempered by mercy and not vice versa, whereby woman and the implied offspring of woman prefigure our promised new creation in the mercy that completes justice. Wives are instructed to submit to their husbands just as the church submits to Christ (Eph 5:24). Not only the submission of woman to man but all deference to the authorities in this life, including the submission of servants to their masters, are ultimately images of the submission of Christ to the cross. The faithful are called to submission in imitation of Christ. The same truth always repeats on all levels of reality, whereby our submission to authority is finally our submission to God. Submission to God is not slavery under law but rather freedom from sin (Rom 6:22)—a paradox made clear by the apostles first being the servants of Christ but finally becoming the friends of Christ (John 15:15). One is enslaved to a curse, not to a blessing, whereby there is no law against love (Gal 5:22–23). Our submission in the natural body to the Covenant of Law prefigures our freedom in the spiritual, or glorified, body in the Covenant of Grace just as the gifts of the Holy Spirit in the present life prefigure the fullness of the Holy Spirit in the promised life to come.

Eve would become the literal mother of mankind through her physical offspring and also the figurative mother of saved mankind through the bloodline of Jesus Christ. Our physical birth in the natural body (first birth) prefigures our resurrection in the spiritual body (second birth) just as the

---

be nothing less than the blood, or life, of Christ, the anointed one, signifying the Spirit of God, fulfilling the law and guaranteeing the indwelling Holy Spirit.

[50] "The rabbis taught: Adam the first was created singly, and why? That disbelievers should not say there were many Creators in Heaven" (Rodkinson, *Talmud: Sanhedrin* 7[15]:113). Adam is singular in that he is the one father of all flesh, but Adam is also threefold in that Eve and the collective offspring of Eve would proceed from him.

original creation through Christ (first creation) prefigures the new creation in Christ (second creation) just as the Covenant of Law (first covenant) prefigures the Covenant of Grace (second covenant). Identifying the second birth with the resurrection does not deny the born-again experience in this life but rather affirms that the gifts of the Spirit in this life are only a deposit on our final inheritance in the kingdom of God (2 Cor 1:22). The born-again experience in this life should be identified with repentance and the corresponding baptism in water. The baptism in water (baptism in the flesh) foreshadows the baptism of fire (baptism of the Holy Spirit) just as repentance foreshadows redemption. Two creations, two births, two baptisms. One savoir, Jesus Christ.

Woman and the implied offspring of woman proceeding from man (Gen 2:23) reflect the Spirit and Son proceeding from the Father (Luke 1:35). The word *children* [H1121] (brought forth in sorrow) has an association in the Hebrew "to build" [H1129], reflecting the body of humanity brought forth and established through the flesh, through the Covenant of Law, and foreshadowing the Body of Christ established in the Spirit, in the Covenant of Grace. The suffering of women in childbirth points to the suffering of Jesus Christ on the cross, while new life being born through the pain of childbirth points to our rebirth coming through the suffering of Christ. The marks of childbirth are stigmata—a flow of water and blood that represent, respectively, law and grace (John 19:34, 1 John 5:6). All pain and suffering ultimately flows from sin just as the suffering in childbirth proceeds from the original sin just as Jesus Christ would die for the forgiveness of sins.

Genesis 3:17–19 And unto Adam he said, Because thou hast hearkened unto the voice of thy wife, and hast eaten of the tree, of which I commanded thee, saying, Thou shalt not eat of it: cursed [is] the ground [H127] for thy sake; in sorrow shalt thou eat [of] it all the days of thy life; 18 Thorns also and thistles shall it bring forth to thee; and thou shalt eat the herb [H6212] of the field [H7704]; 19 In the sweat of thy face shalt thou eat bread [H3899], till thou return unto the ground; for out of it wast thou taken: for dust thou [art], and unto dust shalt thou return.

The curse, following the course of the original rebellion, proceeds from the serpent to the woman to the man and also physical creation. In both cases, the progression is from the spiritual to the physical. The serpent is the embodiment of the spirit of disobedience. Woman is most closely identified with spiritual nature. And man is identified with carnal nature and physical creation. The progression from the spiritual to the natural is an affirmation that personal spirituality—that is, personal morality—is inextricably connected with physical reality. The essence of sin is spiritual, but its manifestation in physical reality is unavoidable. The relationship between the spiritual and physical is not always clear from the perspective of limited understanding, but a relationship must always exist. Everything must proceed from the spiritual because nothing can come into being of itself. And the manifestation of the spiritual cannot be repressed, as evident in the revealing of the Son of man and also the foretold coming of the son of perdition (2 Thess 2:3).

The word *ground* [H127] (cursed is the ground) is cognate with the name *Adam* [H121] (who will return to the ground), which recalls man originally formed from the dust of the ground (Gen 2:7). Adam being formally cursed not directly but rather through the curse of the ground represents an emphasis on the primordial brotherhood of man and earth, which again reflects the connectedness of the spiritual nature of sin and the unavoidable physical manifestation of sin. The implied parity between man obeying woman, representing a material submission to a false spirit, and man disobeying God, or spiritually rejecting the Spirit of God, reflects this unity of reality. The parity between man eating in disobedience, eating by his own hand, and man eating in sorrow, the hand of man being against the hand of God, also reflects this unity of reality. And the manifestation of thorns and thistles reinforces the vision of the spiritual corruption of the physical world.[51]

The word *field* [H7704] (herb of the field) can mean either "cultivated field" or "home of wild beasts," which reflects the dichotomy of life and death in our preservation in exile. God originally gave every *herb* (plant) [H6212] *bearing* [H2232] *seed* [H2233] and also the *fruit* [H6529] of every *tree* [H6086] *yielding* [H2232] *seed* [H2233] to Adam and Eve for meat, while every *green* [H3418] *herb* (plant) [H6212] was originally given to the animals for meat (Gen 1:29–30). Mankind now being given the *herb* [H6212] of the *field* [H7704] after the Fall of Adam is an identification of man with the animal kingdom, which implies a magnified carnal nature in man as a result of the original sin. The primal connection of man with the dust of the ground is relatively neutral in that the earth is inanimate, which is a neutrality reflecting an unconsummated freewill, but the connection of the intellect of man with animal instinct implies a distinct amorality, which is a corruption of freewill and a corresponding loss of freewill. The emphasis, before our fall, on seed-bearing species is an emphasis on life. The life of man was originally sustained expressly by food that embodies life. Life proceeds from life just as the breath of man proceeds from the breath of God. The faithful likewise receive eternal life through eating the flesh and drinking the blood of Jesus Christ, the Seed of woman. The bread and wine that represent the body and blood of Christ are derived from grain and grapes, respectively, a seed and a seed-bearing species.[52]

---

[51] "These [thorns and thistles] are not the natural fruits of the earth, but proceed of the corruption of sin" (Whittingham et al., *Geneva Bible* 3L n. t; Gen 3:18). The coming of thorns and thistles does not represent something new but a corruption of the original domain of plants, likewise the world as a whole, just as sin is not a created thing but a corruption of the good creation of God.

[52] "There is no positive evidence that *animal* food was ever eaten *before* the flood. Noah had the first grant of this kind . . . ." (Clarke 1:79; Gen 9:3). Irrespective of any presumed or actual antediluvian practices, whether those of the lines of Cain or Seth, the first grant, or prophetic declaration, of eating flesh, or sacrificing flesh, that is recorded in the inspired history occurs immediately after the time of the Flood,

ADAM AND EVE

The word *bread* [H3899] (man would eat bread in the sweat of his face) has a connotation "to fight, do battle" [H3898]. The image of eating bread in the sweat of our faces is already vivid, but the etymological shadow of war further stresses our degraded condition and portends the wars and rumors of wars culminating in the end times (Matt 24:6). Bread is a symbol of flesh and likewise the world, both of which became the dominion of sin and death after our fall, whereby eating bread is a symbolic cannibalism, echoing the curse of the serpent to eat the dust of the ground. But the connection between eating bread and suffering is ultimately realized in the commandment to eat the flesh of Christ, which would become the object of the curse on the cross (John 6:53). The Passover bread prefigures Christ as the bread of affliction (Deut 16:3), while the manna in the desert prefigures the flesh of Christ as the bread of God (John 6:32). Bread and wine are, respectively, symbols of the flesh and blood of Christ and likewise of law and grace, whereby the individual commandments to eat the flesh of Christ and drink the blood of Christ are, respectively, the condemnation of the natural body under the law and the exaltation and glorification of the spiritual body by grace through faith in Christ (Matt 26:26–28). The commandment to even now abstain from blood points to the fullness of grace awaiting the Second Advent (Acts 15:29).

The original prophecy that man would die the same day he ate from the tree of knowledge points to many simultaneously true fulfillments (Gen 2:17). Adam did die immediately in the sense that he would be driven from the presence of God. Adam would also die literally, physically, near the end of the first millennium, which is a single day from the perspective of God (2 Pet 3:8). Adam is the embodiment of all humanity and a microcosm of all creation, whereby the death of Adam presages the death of every individual and also the destruction of all creation, all of which was irrevocably determined the very day he ate from the forbidden tree. But the ultimate manifestation of the death of Adam through the tree, least obvious to human eyes, is the death of Jesus Christ on the cross for Adam, that is, the death of Jesus Christ for all mankind. The rejection of Christ in the promised land embodied by the crucifixion is the ultimate reality of the rejection of God in the garden of Eden. Christ is the invisible God made visible (Col 1:15). The spiritual overlapping of the Fall of Man and the Passion of Christ is a vision of Christ as a recapitulation of human history and a corresponding sanctification of creation. God is the font of all life, transcendent, outside simple linear history.[53]

Death entering the whole world through the first man Adam is a horrific validation of both our individual freewill and the unity of all creation (Rom 5:12). A strange but essential juxtaposition, reflecting man as a microcosm of all creation. The truth that the individual cannot be isolated from the rest of reality

---

representing an identification of ritual blood sacrifice, or legally prescribed sacrifice, with the rebirth through the Flood.

[53] "When any divergence is found in the Scriptures, it must not be thought that it is by mere accident, for it is done advisedly" (Rapaport, *Midrash* 58). Adam and also Christ for the sake of, literally in the place of, Adam did die that same day Adam and likewise all Adam-kind ate from the tree of the knowledge of good and evil.

is an affirmation of personal responsibility as the foundation of all morality. God calls us to choose the good and reject the bad (Gen 4:7), to walk before him and be perfect (Gen 17:1). Personal responsibility is the domain of freewill, which is our dominion in the image of God, but personal responsibility should not be confused with self-reliance. Man cannot be perfect of himself, and neither can man afford his own salvation, but rather man is called to make a freewill decision to turn to God. The faithful become perfected, not of themselves, but only through Christ in a personal decision to turn to Christ, heralding a personal relationship with Christ. This is the baptism of repentance that foreshadows the baptism of the Holy Spirit, the Covenant of Law that foreshadows the Covenant of Grace, the natural body that foreshadows the spiritual, or glorified, body (1 Cor 15:46). This is the law that guides us to grace (Gal 3:24). Everyone has sinned, but there is a clear difference between those who reject God and those who seek God. God has given us over to our own desires, in accordance with the sanctity of freewill, but in our accursed state we finally learn the difference between serving the world and serving God, in accordance with the undeniable, or relentless, will of God (2 Chr 12:8).

Exile

Genesis 3:20 And Adam called his wife's name Eve [H2332]; because she was the mother of all living.

Adam naming Eve prefigures God the Father giving the one name of Jesus Christ for our salvation (Acts 4:12). The name *Eve* [H2332] means "life." Eve would become not only the literal mother of all the living on earth, but through Jesus Christ, she would ultimately become the figurative mother of redeemed humanity in eternity. Adam is closely identified with our original creation in the image of God and, thereby, reflects God the Father, while Eve is closely identified with the promise of life, exemplified by our promised redemption through her Seed. The first mother Eve conceiving naturally prefigures the second mother Mary conceiving supernaturally just as our physical birth prefigures our spiritual rebirth just as mortal life prefigures eternal life. The promise of life is plain even though the former things are finite and the latter things are infinite. The promise prefigures the reality. Eve and the offspring of Eve proceeding from Adam reflects the Holy Spirit and the Son proceeding from the Father. The image of the Father, Son, and Holy Spirit being reflected in man, woman, and child is an affirmation that humanity is truly created in the image of God, an image still evident despite the distortion by sin just as the will of God remains undeniable despite our fall (Gen 1:27).[54]

---

[54] "God having named the man, *Adam*, which signifies *red earth*; Adam, in further token of dominion, named the woman, *Eve*, that is, *life*. Adam bears the name of the dying body, Eve of the living soul" (Henry 1:38; Gen 3:20). The dichotomy of justice and mercy is embodied by the union of man and woman.

ADAM AND EVE

Genesis 3:21 Unto Adam also and to his wife did the LORD God make coats of skins, and clothed them.

Adam and Eve trying, after their fall, to cover themselves with fig leaves reflects a denial of blood sacrifice as a necessary recompense for sin. This is the path of flesh in conflict with the path of the Spirit. God replacing their fig leaves (no blood) with animal skins (blood required) represents an animal sacrifice, prefiguring the formal law of Moses and ultimately the death of Jesus Christ for the sins of the world. When flesh became the domain of evil, nakedness, or the display of flesh, became a symbol of sin while clothing, the hiding of flesh, became a symbol of shame. Adam and Eve seeking to cover themselves is a symbolic admission of guilt, while God himself finally covering Adam and Eve represents the consignment of humanity to the law that governs flesh, the first covenant. God giving us over to our own desires is an affirmation of the sanctity of our freewill, while the faithful learning the difference between serving the world and serving God is an affirmation of the undeniable nature of the will of God (2 Chr 12:8). But God covering Adam and Eve finally prefigures Christ clothing the faithful with robes of righteousness (Isa 61:10), a righteousness through Christ in fulfillment of the law (Matt 5:17).[55]

The wearing of animal skins is like wearing a costume in which man mimics the appearance of animals. And man likewise mimics the amorality of the aspiritual nature of animals. The covering of flesh follows the knowledge of nakedness just as physical manifestations always flow from spiritual reality. Man being disguised as an animal represents a distortion of the image of God by the devil, a distortion that recalls the original manifestation of the devil as a serpent (Gen 3:1). The god of this world after the Fall of Man would be the devil, whereby the world would be governed, not by the love of the Spirit in the very image of God, but by the fears of the flesh representing the degradation of the devil (2 Cor 4:4). But man donning animal skins also prefigures Christ assuming flesh just as our condemnation through the one man Adam prefigures our redemption through the one man Jesus Christ.[56]

The more common interpretation of our original nakedness in the garden as being our original innocence is correct in the sense that flesh is not inherently evil just as freewill is not inherently evil. But the original nakedness of Adam and Eve also prefigured their fallen state just as children behave badly even before they're culpable. Nakedness is normal for a child but not for an adult, which implies a spiritual immaturity being linked with the garden. The saints are

---

[55] "Adam and Eve made for themselves aprons of fig-leaves, a covering too narrow for them to *wrap themselves in*, [Isa 28:20]. Such is our own righteousness. But God made them coats fit for them; such is the righteousness of Christ, therefore *put ye on the Lord Jesus Christ*" (Henry 1:39; Gen 3:21). The former things always prefigure the latter things.
[56] "These coats of skin had a significancy. The beasts whose skins they were, must be slain; . . . And probably 'tis supposed they were slain for sacrifice, to typify the great sacrifice which in the latter end of the world should be offered once for all. Thus the first thing that died was a sacrifice, or Christ in a figure [script updated]" (Wesley 1:19; Gen 3:21). The institution of the law from the foundation of the world.

never depicted as nude in heaven but rather clothed in white robes, which of itself testifies that the kingdom of God is not simply a return to the garden of Eden (Rev 7:9). The exposure of the nakedness of Christ on the cross is prefigured by Adam becoming aware of his own nakedness, but the exposure of Adam is an exposure of guilt while the exposure of Christ would be an exposure of innocence. The nakedness of Adam becoming his shame prefigures the nakedness of Christ on the cross embodying the guilt and shame of the whole world. The exposed flesh of Christ on the cross is an image of both his innocence and our guilt, reflecting the universal dichotomy of spirit and flesh. The primordial innocence of the garden is ultimately the peerless innocence of Jesus Christ and finally our promised innocence in Christ.[57]

Genesis 3:22–24 And the LORD [H3068] God [H430] said, Behold, the man is become as one of us, to know good and evil: and now, lest he put forth his hand, and take also of the tree of life, and eat, and live for ever [H5769]: 23 Therefore the LORD [H3068] God [H430] sent him forth from the garden of Eden, to till the ground from whence he was taken. 24 So he drove out the man; and he placed at the east [H6924] of the garden of Eden Cherubims, and a flaming sword which turned every way, to keep the way of the tree of life.

The tree of knowledge prefigures the tree of life just as the first man Adam prefigures the second man Jesus Christ. The image of man becoming like God, knowing good and evil, ironically recalls our original formation in the image of God and also prefigures our sanctification in the Body of Christ. The image of God is still evident in humanity despite our fall just as the will of God—that is, the love of God—is undeniable despite our fall. Adam, the imperfect image of God, chose the bad—in contrast to Jesus Christ, the perfect image of God, who would choose the good. Corrupted man is called to perfection, not of ourselves, but rather in Jesus Christ (Gen 17:1). The tree of life had not been expressly forbidden before our fall through Adam, only the tree of knowledge (Gen 2:16–17), implying that man and likewise creation were not subject to corruption and death before our fall, in accord with the revelation that death originally entered the world through the first sin (Rom 5:12). The tree of life in the garden reflects the presence of God since all life ultimately proceeds from God. In contrast, the tree of knowledge reflects carnal nature, specifically as contrary to spiritual nature. The tree of life is life, while the tree of knowledge is death. The tree of life is spirit, while the tree of knowledge is flesh. The garden of Eden is the way of God, the way of the Spirit, while the present world, outside of the garden, is the way of man, the way of flesh.[58]

---

[57] The supposition, contrary to the literal text, that Adam and Eve were never actually naked but originally clothed in robes of light is a clear example of human bias being added to the Scriptures. Even if Adam and Eve were clothed in light, the emphasis in the account in on their nakedness.

[58] The heavenly court is denoted by the first person plural in Gen 1:26, 3:22, and 11:7, each time in intimate connection with the dispositioning of humanity (Sarna 12; Gen

ADAM AND EVE

The tree of life, also communion with God, is denied in fulfillment of the prophecy that Adam would die the very day he ate from the tree of knowledge. The prophecy that Adam would die refers not only to himself but also to all mankind, figuratively still in him at the time. But the prophecy of the death of man ultimately points to the promise that the natural body will be superseded by the spiritual, or glorified, body. The denial of the tree of life is not merely a punishment but actually a mercy just as the exile of man is a preservation of man and not simply a judgment of man. No man, no sinful man, can be in the presence of God, the fullness thereof, and live (Exod 33:20). The word *ever* (for ever) [H5769] (lest fallen man live for ever) has a connotation "to conceal" [H5956], which in the present context reflects the concealment of sin in the separation of man from God. The image of Adam potentially reaching out his own hand to take from the tree of life is an image of works in contrast to grace. Man entering eternity by his own hand would mean an eternal preservation of the way of flesh, that is, the way of ignorance and suffering. Anyone who embraces eternity outside of grace affirms an eternal suffering in his own person and a corresponding eternal separation from God. And this, of course, speaks of hell. The connection of Adam with the works of his own hands is a connection of man with flesh and likewise with the law that governs flesh. But Adam not being allowed to reach out his own hand is a vision of our promised redemption unfolding despite ourselves.[59]

Our condemnation to till the ground from which we come is an expression of the relationship between justice (condemnation) and creation (ground) that recalls the identification of the name *Elohim* [H430] (justice) with our genesis (creation). The original commandment was given to the first man Adam, even before the fall of creation, whereby law is inextricably tied to the natural order of things. The ground specifically represents carnal nature, whereby the condemnation of flesh to till the ground is an image of flesh being consumed by its own desires, flesh handed over to flesh. A consignment of Adam-kind, mankind, to sin—testifying to the sanctity of freewill as the foundation of the first covenant. The discipline of flesh by flesh is embodied by the internal struggle of every man, as well as by the external struggle of man against man. Again all levels of reality. The condemnation to till the earth is an ironic image of man digging his own grave but also foreshadows the final harvest of mankind, a duality of meaning that foreshadows the perishable body being superseded by the imperishable body. Law heralds grace just as the natural body heralds the spiritual, or glorified, body just as death heralds rebirth. The

---

1:26). God making Adam, or Adam-kind, in his, their, image corresponds to the original creation, Gen 1:26. Adam-kind becoming like God is connected with the First Advent of Christ, 3:22. And God confounding the language of man points to the foretold Second Advent and the concomitant judgment of Adam-kind, 11:7.

[59] God withholding the tree of life after the Fall of Man was a mercy sparing man from a fate of eternal misery (Clarke 1:55; Gen 3:22). The withholding of eternal life in the mortal coil is the call to repentance that must precede redemption.

preservation of humanity, even in condemnation, reflects the law leading Adamkind, specifically the faithful, unto grace (Gal 3:24).[60]

The cherubim placed by God to guard the way of the tree of life embody an undeniable providence (Gen 3:24). The flaming sword placed between man and paradise portends a certain death and destruction unleashed by sin, an irrevocable condemnation that stands between man and eternal life, an utter destruction linked with the second tree. The sword of the cherubim is reflected in the sword of Levi, representing the condemnation of all flesh under the law (Gen 34:26). The image of flames connected with the sword portends a final destruction of all flesh by fire, while the image of the sword connects that final destruction specifically with war. The image of flames also prefigures the baptism of fire—that is, the fullness of the baptism of the Holy Spirit—which connects the final baptism with the final destruction. The foretold destruction by fire in the end times follows the destruction by water in the time of Noah just as the tree of life follows the tree of knowledge just as the baptism of the Holy Spirit follows the baptism in water just as the Covenant of Grace follows the Covenant of Law just as the spiritual, or glorified, resurrection body follows the present physical body.

The emphasis on the gateway to the garden of Eden being in the *east* [H6924] points to the temple also opening to the east (Ezek 8:16). Moses and Aaron, personifying the law and prefiguring the First Advent, would likewise encamp on the east side of the tabernacle (Num 3:38) just as the tribe of Judah, representing the bloodline of Jesus Christ, would also encamp on the east side of the tabernacle (Num 2:3). Joshua would be directed to enter the promised land, which is a temple among nations, across the Jordan from the east (Josh 1:2). And the body of faithful, which is the temple of the Holy Spirit, opens eyes eastward in hope of a new day (1 Cor 6:19). The wise men would follow a star from the east to see the newborn king (Matt 2:1–2) just as the promised coming of the Son of man will be like lightning that comes out of the east (Matt 24:27). The east is the place of the rising sun—the symbolic origin of each new dawn, representing our promised new creation.[61]

Ω Ω Ω

The natures of the one man Adam are twofold just as the natures of the one man Jesus Christ are twofold. Adam was formed of the dust of the ground and animated by the breath of God, wherein the dust of the ground and the breath of God represent the tangible and intangible aspects of life, or abstractly flesh

---

[60] "Punishment is not the last word. . . . The couple's sin has not altered the divine intent to make them fruitful" (Clifford, *New Jerome* 13; Gen 3:20–21). The image of God remains manifest in creation despite having been corrupted by sin.

[61] The symbolic and spiritual import of natural events, such as the rising sun and the changing seasons, has been corrupted by pagans just as everything in creation has been corrupted, but the signs are still recognizable just as the will of God is still recognizable.

ADAM AND EVE

and spirit (Gen 2:7).[62] The original act of creation proceeded through the Son, whereby the twofold natures of the Son, being fully man and fully God, are imprinted upon all creation and, thereby, underlie the manifest dichotomy of flesh and spirit (John 1:1–3).[63] The first man Adam formed in the image of God (Gen 9:6) points to the second man Christ, the only begotten Son of God, who is the perfect image of God, being the incarnation of God (John 3:16). The formation of Adam precedes the birth of Jesus Christ just as the natural body precedes the spiritual body just as law precedes grace. The natural man Adam prefigures the spiritual man Jesus Christ just as all flesh proceeding from Adam prefigures all the faithful being redeemed in Christ. Mortal life foreshadows eternal life just as the original creation of Adam foreshadows our promised new creation in Christ.[64]

The first man Adam and the second man Christ both embody the union of flesh and spirit. Nonetheless, Adam uniquely represents flesh in that natural man is governed by the flesh, the law of the flesh. And Christ uniquely represents spirit because spiritual man is governed by the Spirit, the grace of the Spirit. The first man Adam was formed in the very image of God in an earthly union of flesh and spirit, reflecting the divine union of law and grace, but the image of God embodied by Adam and likewise by all mankind in Adam has become corrupted through sin. The first man Adam is the embodiment of all humanity in that all humanity would proceed from him, whereby the curse of Adam portends the utter destruction of all flesh. The union of flesh and spirit embodied by mortal man is an ironic juxtaposition of death and life, which is a paradox resolved in the death of the natural body heralding the resurrection of the spiritual body. The resolution of this paradox is first manifested in the death and resurrection of Christ and finally in the foretold death and resurrection of the faithful in Christ.[65]

---

[62] Mind, will, soul, spirit, and so forth, are not generally distinguished in the broad view but understood collectively as the intangible aspect of life and, therefore, are commonly thought of collectively as one's spiritual nature or dimension.

[63] The twofold natures of Christ transcend the time of the First Advent just as the blood sacrifice of Christ at the First Advent covers all believers throughout all time.

[64] God is envisioned as creating the universe using the Torah like an architect using a blueprint, *Genesis Rabbah* (Cohen, *Rabbinic Sages* 29). The structure of the Torah is Trinitarian, wherein Jesus Christ, God the Son, is recognized as the true blueprint of all creation, the one through whom all creation proceeds.

[65] "The plot structure [of Biblical narratives] typically consists of an exposition or introduction, a rising tension [usually in conflict with an antagonist], a climax or peaking of the tension, and a resolution and denouement [usually displaying the character of God]" (Waltke 42). Looking at the Bible as a whole, the formal law governing Adam, or fallen man, is the preparative exposition, the First Advent is the climax, and the Second Advent is the final display of the character of God, specifically in the Body of Christ.

ADAM, NOAH, ABRAHAM

1	2
ORIGINAL CREATION	NEW CREATION
ADAM	CHRIST
NATURAL MAN	SPIRITUAL MAN
(FORMED)	(BEGOTTEN)
LAW	GRACE
MORTAL LIFE	ETERNAL LIFE
FLESH	SPIRIT

Our experience of reality is foremost twofold, natural and spiritual, just as the twofold natures of Christ, who is fully man and fully God, relate the visible image of God (Col 1:15). But the fullness of revelation is ultimately threefold, reflecting the Father, Son, and Holy Spirit as the wholeness of truth (Matt 28:19). The manifest threefold pattern is Adam followed by the First and Second Advents of Christ. Adam came first, Christ second, and the faithful now await the final revelation of the Body of Christ. The parallel between the threefold Adam and First and Second Advents and the threefold Father, Son, and Holy Spirit represents an emphasis on our threefold creation, redemption, and sanctification. Adam is the embodiment of creation, reflecting the Father as our creator; the Son is our redeemer, being the person of the Trinity nailed to the cross; and the Holy Spirit is our sanctifier through the agency of indwelling. The threefold successive Adam, First Advent, and Second Advent can also be compared to the threefold image of the dust of the ground being animated by the breath of God and becoming a living being. The living being is something new, transcending the simple sum of the dust and the breath, just as the Body of Christ is something new.[66] All patterns in creation point to the last days, converging in a vision of the fulfillment of the promise of God. The promise of God is our inheritance in the indwelling Holy Spirit, which is our communion with the Father in the Son by the power, or new life, of the Holy Spirit.[67]

Our original creation and our new creation both proceed from the Father through the Son by the power of the Holy Spirit, whereby the image of God is imprinted upon all creation, an image evident despite our fall, in testimony to the undeniable, or relentless, will of God for the welfare of his children (Rom 1:20). The 1-2-3 Trinitarian pattern imprinted upon all creation is specifically an overlapping 1-2, 1-2 pattern, reflecting all creation proceeding through the twofold natures of the Son. The second man Christ is the fulfillment of the first man Adam just as the Second Advent of Christ will be the fulfillment of the First Advent. Our redemption embodied by Christ is the fulfillment of the promise embodied by Adam just as the resurrection of all the dead will be the

---

[66] The threefold image of the breath of life animating a living soul out of the dust of the ground reflects the distinction between spirit, soul, and body, 1 Thess 5:23.

[67] "The early catechetical and liturgical formulas refer to the Father and the Lord Jesus Christ, or to the Father the Creator, his Son Jesus Christ, and the Holy Spirit" (Rusch 2). The emphasis on the relationship between the Father and the Son affirms the universal dichotomy of spirit and flesh, while the emphasis on the Father as the creator affirms the unique identification of the Father with the promise of life.

fulfillment of the resurrection of Christ (1 Cor 15:23). The natural man Adam prefigures the spiritual man Jesus Christ, while Christ, the Head, prefigures the faithful in Christ, the Body of Christ (Col 1:18). This key twofold construction testifies to the primal promise of the communion of the one body of faithful with the one Spirit of God, represented abstractly in the union of flesh and spirit in our original creation. The 1-2 pattern is more obvious than the 1-2-3 pattern in the natural world and also in the Biblical accounting. But this relativity is the limitation of our own finite perception, not a diminishing of the absolute universality of the Trinity. The dimness of our perception reflects the degradation of humanity, specifically the primal rejection of God by Adam, which would be made visible in the rejection of the Son by mankind. The visible sign is the defilement of the Son on the cross—not the unity of the Father, Son, and Holy Spirit—in accordance with our sinful nature (John 14:16–17).

1	2	3
FATHER=CREATOR	SON=REDEEMER	HOLY SPIRIT=SANCTIFIER
1	2	
ADAM=FIRST MAN	CHRIST=SECOND MAN	
	1	2
	FIRST ADVENT=THE HEAD	SECOND ADVENT=THE BODY

The one man Adam reflects the oneness of God. The union of flesh and spirit embodied by Adam reflects the twofold natures of God the Son, who is true man and true God. The threefold progression of the genesis of man—the dust being animated by the breath of God and becoming a living soul—reflects the fullness of truth in the Trinity. Every man is a microcosm of the wholeness of creation, in imitation of the Son of man, who is the visible image of the invisible God of creation. Further, the progression from Adam to Jesus Christ to the Body of Christ represents the natural history of man. This nonuniform threefold pattern of natural history recalls the serial, or simple repeating, pattern identified with the Father, expressly as the God of creation—even though the serial pattern is demarcated by uniform intervals in time. The innate focus on the individual, irrespective of timeframe, recalls the chiastic, or mirrored, pattern of creation, pointing to the incarnation of the singular person of Jesus Christ, our personal redeemer—even though the revelation of the kingdom of God culminating in the conception of Christ is positioned in a very specific and exact way at the center of the Biblical, or historical, timeline. And the faithful in their respective generations coming together to form the members of the one Body of Christ, though they are scattered in a seemingly random fashion, recalls the staircase pattern, pointing to the fulfillment of all things in the last days, in accordance with the sanctifying presence of the Holy Spirit—even though the march of the days and millennia of creation are perfectly uniform in time. The Head is one, the Body is many.[68]

---

[68] The age from Adam to Noah is like our infancy, which is lost to our memory, and is followed by the age from Noah to Abraham, which is like our childhood, a first learning to speak, followed by the age from Abraham to David, which is like a passing puberty, the beginning of fruitfulness and simultaneously a new culpability under the law,

ADAM, NOAH, ABRAHAM

CHAPTER ONE OUTLINE

Key Images

Key images are organized in a twofold progression by order (prime, twofold, threefold) and by level (material, abstract, spiritual). The material level of reality—which is the literal, or immanent, level—is connected via an abstract, conceptual level to a spiritual level—which is the figurative, or transcendent, level. Prime, or singular, images reflect the oneness of God, foremost God the Father. Twofold images are identified with the duality of flesh and spirit, the two covenants of law and grace, and ultimately the twofold natures of God the Son, who is true man and true God. Threefold images relate the threefold movement of God the Holy Spirit in creation and new creation that is finally the revelation of the fullness of Trinitarian reality.

PRIME IMAGES		
Material	Abstract	Spiritual
Adam.	One man.	One man formed in the image of the one God.
The garden of Eden.	Peace on earth.	The promise of the fullness of life that is in communion with God in the kingdom of God.
The serpent.	The spirit of disobedience.	The devil (Eph 2:2).
TWOFOLD IMAGES		
Material	Abstract	Spiritual
The name *God* and the name *Lord God*.	Law and grace. Flesh and spirit.	The perfect union of justice and mercy in the Godhead.
The union of the dust of the ground and the breath of God that becomes, or is, a living soul.	Flesh and spirit.	The union of flesh and spirit in mankind, pointing to the communion of man and God in the Body of Christ.
Male and female.	Justice and mercy. Flesh and spirit.	The union of male and female, reflecting the image of God.
The tree of knowledge and the tree of life.	Death and life. Flesh and spirit.	The Covenant of Law and the Covenant of Grace.
THREEFOLD IMAGES		
Material	Abstract	Spiritual
Man, woman, and child.	Justice; mercy; and the offspring, or union, of justice and mercy.	Father, Son (through the Spirit), and Holy Spirit (indwelling the Body of Christ).
Serpent, Eve, Adam.	Father of lies; mouthpiece of lies; receiver, or embodiment, of lies.	An anti-trinity opposing the one true Father, Spirit, and Son.

---

followed by the age beginning with the kingdom of David, which is like an advanced youth, the beginning of the dominion that points to the Sonship of Christ (Augustine, *City of God* 567). Augustine instinctively looks for a parallel between the progression of individual man and the unfolding of the larger historical context.

ADAM AND EVE

Synopsis

Parallel summaries of the material and spiritual levels of reality are arranged by Biblical chapters and verses and delimited by commentary chapter sections. The material level, or earthly perspective, corresponds to the explicit Biblical text, while the spiritual level corresponds to the implicit heavenly perspective. An intermediary abstract level is not developed, because it would be too intricate to be generally useful.

	THE GARDEN OF EDEN	
	Material	Spiritual
1:1	The revelation of the name *God* (Elohim) in the context of original creation.	Physical creation, the natural body, will be governed by law, not by grace.
2:4	The revelation of the second name *Lord* (YHWH) *God* (Elohim).	A vision of God as the perfect union of justice and mercy.
2:5–6	The Lord God had not caused it to rain upon the earth.	The baptism in water is identified with the Flood, not with the First Creation.
2:7	The Lord God forms Adam from the dust of the ground.	Flesh.
	And the Lord God breathes into his nostrils the breath of life.	Spirit.
	And Adam becomes a living soul.	Man formed in the image of God, the union of flesh and spirit, reflecting the union of law and grace.
2:8–14	Pison, Gihon, Hiddekel, Euphrates.	The four rivers flowing from the one garden, from original creation, point to the conception of Jesus Christ, the Lord of creation, at the end of the fourth millennium from Adam, in the very midst of creation.
2:15	The Lord God places Adam in the garden to dress it and to keep it.	The call of all mankind, from Adam, to grow into the fullness of communion with God.
	THE FIRST LAW	
	Material	Spiritual
2:16–17	The Lord God commands Adam not to eat from the tree of knowledge.	The call to simple obedience to God, pointing to the perfect faithfulness of Christ.
	MALE AND FEMALE	
	Material	Spiritual
2:18	Man should not be alone.	Perfect justice must be tempered by mercy.
2:19–20	Adam gives names to every living thing.	The dominion of human freewill.
	But an help meet was not found for Adam.	Dominion of itself is not enough.
2:21–24	Woman proceeds from man.	Grace proceeds from law.
	A man shall leave his father and his mother and cleave unto his wife.	A prophecy of the marriage of the Lamb.
	Man and woman form one body.	The Body of Christ.
2:25	Man and woman are naked but not ashamed.	Not a perfect innocence, but rather a yet unrevealed nature.
	NAKED	
	Material	Spiritual
3:1–8	The serpent seduces Eve.	The spirit that works in the children of disobedience (Eph 2:2).
	Adam and Eve eat from the tree of the knowledge of good and evil.	Experiential knowledge, walking by flesh in contrast to spirit, ironically foreshadowing the incarnation and specifically the crucifixion.

	Adam and Eve now know they are naked.	The nakedness of Adam and Eve, prefiguring the exposure of Christ on the cross.
	Adam and Eve hide from God.	Our separation from God because of our sins, ultimately embodied by Jesus Christ forsaken on the cross (Matt 27:46).
3:9–13	Adam is naked and afraid.	The way of all flesh, all the earth.
	Serpent, woman, man.	The father of lies forming an anti-trinity.

THREE CURSES

	Material	Spiritual
3:14–19	The serpent is cursed to go on its belly and eat dust.	The dominion of Adam, figuratively flesh, becomes the dominion of the devil.
	The Lord God places enmity between the serpent and woman.	God himself will stand in the breach.
	And man shall rule over woman.	Reflects the submission of Christ, the Seed of woman.
	Children will be brought forth in sorrow.	Prefigures our redemption through the cross.
	And the ground is cursed.	The law that guides us to grace.

EXILE

	Material	Spiritual
3:20	Adam called his wife's name Eve because she was the mother of all the living.	The promise of eternal life through the promised Seed of woman.
3:21	The Lord God clothes Adam and Eve in animal skins.	An animal costume reflecting the degradation of flesh, but ironically also prefiguring the humble condescension of God in the flesh.
3:22–24	Man is denied the tree of life lest he eats and lives forever.	The present natural body will and must pass away (1 Cor 15:44).

CHAPTER TWO

Cain, Abel, Seth

Sacrificial offering is the prime image in the account of Cain, Abel, and Seth, as exemplified by Cain and Abel each individually presenting their respective sacrifices to the one God. The call to acceptable sacrifice is an affirmation of our freewill, our dominion inherited from God that is our creation in the image of God (Gen 9:6). The prime image of individuals presenting individual sacrifices to God immediately diverges into a twofold image of acceptable and unacceptable sacrifices just as freewill is ever an imminent choice between the good and the bad. The call to acceptable sacrifice is the call to choose the good and reject the bad (Gen 4:7), but nevertheless our one salvation is not by works but by the one faith in the one God (Gal 2:16). We cannot save ourselves by our own hands, but rather our deeds are the tangible signs of our intangible faith. Good works are a manifestation of faith just as the material world reflects a spiritual reality just as literal meaning embodies spiritual truth. The call to acceptable sacrifice is ultimately the call to the one perfect sacrifice embodied by the death of the one man Jesus Christ for the sins of the whole world, the one world (Heb 9:28).

In the account of the sons of Adam, the emphasized twofold images are Cain and Abel as two sons, their two individual occupations, and their two representative sacrifices. The essential tension on each level of reality is the conflict between flesh and spirit and likewise between law and grace. Cain and Abel are the first and second sons of Adam just as Adam and Jesus are the first and second sons of God. In each pair, the former embodies the natural while the latter embodies the spiritual. The occupation of Cain, as a tiller of the ground, is connected with the dust of the ground, which is an emblem of death, while the occupation of Abel, as a keeper of flocks, is connected with livestock, which are an emblem of life. The rejection of Cain's sacrifice is an image of our condemnation under the law, while the acceptance of Abel's sacrifice is an image of our redemption by grace. The sacrifices of both brothers are derived from their individual occupations just as our physical deeds reflect our spiritual identity. The two brothers Cain and Abel ultimately evoke an image of one family just as their two occupations evoke an image of one world just as acceptable and unacceptable sacrifices evoke an image of one freewill just as law and grace evoke an image of the one God. Not that the evil embodied by Cain represents any part of God, but rather that freewill is created by God in the image of God.

The threefold Cain, Abel, and Seth is a vision of, respectively, Adam, the First Advent of Christ, and the Second Advent. The curse of Cain recalls the curse of Adam just as Cain killing Abel reflects Adam figuratively, or rather spiritually, killing Christ, as originally manifested in death entering the world through Adam (Rom 5:12). The acceptable sacrifice of Abel points to the perfect sacrifice of Jesus Christ in the First Advent, while Seth replacing Abel is a figurative resurrection of Abel that finally points to the resurrection of all the dead in the Second Advent. The threefold Cain, Abel, and Seth likewise reflect, respectively, the Father, Son, and Holy Spirit. The firstborn Cain recalls the first man Adam formed in the image of God, who is our Creator and therefore our Father. The life and death of Abel prefigures the incarnation of the Son of God, while the figurative resurrection of Abel in the person of Seth prefigures the resurrection of all the dead in Christ, animated specifically by the power of the Holy Spirit. The universal image of the Godhead in creation is a determined testimony to the one will of God that is the sanctification of all the faithful.

FIRSTBORN

Genesis 4:1 And Adam knew [H3045] Eve his wife; and she conceived, and bare [H3205] Cain, and said, I have gotten [H7069] a man [H376] from the LORD [H3068].

Eve previously used the name *God* (Elohim) [H430] in the garden, which evokes the connection of the original creation with justice, a connection that portends a final judgment of creation (Gen 3:2–3). But Eve now, in the context of childbirth, uses the proper name *Lord* (YHWH) [H3068], or literally "the Self-Existent," which evokes an image of life that implicitly acknowledges God as the font of life. The name *Jehovah* (YHWH) encompasses not only the explicit name *I AM THAT I AM* (Exod 3:14) but also the implicit name *I WILL SHEW MERCY ON WHOM I WILL SHEW MERCY* (Exod 33:19). We are rightfully condemned under the law, but we look to our rebirth in grace just as the name *Elohim* points to the name *Jehovah* (YHWH). The promise of life being affirmed despite our condemnation is reflected in the fundamental contrast between pain and hope in childbirth.[1]

The word *knew* [H3045] (Adam knew Eve) has connotations in the Hebrew "to discriminate, distinguish," specifically "to know by experience," and is the root word underlying the word *knowledge* [H1847], used in the name *tree of*

---

[1] In Gen 4:1, the sacred name YHWH is uttered for the first time—not by a man, but by a woman (Sarna 32; Gen 4:1). Further, the Son of man is the Seed of woman, Gen 3:15, whereby it is certainly not happenstance that the risen Lord would be proclaimed first by woman, John 20:18.

knowledge. The knowledge through experience connected with the tree of knowledge represents the medium of flesh, or simply flesh, and likewise the law that governs flesh. The tree of life reflects the wisdom, in contrast to mere knowledge, that comes from the Holy Spirit, the wisdom that gives life, the wisdom of grace. The tree of knowledge points to the tree of life just as the Covenant of Law points to the Covenant of Grace just as knowledge points to wisdom. The tree of life, representing grace, does not replace the tree of knowledge, or the law, just as wisdom does not replace knowledge. Rather, the tree of life is the fulfillment of the tree of knowledge just as wisdom is the fulfillment of knowledge. The fulfillment of law in grace, likewise the fulfillment of knowledge in wisdom, becomes something new, life itself, whereby we inherit the tree of life, not simply the tree of wisdom (Eccl 7:12).

The word *bare* [H3205] (Eve bare Cain) means "to bear, bring forth, beget" and has a connotation "to travail," whereby the pain of childbirth recalls the curse of the flesh and likewise our exile from the garden (Gen 3:16) while the new life of a child embodies our preservation from annihilation and foreshadows our promised rebirth by the Spirit (John 3:7). Man is most closely identified with justice while woman is most closely identified with mercy, whereby the union of man and woman in the conception of new life prefigures the rebirth of the faithful in the promised fulfillment of justice in mercy. The dichotomy of fear and love related in childbirth is the same dichotomy of law and grace resolved in the perfect union of flesh and spirit in the person of Jesus Christ. The union and also the offspring of man and woman both affirm on different levels of reality the prophecy that man and woman are one flesh, but the new life of a child transcends the physical union of man and woman just as our new life in God transcends the simple fulfillment of justice and mercy (Gen 2:24). Our one true redemption is not twofold but rather threefold in the fullness of the Father, Son, and Holy Spirit.[2]

The word *gotten* [H7069] (Eve got Cain) means "to get, acquire," with connotations "to buy" and "of God as victoriously redeeming" and also "of acquiring knowledge, wisdom," reflecting a corrupted humanity being redeemed by the perfect Jesus Christ. The connection of acquiring knowledge or wisdom with our redemption reflects the tree of life as the fulfillment of the tree of knowledge. Likewise, the Covenant of Grace is the fulfillment of the Covenant of Law just as the Second Advent will be the fulfillment of the First Advent. Mercy does not destroy justice but rather completes justice (Matt 5:17). Mercy only destroys justice in the sense that the new life embodied by the union of justice and mercy transcends the simple fulfillment of justice and mercy. This new life is finally represented by the formation of the one Body of Christ from the twofold world order of Jew and Gentile (Eph 2:15).[3]

---

[2] "[S]he [Eve] said, I have acquired a man [Cain], the Angel of the Lord [*Targum of Jonathan ben Uzziel*]" (Etheridge 1:169–70). The first man Adam, likewise the first son Cain, points to the second man Jesus Christ.

[3] "That is, [Eve obtained Cain] according to the Lord's promise, as [Gen 3:15] . . . ." (Whittingham et al., *Geneva Bible* 3L n. b; Gen 4:1). The First Advent of Jesus Christ points to the Second Advent.

ADAM, NOAH, ABRAHAM

The word *man* [H376] (man from the Lord) connotes "man in contrast to woman" and also "man as husband," reflecting Christ as the bridegroom of the faithful. But the word *man* [H376] used to describe Cain is not the same word *man* [H120] used to describe Adam as originally formed from the dust of the ground (Gen 2:7). The original word *man* [H120] has an association "to be red" [H119], reflecting the deposit of life as represented by blood, a life originally bestowed on man but rejected by man. Fallen man is not the same as created man just as the second Adam is not the same as the first Adam. But how can the second Adam, Jesus Christ, be compared with fallen man? The firstborn of the flesh, Cain, is spiritually the firstborn of and into the curse of death, prefiguring, in reverse, Jesus Christ, the firstborn from and out of the curse of death, just as our fall through the one man Adam prefigures, in reverse, our exaltation through the one man Jesus Christ (Rom 5:19). The oneness of individual man is derived from individual freewill and reflects the oneness of God and likewise the one will of God. Accordingly, our corruption of freewill embodies a corruption of the image of God, representing a reverse image when comparing the corrupted with the uncorrupted, the bad with the good. Eve looking to receive a man from the Lord foreshadows the incarnation of Christ as a literal descent from heaven, while the image of descent itself reflects both the degradation of man in the curse and the corresponding condescension of Christ, humbly becoming a curse for the sake of us sinners. The image of descending identified with the incarnation (First Advent) is also a reverse image of the exalting of the faithful in Christ, in the Body of Christ, following the ascending of Christ to the Father, in which Christ will finally present redeemed humanity unto God the Father (Second Advent).[4]

The threefold vision of Adam *knowing* [H3045] Eve, Eve *bearing* [H3205] Cain, and Eve *getting* [H7069] a man from the Lord reflects, respectively, the Fall of Man, the First Advent of Christ, and the Second Advent of Christ. The image of Adam *knowing* [H3045] Eve recalls the experiential knowledge connected with the tree of knowledge and also man heeding woman in his disobedience, while Eve conceiving the first murderer Cain recalls death originally entering the world through the first sin. But the image of Eve *bearing* [H3205] the firstborn son of creation, Cain, also prefigures Mary bearing the child who would become the firstborn son of our new creation, Jesus Christ. The uncomfortable comparison between Christ and Cain reflects the humble condescension of God in the incarnation for the sake of us sinners. The image of Eve *getting* [H7069] a man from the Lord finally prefigures the world

---

[4] The common translation "I have gotten a man with the help of Jehovah" may be better rendered, according to H. L. Ellison, as "I have gotten a man, even the Lord" or, according to M. G. Kline, as "I have gotten a man from the Lord," both reflecting an anticipation of the promised Seed (Coffman 74; Gen 4:1). To speak in terms of better or worse translations is very misleading, for it is completely normal to have layered meanings, even in the original languages.

CAIN, ABEL, SETH

receiving from heaven the Son of God, through whom and in whom the Body of Christ will be revealed in the Second Advent.[5]

Two Sons

Genesis 4:2 And she again bare his brother Abel [H1893]. And Abel [H1893] was a keeper [H7462] of sheep [H6629], but Cain [H7014] was a tiller [H5647] of the ground [H127].

The word *ground* [H127] (Cain tilled) has an association in the Hebrew "to be red" [H119] and is the same word used to describe man being formed from the dust of the *ground* [H127] (Gen 2:7), while the word *tiller* [H5647] (Cain) means "to work" and "to serve" and is the same word used to describe Adam *dressing* [H5647] the garden (Gen 2:15). The occupation of Cain in the world recalls both the occupation of Adam in the garden and also the curse of Adam to toil in the ground. The first son Cain is like the first man Adam. The birthright belongs to the firstborn Cain, but his inheritance from Adam is the curse of the ground, the red earth together with ruddy man.[6]

The word *keeper* [H7462] (Abel) means "to pasture, tend, graze," with connotations "of ruler, teacher" and also "of faithfulness, friendship," while the word *sheep* [H6629] (Abel keeps) has a connotation "multitude (of children)." The occupation of Abel foreshadows Jesus Christ as the good shepherd, while the occupation of Cain recalls Adam appointed to work the earth (John 10:11). The image of sheep migrating represents humanity wandering and searching the earth. A vision of experiential knowledge. Cain and Abel are the first and second sons of Adam just as Adam and Jesus are the first and second sons of God, while the brotherhood of Cain and Abel reflects the brotherhood of mankind and Jesus Christ (Matt 12:50). Mankind should be most closely identified with Cain and not with Abel, since all men are sinners and thereby are personally accountable for the death of Jesus Christ. The faithful are identified with Abel only in the figurative death and resurrection of the baptism of repentance for the forgiveness of sins.[7]

---

[5] "One of the first things noted by literary critics is that biblical authors use words sparingly—each word counts. Therefore, the exegete's attitude should be that every feature in the text is there for a reason and needs to be explained" (Waltke 33). The Word of God is in no way arbitrary just as God is neither arbitrary nor capricious.
[6] The Scriptures don't specifically state that Cain was the firstborn of Eve, and prior offspring are certainly possible given the highly condensed nature of the account (Coffman 75; Gen 4:2). Whether or not Cain was the literal firstborn, the absence of any older siblings in the narrative relates an emphasis that, by itself, identifies Cain as a type of the firstborn, likewise a type of fallen Adam. And not coincidentally the recorded account of the life and deeds of Cain affirms him as a type of the first man Adam.
[7] "[I]t appears evident that Cain and Abel were *twins*. In most cases where a subject of this kind is introduced in the Holy Scriptures, and the successive births of children of the same parents are noted, the acts of conceiving and bringing forth are mentioned in reference to each child; here it is *not* . . . ." (Clarke 1:58; Gen 4:2). The mere possibility

The name *Cain* [H7014] evokes an image of a "spear" [H7013] and also has an association "to chant (lament)" [H6969]. The image of lamentation portends the murder of Abel, likewise the crucifixion of Jesus Christ, and likewise the foretold death of all flesh. Abel would die by the hand of man, figuratively the sword or spear in contrast to pestilence or famine or natural disaster. Jesus Christ would likewise die by the hand of man. The spear that would pierce the side of Christ on the cross recalls the name *Cain* (John 19:34). Abel is the first man murdered at the opening of creation, while Jesus Christ would be the first man murdered at the opening of our new creation. The first son Cain murdering the second son Abel reflects the first son Adam figuratively murdering the second son Jesus Christ. The righteous one, Christ, is, of course, the only begotten Son of God (John 1:18), but Adam and Christ are still figuratively the first and second sons of God in the sense that they are the first and second men as spoken of by Paul (1 Cor 15:47). The lives of Cain and Abel are a microcosm of the unfolding of salvation just as all levels of reality reflect the universal image of God and likewise the undeniable will of God.

The name *Abel* [H1893] evokes an image of "vapour, breath" [H1892], with connotations of "vanity" and "evanescence." The breath of Abel recalls the breath of God originally animating Adam and, thereby, affirms the indwelling Holy Spirit as the true essence of life. But the name *Abel* [H1893] is not the same word used to describe the *breath* [H5397] of life originally breathed into man (Gen 2:7). The connection of breath with vanity evoked by the name *Abel* reflects our fall in Adam and likewise the mortality of Adam-kind, our vain breath. Life had become vain through original sin because death took dominion over flesh, and man had become a corresponding corrupted image of God. But the vain breath of Abel nonetheless prefigures the irrepressible life of Jesus Christ just as finite mortality prefigures eternal life. Cain is a natural man recalling Adam, while Abel is a spiritual man prefiguring Jesus Christ. The hand of Cain is the hand that holds the sword, the spear, whereas the breath of Abel embodies the breath of God, the breath of life. Comparing the imagery connected with the two brothers, the hand of Cain, the hand that holds the spear, is supplanted not merely by the hand of Abel but rather by the intangible breath of Abel. Neither is spiritual man merely a perfection of natural man. Jesus Christ is not merely a perfect man just as mercy is not merely a perfection of justice just as the kingdom of God is not merely a return to the garden of Eden. The birth of Jesus Christ is something new, something radically new, intrinsically, for Christ is the incarnation of God himself, or personally, in the flesh. The perfection of the faithful in Christ is something equally new and radical, the very Body of Christ.

---

that Cain and Abel might have been twins reflects the close kinship between Adam and Christ, while the ambiguity around their conception reflects the mystery of our rebirth in the Body of Christ. The physical conception being most directly identified with Cain and not Abel, by proximity in the text, prophetically contrasts the formation of the natural man Adam with the supernatural birth of the spiritual man Jesus Christ.

CAIN, ABEL, SETH

Two Sacrifices

Genesis 4:3–5 And in process [H7093] of time it came to pass, that Cain brought [H935] of the fruit [H6529] of the ground [H127] an offering [H4503] unto the LORD. 4 And Abel, he also brought [H935] of the firstlings [H1062] of his flock [H6629] and of the fat [H2459] thereof. And the LORD had respect [H8159] unto Abel and to his offering [H4503]: 5 But unto Cain and to his offering [H4503] he had not respect. And Cain was very wroth [H2734], and his countenance fell [H5307].

The word *process* [H7093] (in process of time) means "end" and has a connotation "time of final punishment" and is derived from the root "to cut off" [H7112]. The word *brought* [H935] (unto the Lord) is a general term, but Cain and Abel bringing their offerings specifically into the presence of God is an image of judgment that prefigures the end of time. The image of creation being cut off in the end times has parallel eschatological implications for the individual just as the judgment of creation presumes the judgment of individuals. The death of the individual prefigures the destruction of creation, while the destruction of creation is the death of all individuals. The death of the individual is ultimately equivalent to the end of creation since both the individual and creation have infinite value to God. The individual is not simply a microcosm of all creation by mere symmetry, but rather the individual is a literal embodiment of all creation as the embodiment of the fullness of the promise of life that proceeds from the Lord God. An understanding of the formation and destruction of creation as a whole is inseparable from an understanding of the life and death of the individual.[8]

The word *offering* [H4503] (offerings of Cain and Abel) means "gift, tribute, offering." The ambiguity between love gifts and disingenuous tributes reflects our freewill, which is a dominion affirmed in the disparate offerings of the first and second born sons Cain and Abel. But freewill also implies an offering from the heart, which emphasizes the unity between the individual and his offering. Cain offering the *fruit* [H6529] of the *ground* [H127] recalls Adam eating the *fruit* [H6529] of the tree of knowledge (Gen 3:6) and also recalls the curse of the *ground* [H127] that Adam incurred (Gen 3:17). The first son Cain rejecting the counsel of God is an affirmation of the first man Adam rejecting the commandment of God, whereby the fruit of the ground is cursed just as the ground itself is cursed. The curse of Adam being affirmed in his son Cain finally portends the condemnation of all flesh in the end times.

The word *flock* [H6629] (linked with Abel) has a connotation "multitude (of children)," representing the multitude of mankind, while the word *fat* [H2459] (also linked with Abel) has a connotation "choicest, best part," representing the

---

[8] "*In process of time—At the end of days*, either at the end of the year when they kept their feast of *in-gathering*, or at the end of the days of the week, the seventh day; . . ." (Wesley 1:20; Gen 4:3). The one reflects the other, and the two converge in the end of ends.

perfection of mankind. The figuratively perfect sacrificial firstborn of the flock offered by Abel prefigures the literally perfect sacrifice of the Son of man. The word *firstlings* [H1062] (offered by Abel) has a connotation "right of the firstborn." Abel was the second born, but he offered the sign of the firstborn, the firstborn of his flock. The birth of Jesus Christ in the flesh would likewise follow the formation of Adam from the dust, but Christ and not Adam would assert possession of the birthright of the firstborn, which is the image of God.[9]

The word *respect* [H8159] (Lord had respect unto Abel) means "to gaze" in the Hebrew, implying an intimate and personal presence of God, a nearness that recalls the presence of God in the garden and foreshadows the incarnation of Jesus Christ. Whether or not acceptable sacrifices had been explicitly explained beforehand, Abel's spiritual understanding is a seal placed upon him by the Holy Spirit, marking him as a type of Christ. It was by faith that Abel offered God a better sacrifice than that of Cain (Heb 11:4). In contrast, Cain's ignorance of acceptable sacrifices is a sign of his separation from the Spirit, which marks him as a type of Adam, likewise flesh, and likewise this world. Cain's ignorance of acceptable sacrifices and the closely related murder of Abel both embody the same spirit of disobedience just as small sins and big sins both reflect the same sinful nature. Cain and Abel and also their respective offerings are reflections of Adam and Jesus Christ, in testimony to the unity of creation and likewise the oneness of the Creator. Man is called to be perfect in both small things and large things (Jas 2:10).[10]

The word *wroth* [H2734] (Cain was wroth) means "to burn, be kindled, of anger," while the word *fell* [H5307] (Cain's countenance fell) has a connotation "of violent death." The faithlessness of Cain becomes a consuming fire, a personal degradation that finally portends the death of all flesh in the foretold destruction by fire in the end times. The offerings of the two brothers are direct reflections of their occupations just as our physical deeds are direct reflections of our spiritual identity. The offerings of Cain and Abel represent summations of their personal characters just as the summations of their lives is implied by the underlying theme of the end of time. Physical enactments, such as sacrificial offering, reflect a spiritual reality just as all creation reflects a spiritual reality. Jesus Christ is likewise the ultimate visible image of the invisible God.[11]

---

[9] ". . . Abel was preferred before the elder brother; so to . . . Isaac . . . Jacob . . . Phares [Pharez] . . . David . . . and as the reason why all these parables and others like them preceded, not only of words but also of deeds, in like manner to the people of the Jews was preferred the Christian people . . . . [Augustine, *Expositions on the Psalms*]" (Schaff, *Nicene and Post-Nicene Fathers: First Series* 8:370). Not simply the Gentiles, but rather Jews and Gentiles together in the one Body of Christ.

[10] Cain's grain offering was a thank offering while Abel's blood sacrifice was a sin offering, by which Abel acknowledged his own fallen nature but Cain did not (Jamieson et al. 1:70; Gen 4:7). All levels of reality reflect the same truth that is ultimately the one image of God.

[11] ". . . *Cain's* was only *a sacrifice of acknowledgment* offered to the Creator; the meat-offerings of *the fruit of the ground* were no more: but *Abel* brought *a sacrifice of atonement*, the *blood* whereof was shed in order to remission, thereby owning himself a sinner,

CAIN, ABEL, SETH

Genesis 4:6–7 And the LORD said unto Cain, Why art thou wroth? and why is thy countenance fallen? 7 If thou doest well [H3190], shalt thou not be accepted [H7613]? and if thou doest not well [H3190], sin [H2403] lieth at the door. And unto thee [shall be] his desire [H8669], and thou shalt rule [H4910] over him.

The word *well* [H3190] (do thee well) means "to be good, well, glad, pleasing," which reflects the ever-present equality between spiritual purity and material well-being. The word *sin* [H2403] (sin waits to enter thee) carries a connotation "water of purification from sin (uncleanness)" and is derived from the root "to miss (a goal or way)" [H2398], which again connects the physical with the spiritual. The word *accepted* [H7613] (if thou doest well) is derived from the root "to be high, exalted, rise" [H7311], which is explicitly our exaltation by God in the present context. Our promised material prosperity is not, however, the mere exaltation of the perishable body in corruptible wealth—rather the exaltation of the imperishable body, which is our promised incorruptible wealth. Our intangible acceptance by God through an intangible faith, which necessarily underlies right sacrifice, is ultimately our tangible exaltation in the Body of Christ that is necessarily a true body.[12]

The word *rule* [H4910] (rule over sin) means "to rule, have dominion, reign," which recalls the dominion of freewill originally formed in Adam. Cain, like all humanity, must choose between the good and the bad, between life and death (Deut 30:19). Our freewill is inviolable as our inherited dominion, or birthright, in the sacrosanct image of God. The word *desire* [H8669] (sin's desire) means "longing" and has an association "to be abundant (overflow)" [H7783], which reflects the nature of desire as being the overflow of the heart, that is, desire as being a revelation of the inner self. Cain could turn back to God and be accepted, but it is simply not his will, not his nature. God does not reject us, but rather we reject God. To reject God is to reject the image of God, even freewill, whereby our rejection of the Holy Spirit is not freedom but rather enslavement to the spirit of disobedience, which is finally the annihilation of freewill. The fulfillment of evil is an incapacity to do good, while true freewill is the personal choice to do good and not evil.

Cain rejecting God is a reenactment of the original fall in Adam just as all men reenact the original fall through their own sins. All mankind inherited death from Adam, and yet no man can reject his inheritance in death, because all men sin (Rom 5:12). Only Jesus Christ could reject the inheritance from Adam because only Jesus Christ is perfectly sinless, innately and infinitely, as the God-man. The progressive degradation of humanity following our fall in Adam is not an accident of history but rather an unavoidable manifestation of the

---

deprecating God's wrath, and imploring his favour in a Mediator. . . . *Abel* offered with an eye to God's will as his rule, and in dependence upon the promise of a Redeemer" (Wesley 1:21; Gen 4:4). The institution of the law from the foundation of the world.
[12] The rendering "shalt thou not be accepted" can be understood as "shalt thou not have the excellency," reflecting the dominion of the firstborn (Jamieson et al. 1:69–70; Gen 4:7). The acceptance by God is an exaltation in God, namely, the Body of Christ.

embrace of the spirit of disobedience. But the perfection of God implies that anyone who can be redeemed will be redeemed. No one will be damned by some accident of history, including accidents of genetics. This is the promise that not a single child of God will be lost (Matt 18:14). In the communion of the blood of Christ, our inheritance is no longer death in Adam under the law—a death that comes by the hand of man, the way of flesh—but rather true life in Jesus Christ by grace through faith—an eternal life that comes by the hand of God, the way of the Spirit.[13]

Genesis 4:8 And Cain talked with Abel his brother: and it came to pass, when they were in the field [H7704], that Cain rose up [H6965] against Abel his brother, and slew [H2026] him.

The word *field* [H7704] (Abel slain in the field) can mean either "cultivated field" or "home of wild beasts," which is a contrast between civilization and wilderness and likewise between spirit and flesh. Cultivated fields recall the garden and the uncorrupted dominion of man formed in the image of God, while the wilderness reflects our exile from the garden that is our exile from the presence of God. The ambiguity between civilization and wilderness reflects our ever-present freewill choice between the good and the bad, a dichotomy affirmed in the closely related contrast between our preservation by the fruit of the ground and our curse in the dust of the ground. The word *slew* [H2026] (Cain slew Abel) can describe the act of either man or God and can be applied to slaying either man or beast. The juxtaposition of slaying either man or beast again reflects freewill. The implicit relationship between man and beast reflects the brotherhood of flesh and earth, the preference of the natural body for the way of flesh. The account of Cain and Abel affirms that death proceeds not from the hand of God, the way of the Spirit, but rather from the hand of man, the way of flesh. The ambiguity between acts of man and acts of God reflects an undeniable and unassailable providence, the sovereignty of God being manifest despite the corruption of creation.

Cain defiling the ground with the blood of Abel recalls Adam originally defiling his flesh, a flesh formed from the ground, while the ground figuratively condemning Cain recalls the original curse of flesh through the ground (Gen 3:17). The image of Cain talking to Abel precedes the image of Cain killing Abel just as the word of flesh, the spirit of disobedience, precedes the literal death of flesh, while Abel dying ultimately through the original sin of Adam prefigures Christ dying for the sins of all mankind. Death reverberated from the first man to the first son to all mankind just as Adam is the embodiment of all mankind, whereby sin would multiply just as men would multiply. But grace would surpass even sin just as Jesus Christ would surpass Adam. The image of Christ

---

[13] "As all mankind were represented in *Adam*, so that great distinction of mankind into the children of God and the children of the wicked one, was here represented in *Cain* and *Abel*, . . ." (Wesley 1:20; Gen 4). The innate bifurcation of freewill is the inevitable bifurcation of humanity.

superseding Adam will be finally manifested in the spiritual body, the Body of Christ, superseding the natural body, the body of Adam (Rom 5:20).[14]

The word *rose* [H6965] (Cain rose up) has connotations "to confirm" and "to establish," which reflects our actions testifying to our true self. The darkness of Cain instinctively snuffed out the light of Abel, in testimony against a world that hates the children of God (1 John 3:12–13). The children of the devil follow after the lusts of their father, who was a murderer from the beginning and the father of lies (John 8:44). The firstborn Cain killing the second born Abel reflects the first man Adam killing the second man Christ, that is, Adam calling death into the world through the original sin. The conflict between Adam and Jesus and likewise between Cain and Abel is the conflict between flesh and spirit. Adam and likewise Cain embody the curse of the natural body, but Abel prefigures Jesus Christ who is our blessing in the spiritual, or glorified, body.[15]

Genesis 4:9 And the LORD **said unto Cain, Where [is] Abel thy brother? And he said, I know [H3045] not: [Am] I my brother's keeper [H8104]?**

The word *know* [H3045] (I know not) has connotations in the Hebrew "to discriminate, distinguish," specifically "to know by experience," and is the root word underlying the word *knowledge* [H1847] used to denote the tree of knowledge. Cain not obeying, spiritually not knowing, the natural-law prohibition against murder recalls Adam not obeying, spiritually not knowing, the original commandment. Cain shamelessly claims that he doesn't know the whereabouts of Abel, while Adam, symbolically not knowing even his own whereabouts, hid himself from the presence of God (Gen 3:8). The way of flesh never knows the way of the Spirit. The way of flesh seeks to hide the body of Abel, while the way of the Spirit seeks to reveal the Body of Christ. The faithful man names himself HERE I AM in imitation of the name of God I AM, whereby the faithful are identified with life (Gen 22:1, Mark 14:62). The faithless man names himself I KNOW NOT in imitation of Cain, likewise the serpent, not knowing the life in God, whereby the faithless profess an

---

[14] "In the beginning, He figured forth the pruning-hook by means of Abel, pointing out that there should be a gathering in of a righteous race of men. He says, 'For behold how the just man perishes, and no man considers it; and righteous men are taken away, and no man layeth it to heart.' These things were acted beforehand in Abel, were also previously declared by the prophets, but were accomplished in the Lord's person; and the same [is still true] with regard to us, the body following the example of the Head [Irenaeus of Lyon, *Against Heresies*]" (Roberts et al., *Ante-Nicene Fathers* 1:512). Christ the Head is followed by the Body of Christ just as the first man Adam is followed by the second man Jesus Christ.

[15] "In killing his brother, he directly struck at God Himself; for God's acceptance of Abel, was the provocation pretended; and for that very reason he hated Abel, because God loved him" (Henry 1:42; Gen 4:8). The crucifixion relates the killing of the one true living and breathing God, not in the spirit, but in the flesh, which is ironically our own flesh, and this is why the crucifixion embodies the death of all flesh, the life of which is the Spirit, or breath, of God.

annihilation of self, represented by their ignorance and finally affirmed by their death. Cain claiming to not know anything about Abel is ultimately prophetic in the sense that Cain not knowing about Abel prefigures the natural man not being able to recognize Jesus Christ as the incarnation of God. The way of flesh is ignorance, but the faithless still prophesy despite themselves because the image of God in creation is irrepressible despite our corruption of creation. Likewise, the grace of God is undeniable despite our sins and despite even our sinful nature. Caiaphas, for example, would unknowingly prophesy that the one must die for the sake of the many (John 11:49–50).

The word *keeper* [H8104] (my brother's keeper) means "to keep" and "to watch" and "to preserve" and is the same word used to describe Adam put in the garden of Eden to *keep* it (Gen 2:15). Cain being implicitly called to be the keeper of Abel recalls the preordained occupation of man, both before and after our fall, to grow in unity with the Spirit of God and likewise to guard against the spirit of disobedience. The covenantal nature of the call to keep our brother reflects our original creation under the law, while the murder of Abel reflects the death of all mankind in the original condemnation of Adam. But the murder of Abel also prefigures the execution of Christ just as the law prefigures grace. The murder of Abel is the curse of the law, but the victory of Christ over death is the blessing by grace. Cain should have been his brother's keeper just as Adam should have guarded the garden in obedience to God, and therefore Cain's ignorance of his divine calling affirms the separation from the Spirit established by Adam. Cain killing Abel despite clear forewarnings from God is a testimony to flesh being governed by the spirit of disobedience in conflict with the Holy Spirit. The natural man embraces his inheritance from Adam, while the spiritual man seeks his inheritance in Jesus Christ.

JUDGMENT

Genesis 4:10–11 And he said, What hast thou done? the voice of thy brother's blood [H1818] crieth unto me from the ground. 11 And now [art] thou cursed [H779] from the earth [H127], which hath opened her mouth to receive [H3947] thy brother's blood [H1818] from thy hand [H3027];

The word *hand* [H3027] (hand of Cain) connotes "strength" and "power," which reflects not only the dominion of the hand of man but also the personal responsibility implied by personal power. The word *cursed* [H779] (Cain cursed) is the same Hebrew word used to describe the original *curse* [H779] of Adam through the ground (Gen 3:17), while the word *earth* [H127] (cursed from) is the same word used to describe both Adam formed of the *ground* [H127] (Gen 2:7) and also the curse of the *ground* [H127] because of Adam (Gen 3:17). The curses of Adam and Cain are both intimately connected to the earth—reflecting, not only the preference of natural man for the material in conflict with the spiritual, but also the unity of all creation. The ground is a metaphor for this world and likewise for flesh. But most relevant to the present context, the ground also represents the law that governs flesh. The ground expressly embodies the curse of the law. The curse of man proceeds from the hand of man. And the connection between the ground and the curse reflects the inseparable relationship between flesh and the law that governs flesh. The curse does not come after the sin, but rather the curse is the spiritual reality of sin, a universal equality evident in both natural law and the formal law.[16]

The word *receive* [H3947] (earth receives Abel's blood) has connotations "to take in marriage" and "to buy," which reflects Christ as a bridegroom of blood who takes possession of the church (Exod 4:25). The Bride of Christ is the body of faithful (Isa 62:5), a bride purchased at a price (1 Cor 6:19–20). The word *blood* [H1818] (brother's blood) is synonymous with "life" and has a symbolic connotation "wine," affirmed in the memorial of bread and wine (Matt 26:28). The blood of righteous Abel spilled by sinful Cain prefigures the blood of Christ spilled for the sins of the world, while the image of God speaking directly to Cain reflects the humble condescension of the incarnation of Jesus Christ. The silence of the flesh implied by spilled blood prefigures the death of Christ and the corresponding age of the material church between the First and Second Advents—which is now a famine, or silence, of the Word of God manifested as the physical absence of Christ (Amos 8:11). The image of Abel's blood crying out from the ground is a vision of our condemnation under the law, figuratively the ground, while not man but only God hearing the cry of Abel's blood is a testimony that natural man cannot enter into the mystery of Christ. The image of blood crying out affirms that our life is in the blood. The dichotomy of silence and crying connected with the blood of Abel reflects the universal duality of death and resurrection.[17]

The image of Abel's blood being received by the earth is finally a vision of life, represented by blood, returning to the Holy Spirit, represented by the earth, that in turn prefigures all the faithful reborn in the Body of Christ (Eph 5:30). The words *earth* [H127] and *Spirit* (Ruwach) [H7307] normally both have feminine gender, reflecting a common relationship to the Father, while the material nature of the earth is an affirmation that the spiritual body, the Body of Christ, is a true body. The Holy Spirit proceeds from God the Father just as woman was originally taken from the side of man (Gen 2:22). The Spirit accomplishes the will of the Father just as woman submits to man (Eph 5:23). Thus, to say woman is less than man would be like saying that the Holy Spirit is less than the Father, which would, of course, be blasphemy. The comparison of the earth, as a feminine image, to the Holy Spirit does not conflict with comparisons of the earth to flesh, likewise with the law that governs flesh, since the law leading us to grace is the embodiment of the Holy Spirit just as flesh is

---

[16] Abel's plural "bloods" is understood in Rabbinic thought to refer collectively to his blood and his offspring's blood and, thereby, reflects the maxim that destroying one life is like destroying an entire world (Cohen, *Rabbinic Sages* 311). Humanity innately exists as a community of individuals, reflecting the triune reality of God.

[17] "How mysterious you are, God, dwelling on high in silence! [Isa 33:5]" (Augustine, *Confessions* 21). The silence of God is the voice of man. The freewill of man is allowed only by the humble condescension of God.

the revelation of spirit just as repentance is the revelation of faith.[18] The comparison of the earth to woman does not conflict with comparisons of the earth to man, since all levels of reality always reflect aspects of both the masculine and the feminine, that is, both flesh and spirit.[19]

Genesis 4:12   When thou tillest [H5647] the ground, it shall not henceforth yield unto thee her strength [H3581]; a fugitive [H5128] and a vagabond [H5110] shalt thou be in the earth.

The word *tillest* [H5647] (Cain tillest) means "to work" and "to serve" and is the same word used to describe the original commandment for Adam to *dress* [H5647] the garden of Eden (Gen 2:15) and also the curse of Adam-kind in Adam to *till* [H5647] the ground in separation from Eden (Gen 3:23). The fates of both Adam and Cain are intimately linked to the ground just as flesh and earth are brothers in blood. But the curse of Cain is magnified compared with the curse of Adam just as the wanton murder of Abel is a greater sin than the juvenile disobedience of Adam. The first man Adam was exiled from the garden of Eden. The first son Cain is exiled from the ground itself. Adam would eat bread in the sweat of his face. Cain would, at least figuratively, not eat bread at all. Evil always multiplies like a cancer, whether in the individual or in society or in the natural world. The increasing degradation of creation on all levels of reality is a prophecy, affirming and reaffirming, that the curse of the flesh in the absence of grace will be magnified in the curse of the spirit, that the first death will be magnified in the second death (Rev 21:8). But the hope of the faithful in God is proved in the preservation of man despite sin. The grace of God is greater than the sin of man (Rom 5:20).

The word *strength* [H3581] (earth will not yield its strength) means "strength" and "power" but also has a connotation of "reptile, unclean creeping thing." Cain will not be able to overcome the ground, to harvest its strength, just as mankind will not be able to overcome flesh, or the law that governs flesh, that is, in the absence of grace. Our lost strength being identified with reptiles recalls our original fall being conceived of the serpent and, thereby, reflects our enslavement to sin, our lost strength, being under the yoke of the god of this world, the devil (2 Cor 4:4). The concomitant emphasis on uncleanness reinforces the image of our condemnation under the law. All men, even the faithful, embody the degradation, or lost strength, of Cain since all men, even

---

[18] The spiritual realities of the heavenly bodies, likewise the earth, have been distorted by pagans just as everything in creation has been corrupted and distorted, but the signs are still recognizable just as the will of God is incontrovertible. And since the devil can only corrupt, not create, it is completely normal to find triune roots in pagan traditions, such as the earth, the so-called mother earth, being identified with the feminine.

[19] "[T]*hy brother's bloods*, in the plural; which the Jews generally understood of the posterity that would have descended from Abel, had he not been murdered; . . . or it may respect the blood of the seed of the woman, of all the righteous ones that should be slain in like manner" (Gill 1:28; Gen 4:10). Both readings are correct, reflecting the unity of Christ and the Body of Christ.

the faithful, are sinners. All men, including the faithful, are personally responsible for the death of Christ for the sins of the world, a death prefigured in the murder of Abel. But the faithful in Christ are nevertheless redeemed by grace through Christ and, thereby, die with Christ. Figuratively like Abel, literally with Christ. The dichotomy of condemnation and redemption—evident in the connection of the body of faithful with both faithless Cain and faithful Abel—is the condemnation of the natural body under the law in contrast to the promise of rebirth in the spiritual, or glorified, body by grace. Our transitory degradation, our lost strength, in this life foreshadows an eternal degradation in the absence of grace, but our preservation in the flesh despite sin foreshadows our redemption in the strength of Christ, that is, by the grace of the Holy Spirit through faith in Christ.

The word *fugitive* [H5128] (linked with Cain) means "to quiver, tremble" with a connotation "to stagger like a drunkard," while the word *vagabond* [H5110] (also linked with Cain) means "to move to and fro, wander" and "to shew grief." And these images are all reflections of chaos in contrast to cosmos, flesh in contrast to spirit, death in contrast to life. The increasing degradation of Cain, as compared with Adam, portends an increasing hopelessness of apostate mankind, an aimless lamenting of the soul, that is, outside of grace. The condemnation of Adam embodies the condemnation of all mankind since all mankind was still in Adam at the time of our fall, while the condemnation of Cain is most closely identified with the condemnation of antediluvian mankind since the line of Cain would be cut off in the floodwaters. The line of Cain, spiritually the seed of the serpent, being cut off in the floodwaters prefigures the faithless, the children of the devil, cut off in the foretold destruction by fire (Rev 20:9). At the same time, the narrowing of Adam's descendants—as represented by the line of Cain following the death of Abel—signifies a focusing of evil in Cain that is a focusing of condemnation on the person of Cain, which finally prefigures a singular individual in the end times, the man of lawlessness (2 Thess 2:3). The parallel between increasing universal wickedness and the magnification of evil in individuals testifies to individual freewill being a microcosm of all creation, namely, the body of anti-christ in the case of corrupted freewill. The progressive revelation of evil in the world is a dark imitation of the progressive revelation of grace just as the foretold son of perdition will be a malevolent counterfeit of the Son of God.

Genesis 4:13–14 And Cain said unto the LORD, My punishment [H5771] [is] greater than I can bear [H5375]. 14 Behold, thou hast driven me out [H1644] this day from the face [H6440] of the earth [H127]; and from thy face [H6440] shall I be hid; and I shall be a fugitive and a vagabond in the earth; and it shall come to pass, [that] every one that findeth me shall slay [H2026] me.

The word *driven out* [H1644] (the Lord hast driven me out) means "to drive out, cast out" and has a connotation "divorced." The divorce of mankind from God foreshadows a new marriage of the faithful with God just as the fall of all mankind through the one man Adam foreshadows the exaltation of all the faithful by and in the one man Jesus Christ, in the Body of Christ. The dichotomy of divorce and marriage in the Scriptures reflects the condemnation of the natural body under the law, the original creation under the law—in contrast to the exaltation of the spiritual, or glorified, body by grace, which is the promised new creation (1 Cor 15:44).[20]

The word *face* [H6440] (face of the earth) is the same word translated *presence* [H6440] in describing the presence of God (Gen 3:8), while the word *earth* [H127] (face of the earth) is the same word translated *ground* [H127] in describing the ground cursed because of Adam (Gen 3:17). The firstborn Cain being driven from the face of God recalls the first man Adam being driven from the face of God, but the exile from the earth heaped on top of the exile from the garden is a palpable escalation of condemnation, compared even with the original exile from the garden. The degradation of Adam-kind is magnified outside the personal presence of God. The way of Cain is the word that speaks abusively about whatever it doesn't understand, and it is finally destroyed by its own instincts (Jude 1:10–11).

The word *slay* [H2026] (slay Cain) is the same word used to describe Cain *slaying* Abel (Gen 4:8) but not the same word *kill* [H7523] used in the commandment "thou shalt not kill" (Exod 20:13). The word *slay* [H2026] means "to kill, slay" and is used to describe the slaying of either man or beast, while the word *kill* [H7523] means "to murder, slay" and is used, with a moral connotation, specifically of slaying human beings. The relative moral neutrality of the word *slay* [H2026] reflects a fundamental amorality of Cain and figuratively of all mankind, while the increasing moral clarity of the word *kill* [H7523] reflects not only an increasing condemnation under the law but also an increasing revelation of grace. Cain fearing he will be slain portends the righteous judgment of fallen mankind, that is, the judgment outside of grace. Fear is the nature of flesh, but love is the nature of the Spirit.[21]

The word *punishment* [H5771] (Cain's punishment) means "punishment of iniquity" and has an association "to bend, twist" [H5753], which reflects the corruption and distortion, through sin, of the image of God embodied by man. The word *bear* [H5375] (Cain cannot bear) means "to lift, carry, take," which reflects the inability of man to exalt himself, specifically above sin and death. Cain proclaiming that he could not bear his punishment is finally a prophecy of our utter condemnation outside of grace, while Cain's fear of death is a

---

[20] "[T]he covenant between them [God and humanity] had the nature of a matrimonial contract; which covenant man broke . . . by committing idolatry, that is, spiritual adultery, not giving credit to him [God], but believing the devil before him; wherefore he [God] wrote him [humanity] a bill of divorce, and sent him away . . . from his house and habitation . . . ." (Gill 1:25; Gen 3:24). The one true God is personal and intimate and, though simultaneously transcendent, is in no way detached from reality.

[21] Cain's lament, "My punishment is greater than I can bear," shows great misery but no sign of penitence or cry for pardon (Jamieson et al. 1:71; Gen 4:13). Cain loves himself but simultaneously hates his brother, wherein the two realities are understood to be the one and same reality.

prophecy of the death of all flesh. Cain, like Adam, like all mankind, would not be able to bear his own iniquity, in stark contrast to Jesus Christ who would be able to bear the sins of the whole world (1 John 2:2).[22]

Genesis 4:15 And the LORD said unto him, Therefore whosoever slayeth [H2026] Cain, vengeance shall be taken on him sevenfold. And the LORD set [H7760] a mark [H226] upon Cain, lest any finding him should kill [H5221] him.

The word *kill* [H5221] (kill Cain) means "to smite" and has a connotation "to slaughter" in the Hebrew, while the previous word *slay* [H2026] (slay Cain) means "to kill, slay" and is used to describe the slaying of either man or beast. The more emphatic word *kill* [H5221], used by God, replacing the more neutral word *slay* [H2026], previously used by Cain, points to a fulfillment of the curse that transcends the cursing of the one man Cain (Gen 4:14). Cain is preserved, but his fear reflects a universal foreboding, a prophetic foreboding. The person of Cain is the epitome of fallen man preserved in the call to repentance, whereby the figurative smiting of Cain contrary to the mark of God, as embodied by Cain's own fear, portends the suffering of Christ, the Head of the Body, in the place of fallen man. This is likewise the suffering of the faithful, the Body of Christ signified by the Heel, in imitation of Christ (Gen 3:15). The connecting of the affliction of the imperfect church and the affliction of the perfect Messiah reflects the essential condescension of the grace of God. And the connecting specifically of the ruthless murderer Cain with the perfectly righteous Jesus Christ is a graphic affirmation that grace is not deserved.

The word *set* [H7760] (set a mark upon Cain) means "to put, place, set" and has connotations "to ordain" and "to appoint." The appointment of flesh to mortal life prefigures the ordination of the faithful unto eternal life. The word *mark* [H226] (mark upon Cain) means "sign" and has a connotation "miracle." The promise of life implied by life is a miraculous sign. The mark of life placed upon Cain, fallen man, foreshadows the seal of the Holy Spirit placed upon the children of God, the faithful, just as the breath of life, mortal life, foreshadows the fullness of the indwelling Holy Spirit, eternal life (2 Cor 1:22). The Spirit of God will not always strive with man, neither with the individual in the natural body nor with the present order of creation as a whole (Gen 6:3).[23]

The mark of the beast will be a mark of death in a dark imitation of the mark of God just as the son of perdition will be a counterfeit of the Son of God (Rev

---

[22] "... 'One of the clearest marks of sin is our almost innate desire to excuse ourselves ....' [J. M. Boice]. ... '... One of the first signs of new life is that the individual takes sides with God against himself' [D. G. Barnhouse]" (Guzik 54–55; Gen 4:13–15). Repentance, pivoting to the Holy Spirit, must precede the redemption of the Spirit, in accordance with the absolute sanctity of freewill.

[23] "'What the soul [human spirit] is to the human body, the Holy Spirit is to the Body of Christ, which is the Church' [Augustine, *Sermons*]" (Rom. Catholic Church, *Catechism* 230). Whether looking at triune man or triune creation as a whole, all levels of reality are observed to reflect the same triune reality of God.

13:13–16). The firstborn Cain is the epitome of fallen man preserved until the final judgment. The person of Cain himself is preserved, but the curse appointed to his potential slayer points to some shadowy figure in the future that will violate the mark of life, some man of lawlessness who will desire the death of all flesh in the end times (2 Thess 2:3). The identification of the antichrist with a potential avenger of blood seeking Cain is also implied by the absence of any other peoples being explicitly described in the text. The foretold sevenfold vengeance linked with the violation of the mark of life specifically portends the final judgment linked with the millennial kingdom, corresponding to the seventh millennium of creation and prefigured by the seventh day of creation (Rev 20:5). In contrast, the faithful will receive the seventy-times-seven forgiveness that will transcend the sevenfold curse (Matt 18:21–22) just as our new creation in God the Son (Rom 12:5) will transcend our original creation through God the Son (John 1:3).[24]

Genesis 4:16 And Cain went out from the presence of the LORD, and dwelt in the land of Nod, on the east of Eden.

The connection between exile and the east is our expectation of the dawning of a new creation, something truly new and not merely another sunrise, like lightning coming out of the east and shining even unto the west (Matt 24:27). The promised new creation is not merely a renewed communion with God but a new communion, the fullness of communion with God that is in God.

Genesis 4:17 And Cain knew his wife; and she conceived, and bare Enoch: and he builded a city, and called the name of the city, after the name of his son, Enoch.

The building of cities in the time leading up to the destruction by water portends the cities of men opposing the city of God in the last days, culminating in the end times with fallen man calling down upon himself the foretold destruction by fire.

Genesis 4:18 And unto Enoch was born Irad: and Irad begat Mehujael: and Mehujael begat Methusael: and Methusael begat Lamech.

The prolificacy of the line of Cain portends the multitudes opposing God throughout history and particularly in the end times.

Genesis 4:19–20 And Lamech took unto him two wives: the name of the one [was] Adah, and the name of the other Zillah. 20 And Adah bare

---

[24] ". . . Cain expected to fall by the hands of some person who, from his *consanguinity*, had the right of the avenger of blood; . . ." (Clarke 1:60; Gen 4:10). The avenger of blood is spiritually the serpent, coming by a consanguinity not of the flesh but of the spirit, not of living blood but of spilled blood.

CAIN, ABEL, SETH

Jabal: he was the father of such as dwell in tents, and [of such as have] cattle.

And the peoples not living in cities, or so-called developed areas, will also oppose God in the end times.

Genesis 4:21–22 And his brother's name [was] Jubal: he was the father of all such as handle the harp and organ. 22 And Zillah, she also bare Tubal-cain, an instructer of every artificer in brass and iron: and the sister of Tubal-cain [was] Naamah.

A prophecy of the expansion of human knowledge, especially science and technology, and that the final expansion of knowledge will be intimately linked with the final apostasy.

Genesis 4:23–24 And Lamech said unto his wives, Adah and Zillah, Hear my voice; ye wives of Lamech, hearken unto my speech: for I have slain a man to my wounding, and a young man to my hurt. 24 If Cain shall be avenged sevenfold, truly Lamech seventy and sevenfold.

The basic logic of expanding a scale from 7 to 77, especially in the context of Lamech representing the seventh generation from Adam, connects the seventh-day Sabbath to the seventh-millennium Sabbath. And the same logic also looks beyond the seventh millennium into eternity. The avenging of blood identified with the number 7 is the judgment of God Almighty, likewise the eternal consequences of that judgment, as linked with the seventh millennium.

NEW LIFE

Genesis 4:25 And Adam knew his wife again; and she bare a son, and called his name Seth [H8352]: For God [H430], [said she], hath appointed [H7896] me another seed [H2233] instead of Abel, whom Cain slew.

The name *God* (Elohim) [H430] (appointed another seed) invoked by Eve is identified with the original creation just as the son Seth, conceived by Eve, embodies a new creation—a new creation recalling the original creation, a new creation affirming the original creation (Gen 1:1). The antediluvian emphasis on God as *Elohim*, in contrast to *Jehovah* (YHWH), reflects the perspective of the natural man, carnal man, but nonetheless the name *Elohim* points to the name *Jehovah* just as our original creation points to our new creation just as our preservation under the law points to our redemption in grace. The first prefigures the second, while the second fulfills the first. But their synthesis is a third that is singular in its kind. This third revelation is the final revelation of the Trinity in the resolution of our duality in the one Body of Christ.[25]

The death of Abel recalls our death in Adam, while the birth of Seth prefigures the birth of Jesus Christ and likewise our promised rebirth in Christ. Abel represents Adam; Seth represents Jesus. But the death of Abel also prefigures the death of Christ for the sake of Adam. And the symbolic resurrection of Abel in Seth prefigures the resurrection of Christ, likewise the resurrection of the faithful in Christ. Abel represents the death from Adam; Seth represents the life in Christ. Abel represents both the person of Adam and the death of Jesus for Adam because the fundamental vision in each case is the nature of flesh, the condemnation of flesh. Adam is the natural man, the embodiment of flesh, while the death of Jesus would be the fulfillment, or completion, of the incarnation of the image of God in Adam, in the flesh of mere man. Seth represents both the person of Jesus and the promise of life in Jesus because the fundamental vision in each case is the essence of the Spirit, the grace of the Spirit. Jesus is the spiritual man, the embodiment of the Spirit, while the promise of life in Christ will be fulfilled in the resurrection of the dead through the power of the Spirit. Abel and Seth therefore reflect not only the persons of Adam (natural man) and Jesus Christ (spiritual man) but also the First Advent (incarnation in the flesh of man) and the Second Advent (glorification in the Spirit). The incarnation of Christ in the flesh in the First Advent recalls the formation of natural man in the original creation, while the glorification of the Body of Christ in the Second Advent will be the new creation of spiritual man. Likewise, the persons of Adam (natural man) and Jesus Christ (spiritual man) can be compared to the First Advent (incarnation in the flesh) and the Second Advent (glorification in the Spirit). The repeating twofold image of death and life reflects the union of flesh and spirit in every man, including Christ, while the convergence, or the resolution, of flesh and spirit in the last days reflects the fulfillment of the promise of life in the resurrection of the dead in Christ.

The word *seed* [H2233] (seed appointed to Eve) is the same word used to describe the promised *Seed* of woman in the original curse, while Eve proclaiming that Seth is appointed in the place of Abel prefigures the fulfillment of the promised Seed in the person of Jesus Christ (Gen 3:15). Abel and Seth both reflect Jesus Christ since Seth is the figurative resurrection of Abel. In contrast, murderous Cain reflects the foretold seed of the serpent that seeks to corrupt the Body of Christ, the Head and the Heel. Abel represents both Adam and Christ since Abel is the object of the curse, which is a superimposition of

---

[25] "... He [the Son] is begotten of the Father . . . the Father is not begotten . . . . [T]he Holy Spirit proceedeth from the Father . . . . We have an analogy in Adam, who was not begotten (for God Himself moulded him), and Seth, who was begotten (for he is Adam's son), and Eve, who proceeded out of Adam's rib (for she was not begotten). These do not differ from each other in nature, for they are human beings: but they differ in the mode of coming into existence [John of Damascus, *Exposition of the Orthodox Faith*]" (Schaff and Wace, *Nicene and Post-Nicene Fathers: Second Series* 9.2:8). The individual is triune just as the family unit is triune just as God is triune.

images that itself reinforces Abel as a vision of the redemption of fallen man in Christ. Cain, when compared with Abel, is most closely identified with Adam, in contrast to the incarnation of Christ, since murderous Cain embraces his inheritance in death from Adam, whereby the firstborn Cain is an image of the condemnation of fallen man outside of grace. The faithlessness of Cain and his corresponding unacceptable sacrifice reflect the disobedience of Adam, whereas the faithfulness of Abel and his corresponding acceptable sacrifice reflect the obedience of Jesus Christ even unto death (Phil 2:8). Cain and Abel are both correctly compared to Christ—that is, aspects of Christ—but the key distinction is that Cain is the embodiment of death under the law while Abel is the embodiment of the hope of life in grace, the promise of life even through death.

The word *appointed* [H7896] (God hath appointed) means "to put, set" and is the root word from which the name *Seth* [H8352] (Seth in place of Abel) is derived. The image of Seth being appointed to replace Abel reflects the spiritual body preordained to replace the natural body—a promise intimated, even before our fall, by the conditioning of the natural body by the original commandment. The two brothers Abel and Seth can be compared to Adam and Christ and also to the First and Second Advents. In each twofold comparison, the former emphasizes the natural while the latter emphasizes the spiritual. However, the three brothers Cain, Abel, and Seth, as a group, should be compared specifically to Adam, the First Advent, and the Second Advent, reflecting the threefold Father, Son, and Holy Spirit. A repeating, overlapping twofold pattern always underlies the threefold. Cain is a natural man reflecting Adam formed from the dust, whereby Cain is the embodiment of our original creation and, thereby, reflects the creator, our Father, since man is made in the image of God. Abel is a spiritual man reflecting Jesus Christ as the man from heaven, whereby the death of Abel at the hands of Cain embodies the death of Christ spiritually at the hands of Adam. Seth embodies the bloodline of Christ, whereby Seth and his progeny represent the multitudes of faithful called to eternal life in the Body of Christ, which is our sanctification in the Holy Spirit. Cain, Abel, and Seth reflect Adam, the First Advent, and the Second Advent as the embodiments of fallen man (Cain), the sacrifice of Christ (Abel), and the resurrection of all the dead in Christ (Seth). Cain, Abel, and Seth reflect God the Father, God the Son, and God the Holy Spirit as identified with man, or Adam-kind, originally created in the image of God, specifically the Father (Cain), the death of the Son as our redeemer (Abel), and our promised rebirth by the Spirit, who is our sanctifier (Seth).[26]

Genesis 4:26 And to Seth, to him also there was born a son; and he called [H7121] his name Enos [H583]: then began [H2490] men to call [H7121] upon the name [H8034] of the LORD [H3068].

---

[26] The name *Seth* sounding like the word *granted* (appointed) represents a purposeful play on words in the Hebrew (Viviano, *Collegeville* 46; Gen 4:17–26). The affirmation of relationships in the very sounds of words testifies to the image of God being impressed upon all creation and especially upon the most fundamental aspects of creation.

The name *Lord* (YHWH) [H3068], or at least the meaning of the name *Lord* (YHWH), would not be revealed until the time of Moses, whereby antediluvian man using the name *Lord* implies a profound misconception of the Godhead at that time (Exod 6:3). Antediluvian man calling upon the name of the Lord in ignorance of the nature of the Godhead, specifically before the floodwaters, parallels the ignorance of salvation by grace through faith in the Son that exists in natural man, specifically before the baptism of repentance, also signified by water. The fruit of the tree of knowledge is experiential knowledge, the way of flesh, the way of ignorance and suffering and death. But the fruit of the tree of life is spiritual understanding, the way of the Spirit, the wisdom that gives life. Ignorance is always the mark of the spirit of disobedience and is finally sealed by death, which is an ignorance of life itself.[27]

The name *Enos* (Enosh) [H583] (born to Seth) means "man, mankind" [H582] and has an association "to be weak, sick" [H605] but is not the same name *Adam* [H120] that similarly means "man, mankind" (Gen 2:19). The negative images of weakness and sickness associated with the name *Enos* reflect the condemnation of the natural body under the law, foreshadowing Jesus Christ bearing our infirmities in obedience to the law (Isa 53:4). The new name for man *Enos* foreshadows our new creation in Christ, a new creation that comes not by our strength, not by the law, but by our weakness, that is, only by grace. The birth of Seth in the place of Abel specifically prefigures the resurrection of Jesus Christ, while the offspring of Seth, embodied by Enos, prefigure the faithful redeemed in Christ. The redeemed are the offspring of Christ, the Body compared with the Head (Col 1:18). The figurative resurrection of Abel in Seth is fulfilled through the figurative resurrection of Seth in his progeny just as the resurrection of Christ as and with the firstfruits of the grave will be fulfilled through the harvest of the faithful in the resurrection of the dead (1 Cor 15:20, Matt 27:52–53). The law commands, or rather prophesies, that a man should raise offspring for a dead brother (Deut 25:5).

The word *began* [H2490] (men began to call upon the name of the Lord) has associations "to pierce" [H2490] and also "to profane" [H2490], which prefigure the crucifixion of Christ (Lev 19:12). The word *call* [H7121] (call upon the name) means "to call, proclaim, read (aloud)," in contrast to an inward appeal, or silent prayer. The adamant calling out reflects the irrepressible manifestation of the spiritual in the physical, which in this case is a revelation of apostasy. The anti-spirit moving in antediluvian mankind opposed the proclamation of the bloodline of Christ represented by the person of Enos. The word *name* [H8034] (name of the Lord) is synonymous with "reputation, fame," whereby calling upon the name of the Lord, in contrast to simply calling upon the Lord, is an emphasis on the glory of God, which in the present context is a

---

[27] The first observed name of a person in the Torah that is derived from the divine name YHWH is that of Moses's mother, Exod 6:20, which accords with the idea that the name YHWH did not become prominent until the time of Moses, Exod 3:13–16, 6:3 (Sarna 40; Gen 4:26). The life and times of Moses prefigure the revelation of Jesus Christ, the Seed of woman, at the time of the First Advent.

CAIN, ABEL, SETH

desecration of the glory of God that prefigures the desecration of the person of Jesus. The name *Lord* (YHWH) [H3068] means "the Self-Existent," whereby the desecration of the name *Lord* reflects a fundamental contempt for life, which is the satanic desire to corrupt all flesh, spiritually the desire to corrupt the Body of Christ. The reassertion of the line of Abel through Seth represents the line of Christ being heralded with blasphemy in the time of Adam, the embodiment of all mankind, or the whole world. This primordial blasphemy of the body of Adam portends Jesus Christ being rejected by the world, the whole world represented by the complicity of the Jews and Romans, that is, the Jews and Gentiles (John 1:10). Lord God have mercy.[28]

☙ ☙ ☙

The 1-2-3 pattern evident in the account of Cain, Abel, and Seth is specifically an overlapping 1-2, 1-2 pattern reflecting the twofold natures of the Son, being fully man and fully God. The structuring of the narrative deals, first, with the twofold relationship between Cain and Abel and, second, with the twofold relationship between Abel and Seth. Cain is the natural man whose offering is not acceptable to God, while Abel is the spiritual man whose offering is acceptable to God. Abel is then killed but Seth is raised up to replace Abel, representing not the resurrection of Christ in isolation but also and together with the promised resurrection of the faithful in Christ. Cain reflects Adam, while Abel reflects Christ. Abel specifically reflects the First Advent of Christ, while Seth points to the Second Advent. The 1-2-3 pattern evident in the Biblical narrative reflects the Trinity, while the underlying 1-2, 1-2 pattern reflects the twofold natures of the Son. The singularity implied by the unity of the pattern reflects the oneness of God. The primordial image of God is oneness, testifying to the one God being the one font of all life. Our personal experience of reality is, however, twofold just as the twofold natures of Jesus Christ relate the visible image of God (Col 1:15). And the fullness of progressive revelation is finally threefold, reflecting the wholeness of truth in God the Father, God the Son, and God the Holy Spirit (Matt 28:19).

---

[28] "[M]any eminent men have contended that [the underlying Hebrew of Gen 4:26], which we translate 'began,' should be rendered 'began profanely,' or 'then profanation began,' and from this time they date the origin of idolatry. Most of the Jewish doctors were of this opinion, and Maimonides has discussed it at some length in his treatise on idolatry [*Mishneh Torah*]; . . ." (Clarke 1:63–64; Gen 4:26). If antediluvian mankind had begun to call upon the Lord's name in a positive way, then certainly they would not have been condemned in the Flood.

ADAM, NOAH, ABRAHAM

1	2	3
ADAM	FIRST ADVENT	SECOND ADVENT

1	2	
CAIN (NOT ACCEPTED)	ABEL (ACCEPTED)	
	1	2
	ABEL (DEATH)	SETH (ABEL RESURRECTED)

The lives of Cain, Abel, and Seth reflect the same images of birth, death, and rebirth evident in the lives of Adam and also Jesus, but the progression from Adam to Jesus represents the fundamental genealogy that points linearly to the last days and the final fulfillment of our promised inheritance in the fullness of the indwelling Holy Spirit. Adam as the first man and our universal progenitor is the embodiment of all mankind and likewise of all creation, whereby his person uniquely prefigures our new creation in the person of Jesus Christ, that is, in the Body of Christ. In contrast, the account of Cain, Abel, and Seth represents a genealogy perpendicular to the fundamental bloodline from Adam through Seth to Jesus Christ. The account of the sons of Adam, compared with the promised redemption through the fundamental bloodline, represents a kind of refrain of the main chorus, a refrain that repeats at regular intervals throughout the Scriptures, as with the subsequent accounts of the sons of Noah followed by the sons of Abraham.

1	2	3
ADAM	FIRST ADVENT	SECOND ADVENT
CAIN	ABEL	SETH

The refrain represented by the account of the sons of Adam is an echo of the main chorus represented by the account of Adam and Jesus Christ just as the song we sing in this life is an echo of the harmony in heaven (Rev 5:9). The promise of redemption being manifested in the personal lives of the patriarchs reflects the will of God for the sanctification of the very essence of our individual personhoods, not merely as a multitude forming one body in a collective. Though we are a community, or family, of faithful, we are also individuals whose freewill is eternally sacrosanct just as the Son is eternally begotten. The song, or story, of salvation impressed upon all creation is our sanctification by the Holy Spirit in the Body of Christ to be finally harmonized, or spoken forth, in the Second Advent. The image of God proceeding from the Father and being originally embodied by father Adam is a relating of the eternal fatherhood of God that is our promised sonship.

1	2	3
GOD THE FATHER	GOD THE SON	GOD THE HOLY SPIRIT
CREATOR	REDEEMER	SANCTIFIER
ADAM	FIRST ADVENT	SECOND ADVENT
IMAGE OF GOD	HEAD OF THE BODY	BODY OF CHRIST

CAIN, ABEL, SETH

CHAPTER TWO OUTLINE

Key Images

PRIME IMAGES		
Material	Abstract	Spiritual
Sacrificial offering.	Substitution.	The death of Jesus Christ for the sins of the world.

TWOFOLD IMAGES		
Material	Abstract	Spiritual
Cain and Abel.	First and second sons. Faithless and faithful. Flesh and spirit.	Adam and Christ.
Abel and Seth.	First and second seeds of woman. Death and life. Death and resurrection. Flesh and spirit.	The First and Second Advents.
A tiller of the ground and a keeper of sheep.	Plant and animal. Death and life. Flesh and spirit.	Natural body and spiritual body.
Grain offering and animal offering.	Unacceptable and acceptable. Body and blood. Flesh and spirit.	Curse and blessing.

THREEFOLD IMAGES		
Material	Abstract	Spiritual
Cain, Abel, and Seth.	The call of man, the death of man, the rebirth of man.	Adam, First, Second Advents. Creator, Redeemer, and Sanctifier. Adam, Christ, Body of Christ. Father, Son, and Holy Spirit.

Synopsis

	FIRSTBORN	
	Material	Spiritual
4:1	Cain is born.	Recalls the creation of Adam.

	TWO SONS	
	Material	Spiritual
4:2	Abel is born.	Foreshadows the incarnation of Christ.
	Abel is a keeper of sheep.	Foreshadows Jesus Christ being the good shepherd (John 10:11).
	But Cain is a tiller of the ground.	Recalls the curse of the ground (Gen 3:17).

	TWO SACRIFICES	
	Material	Spiritual
4:3–5	The offering of Abel is accepted, but the offering of Cain is rejected.	The law requires blood sacrifice, prefiguring the crucifixion of Christ (Heb 9:22).
4:6–7	The Lord tells Cain to rule over sin.	The call back to our lost dominion, that is, the call to repentance.
4:8	Cain slays Abel.	Adam spiritually kills Christ, that is, Christ dies for the sins of all mankind in Adam.
4:9	Cain professes that he does not know the whereabouts of Abel.	The natural man (Adam-kind) cannot comprehend the coming and going of the spiritual man (Christ-kind).

ADAM, NOAH, ABRAHAM

	JUDGMENT	
	Material	Spiritual
4:10–12	The ground will no longer yield her strength to Cain.	The law condemns the natural body.
4:13–15	The Lord marks Cain to preserve him from death.	The natural body will be preserved until the final judgment in the end times.
4:16–24	And Cain knew his wife, and she conceived.	The prolificacy of antediluvian man portends multitudes opposing God in the end times.
	The offspring of Cain become instructors of various arts and sciences.	A prophecy of the expansion of human knowledge in the end times.
	NEW LIFE	
	Material	Spiritual
4:25	Seth is born and figuratively replaces Abel.	The resurrection of Jesus Christ heralding the resurrection of all the faithful in Christ.
4:26	To Seth a son is born.	The offspring of Seth representing the faithful reborn in Christ.

NOAH

יהוה

CHAPTER THREE

Noah

The prime images in the account of the Flood are the one righteous man Noah and the one ark and the one destruction by water. Noah is a new Adam, a new father of humanity, prefiguring Jesus Christ, who is the ultimate progenitor of our redemption. The account of Noah and the Flood is not, however, a simple repetition of the account of the First Creation. Adam was preserved despite sin, but Noah is saved through righteousness in a progression reflecting the fulfillment of law in grace. The one wooden ark parallels the one man Noah, representing the only redemption afforded to antediluvian man. Likewise, the one wooden cross of Christ is the primary symbol of the First Advent, relating the only redemption afforded to humanity (Acts 4:12). The death and resurrection of the world through the floodwaters is a baptism in water of all creation that prefigures the redemption of all creation through the incarnation of Jesus Christ. Sin would continue after the Fall of Man just as sin would continue after the Flood just as sin would continue after the First Advent, but our original creation will be fulfilled in our new creation just as the First Advent will be fulfilled in the Second Advent just as the baptism in water will be fulfilled in the baptism of the Holy Spirit.

The twofold images emphasized in the account of the Flood are the clean and unclean animals preserved in the ark, the raven and the dove sent forth from the ark, the green herbs and meat given as food, and also the distinction between the flesh and blood of meat. Each pair reflects the fundamental tension between flesh and spirit and likewise between law and grace—a tension ultimately resolved only in the sinless person of Jesus Christ. The unclean animals are figuratively preserved by virtue of the clean animals. Christ redeems sinners, the clean being sacrificed for the unclean (1 Pet 3:18). The raven is aloof, while the dove is faithful. Adam rejected the presence of God, while Jesus Christ would be faithful even unto death. Green herbs are a symbol of the earth, while the meat of animals is a symbol of life. Adam embodied the dust of the ground, while Jesus Christ embodies life. The flesh and blood of animal meat prefigures the death of Christ in the flesh, through which the faithful receive the blood of the new covenant.

ADAM, NOAH, ABRAHAM

The threefold progression of the Father, Son, and Holy Spirit are reflected in the threefold entering of Noah, his sons, and their wives into the ark. Noah represents the father of humanity just as God the Father is the spiritual progenitor of our creation. Noah's sons reflect God the Son, while their wives reflect the Bride of Christ sanctified by the indwelling Holy Spirit. The flight of the raven followed by the first and second flights of the dove reflects, respectively, the formation of Adam followed by the First and Second Advents of Christ. The raven found no rest just as Adam was exiled from the garden. The dove found no life in its first flight just as Christ would be rejected in the First Advent, but the dove brought back a sign of life to Noah in its second flight just as Christ will present a multitude to the Father upon the Second Advent. Green herbs followed by meat and blood also reflect Adam followed by the First and Second Advents of Christ. Animals are a higher form of life than plants just as the life in Christ is greater than the life of Adam. The meat given as food prefigures the commandment to eat the flesh of Christ in imitation of the First Advent (John 6:53–54), while animal blood being forbidden prefigures the blood, or life, of the new covenant not being fully manifested until the resurrection of the Body of Christ in the Second Advent (Matt 26:27–29). The threefold successive Adam and First and Second Advents of Christ finally reflect the universal Trinity as Creator, Redeemer and Sanctifier.

Promise

Genesis 5:1–2 This [is] the book of the generations of Adam. In the day that God created man, in the likeness of God made he him; 2 Male and female created he them; and blessed them, and called their name Adam, in the day when they were created.

The individual is formed in the image of God; likewise the union of man and woman is formed in the image of God; and likewise the generations of humanity are formed in the image of God. All creation as a whole and every layer of creation, though corrupted, still embody the one image of God.

Genesis 5:3–20 And Adam lived an hundred and thirty years, and begat [a son] in his own likeness, after his image; and called his name Seth: 4 And the days of Adam after he had begotten Seth were eight hundred years: and he begat sons and daughters: 5 And all the days that Adam lived were nine hundred and thirty years: and he died. 6 And Seth lived an hundred and five years, and begat Enos: 7 And Seth lived after he begat Enos eight hundred and seven years, and begat sons and daughters: 8 And all the days of Seth were nine hundred and twelve years: and he died. 9 And Enos lived ninety years, and begat Cainan: 10 And Enos lived after he begat Cainan eight hundred and fifteen years, and begat sons and daughters: 11 And all the days of Enos were nine hundred and five years: and he died. 12 And Cainan lived seventy years, and begat Mahalaleel: 13 And Cainan lived after he begat Mahalaleel eight hundred and forty

years, and begat sons and daughters: 14 And all the days of Cainan were nine hundred and ten years: and he died. 15 And Mahalaleel lived sixty and five years, and begat Jared: 16 And Mahalaleel lived after he begat Jared eight hundred and thirty years, and begat sons and daughters: 17 And all the days of Mahalaleel were eight hundred ninety and five years: and he died. 18 And Jared lived an hundred sixty and two years, and he begat Enoch: 19 And Jared lived after he begat Enoch eight hundred years, and begat sons and daughters: 20 And all the days of Jared were nine hundred sixty and two years: and he died.**

The individual, formed in the very image of God, is as nothing to the present fallen world, which hates God and is separated from God. But the individual has infinite value to God, and therefore individual names are recorded in the Word of God for their own sake, as a sign of the innate value of the individual. Further, the marking of generations, which is closely connected with individuals and individual names, is a prophecy of all creation moving inexorably into the last days and finally unto the Day of the Lord, when the redemption of the individual, the family, and the generations of man will be realized.

Genesis 5:21–24 **And Enoch lived sixty and five years, and begat Methuselah: 22 And Enoch walked with God after he begat Methuselah three hundred years, and begat sons and daughters: 23 And all the days of Enoch were three hundred sixty and five years: 24 And Enoch walked with God: and he [was] not; for God took him.**

The one man Enoch walking with God and being taken by God prior to the judgment of the world by the floodwaters is a prophecy of the resurrection and rapture of the one Body of Christ that will similarly precede the yet future judgment of the world by fire. First water, second fire, and finally the lake of fire, or water of fire.[1]

Genesis 5:25–27 **And Methuselah lived an hundred eighty and seven years, and begat Lamech: 26 And Methuselah lived after he begat Lamech seven hundred eighty and two years, and begat sons and daughters: 27 And all the days of Methuselah were nine hundred sixty and nine years: and he died.**

The long but mortal life of Methuselah—surpassing even that of the first man Adam, the father of all the living—prefigures a vain covenant with death

---

[1] "[H]e [Enoch] was transported into heaven without dying, and thus the doctrine of immortality was plainly taught under the old dispensation. . . . The voice of early ecclesiastical tradition is almost unanimous in regarding Enoch and Elijah as the 'two witnesses' [Rev 11:3]" (*New Unger's Bible Dictionary*, s.v. "Enoch"). Enoch and Elijah are the only ones known to have been set apart without seeing death, or dying in the natural body, Heb 11:5, 2 Kgs 2:11.

being attempted in the end times—in opposition to and in imitation of the promise of true, eternal life in Jesus Christ, the new Adam (Isa 28:15, 28:18).[2]

Genesis 5:28–31 And Lamech [H3929] lived an hundred eighty and two years, and begat a son: 29 And he called [H7121] his name [H8034] Noah [H5146], saying, This [same] shall comfort [H5162] us concerning our work [H4639] and toil [H6093] of our hands, because of the ground which the LORD [H3068] hath cursed [H779]. 30 And Lamech lived after he begat Noah five hundred ninety and five years, and begat sons and daughters: 31 And all the days of Lamech were seven hundred seventy and seven years: and he died.

The name *Lord* (YHWH) [H3068] (hath cursed) compared with the name *Lord* (YHWH) [H3068] *God* (Elohim) [H430] used at the time of the original curse relates a shift in emphasis from justice to mercy and likewise from law to grace, a shift typical of progressive revelation. The law governs natural man, condemning fallen man, while grace governs spiritual man, exalting the faithful in the Body of Christ. This shift from law to grace is also evident in the shift from the perishable to the imperishable, from the profane to the sacred. But the truth of the name *Lord* [H3068] would not be explicitly revealed until the time of Moses (Exod 6:3). Antediluvian man proclaiming, without understanding, the one man Noah as the comforter from the curse of the *Lord* (YHWH) [H3068] prefigures Caiaphas proclaiming, without understanding, the death of the one man Jesus so that the whole nation would not perish, the whole nation representing the whole of creation (John 11:49–50).[3]

The word *name* [H8034] (name of Noah) is synonymous with "reputation, fame," consistent with the obvious prophetic nature of names in the Scriptures. A name is always a symbol of the person or thing to which it is applied, even if a deeper meaning is not evident. A name, if nothing else, will acquire certain connotations from the nature of the person or thing to which it is applied. The name *Noah* [H5146] is derived from the root "to rest" [H5117], recalling the rest and peace in the garden of Eden and foreshadowing the promised peace in the fullness of the Holy Spirit that will be manifested in the kingdom of God. Noah represents a new Adam just as the Flood represents a new creation, whereby Adam and Noah both prefigure our new creation in the Body of Christ. Every man is actually a blurred, or partial, image of Christ in the progressive revelation of the generations pointing to the one Body of Christ. The word *called* [H7121] (called his name Noah) means "to call, proclaim, read (aloud)" and is the same

---

[2] Jesus Christ is the promised new Adam, not merely another Adam, for Adam was the created, or reflected, image of God whereas Christ is the actual, or perfect, image of God, being literally God in the flesh.

[3] "Lamech [naming his son *Noah*] had respect to the promise, [Gen 3:15], and desired to see the deliverer... he also spake this [his son's name] by the Spirit of prophecy, because Noah delivered the Church, and preserved it by his obedience" (Whittingham et al., *Geneva Bible* 3R n. h; Gen 5:29). All creation, including the actual flow of history, is a prophecy of the coming of the Lord, the image of God made visible.

word used to describe antediluvian man originally *beginning* (profanely) [H2490] to *call* [H7121] upon the name of the Lord at the time of the birth of Enos (Gen 4:26). The use of the name of the Lord in vain, connected with the reassertion of the line of Christ through the offspring of Seth, prefigures the rejection of Christ and finally the death of Christ, a death that will be imitated by the death of all flesh, a final destruction by fire foreshadowed in the destruction by water.[4]

The word *work* [H4639] (because of the curse) means "deed, work," while the word *toil* [H6093] (because of the curse) means "pain, toil." The word *toil* [H6093] is the same word rendered *sorrow* [H6093] to describe man eating in sorrow because of the original curse (Gen 3:17). The progression of emotional intensity from the word *work* [H4639] to the word *toil* [H6093] reflects the degradation of the work of man in exile, a work degraded in exile but not abandoned, as preordained in the garden. The intimate relationship between the suffering of mankind and the curse of the ground recalls the original formation of man from the dust of the ground. The red earth and ruddy man are brothers in blood in that all creation has been corrupted through the original sin, whereby earth and man would both be condemned together in the floodwaters. Yet this is a figuratively complete destruction of the original creation that prefigures a literally complete destruction, including the natural body and finally sinful nature itself (Rev 20:14). A remnant would be preserved even through the floodwaters. And dry land would again appear in an ironic testimony to the required death and resurrection manifested in the baptism in water, that is, the baptism of repentance for the forgiveness of sins. The faithful will likewise be preserved even through the foretold destruction by fire. And the baptism in water will be fulfilled by the baptism of the Holy Spirit just as the destruction by water will be completed in the foretold destruction by fire.[5]

The use of the word *comfort* [H5162] (Noah shall comfort) is ironic in that the prophecy of the comfort of God would be realized in a preservation of Noah, likewise mankind in Noah, not from the floodwaters but rather through the floodwaters. The perfect compassion of the Lord God is not the absence of justice but rather the fulfillment of justice in mercy. The preservation of a remnant is a figurative death and resurrection in which the destruction of a majority reflects the death of the tangible natural body, while the preservation of a minority reflects the resurrection of the yet unseen intangible, or tangible and intangible, spiritual body. The image of a remnant is sometimes interpreted to mean that only a small minority of mankind will ultimately saved, but another

---

[4] "Noah is the first [recorded] man to be born after the death of Adam, according to the chronology of [Gen 5:28–29], and he becomes a second Adam, the second father of humanity" (Sarna 49; Gen 6:9–9:17). The death of Adam followed by the birth of Noah is itself an image of death and resurrection.

[5] "Assuming these genealogies are consecutive, Seth died when Noah was 14 years old. Noah could have known Adam's son!" (Guzik 59; Gen 5:28–32). More abstractly, the long life of Adam spans almost the entire period before the birth of Noah, and thereby Adam embodies the entire antediluvian period. And the death of father Adam under the curse, likewise the death of Christ for Adam in fulfillment of the curse, is appropriately manifested in the death of all flesh represented by the floodwaters.

interpretation of the remnant image, with respect to humanity as a whole, is that the salvation of the many comes through the few and, ultimately, the One. Humanity was saved in the remnant embodied by the one man Noah just as all nations are saved, or preserved, in the one nation Israel just as all creation, earth and heaven, will be saved in the one man Christ. The emphasis on the one testifies to the oneness of the Lord God and likewise to the immeasurable value to God of the individual created in the image of the Lord.[6]

The birth of Noah marks the tenth generation of man as descended through Seth from the first man Adam (Luke 3:36–38). The number 10 is a recurring mark of death and destruction, as exemplified by the destruction in the floodwaters in the tenth generation, the ten plagues at the time of the Exodus (Exod 7–11), and the ten horns of the red dragon (Rev 12:3). The Decalogue, or Ten Commandments, is also connected with death since the law condemns us to death (Rom 7:10). The violation of the ten concubines of David is a graphic connection of the number 10 specifically with defilement (2 Sam 16:22). The persistent repetition of numbers with consistent relationships in the Scriptures is an affirmation that the same spiritual truth is manifested on all levels of reality, while the character of repetition itself reflects the undeniable, or relentless, nature of the will of God for the welfare of humanity.[7]

Genesis 5:32 And Noah was five hundred years old: and Noah begat Shem, Ham, and Japheth.

Noah is the new Adam, and his three sons reflect the triunity of the Lord God, likewise the threefold totality of creation formed in the image of God.

Justice and Mercy

Genesis 6:1–4 And it came to pass, when men began to multiply on the face of the earth, and daughters were born unto them, 2 That the sons of God [H430] saw the daughters of men [H120] that they [were] fair [H2896]; and they took them wives of all which they chose. 3 And the Lord said, My spirit [H7307] shall not always strive [H1777] with man, for that he also [is] flesh: yet his days [H3117] shall be an hundred and twenty years. 4 There were giants [H5303] in the earth in those days [H3117]; and also after [H310] that, when the sons of God came in unto

---

[6] Two seemingly new sources of comfort received through Noah are the eating of meat as a respite from tilling the ground and the drinking of wine as a source of refreshment and cheer (Gill 1:35–36; Gen 5:29). The identification of Noah, as a new Adam, with the First Advent is therein reinforced, since the twofold comfort of meat and drink points to the commandment to eat the flesh and drink the blood of Christ, John 6:53.
[7] "By presenting ten generations both before and after the Flood, the narrator sets the Flood as the great divide between Adam and Abraham" (Waltke 111). The Flood being the great divide between fallen Adam and faithful Abraham foreshadows the First Advent being the great divide between the natural and glorified bodies.

the daughters of men, and they bare [children] to them, the same [became] mighty men which [were] of old, men of renown.

The name *God* (Elohim) [H430] evokes an image of "rulers" and "judges" in the Hebrew, whereby the *sons of God* evokes an image of the offspring of justice, or wrath, the object of the curse. The word *men* [H120] has an association "to be red" [H119], whereby the *daughters of men* or, equivalently, the *daughters of Adam* evokes an image of the daughters of blood, the sacred life represented by blood. The offspring of the union of the sons of God and the daughters of men represent the literal corruption of flesh by the serpent, specifically by the host of fallen angels (Jude 1:6).[8] The word *fair* [H2896] (daughters of men are fair) recalls the same word used to describe the original creation as very *good* [H2896], whereby the corruption of the daughters of men reflects the corruption of creation (Gen 1:31). The connection of daughters with uncorrupted creation equally points to the promised Seed of woman that would strike the head of the serpent (Gen 3:15). Any presumed unions between the offspring of Cain, the embodiment of death, and the offspring of Seth, representing the life in the blood, could be viewed as a reflection of the union of the sons of God and the daughters of men, wherein the offspring of Cain and that of the fallen angels would both represent the same manifest dominion of the serpent condemned in the floodwaters and finally in the lake of fire. Identifying Cain with the sons of God while identifying Seth with the daughters of men is, however, exactly opposite to the common modern interpretation.[9] The controversy over the interpretation of the identity of the sons of God, those who go into the daughters of men, is actually one of many inflection points in the Scriptures where the faithful are called upon to discern the counterfeit from the genuine, to discern anti-christ from Christ (2 Cor 11:14).[10]

The word *giants* [H5303] (giants in the earth) literally means "giants" and is derived from the root "to fall, lie" [H5307], which again identifies the origin of the giants with the fallen host of heaven and with the corresponding fall of mankind (Isa 14:12).[11] The presence of giants in the earth reflects the

---

[8] The technical question is whether the conception of giants was the result of a physical contact, or literal sexual union, with the fallen angels or via a spiritual contact, that is, some form of demonic possession in which the demons conceived themselves.

[9] Coffman asserts that in the preceding two chapters of Genesis the sons of God and the daughters of men are firmly established to be, respectively, the offspring of Seth and Cain (Coffman 98–99; Gen 6:1–2). An innate parallel exists between the earthly and the heavenly, such that opposing views are commonly found to be not mutually exclusive but complementary, either directly or in reverse.

[10] From the parallel usages in Job 1:6, 2:1, and 38:7, the term *sons of God* must be considered a reference to the angelic host (Sarna 45; Gen 6:2). The purely naturalistic reading of the Scriptures should be recognized as an anti-supernatural bias that is in direct opposition to the Bible and the God of the Bible.

[11] The evil one can be viewed as only corrupting, not creating, for only God can create anything, especially new life. Therefore one must infer that the giants were not the offspring of women and angels, representing a new hybrid form of life, but rather the

corruption of both ruddy man and the red earth, while the linking of large physical size with the rejection of God reflects our colossal apostasy and our corresponding self-aggrandizing pride. The word *days* [H3117] (giants in those days) recalls the same word used to describe Adam cursed to die the same *day* he ate from the tree of knowledge (Gen 2:17). But one day is with the Lord as a thousand years, and a thousand years as one day (2 Pet 3:8). The long life of Adam is the personification of the antediluvian era, while the death of Adam near the time of the birth of Noah prefigures the condemnation of antediluvian man in the floodwaters. The word *after* [H310] (giants also after the Flood) has a connotation "of hinder-part," which in context recalls the prophecy of the seed of the serpent following the Seed of woman (Gen 3:15). The word *after* [H310] is derived from the root "to remain behind, delay, tarry" [H309], which in context portends a final judgment being delayed until the end times. The offspring of the sons of God and the daughters of men would be seen after the Flood of Noah just as sin would continue in the world after the Flood. The dominion of the serpent would be severely diminished, though not eradicated, after the Flood just as sin is greatly diminished, though not completely removed, after the repentance in the baptism in water. Sin would likewise persist even after the baptism of the cross of Christ.[12]

The word *spirit* (ruwach) [H7307] (Spirit of God) evokes an image of "breath, wind," while the word *strive* [H1777] (Spirit will not always strive) has a connotation "to judge." The Spirit of God not always striving with man portends not only the immediate judgment of mankind in the floodwaters but also a final destruction in the end times of the natural body and likewise the original creation. But the Spirit of God not always striving with man also implies an end of judgment and a corresponding end of the contention between flesh and spirit. Our rebirth through fire is foreshadowed by the preservation of humanity through the floodwaters just as the promised spiritual, or glorified, resurrection body is prefigured by the present natural body. The judgment of all flesh being closely identified with the sons of God corrupting the daughters of men portends the final condemnation of the spirit of disobedience being embodied by the serpent (Rev 20:10).[13]

---

incarnation of the fallen angels themselves, as is consistent with the word *giants* [H5303] being derived from the root "to fall, lie" [H5307]. And even in the act of corrupting creation that is formed in the image of God, the evil one, a created being himself, necessarily imitates the Creator, or works within the bounds of creation, wherein the incarnation of fallen angels should be recognized as a dark imitation, or anticipation, of the conception of Christ, not as a hybrid being, which would be neither man nor God, but as himself, God the Son.

[12] "Jehovah resolved to destroy the human race, but He allowed a respite of 120 years, during which time Noah sought to bring the people to repentance [Gen 6:1–9, 1 Pet 3:20, 2 Pet 2:5]" (*New Unger's Bible Dictionary*, s.v. "Noah"). The Flood is closely linked with the call to repentance from sin and, thus, is correctly connected with the baptism of repentance, which is, not coincidentally, signified by immersion in water.

[13] The 120 years of the life Moses, Deut 34:7, recalls the 120 years identified with the wooden ark, Gen 6:3. And both periods point to the one life of Jesus Christ fulfilling

NOAH

Genesis 6:5–6 And GOD [H3068] saw that the wickedness [H7451] of man [H120] [was] great [H7227] in the earth, and [that] every imagination of the thoughts of his heart [H3820] [was] only evil continually. 6 And it repented [H5162] the LORD [H3068] that he had made man on the earth, and it grieved [H6087] him at his heart [H3820].

The word *wickedness* [H7451] (of man) means "bad" and "evil" and has a connotation of "misery." Immorality and physical suffering are inseparable in practice just as spirit and flesh are inseparable in life. The word *man* [H120] (wickedness of) corresponds to the name *Adam* [H120], which is a persistent reminder of the inheritance of all mankind from Adam, namely, the fundamental conflict between spirit and flesh embodied by corruption and death. The word *great* [H7227] (great wickedness) means "much, many, great" and recalls the original *multiplying* [H7231] of mankind on the face of the earth (Gen 6:1). But antediluvian Adam-kind had chosen to multiply the bad and not the good just as Adam had chosen to disobey the original commandment of God. Israel would likewise reject the incarnation of Jesus Christ. The last generation will likewise reject life itself in the end times. The circumstances change, but the underlying spirit of rebellion remains the same. The progression of apostasy from disobedience to murder to an utter rejection of God, likewise the life in God, is our hopelessness outside the grace of God (Eph 2:2).[14]

The word *heart* [H3820] (heart of man, heart of the Lord) means "inner man, mind, will, heart." The heart of God is evident in the Holy Spirit, while the heart of man is our inheritance in the Holy Spirit. There is only one Spirit just as there is only one God. There was only God before, or outside, the beginning and nothing except God, whereby the spirit of disobedience should not be considered a fundamental spirit, rather a mere corruption of the spirit of love. Likewise, fallen creation is not something of itself but rather a corruption of the breath of life, a corruption of the image of God. The use of the same word *heart* [H3820] for both the *heart* [H3820] of man and the *heart* [H3820] of God emphasizes an intimate, even familial, relationship between man and God, a kinship reflecting the origin of our spirit in the Holy Spirit and dramatically affirmed in the incarnation of Jesus Christ. The word *grieved* [H6087] (grieved the heart of the Lord) means "to hurt, pain, grieve," wherein God is not indifferent but passionate. The passion of the Lord God is a divine suffering that would be manifested most clearly on the cross. The intimate relationship between man and God is founded in the Lord God originally breathing the

---

the 12x10 law and prophets, Matt 5:17, that is, the 10 commandments being nailed to the wooden cross in place of each of the 12 tribes of Israel, Acts 26:6–8.

[14] "[T]he conditions of the world before the coming of Jesus will be like the conditions of the world before the flood [Matt 24:37]: exploding population [Gen 6:1], sexual perversion [Gen 6:2], demonic activity [Gen 6:2], constant evil in the heart of man [Gen 6:5], and widespread corruption and violence [Gen 6:11]" (Guzik 63; Gen 6:5–8). And also expected is a relative material prosperity—at least in the Roman West, according to the temporal blessing of Japheth—funding the excesses of the body and soul. For men are, after all, the most evil, not when they are starving, but when they are gorging.

breath of life into man, whereby the breath of life prefigures the fullness of the indwelling Holy Spirit just as the very good image of God originally embodied by Adam prefigures the perfect image of God that will finally be embodied in the Body of Christ.[15]

The word *repented* [H5162] (Lord repented) has a connotation "to suffer grief" and is the same word rendered *comfort* [H5162] in the prophecy that Noah would be a comfort from the curse (Gen 5:29). The repentance of the Lord is a comfort through death and not from death. The same images of regret and repentance being applied to man and to God reflects the humble condescension of Christ. Our surprise at God repenting at the time of the Flood is the same surprise of John the Baptist at Jesus Christ seeking the baptism in water, that is, the baptism of repentance for the forgiveness of sins (Matt 3:13–15). The meaning of divine repentance is ultimately realized in the death and resurrection of Jesus Christ, in which Christ repents not for his own sins but for the sins of the world. The image of divine repentance does not reflect an evolution of God or an absence of divine foreknowledge, but rather divine repentance means divine empathy manifested as divine action, intercession, just as our individual repentance is a contrite spirit manifested as a willful turning from evil.[16]

The surprising image of God repenting at the time of the Flood is also a testimony to the relationship between the Flood (first destruction), the incarnation (First Advent), and the baptism of repentance (first baptism). The divine repentance in the First Advent of Christ will be fulfilled in the divine redemption in the Second Advent just as the destruction by water in the first destruction will be fulfilled by fire in the foretold second destruction. The baptism in water (the baptism of repentance) will likewise be fulfilled in the baptism of the Holy Spirit (the baptism of redemption) just as the natural body (the first body) will be fulfilled in the spiritual, or glorified, body (the second body). The delayed death of the natural body until old age, likewise the delayed destruction of antediluvian man until the second millennium, and likewise the delayed destruction of all flesh until the end times are all reflections of the same call to repentance. The baptism of Christ being reflected in both the baptism of the world and the baptism of the individual is itself a prophecy of our promised new creation in the Body of Christ.

Genesis 6:7 And the LORD said, I will destroy [H4229] man [H120] whom I have created from the face [H6440] of the earth; both man [H120], and beast [H929], and the creeping thing [H7431], and the fowls [H5775] of the air [H8064]; for it repenteth me that I have made them.

---

[15] God will proclaim to the righteous in the hereafter, "See, I am the same as you!"— *Sifra* (Cohen, *Rabbinic Sages* 386). When he shall appear, we shall be like him, for we shall see him as he is, 1 John 3:2.

[16] The Rabbinic understanding of repentance is related in the contrast between man lamenting his subjugation and God delighting in His subjugation as a display of His great and perfect mercy, *Pesachim* (Cohen, *Rabbinic Sages* 19). The absolute necessity of the incarnation can be perceived even in the contrast between man and God.

NOAH

The word *destroy* [H4229] (man and beast) means "to wipe out," which portends an utter destruction of all flesh and likewise an utter destruction of all sin. The word *face* [H6440] (destroy from the face of the earth) recalls Adam hiding from the *presence* [H6440] of God (Gen 3:8) and also Cain being driven from the *face* [H6440] of the earth (Gen 4:14). The progression from Adam, driven from the garden, to Cain, driven from the earth, to antediluvian man, driven from life itself, reflects the inevitable descent into the utter darkness that exists apart from the light of God and, thereby, points to a final destruction in the end times. The destruction in the floodwaters is a fulfillment of the original condemnation of creation but not the final fulfillment. The death of each individual is an affirmation of the death of Adam but not the final affirmation. The final fulfillment of the curse will be the literal death of all flesh in the end times, the end of the natural body and likewise the end of the original creation. The completion of prophecy will not be fully revealed until the last days.[17]

The depravity of antediluvian man is closely identified with murderous Cain, particularly since antediluvian man comprised to some presumably large degree the literal offspring of Cain. The seed of the serpent is also closely identified, by the sign of murder, with the offspring of the first murderer Cain, particularly since one could say that murder is the figurative offspring of Cain. In contrast, Adam is identified with both Cain and Abel—that is, both the seed of the serpent and the Seed of woman—since Adam is the father of both Cain and Abel. The destruction of antediluvian man, driven from life itself, is a fulfillment of the curse of Cain, driven from the face of the earth, while the long delay between the murder of Abel and the advent of the floodwaters foreshadows the long delay that even now separates the crucifixion of Christ and the foretold destruction of all flesh by fire. The literal line of Cain, or at least the formal paternal line, would be cut off in the floodwaters, but a spiritual genealogy would ultimately continue through Ham. The seed, or offspring, of the serpent are literally the giants, but the seed of the serpent are spiritually all those who reject God. Likewise, the seed of Abraham are literally the Israelites but spiritually all the faithful in Christ (Gal 3:7). All flesh has been corrupted, not simply one bloodline, and therefore all flesh has been cursed. Only Christ has rejected the inheritance in death from Adam.

---

[17] Exorcisms are characterized by six distinct stages: presence, pretense, breakpoint, voice, clash, and expulsion (Martin 17–24). The reported six stages of the exorcism of an individual seem to be a microcosm of the exorcism of creation as a whole as embodied by the six millennia demarcating creation. The alien presence reflects the serpent in the garden of Eden. The demonic pretense of hiding among us reflects the primeval collusion between corrupted flesh and corrupted spirit, specifically the corruption of the daughters of men by the sons of God. The breakpoint is characterized by suffering and fear, which reflects the call of the faithful through the baptism in the floodwaters, ultimately as embodied not by Noah but by Abraham in the call to be the father of all the faithful. The voice of evil reflects the dark calling to oppose the kingdom of David and to reject the conception of Jesus Christ as king of kings. The clash reflects the crucifixion of Christ and the persecution of the faithful in imitation of Christ. And the expulsion reflects the coming final judgment in the end times.

ADAM, NOAH, ABRAHAM

The word *man* [H120] (destroy man) corresponds to the name *Adam* [H120], whereby God declaring the death of mankind in their apostasy is a fulfillment of the prophecy of the death of Adam in his disobedience (Gen 2:17). The word *beast* [H929] (destroy beast) is used in the Scriptures to denote both clean and unclean animals, also both domesticated and wild animals, which is an ambiguity that reflects freewill. The context of destruction specifically implies a corrupted freewill, while the destruction of man and beast together implies a universal carnal nature. The word *creeping* [H7431] (destroy the creeping thing) recalls the serpent cursed to go upon its belly (Gen 3:14). The rendering *fowls* [H5775] of the *air* [H8064] (destroy) literally means "flying creatures of the sky" but figuratively represents the fallen angelic host connected with the serpent. Likewise, the sky typically represents heaven. The death that comes by water is manifested on all levels of reality—including the heavenly, the earthly, and ultimately that of the individual.

The destruction in the floodwaters was a literal, physical destruction of man and beast and creeping thing and fowl, but it was also a spiritual destruction of evil, as evident in the origin of the destruction being in the depravity of antediluvian man. The end of the universal apostasy of Adam-kind embodied by the Flood marks an end to the overt dominion established by the serpent after the Fall of Adam. The Flood was a separation of man and serpent in the second millennium, counting from Adam, that recalls the division of the waters below the firmament from the waters above the firmament on the second day of creation (Gen 1:6–8). Adam, who was originally seduced by the serpent, dying near the time of Noah's birth also reflects the end of the overt dominion of the serpent since Adam, more than any other man, is the embodiment of fallen creation (Gen 5:5). The end of apostasy, the end of the overt dominion of the serpent of the garden, is marked in the life of the individual by the baptism of repentance that also comes by water.

The destruction by water would not be a complete destruction, since Noah and his family would be preserved. Sin would also continue in the world just as flesh would continue. Sin would continue after the Flood just as sin would continue after the First Advent just as sin continues after the baptism in water, but the destruction by water will be fulfilled in the foretold destruction by fire just as the First Advent will be fulfilled in the Second Advent just as the baptism in water will be fulfilled in the baptism of the Holy Spirit. Mankind was preserved through the floodwaters just as the faithful will be preserved through the final destruction by fire. Noah represents a new Adam just as the postdiluvian world represents a new earth. The promise of a new Adam and a new creation do not, however, represent a mere return to the garden of Eden but rather something new, our new creation in the Body of Christ.

The Flood is a vision on a global scale of the death and resurrection of Christ, affirming the life of Christ as a sanctification of all creation. The degradation of the dominion of the serpent in the time of Noah prefigures death itself and likewise the devil being overwhelmed by the blood of the Lamb from the time of the incarnation. The relative suppression of overt blasphemy after the Flood reflects an end to the overt dominion of the serpent, whereby the serpent was degraded from tempter to accuser. The sons of God taking the daughters of men would become the exception and not the rule after the destruction in the floodwaters. But the answer to the accusations of the devil would not be revealed until the victory of Jesus Christ over death (1 Cor 15:56–57). The devil would continue to tempt Adam-kind after the Flood, though primarily through the desires of the flesh, manifested in extreme cases as demonic possession, but the devil will not again overtly speak in the person of the serpent, not again that is until the coming end times when the Restrainer will be removed and the accuser will be finally revealed as the tormentor (2 Thess 2:7). The final revelation of satan as tormentor is even now manifest in the persecution of the earthly church, but the depths of that dark revelation will not be realized until the end times. The evil one is tempter, accuser, and tormentor, but the emphasis evolves through the different epochs in a dark progression pointing inexorably to the second death in the lake of fire. The degradation of the devil in this progression is, not solely a degradation in power, but an increasing opposition to the image of God. This is the dragon, that old serpent, which is the devil, and satan (Rev 20:2). The dragon who is revealed to be the serpent, devil, and satan.[18]

Genesis 6:8–9 But Noah found [H4672] grace [H2580] in the eyes [H5869] of the LORD. 9 These [are] the generations of Noah: Noah was a just [H6662] man [and] perfect [H8549] in his generations, [and] Noah walked with God.

The word *found* [H4672] (found grace) means "to attain to, find" but not specifically to earn or buy a thing, while the word *grace* [H2580] means "favour, grace" and has a connotation of "acceptance."[19] Salvation is by grace alone, a grace that comes only through the one faith in the one true God, the one true God revealed from the beginning by his personal presence, a presence ultimately revealed in the person of the one man Jesus Christ. Works, or equivalently the law, cannot redeem man; on the contrary, the law is the irrevocable condemnation of man. But the mortality of the natural body prefigures the immortality in the spiritual, or glorified, resurrection body just as the transitory preservation of Noah and his family prefigures the everlasting redemption of all the faithful. The Flood is a global renewal prefiguring the totality of our rebirth in Jesus Christ. The death and resurrection of the faithful in the Body of Christ is the rebirth of all creation. The grace that Noah and his family found in the Lord foreshadows the blessing of the Son, likewise the blessing of the faithful in the Son, by the Father. All mercies prophesy the

---

[18] The vast majority of reported psychic disturbances are not demonic possessions but physical illnesses (Martin 298). Wars and rumors of wars are likewise mistaken for the foretold final tribulation period.

[19] The words *Noah* and *grace* constitute an anagram in the Hebrew (Sarna 47; Gen 6:8). Yet another subtle sign that every jot and tittle has meaning.

renewal of all creation in the Body of Christ. Noah figuratively, or spiritually, walking with God prefigures the faithful in Christ literally walking with God.[20]

The word *eyes* [H5869] (eyes of the Lord) has a connotation "spring (of water)," which in the present context is an image of the font of life. The breath of life and the tree of life and the bread of life and the water of life are other perspectives of the life that proceeds from God, but all life is one just as God is one. Noah finding grace in the eyes of the Lord is not strictly a figure of speech but rather testifies to man finding life literally in the Lord and nowhere else. The word *just* [H6662] (Noah was just) means "just, righteous" and has a connotation of "lawful," while the word *perfect* [H8549] (perfect in his generations) means "complete, sound" and has connotations of "innocent" and "entirely in accord with truth and fact." Our justification through the law is the cross, while our wholeness is the Body of Christ. Noah figuratively walking with God prefigures Jesus Christ literally walking as God. The figurative perfection of Noah prefigures the literal perfection of Jesus Christ and likewise the literal perfection of the faithful in Christ. Calling Noah perfect is not divine hyperbole but rather a prophecy of Christ just as calling mere men the very children of God points to our perfection in Christ (John 1:12).[21]

Genesis 6:10 And Noah begat three sons, Shem, Ham, and Japheth.

The three sons Ham, Shem, and Japheth recall the three sons Cain, Abel, and Seth just as Noah recalls Adam just as the Flood recalls the Creation. The common ordering of the names of Noah's sons (Shem, Ham, Japheth) reflects Jesus Christ supplanting Adam, as represented by Shem supplanting Ham.[22]

The Ark

Genesis 6:11–13 The earth also was corrupt [H7843] before God [H430], and the earth was filled with violence [H2555]. 12 And God [H430]

---

[20] "Noah and Enoch are the two antediluvians of whom it is said that they 'walked with God' [Gen 5:24, 6:9]. Enoch, 'translated that he should not see death' [Heb 11:5], becomes a type of the saints who will be 'caught up' before the great tribulation [1 Thess 4:14–17, Rev 3:10, Dan 12:1, Matt 24:21]; Noah, preserved through the Flood, is a type of the Israelitish people who will be preserved through the tribulation [Jer 30:5–9]" (Scofield 13 n. 2; Gen 6:9). Noah and Enoch, representing the certainty of death in contrast to the promise of life, likewise the law and the prophets, foreshadow Moses and Elijah, Matt 17:4, and finally the foretold two witnesses, Rev 11:3.

[21] Some commentators view the perfection of Noah as a reference to the purity of his bloodline not having been corrupted by the sons of God taking the daughters of men, Gen 6:2 (Guzik 64; Gen 6:9–10). Not merely Noah's bloodline in the natural, but rather the Messianic bloodline in the natural and the spiritual.

[22] "Although Shem is unanimously declared by the Rabbis to have been the youngest son of Noah . . . yet he is always named first, being the most important of the three brothers" (*Jewish Encyclopedia*, s.v. "Shem"); "Japheth is considered by the Talmudists [Rabbis] to have been the eldest son of Noah . . . ." (*Jewish Encyclopedia*, s.v. "Japheth").

looked upon the earth, and, behold, it was corrupt; for all flesh had corrupted his way upon the earth. 13 And God [H430] said unto Noah, The end [H7093] of all flesh is come before me; for the earth is filled with violence through them; and, behold, I will destroy them with the earth.

The name *God* (Elohim) [H430] (corrupt before God) evokes an image of "rulers" and "judges," which is an emphasis on justice and the implied authority and power required to administer justice. The name *God* (Elohim) [H430] is the original name identified with our original creation, emphasizing our original creation under the law and also foreshadowing the subsequent condemnation of mankind by the law (Gen 1:1). The parallels between the original creation and the first destruction affirm the Flood as a new creation, a death and resurrection of creation. But the Flood would not be the final revelation of our new creation just as Noah would not be the final figure of Messiah. The name *Lord* (YHWH) [H3068] also being used in the account of the Flood points to the ultimate fulfillment of our promised new creation in the Body of Christ. Sin would continue in the world after the Flood just as the believer still sins after the baptism in water just as the faithful still die physically even after the victory of Christ over death. The condemnation of the natural body under the law is irrevocable, but the faithful look to the resurrection of the spiritual, or glorified, body by grace through faith in Christ.

The word *corrupt* [H7843] (earth was corrupt) means "to go to ruin" with a connotation "to pervert," while the word *violence* [H2555] (earth filled with violence) means "violence, wrong" and has a connotation of "hatred characterized by violence." The world full of violence is reflected in the microcosm of the individual. An utter corruption of the world reflects an utter darkness of the soul. Our sin had corrupted not only our individual lives but also our entire physical reality. The red earth and ruddy man are brothers in blood, and thus dust and flesh would be destroyed together. The foundation of physical reality is spiritual reality and not vice versa. Accordingly, death should be understood as the material manifestation of our separation from God—that is, our separation from God is the spiritual, or true, meaning of physical death. Our suffering does not proceed from God, rather from our freewill separation of ourselves from God. The existence of sin is a graphic testimony to the sanctity of our freewill, while the fruition of sin in suffering and finally death is a graphic testimony to the long-suffering of our Lord and God in the call to repentance. The world full of violence is expressly the maturity, or fullness, of evil. Maturity is always the natural time of harvest, whereby the end times will inevitably recall the days of Noah (Matt 24:37). The destruction in the floodwaters portends the foretold destruction by fire, but the preservation of Noah through the floodwaters prefigures the redemption of the faithful through the fire of judgment.

The word *end* [H7093] (end of all flesh) is derived from the root "to cut off" [H7112], recalling man cut off from God in the original exile from the garden, also portending the final judgment connected with the kingdom. The Flood of Noah would not, however, literally destroy all flesh, since mankind would be preserved through Noah and the natural body would likewise continue. The Flood is called a complete destruction because it is itself also a prophecy, a graphic prophecy, of the foretold second destruction, coming by fire, that will be the literally complete destruction of sin and death and the corresponding end of the natural body. The Flood directly reflects the baptism in water but also foreshadows the baptism of the Spirit just as the baptism in water itself points to the baptism of the Spirit. The foretold death of Adam after eating from the tree of knowledge is likewise a prophecy of the death of all flesh in the end times. Nothing in this world, not even the First Advent of Jesus Christ, is a final fulfillment of the promise of life, rather the present things are the deposit on our inheritance (2 Cor 1:22). The first creation points to the second just as the first destruction points to the second. Even the First Advent of Christ points to the Second Advent. The First Advent is the firstfruits of the grave, pointing to the harvest of all the faithful in the Second Advent (1 Cor 15:23, Lev 23:10–12). All creation prefigures the promised new creation. All revelation points to the fulfillment of all things in the last days in the promised communion of the creation with the Creator in the Body of Christ in accordance with the fullness of the indwelling Holy Spirit.[23]

Genesis 6:14 Make thee an ark [H8392] of gopher wood [H6086]; rooms shalt thou make in the ark, and shalt pitch [H3722] it within and without with pitch [H3724].

The word *wood* [H6086] (ark of wood) has a connotation "gallows," which foreshadows the wooden cross of the crucifixion. The word *pitch* [H3722] (pitch the ark) literally means "to cover over" but has connotations "to pacify" and "to make propitiation," while the other word rendered *pitch* [H3724] (cover with pitch) has a connotation "the price of a life, ransom." The life of Jesus Christ is a ransom for many (Matt 20:28). The ark of Noah was covered with pitch just as the brazen (brasen) altar was covered with the blood of animals just as the cross was covered with the blood of Christ. The call of Noah to build the ark is the call of mankind to repentance, a repentance embodied by the faithful in Christ being nailed to the cross with Christ, while Noah and his family passing safely through the floodwaters prefigures Christ and likewise the faithful in Christ passing through death (Rom 6:4). The Flood is the first destruction; the law is the first covenant; the death and resurrection of Jesus Christ is the First Advent. The advent of the floodwaters was the condemnation of a corrupt world just as the law is the condemnation of sinful man, but the condemnation

---

[23] In the Flood is seen a type of the coming final judgment of creation because of the insurrection of mankind against God (Coffman 123; Gen 8:1). The Flood of Noah is a huge, literal event to be viewed simultaneously as a mere type, or shadow, of things to come, but it is absolutely correct to do so. And therein one should recognize that all creation is a promise, or prophecy, of a new creation and that the reality of the new creation will necessarily dwarf the promise represented by the present creation.

of Christ under the law in the place of sinful man has become the sanctification of all creation.[24]

The image of passing through water is a baptism in water that signifies the baptism of repentance for the forgiveness of sins (Mark 1:4). Peter explicitly tells us that the baptism of creation in the floodwaters parallels the baptism of the church in water (1 Peter 3:20–21). Christ calls his own passion a baptism (Luke 12:50), whereby our imitation of Christ is likewise a baptism (Mark 10:39). The First Advent points to the Second Advent just as the firstfruits point to the harvest just as the first baptism points to the second baptism. The nation of Israel was baptized in the Red Sea when coming out of the land of Egypt (Exod 14:29) just as the subsequent generation was baptized in the Jordan when entering into the promised land (Josh 1:2). The ubiquitous cleansing in water required by the Levitical code is also an image of the baptism in water. The law precedes grace just as the baptism in water precedes the baptism of the Holy Spirit just as repentance precedes redemption. The universal baptism in water is a figurative death and resurrection that represents the death and resurrection of the world, likewise the death and resurrection of Jesus Christ, and likewise the death and resurrection of the faithful in Christ. The connection of the baptism of the world in the floodwaters and the baptism of Christ in the flesh is an affirmation that Christ is our new creation, while our imitation of Christ in baptism is an affirmation of the oneness of the Body of Christ. The baptism in water is both our spiritual repentance in the flesh and also our literal death in the flesh.[25]

The word *ark* [H8392] (Noah's ark) literally means "chest, box" and is the same word used to describe the *ark* [H8392] of bulrushes that preserved the infant Moses in the Nile (Exod 2:3). The word *ark* [H727] used to describe the *ark* of the covenant has a similar literal meaning "ark, chest" but is a distinct Hebrew word. Despite the differences, all three arks evoke an image of death and resurrection. Noah's ark and Moses's ark of bulrushes would both literally deliver flesh from death to life. The ark carrying the law would likewise deliver flesh literally from death to life (Num 10:35) but would also spiritually deliver flesh from death to life since the law guides men to faith in Christ (Gal 3:24). The former things are dominated by the literal, representing the natural body, while the latter things are expressly the union of the literal and spiritual, testifying to the spiritual body being a true body. The three arks are also connected with death and resurrection by the sign of water that marks the call to the death of sin. Noah would be delivered through the floodwaters just as the

---

[24] "[T]he word translated 'pitch' in [Gen 6:14] is the same word translated 'atonement' in [Lev 17:11], etc. It is atonement that keeps out the waters of judgment and makes the believer's position 'in Christ' [in the Body of Christ] safe and blessed" (Scofield 14 n. 3; Gen 6:14). The baptism in the floodwaters is the baptism of the cross.

[25] The act of repentance is considered equal to rebuilding the temple and offering the required sacrifices, *Leviticus Rabbah* (Cohen, *Rabbinic Sages* 105). All the faithful, through repentance in Christ, participate together in the death and resurrection of the one true temple, who is the Christ, wherein Noah building the ark and also Solomon building the temple should be recognized as foreshadowing the incarnation of Jesus Christ.

infant Moses would be delivered through the waters of the Nile just as the ark of the covenant would lead the Israelites through the waters of the Jordan into the promised land. Ultimately, the world saved through Noah and also Israel saved through Moses both prefigure man and creation being redeemed together through Jesus Christ and in Jesus Christ, who is the true ark, or embodiment, of the covenant. The vastly different size scales of the first two arks, Noah's ark and Moses's ark, reflect overall creation compared with individual man. Adam is likewise the father of all mankind and the embodiment of all creation, while his mere descendant Jesus would be a lowly Nazarene cut off without offspring. The former represents pride, while the latter represents humility. The similarities between the first two arks and the third ark reflect the natural prefiguring the spiritual, while the distinctions between the third ark and the first two arks reflect the transcendence of the spiritual, or glorified, body compared with the natural body. The singularity of the third ark compared with the duality of the first two arks reflects the unity of the spiritual body compared with the conflict of the natural body.[26]

By faith Noah built the ark in reverent fear of things forewarned but not yet seen, by which he condemned the world and became heir of the righteousness that comes by faith (Heb 11:7). The imperfect faithfulness of Noah prefigures the perfect faithfulness of Jesus Christ just as the fear in the flesh points to the love in the Spirit. Faith is the mark placed upon the children of God by the Holy Spirit, a mark manifested as our recognition of the Word of God, both in reading the Scriptures and also living out our personal morality. All men sin. And thereby the world seeks to condemn the children of God as hypocrites. But the truth remains that there is a clear distinction between the faithful in Christ and the faithless separated from Christ just as there is a clear distinction between the books of men and the Book of God. The figurative condemnation of mankind by Noah is the condemnation of flesh under the law, which ultimately prefigures the literal condemnation of mankind by the Son. The reality of our oneness in the Body of Christ should not be understated, but the condemnation being by Noah is literal only in the sense that the faithful are one with Christ. The duality of our inviolable freewill and our oneness with Christ is the duality of flesh and spirit, a paradox that is prefigured in the natural body and finally resolved in the Body of Christ.[27]

Genesis 6:15–16 And this [is the fashion] which thou shalt make it [of]: The length of the ark [shall be] three hundred cubits, the breadth of it fifty cubits, and the height of it thirty cubits. 16 A window shalt thou make to the ark, and in a cubit shalt thou finish it above; and the door of

---

[26] "This call to Noah was a type of the gospel call to sinners. Christ is an Ark already prepared, in whom alone we can be safe, when death and judgment come; . . ." (Henry 1:53; Gen 7:1, 7:4). The wooden ark prefigures the wooden cross.

[27] "This *ark* was like the hulk of a ship, fitted not to sail upon the waters, but to float waiting for their fall" (Wesley 1:32; Gen 6:14). The course of faith.

NOAH

the ark shalt thou set in the side thereof; [with] lower, second, and third [stories] shalt thou make it.

The exacting design of the ark testifies to the narrow way unto life and, accordingly, a literal heavenly domain paralleling the earthly domain (Matt 7:14). Not all the details concerning Noah's ark are recorded, and therefore all the details that are recorded are expected to have significance beyond the commonplace. The one door is the one salvation in the one man Jesus Christ. The window is the light of the Holy Spirit. The design itself, the conception of the ark, should be identified with the Father. The repetition of the number 3, especially with respect to the basic shape and structure of the ark, affirms that the triunity of God is the proper foundation for understanding all things. The number 5 points to the fifth millennium, reflecting the ubiquitous connection between the wooden ark of Noah and the wooden cross of Christ.

Genesis 6:17–18 And, behold, I, even I, do bring a flood of waters upon the earth, to destroy all flesh, wherein [is] the breath of life, from under heaven; [and] every thing that [is] in the earth shall die. 18 But with thee will I establish my covenant; and thou shalt come into the ark, thou, and thy sons, and thy wife, and thy sons' wives with thee.

God takes full responsibility for the destruction of all flesh because God necessarily foreknew the fall of all creation in Adam and the resulting condemnation of all mankind, all Adam-kind. Nonetheless, God has in no way sinned in the act of creation, for it is still man himself, in accordance with the inviolable sanctity of freewill, that has rejected God. And thereby it is man that has condemned himself. And we know that God has not sinned, because God has not ceased being God, as evident from creation not having unraveled. God in love chooses to allow the freewill of man, that is, God chooses to allow man to exist, which is a divine condescension and humble self-limitation. And to truly allow freewill necessarily means to allow freewill throughout all creation. And the absolute necessity that the freewill of man be allowed in all creation, all space and time, harks back to the original act of creation in which God, limiting himself, allowed the emergence of those who would be saved together with those who would not be saved. And God, who is perfect in love and mercy, has done all these things and suffered along with us, not for his own sake, but in order that we may live and truly live. And the faithful understand and affirm that if a person can be saved under any circumstances whatsoever, then the Lord God will surely save him.

Genesis 6:19–22 And of every living thing of all flesh, two of every [sort] shalt thou bring into the ark, to keep [them] alive with thee; they shall be male and female. 20 Of fowls after their kind, and of cattle after their kind, of every creeping thing of the earth after his kind, two of every [sort] shall come unto thee, to keep [them] alive. 21 And take thou unto thee of all food that is eaten, and thou shalt gather [it] to thee; and it shall

be for food for thee, and for them. 22 Thus did Noah; according to all that God commanded him, so did he.

A living, physical creation is the essential extension of man, who is a living soul having freewill and, therefore, having dominion over a true, literal creation. The life of man is innately connected, eternally, with the life of creation and likewise with the act, or promise, of creation just as the life of God, specifically God the Holy Spirit, is intimately connected with the life of man in creation.

Genesis 7:1 And the LORD said unto Noah, Come thou and all thy house into the ark; for thee have I seen righteous before me in this generation.

The righteousness of the one man Noah pleases the Lord and, therein, saves his family, preserves natural creation, and guarantees future generations. The imperfect righteousness of the one man Noah prefigures the perfect righteousness of the one man Jesus Christ.

Genesis 7:2–3 Of every clean [H2889] beast thou shalt take to thee by sevens [H7651], the male and his female: and of beasts that [are] not clean [H2889] by two [H8147], the male and his female. 3 Of fowls also of the air by sevens [H7651], the male and the female; to keep seed [H2233] alive upon the face of all the earth.

The word *clean* [H2889] (clean beasts) means "clean" and "pure" and has a connotation of "ethically pure," which reflects the relationship between physical purity and spiritual purity. The *seed* [H2233] kept alive on the earth is ultimately the promised Seed of woman, the clean Seed, Jesus Christ. The preservation of both clean and unclean animals is a sign that sin, though abated, would continue in the world after the Flood. The believer likewise continues to sin after the baptism in water just as sin would continue in the world after the crucifixion of Christ. The postdiluvian world would degenerate from the time of Noah just as the antediluvian world degenerated from the original creation. But where sin abounds, grace abounds much more (Rom 5:20). The destruction by water foreshadows the destruction by fire, but the baptism in water foreshadows the baptism of the Holy Spirit just as the First Advent of Christ foreshadows the Second Advent. The juxtaposition of sin increasing and grace increasing in the world reflects the duality of flesh and spirit and likewise the death of the natural body in contrast to the rebirth in the spiritual, or glorified, body. The first foreshadows the second, while the second fulfills the first. The preservation of both clean and unclean animals together in the ark is also a sign that the clean saves the unclean just as Christ would redeem Adam, that is, fallen man. The connection of the unclean with the clean, both in the preservation of flesh despite sin and also in the redemption of flesh from sin, reflects the same suffering endured in the call of the sinful to repentance.[28]

The word *sevens* [H7651] (clean by sevens) has an association "to swear" [H7650], which is an emphasis on covenant, that is, the promises of God. The oath of God is the promise of life, a promise affirmed in the preservation of the seed of life. The number 7 also recalls the 6+1 days of creation, which reinforces an image of covenant, as implied by the original creation of life. The seed of life preserved in the ark recalls the original breath of life just as the Flood recalls the Creation. The covenant of God is the relationship between man and God established by God for the welfare of man, whereby the essence of covenant is embodied by creation itself. The connection of the number 7 specifically with clean animals is a sign that creation (the embodiment of freewill) is very good irrespective of evil (the essence of evil being the corruption of freewill) and likewise that the will of God (despite the sinful nature of man) cannot be denied or confounded.[29] The word *two* [H8147] (by two) is applied to both clean and unclean animals for the counting by pairs of male and female. The pair is a fundamental unit of counting just as the union of male and female is a fundamental image of the oneness of God. The union of male and female is a symbol of life through procreation just as God is the font of life in creation, whereby the pairs saved through the floodwaters reflect the promise of life in our foretold new creation. The word *two* [H8147] has a connotation "double portion," which connects the twofold union of man and woman to the oneness of the firstborn, to whom belongs the double portion (Deut 21:17). This is ultimately the oneness of the Body of Christ that proceeds from God the Father through the power of God the Holy Spirit. The image of single pairs of unclean animals represents the singleness, or isolation, of fallen man outside communion with God. The sevenfold larger number of clean animals compared with unclean animals is an affirmation that grace is greater than sin and also that grace is expressly reflected by the sevenfold creation, that is, the seven days of creation.[30]

Genesis 7:4–6 For yet seven days, and I will cause it to rain upon the earth forty days and forty nights; and every living substance that I have made will I destroy from off the face of the earth. 5 And Noah did according unto all that the LORD commanded him. 6 And Noah [was] six hundred years old when the flood of waters was upon the earth.

---

[28] "Christ was represented also in Noah, and in that ark of the whole world. For why were all kinds of animals shut in, in the ark, but to signify all nations? [Augustine, *Tractates on the Gospel of John*]" (Schaff, *Nicene and Post-Nicene Fathers: First Series* 7:67). The death and resurrection of Christ is the death and resurrection of the whole world.
[29] "Which [of every clean beast] might be offered in sacrifice, whereof six were for breed and the seventh for sacrifice" (Whittingham et al., *Geneva Bible* 4R n. b#1; Gen 7:2). A subtle testimony to the 6+1 days of creation.
[30] The symbolic significance of numbers in creation has been distorted by pagans just as everything in creation has been corrupted, but the signs and patterns of creation can still be perceived just as the image of God can still be discerned.

The six hundred years that mark the completion of the seven days by the forty days and forty nights is the sixth millennium that is connected to the final Sabbath, or Day of the Lord, by the tribulation period.[31]

Renewal

Genesis 7:7 And Noah went in, and his sons, and his wife, and his sons' wives with him, into the ark, because of the waters [H4325] of the flood [H3999].

The word *waters* [H4325] (waters of the Flood) has connotations of "purification" and also "distress" and "violence," which are images of the judgment under the law of the natural body in this life. Water is an emblem of flesh and likewise the law that governs flesh, exemplified by ceremonial purification by water before the brazen (brasen) altar. Fire is an emblem of spirit and likewise the grace that governs spirit—that is, the grace that redeems us through the Holy Spirit—exemplified by the complete purification in the fire on the altar (Lev 1:9). The palpable dichotomy of degradation and exaltation manifest in the natural body reflects the duality of flesh and spirit and finally the death of the natural body and the rebirth of the spiritual body. The synthesis of law and grace is evident on all levels of reality in a myriad of paired images that represents universality. Water and fire, dust and breath, flesh and spirit, bread and wine, body and blood, earth and sky, night and day, man and woman, barrenness and fertility, and finally death and life, or death and rebirth, all reflecting the duality of justice and mercy.[32]

The word *flood* [H3999] (went in because of) is derived from the root "to conduct, bear along, especially in procession" [H2986], which reflects the first covenant leading us to the second covenant and likewise repentance leading us to redemption.[33] The law, the first covenant, does not justify us but rather condemns us and calls us to repentance (Rom 3:20). The baptism in water is

---

[31] The formal tribulation period precedes the seventh, or Sabbath, millennium, but the final destruction by fire establishing the new creation follows the Sabbath millennium, such that there is a first and second destruction by fire, likewise a first and second casting into the lake of fire, and likewise a first and second death—testifying to the resurrection of life being separated from the resurrection of damnation, likewise the resurrection and rapture preceding the formal second coming of Christ, likewise the First and Second Advents of Christ, and likewise the first and second men Adam and Jesus Christ, Rev 19:20, 20:14–15.

[32] The accounts of the Creation and the Flood show an alternating literary structure organized into seven parallel elements, with Gen 1:1–6:8 paralleling 6:9–11:32 (Waltke 19–20). Noah corresponds to Adam in the context of sin, 3:7 ↔ 9:22, while Noah corresponds to Abraham in the context of blessing, 6:8 ↔ 11:31, reflecting the nexus of curse and blessing exemplified by the Flood of Noah and ultimately embodied by the Passion of Christ.

[33] Root per *Strong's*, not *Brown-Driver-Briggs*, but the link between the ark being carried by floodwaters and the idea of a procession is clear regardless of the exact etymology.

likewise a sign of repentance for the forgiveness of sins that prefigures the baptism of the Holy Spirit (Acts 19:4–6). Water points to fire and spirit just as the law points to grace just as repentance points to redemption just as the natural body points to the spiritual, or glorified, body. Even Jesus Christ would first seek the baptism in water, and only after which, or simultaneously, would the Spirit formally descend upon him (Matt 3:16). The exceptions in the New Testament to the normal ordering of the baptism of repentance, represented by water, followed by the baptism of the Holy Spirit, represented by the laying on of hands, are not accepted but rather quickly remedied (Acts 10:47–48). Nevertheless, this ambiguity in the proper ordering of the two baptisms is also a prophecy of the final synthesis of law and grace in the Body of Christ, a union embodied by the simultaneously sequential and concurrent baptism in water and baptism of the Spirit experienced by Jesus.

The threefold progression of Noah, his sons, and finally the women entering into the ark reflects the Father, Son, and Holy Spirit. Noah's wife being listed before his sons' wives prefigures the Spirit calling the one nation of Israel before the nations of the Gentiles, while their presence in the ark together reflects the unity of Jew and Gentile in the Body of Christ. The Flood is closely identified with the Passion of Christ. The identification of the Father, Son, and Holy Spirit with Noah's ark is an affirmation that the fullness of deity is present in Jesus Christ and likewise present in the redemption of the faithful in Christ. The received ordering God the Father, God the Son, and God the Holy Spirit reflects the Holy Spirit proceeding from the Father through the Son and also from the Son to indwell the creation (Matt 28:19). The Holy Spirit does indwell all humanity in the natural body but only in part, an indwelling manifested most obviously as the breath of life. In contrast, the spiritual, or glorified, body will be animated by the fullness of the Holy Spirit, the very presence of God. The sign of the Holy Spirit is life, but the seal of the Holy Spirit is faith. The Father, Son, and Holy Spirit are equally reflected by the image of man, woman, and child, which is a reversal of woman and child as compared with the threefold Noah, his sons, and their wives. This reversal itself reflects the unity of the Holy Spirit in the procession through the Son and with the Son and from the Son. The former image of a wife as the embodiment of the third person of the Trinity reflects the Spirit indwelling the Bride of Christ, while the latter image of progeny as the embodiment of the third person of the Trinity reflects the fullness of the Holy Spirit present in the Body of Christ. The second person of the Trinity being reflected by both woman and child testifies to the Spirit and Son both proceeding from the Father, specifically the conception of the Son through the Holy Spirit (Luke 1:35).[34]

---

[34] "... 'It is the Father who generates, the Son who is begotten, and the Holy Spirit who proceeds' [Lateran Council IV, AD 1215]" (Rom. Catholic Church, *Catechism* 75). The words *Father*, *Son*, and *Spirit* have literal meanings, which is a reality that can be ignored only in opposition to the Word of God.

Genesis 7:8–9 Of clean beasts, and of beasts that [are] not clean, and of fowls, and of every thing that creepeth upon the earth, 9 There went in two and two unto Noah into the ark, the male and the female, as God had commanded Noah.

Each contrast—the beast and the creeping thing, the fowl and the beast, man and animal, the clean and the unclean—testifies to the universal juxtaposition of grace and law. Each pair—male and female—represents the essential union of law and grace.

Genesis 7:10–11 And it came to pass after seven days, that the waters of the flood were upon the earth. 11 In the six hundredth year of Noah's life, in the second month, the seventeenth day of the month, the same day were all the fountains of the great deep broken up, and the windows of heaven were opened.

The parallel between the fountains of the deep and the windows of heaven reflects the universal relationships between earth and heaven, flesh and spirit, and law and grace. The connection between the earthly and heavenly domains, particularly in the context of destruction, points to a coming new creation that will necessarily arise out of the death and resurrection of all creation, heaven and earth (Rev 21:1). Further, the emphasis on the specific timing of the first destruction (by water) is a testimony that the time of the yet future second destruction (by fire) has been preordained from the foundation of the world. And what is the preordained time of completion if not the Sabbath millennium, representing the fulfillment of a prophetic week in the Day of the Lord?

Genesis 7:12 And the rain was upon the earth forty days and forty nights.

The forty days of rain in the time of Noah foreshadow the forty days Moses would stay on Sinai (Exod 34:28) and also the forty years that Israel would wander in the desert (Deut 8:2) and also the forty days that Christ would be tempted by the devil (Mark 1:13). The forty days of rain represent a destruction that heralds the rebirth of creation through the floodwaters. The forty days on Sinai represent a separation that prepares the formal law for the Israelites as the governance of repentance in the flesh. The forty years in the desert represent a deprivation that prepares the Israelites to enter into the promised land. The temptation of Christ is a microcosm of the life of Christ, the life revealed to sanctify creation by grace through faith. Each period of forty days or years is a purification that precedes a renewal, or more abstractly a death that precedes a rebirth. The ubiquitous prophecy of death and resurrection is ultimately embodied by the death and resurrection of the one man Jesus Christ but will finally be completed in the death and resurrection of the faithful in Christ and the corresponding renewal of all creation in the Body of Christ. The implicit comparison of days and years is a parallel between the daily cycles of night and day and the annual cycles of winter and summer, a parallel that testifies to a consistency between the different levels of reality. The ambiguous distinction between days and years also prefigures a fading of time itself in fulfillment of the promise of eternity. All patterns point to our new creation in the last days.[35]

The persistent and purposeful repetition of certain numbers and symbols in the Bible is undeniable, but spiritual interpretations should always be disciplined by literal context, in acknowledgment of the correspondence between the physical and the spiritual. The study of Biblical symbols is distinct from occult practices. Biblical symbols are merely a symbolic language akin to literal language, while the occult is a seeking of knowledge separated from the Spirit. The spiritual is the foundation of the natural and not vice versa, but their essential correspondence allows one in principle to perceive either level of reality by its counterpart, though never outside the light of the Spirit. Our initial perception of the spiritual is normally through the natural since we are carnal beings exiled from the fullness of the Holy Spirit. The call to walk not by sight but by faith is not the call to close our eyes but rather to see the spiritual significance of the physical, the true meaning of the physical (2 Cor 5:7). The abstract symbols evident in the Scriptures testify to the spiritual meaning underlying simple literal meaning, whereby symbolic language is the natural language of the Spirit. The use of symbols in the Scriptures also reflects the same spiritual truths being manifested on all levels of reality, in agreement with the image of God being impressed upon all creation. The strange rambling that pervades the occult represents an arbitrariness, a detachment from the literal that is a rejection of God in creation. This rejection stands in stark contrast to the faithful perceiving the Creator in the creation despite the corruption of flesh (Rom 1:20). To ignore the obvious symbolism in the Scriptures is to ignore the movement of the Spirit in the Scriptures.[36]

Genesis 7:13–17 In the selfsame day entered Noah, and Shem, and Ham, and Japheth, the sons of Noah, and Noah's wife, and the three wives of his sons with them, into the ark; 14 They, and every beast after his kind, and all the cattle after their kind, and every creeping thing that creepeth upon the earth after his kind, and every fowl after his kind, every bird of every sort. 15 And they went in unto Noah into the ark, two and two of all flesh, wherein [is] the breath of life. 16 And they that went in, went in male and female of all flesh, as God had commanded him: and the LORD shut him in. 17 And the flood was forty days upon the earth; and the waters increased, and bare up the ark, and it was lift up above the earth.

---

[35] "Forty, a symbolic number in the Bible, is often connected with purification and the purging of sin" (Sarna 54; Gen 7:4); "Forty will become a number associated with a time of testing and purification, especially before coming into something new and significant" (Guzik 70; Gen 7:10–12).

[36] "The Spirit . . . makes us hear the Father's Word, but we do not hear the Spirit himself. We know him only in the movement by which he reveals the Word to us and disposes us to welcome him in faith" (Rom. Catholic Church, *Catechism* 197). The subtlety of the Spirit is a testimony to the abstract and symbolic character of reality.

Noah's family represents all the faithful throughout all the ages, while every beast and all the cattle, and so forth, represent creation as a whole, the physical and the spiritual. The procession of people together with creatures into Noah's ark is a prophecy of man and earth and heaven being redeemed together in the one Body of Christ. The procession by pairs, male and female, signifies a redemption that is in accordance with law and grace, while Noah's family caring for the animals reflects grace subsuming law.

Genesis 7:18 And the waters prevailed, and were increased greatly upon the earth; and the ark went upon the face [H6440] of the waters [H4325].

The ark of Noah upon the *face* [H6440] of the *waters* [H4325] recalls the Spirit of God moving upon the *face* of the *waters* in the original act of creation, wherein the renewal of the world through the floodwaters is again related to the original creation (Gen 1:2). The one man Noah recalls the one man Adam, while the enclosed ark of Noah recalls the enclosed garden of Eden. Noah and his family exiting the ark ironically recalls Adam and Eve exiled from the garden. The paradox of the preservation of Adam in his condemnation and likewise the paradox of the preservation of Noah through the condemnation of all flesh reflect the law that both condemns us to death and leads us to life. This is the same conflict between the death of the natural body and the promised rebirth in the spiritual, or glorified, body. The original creation and also the advent of the floodwaters both point to the renewal of creation in Christ just as the law points to grace.[37]

The image of man and woman, the embodiment of justice and mercy, exiting the garden, likewise exiting the ark, prefigures water and blood, spiritually law and grace, flowing from the side of Christ on the cross (John 19:34). Noah is the father of postdiluvian mankind just as Adam is the father of all mankind, wherein Adam and Noah both prefigure Jesus Christ being the progenitor of redeemed mankind. The baptism in the floodwaters prefigures the baptism of Jesus Christ on the cross. The wooden ark prefigures the wooden cross. The ark of Noah passing through the storm prefigures Christ passing through persecution and finally death, likewise the faithful in Christ passing through persecution and finally death. The original creation (first creation), the Flood (first destruction), and the incarnation of Jesus Christ (First Advent) all point to a fulfillment of all things in the last days—namely, a convergence of the glorious reappearing of Christ (Second Advent) and the foretold destruction by fire (second destruction) and our promised new creation (second creation).[38]

---

[37] "[T]he world returns [in the Flood] to the watery chaos that existed before creation . . . [I]t entails the destruction of the entire cosmos and a reversion to primeval chaos" (Viviano, *Collegeville* 49; Gen 7:6–7:24). Since the Lord God does not lie, dramatic hyperbole must point to a literal fulfillment of all prophecy in the end times. The Flood of Noah, for example, was a huge, literal event representing the death and resurrection of the world and pointing to the end times.

[38] A second destruction of the world is foretold in 2 Pet 3, not by water but by fire (Coffman 130; Gen 8:20–22). Water and fire, water and spirit, water and blood, flesh

NOAH

Genesis 7:19–24 And the waters prevailed exceedingly upon the earth; and all the high hills, that [were] under the whole heaven, were covered. 20 Fifteen cubits upward did the waters prevail; and the mountains were covered. 21 And all flesh died that moved upon the earth, both of fowl, and of cattle, and of beast, and of every creeping thing that creepeth upon the earth, and every man: 22 All in whose nostrils [was] the breath of life, of all that [was] in the dry [land], died. 23 And every living substance was destroyed which was upon the face of the ground, both man, and cattle, and the creeping things, and the fowl of the heaven; and they were destroyed from the earth: and Noah only remained [alive], and they that [were] with him in the ark. 24 And the waters prevailed upon the earth an hundred and fifty days.

The death of all flesh is identified with the deluge, or baptism, of dry land, reflecting the ubiquitous relationship between ruddy man and the red earth, between the way of all flesh and the way of the dust of the ground, or earth, from which the flesh is formed (Gen 3:19, Josh 23:14). The freewill of man, created in the very image of God, implies a physical body and also a physical dominion, though that which is merely physical inevitably dies when cut off from the spiritual. The simple existence of God likewise implies creation and also incarnation and ultimately death and resurrection.

Genesis 8:1–2 And God remembered Noah, and every living thing, and all the cattle that [was] with him in the ark: and God made a wind [H7307] to pass over the earth, and the waters asswaged; 2 The fountains also of the deep and the windows of heaven were stopped, and the rain from heaven was restrained [H3607];

The word *wind* [H7307] (asswaged the waters) is the same word used to describe the *Spirit* (Ruwach) [H7307] of God moving upon the face of the waters in the original creation, which again reflects the Flood as a new creation (Gen 1:2). The word *wind* [H7307] is also the same word used to describe the Lord causing a strong east *wind* to part the Red Sea in the Exodus, which reflects the parallel between the baptism in the floodwaters and the baptism of the Israelites (Exod 14:21). The connection between the Spirit and the baptism in water is the call of the faithful to repentance by the Spirit. The image of creation connected with the baptism in water points to our promised new creation in Christ. Water is a symbol of flesh and likewise the law that governs flesh, whereby the baptism in water is an image of the death and resurrection of flesh under the law. The flesh that precedes flesh, the baptism that precedes baptism, is the natural body that precedes the spiritual, or glorified, body and likewise the original creation that precedes our new creation. To say that the spiritual body is flesh is to say that the spiritual body is a true body. The Body

---

and blood, and body and blood all represent the natural and the spiritual, also law and grace, and ultimately Jesus Christ, who is fully man and fully God.

of Christ comes by both water and blood just as our redemption comes by the baptisms in water and of the Spirit (1 John 5:6). Our condemnation under the law is death, but our hope is the promise of eternal life by grace.

The word *restrained* [H3607] (rain restrained) means "to shut up, restrain, withhold" in the Hebrew, implying that the flame of life would naturally and immediately be extinguished in the absence of divine intervention, which is ultimately the intercession of the Son. Our existence implies not only the existence of God but also the perpetual mercy of God. The natural body, the original creation, will be preserved until the fulfillment of all things in the last days just as Jesus Christ will always live to intercede for us in the spiritual, or glorified, body, in the promised new creation in eternity (Heb 7:25). The restraint of the floodwaters is an image of the victory of Christ over death just as passing through the floodwaters is the death and resurrection of Jesus Christ. The victory of Christ over death is in accordance with the law, whereby the restraint of the floodwaters likewise prefigures the restraint of lawlessness (2 Thess 2:7). The emphasis on rain coming from heaven is an affirmation that the baptism in water proceeds from heaven (Matt 21:25) just as the incarnation of God in the flesh proceeds from heaven (1 Cor 15:47).

The image of God remembering Noah and his family in the ark implies that God had previously forgotten them in the ark. Divine forgetfulness, like divine repentance, is a startling, seemingly impossible, image of our relationship with God, but such images are ultimately made clear in the Passion of Jesus Christ (Matt 19:26). The baptism of the world in the floodwaters should always be likened to the baptism of Christ for the world, that is, the death and resurrection of Christ (1 Pet 3:20–22). The image of God forgetting Noah in the wooden ark is a vision of the Father forsaking the Son on the wooden cross (Mark 15:34). The image of God remembering Noah could be discounted without this essential comparison between the Flood and the Passion of Christ. God forgetting man in the ark is a prophecy of God no longer remembering the sins of man (Heb 10:17), wherein the faithful are nailed to the cross with Christ (Gal 2:20). God finally remembering man in the ark is a vision of the Father remembering the Son on the cross and likewise remembering the faithful in the Son. The Father remembering the Son is the Father accepting the life of Jesus Christ as a perfect fulfillment of the law (Matt 5:17) and as a corresponding sanctification of the world, that is, all creation (1 John 2:2).

Since God in divine triunity is omniscient, the transcendent significance of God forgetting is not literal in the human sense but rather relates to God putting a thing outside the fullness of his presence, or outside the fullness of the experience of his presence.[39] The thing that God puts outside the fullness of his presence is sin and likewise sinful man (Exod 33:20). This is both fallen man in the wooden ark and also Christ embodying sin on the wooden cross (Gal 3:13). In contrast, the immanent significance of God forgetting is quite literal in the

---

[39] God is also omnipresent, and thus our being outside the fullness of the presence of God relates, not to the glory of God, but to our degraded perception and experience of the glory of God, our not yet being glorified by God, in God, and through God.

human sense and relates to God putting off the mantle of power in the incarnation in the flesh of man (Phil 2:6–8). The condescension of Christ includes humbly putting off omniscience in the Spirit—or putting on forgetfulness and likewise forsakenness—and therein the convergence of the spiritual and natural aspects of divine forgetfulness is manifest in the redemption of the chosen people (Mark 13:32). Jesus Christ is true God and true man—yes fully divine but also literally human, without mingling or contradiction of the two natures. The Lord God putting sin outside the fullness of his presence in the call to repentance in the present world is a prophecy of the Lord purifying us of our sins, that is, forgetting our sins in our redemption that will mark the next world (Jer 31:31–34).[40]

Genesis 8:3–6 And the waters returned from off the earth continually: and after the end of the hundred and fifty days the waters were abated. 4 And the ark rested in the seventh month, on the seventeenth day of the month, upon the mountains of Ararat. 5 And the waters decreased continually until the tenth month: in the tenth [month], on the first [day] of the month, were the tops of the mountains seen. 6 And it came to pass at the end of forty days, that Noah opened the window of the ark which he had made:

The Flood beginning in the midst of the second month of the year echoes the Flood coming in the midst of the second millennium from Adam (Gen 7:11). The one hundred and fifty days, or five months, of the abating of the floodwaters points to the death and resurrection of Jesus Christ marking the fifth millennium from Adam. The ark finally resting upon Ararat in the seventh month points to the rest and peace of the seventh, or Sabbath, millennium from Adam being heralded by the final tribulation period. The resting of the seventh month being affirmed by the tenth month and reaffirmed by forty days reflects the law being subsumed by grace.

Genesis 8:7–11 And he sent forth a raven [H6158], which went forth to and fro, until the waters were dried up from off the earth. 8 Also he sent forth a dove [H3123] from him, to see if the waters were abated [H7043] from off the face of the ground; 9 But the dove [H3123] found no rest for the sole of her foot, and she returned unto him into the ark, for the waters [were] on the face of the whole earth: then he put forth his hand, and took her, and pulled her in unto him into the ark. 10 And he stayed yet other seven days; and again he sent forth the dove [H3123] out of the ark; 11 And the dove [H3123] came in to him in the evening; and, lo, in her

---

[40] Gen 6:9–9:19 shows a chiastic literary construction with God remembering Noah in 8:1 as the pivot (Waltke 125). God remembering Noah in the wooden ark connects the antediluvian and postdiluvian worlds just as the Father remembering the Son on the wooden cross, the tree of the cross, connects this life and the next.

mouth [H6310] [was] an olive [H2132] leaf [H5929] pluckt off: so Noah knew that the waters were abated [H7043] from off the earth.

The word *raven* [H6158] (raven sent forth) has an association "to become evening" and "to grow dark" [H6150], implying a contrast between the darkness and light represented by the raven and dove. The raven never returning to Noah is an image of apostasy, while the dove returning immediately is an image of faithfulness. Correspondingly, the dove is a clean bird while the raven is unclean, as prescribed by the Levitical code (Lev 1:14, 11:15). The image of the raven going to and fro is a vision of vain searching, groping in the darkness, while the raven waiting until the waters recede portends the persistence of sin after the Flood. The ark carries both clean and unclean animals just as the individual continues to sin after the baptism in water just as sin would continue in the world even after the crucifixion. The persistence of sin does portend the second destruction (by fire) in fulfillment of the first destruction (by water), but the natural body foreshadows the spiritual, or glorified, body just as the baptism in water foreshadows the baptism of the Holy Spirit just as the First Advent of Christ foreshadows the Second Advent.[41]

The word *dove* [H3123] (dove sent forth) is probably related to the word "wine" [H3196], foreshadowing our atonement through the blood of Jesus Christ.[42] In any case, the raven is the first bird sent forth and is an image of Adam, the first son in creation, while the dove is the second bird and is an image of Jesus Christ, the second Son of creation. Christ is, of course, the only begotten Son of God (John 1:18), but Adam and Christ are still figuratively the first and second sons of God in the sense that they are the first and second men as spoken of by Paul (1 Cor 15:47). The raven found no rest, flying to and fro, just as Adam did not endure in the garden. The raven, according to its own nature, preferred to stay separated from the ark just as Adam, of his own freewill, chose to disobey God and, thereby, chose to leave the garden of God. The dove replaces the raven in the search for deliverance just as Christ replaces Adam, while the first and second flights of the dove specifically prefigure the First and Second Advents of Christ. The first flight of the dove finds no rest just as Christ would be rejected upon the First Advent, but the second flight of the dove brings back a sign of life to Noah just as Christ will present living souls to the Father upon the Second Advent. The dove is the harbinger of a renewed creation, while Christ is the embodiment of our new creation. The dove also connects the baptism in the floodwaters to the baptism in water since the Holy

---

[41] "Some make this creature [the raven] to be an emblem of the law, first sent forth, but brought no good tidings . . . rather it is an emblem of unregenerate men, who are, like it, black through original sin and actual transgressions; are unclean and polluted . . . ." (Gill 1:47; Gen 8:7). Natural man and the law that governs natural man reflect the same reality on different levels, namely, the undeniable justice of God.

[42] Cognate relationship per *Strong's*, not *Brown-Driver-Briggs*, but the image of atonement marking the story of the dove is clear regardless of exact etymology.

NOAH

Spirit would descend in the form of a dove upon the baptism of Jesus in the Jordan River (Matt 3:16).[43]

The word *leaf* [H5929] (olive leaf) is derived from the root "to go up, ascend, climb" [H5927], while the word *olive* [H2132] has connotations of "beauty" and "fresh (thriving)," which are all images of glorification. Noah, the revealed father of mankind, sends forth the dove just as the Father sends forth the Son. The dove, olive leaf in mouth, is a revelation of life after the Flood just as Jesus Christ would be revealed as the embodiment of new life after the crucifixion of the natural body. The word *mouth* [H6310] (mouth of the dove) has a connotation "devouring sword," whereby the dove, with olive leaf in mouth, specifically represents the sword proceeding from the mouth of Christ, the Word of God that establishes the new creation (Rev 1:16). The word *abated* [H7043] (waters abated) has connotations "to be trifling (of little account)" and also "to be cursed." Water is a symbol of flesh and likewise the law that governs flesh. The floodwaters are cursed in the sense that they would never again be allowed to rise just as we live only one life in the natural body. Christ would likewise die only once just as the present world will pass away once and for all.[44]

Genesis 8:12 And he stayed yet other seven days; and sent forth the dove; which returned not again unto him any more.

The third and final flight of the dove, in never returning again to the ark, represents our eternity in Christ following the millennial kingdom of Christ. The dove not returning to Noah should not be understood as prefiguring a separation of the faithful from the Father in eternity. The dove does not return to Noah on the ark, but rather Noah exits the ark and joins the dove in the renewal of creation. Our new creation in Christ is, not our ascension to God, but rather the humble condescension of God to man. The faithful will be perfected but not of ourselves, rather only in Christ. The preservation of Adamkind in the ark recalls our original creation in the garden, whereby the dove not returning to the ark affirms that our promised new creation is not simply a return to the garden of Eden, likewise not simply a perfection of the natural body. The Body of Christ is something new. If the garden had embodied the fullness of the promise of God—that is, the fullness of the presence of God—

---

[43] "The dove is an emblem of a gracious soul, which finding no rest in this world, returns to Christ as to its Ark; . . ." (Henry 1:58; Gen 8:6–12). The Body of Christ.

[44] "The water [of the Deluge], then, is that in which the flesh is dipped, that all carnal sin may be washed away. All wickedness is there buried. The wood [of the ark] is that on which the Lord Jesus was fastened when He suffered for us. The dove is that in the form of which the Holy Spirit descended, as you have read in the New Testament, Who inspires in you peace of soul and tranquility of mind. The raven is the figure of sin, which goes forth and does not return, if, in you, too, inwardly and outwardly righteousness be preserved [Ambrose, *On the Mysteries*]" (Schaff and Wace, *Nicene and Post-Nicene Fathers: Second Series* 10:318). All signs and symbols working together, telling the one story of our salvation, is a testimony to the providence of God, working all things together for good to the faithful, Rom 8:28.

then the original blasphemy of man could never be forgiven (Heb 6:4–6). Only the Body of Christ embodies the fullness of the promise of God. The Flood of Noah prefigures the Passion of Christ, whereby the dove not returning to the wooden ark also affirms that Jesus Christ would die only once on the wooden cross. Jesus Christ is not continually nailed to the cross just as the faithful in Christ are not continually nailed to the cross, but rather together once and for all and never again (Heb 9:24–28). God the Father not literally but truly forgets our sins in our redemption from our sinful nature through God the Holy Spirit in God the Son (Heb 8:12).[45]

Genesis 8:13–14 And it came to pass in the six hundredth and first year, in the first [month], the first [day] of the month, the waters were dried up from off the earth: and Noah removed the covering of the ark, and looked, and, behold, the face of the ground was dry. 14 And in the second month, on the seven and twentieth day of the month, was the earth dried.

The year of the Flood—counted from the second month of Noah's six hundredth year to the second month of Noah's six hundredth and first year—corresponds to the completion of an annual cycle of seasons and, thereby, represents a new creation, or abstractly a new day, reinforcing the image of new creation and new dawn innate in the Flood (Gen 7:11, 8:14). The year of the Flood points to the Day of the Lord (2 Pet 3:10).

Covenant

Genesis 8:15–19 And God spake unto Noah, saying, 16 Go forth of the ark, thou, and thy wife, and thy sons, and thy sons' wives with thee. 17 Bring forth with thee every living thing that [is] with thee, of all flesh, [both] of fowl, and of cattle, and of every creeping thing that creepeth upon the earth; that they may breed abundantly in the earth, and be fruitful, and multiply upon the earth. 18 And Noah went forth, and his sons, and his wife, and his sons' wives with him: 19 Every beast, every creeping thing, and every fowl, [and] whatsoever creepeth upon the earth, after their kinds, went forth out of the ark.

The seed of life proceeding from the side of the ark (Gen 6:16) recalls Eve proceeding from the side of Adam (Gen 2:21) and foreshadows water and blood proceeding from the side of the crucified Jesus Christ (John 19:34). Noah and his family proceeding from the ark, likewise Eve and the progeny embodied

---

[45] "This [dove] some take to be an emblem of the Gospel, bringing the good tidings of peace, pardon, righteousness, and salvation by Jesus Christ: rather it is an emblem of a sensible sinner, and true believer in Christ, being mournful, timorous . . . mourn for their iniquities; tremble at the sight of their sins, and the curses of the law . . . ." (Gill 1:47; Gen 8:8). The Gospel is the call to repentance, wherein the Gospel call and the response of repentant man reflect the same reality on different levels, namely, the unmerited mercy of God.

by Eve proceeding from the side of Adam, represents the promise of life. The symbols of water and blood represent flesh and spirit and likewise law and grace, whereby the implied intermingling of water and blood on the cross is a vision of the perfect union of flesh and spirit in the Body of Christ, the fulfillment of the promise of life. Noah and his family entered the ark hierarchically—Noah and his sons followed by their wives—reflecting the presence and progression of the Father, Son, and Spirit in the call of man to repentance. But Noah and his family exit the ark by pairs—Noah and his wife followed by his sons and their wives—prefiguring the redemption of man in the resolution of justice and mercy on the cross.[46]

The prophecy that Noah would be fruitful and multiply recalls the prophecy that Adam would be fruitful and multiply, while both prefigure a multitude being reborn in Christ (Gen 1:28). Noah exiting the ark recalls Adam being exiled from the garden, while both foreshadow the death and resurrection of Jesus Christ. Noah being preserved after the Flood recalls Adam being preserved after the Fall of Man, while both prefigure our eternal redemption coming through the Passion of Christ. The garden and the ark are both manifestations of the promise of life that proceeds from God, while the cross is the deposit on that promised inheritance of life in the Body of Christ, a life from God and through God and in God. Sin would persist after the Flood just as sin persisted after the original condemnation just as sin now persists even after the First Advent, but our transitory preservation in the natural Adamic body prefigures our eternal redemption and perfection in the spiritual, or glorified, resurrection body in the Body of Christ.[47]

Genesis 8:20–21 And Noah builded an altar [H4196] unto the LORD [H3068]; and took of every clean beast, and of every clean fowl, and offered [H5927] burnt offerings [H5930] on the altar. 21 And the LORD [H3068] smelled [H7306] a sweet [H5207] savour [H7381]; and the LORD [H3068] said in his heart, I will not again curse the ground any more for man's sake; for the imagination of man's heart [is] evil from his youth; neither will I again smite any more every thing living, as I have done.

---

[46] "A suggestive word was made use of by the evangelist, in not saying pierced, or wounded His side, or anything else, but 'opened;' that thereby, in a sense, the gate of life might be thrown open.... This was announced beforehand, when Noah was commanded to make a door in the side of the ark ... Because of this, the first woman was formed from the side of the man when asleep ... Truly it pointed to a great good ... This second Adam bowed His head and fell asleep on the cross, that a spouse might be formed for Him from that which flowed from the sleeper's side [Augustine, *Tractates on the Gospel of John*]" (Schaff, *Nicene and Post-Nicene Fathers: First Series* 7:434–35). The theme of salvation imprinted upon history is the triune image of God, redeeming the faithful unto the Father in the Son by the power of the Holy Spirit.

[47] "The same hand that at first brought them [the animals] to *Adam* to be named, now brought them to *Noah* to be preserved" (Wesley 1:34; Gen 7:7). The dominion of Adam preserved in Jesus Christ.

ADAM, NOAH, ABRAHAM

The Lord [H3068] vowing after the Flood to never again curse the ground is a prophecy that Christ would die only once, likewise that the faithful in Christ would die only once. Only the faithless will suffer the second death (Rev 21:8).[48] The word *altar* [H4196] (built by Noah) is derived from the root "to slaughter for sacrifice" [H2076], which prefigures the sacrifice of Christ on the cross.[49] The imperfect sacrifice of clean animals is a prophecy fulfilled in the perfect sacrifice of the sinless Christ. The sacrificial offering of Noah being closely linked with the Flood points to the sacrificial offering of Jesus Christ as the death and resurrection of all creation, that is, the sanctification of creation in Christ. The word *burnt* [H5930] (burnt offerings) evokes an image of "that which goes up to heaven" and is derived from the root word *offered* [H5927], meaning "to go up, ascend, climb," literally referring to the smoke and savor rising from the altar sacrifice but spiritually prefiguring the resurrection and ascension of Jesus Christ.

The implied equality between the sweet savor rising from Noah's sacrifice and the vow of God to never again curse the ground is an affirmation of our redemption in the resurrection and ascension of Jesus Christ. The words *smelled* [H7306] and *savour* (savor) [H7381] (Lord smelled a sweet savour) are related to the word *Spirit* (Ruwach) [H7307] (Spirit of God), which is a connection that reflects the testimony of the Holy Spirit concerning the sacrifice of the cross. The faithful looking to the sacrifice of Christ and ultimately participating in the sacrifice of Christ is the visible manifestation of the invisible faith that itself is the seal of the Holy Spirit. The baptism in water prefigures the baptism of the Spirit just as the breath of life prefigures the fullness of the indwelling Spirit. The word *sweet* [H5207] (sweet savour) means "quieting, soothing" and is derived from the root "to rest" [H5117], which recalls the rest in the garden and foreshadows our promised peace in the kingdom.[50]

The pronouncement that man's heart is evil from his youth is a prophecy that sin would continue after the Flood and, further, that the condemnation of original sin in the natural body is binding from and in the very youth of creation. But the universal apostasy established by the serpent was ended in the floodwaters. A people will be set aside for the Lord. The overt temptation of Adam is now succeeded by a covert temptation of mankind through the desires of the flesh, the evil of our own hearts. The narrative of the serpent explicitly tempting Adam in the garden is succeeded by the narrative of satan invisibly encouraging the suffering of Job (Job 1:12, 2:6). Our explicit tempter has

---

[48] "The word for God here is not *Elohim* but *Jehovah* (Yahweh), as frequently used in connection with God's covenant actions and in exhibitions of his grace" (Coffman 129; Gen 8:20–22). The personal name of God relates the grace that exists only in God and that comes only by a personal relationship with God.

[49] H4196 is coded incorrectly as H4096 on page 258 of *Brown-Driver-Briggs*, per *Green's Interlinear* and also *Strong's*.

[50] "My faith, Lord, calls upon you. It is your gift to me. You breathed it into me by the humanity of your Son, by the ministry of your preacher" (Augustine, *Confessions* 3). Not mere predestination, but an authentic freewill decision in accordance with the humble condescension of the Lord God in the flesh.

become our implicit accuser, wherein our duplicity has become complicity. The restriction of the dominion of the serpent to the desires of the flesh reflects the corruption of flesh and a corresponding internalization of the spirit of disobedience in the flesh, an internalization reflected, for example, in the dramatically decreased life spans after the Flood. The physical serpent not having entered the ark is also implied by his omission from the account, further affirming the personal degradation of the serpent that parallels the end of the formal bloodline of Cain.[51]

The degradation of the serpent from a manifest tempter to a hidden accuser at the time of the Flood parallels the victory of Christ over the dominion of death, over the dominion of the devil, at the time of the First Advent. The folding of the Biblical timeline implied by the comparison of the Flood and the First Advent testifies to the life of Christ being a recapitulation of creation. The life of Christ is a recapitulation of both natural history and human history because the life of Christ is a sanctification of all levels of life, our uttermost redemption (Heb 7:25). The death and resurrection of Christ is truly the death and resurrection of all creation. An overt sinfulness exists before the baptism in water, as implied by the act of repentance, just as an overt dominion of the serpent was manifest in the universal apostasy before the advent of the floodwaters. But the same sinful nature, though suppressed, still persists after the baptism in water just as the dominion of the serpent, though internalized, would persist after the floodwaters subsided. Sin would continue even after the incarnation, but the First Advent points to the Second Advent just as the baptism in water points to the baptism of the Spirit. The true baptism of the faithful is ultimately the participation in the perfect baptism of Christ.[52]

Genesis 8:22 While the earth remaineth, seedtime and harvest, and cold and heat, and summer and winter, and day and night shall not cease [H7673].

The word *cease* [H7673] (day and night shall not cease) has connotations "to rest, desist from labour" and "to keep, observe (Sabbath)," which recalls the original seventh day in the garden of Eden and foreshadows the promised peace of the seventh millennium in the kingdom of God.[53] Each pair, night and day,

---

[51] "That the constitution of man was then much altered appears in the greatly contracted lives of the postdiluvians; . . ." (Clarke 1:79; Gen 9:3). The Flood of Noah parallels the death and resurrection of Christ, while the degradation of life spans after the Flood parallels the persecution of the church after the First Advent.

[52] "If the works of the Logos' Godhead had not been done by means of the body, humanity would not have been divinized [sanctified]. Furthermore, if the properties of the flesh had not been reckoned to the Logos, humanity would not have been completely liberated from them [Athanasius, *Orations Against the Arians*]" (Norris 91). We must be made perfect in order to enter into the fullness of the presence of God, not of ourselves but rather only in Christ.

[53] "You fool [angels proclaim]! do you not know that this world [the hereafter] is like a Sabbath and the world from which you have come [this life] like a Sabbath-eve?

and so forth, is a contrast between death and rebirth, between curse and blessing, between law and grace, and between flesh and spirit. Every sunrise is a prophecy of our resurrection. The harvest of crops foreshadows the harvest of humanity. The pairwise images of day and night, also summer and winter, specifically identify life with the light of God, while death is identified with the darkness that exists in separation from God. The implication that day and night will not remain forever and likewise that the earth will not remain forever is a prophecy of the end of the natural body and likewise the end of the present creation. The way of all flesh, all the earth, and likewise the law that governs flesh will continue as long as the earth remains. Sin continued after the Flood and even after the First Advent. Mankind continues to live and die and to do good and evil, but the earth will not endure forever just as flesh will not live forever. Flesh and dust are brothers and will finally perish together in the end times, but mortality foreshadows immortality just as this world foreshadows the next. Creation foreshadows new creation just as birth foreshadows rebirth.[54]

Genesis 9:1–2 And God blessed [H1288] Noah and his sons, and said unto them, Be fruitful, and multiply, and replenish the earth. 2 And the fear of you and the dread of you shall be upon every beast of the earth, and upon every fowl of the air, upon all that moveth [upon] the earth, and upon all the fishes of the sea; into your hand are they delivered.

The word *blessed* [H1288] (God blessed Noah) is used in the Scriptures to denote both God *blessing* [H1288] man (Num 23:20) and also man *cursing* [H1288] God (Job 2:9), an ambiguity that reflects our freewill and ironically affirms our continued dominion after the Flood. The dominion of our freewill is our inheritance from God that is our original creation in the image of God, prefiguring our rebirth in the Body of Christ. The inviolable freewill of man points to the unassailable dominion of Jesus Christ just as the promise of life points to the fulfillment of the promise. The promised unity of the Holy Spirit in the Body of Christ is not in any way an annihilation of personal freewill. The existence of suffering and death in the world is a graphic testimony that God will never violate our freewill, even the choice to separate ourselves from life. The freewill of the faithful continues after death and resurrection just as the dominion of man would continue after the death and resurrection of the world in the floodwaters and even after the death and resurrection of Jesus Christ in the place of the faithful. Finally, however, the freewill of the faithless, in stark contrast with the faithful, is annihilated in the fullness of the slavery to sin. The faithful in Christ choose the good and reject the bad, but the faithless from Adam cannot choose the good, because they are quite literally addicted to the

---

[*Midrash Rabbah*]" (Cohen, *Rabbinic Sages* 109). Yes, the seventh day, but also the eighth day, representing eternity.

[54] The pronouncement of temperature extremes implies some fundamental change in the habitat of the earth that in turn seems related to the hugely decreased life spans as compared with antediluvian mankind (Guzik 74; Gen 8:21–22). Such a dramatic change in the physical world implies an equally dramatic change in the spiritual world.

bad. The bad is not something of itself but rather a corruption of the good just as faithlessness is a corruption of faithfulness. Freewill, by its nature, can corrupt itself, but a corrupted freewill of itself has no means to purify itself, no means apart from grace.

The blessing of Noah to be fruitful and multiply recalls the blessing of Adam to be fruitful and multiply, while both point to the promised redemption of the faithful in Christ. A blessing is not, however, strictly a commandment but also a prophecy. The representation of God as commanding is not only an affirmation of the undeniable, or relentless, will of God but also of the perfect foreknowledge of God. The blessing to be fruitful and multiply, for example, does not mean that God has commanded indiscriminate overpopulation. Likewise, our foretold blessing in the Son that would come by his suffering was not a commandment to carry out the crucifixion but rather an explanation of the crucifixion. The blessing of fruitfulness literally foretells our burgeoning world populations but finally points to the multiplication of the faithful in Jesus Christ. Our increasing populations, even with increasing suffering, prefigures the increasing numbers of faithful called to Christ just as the promise of life embodied by Adam, despite our fall, prefigures the fulfillment of the promise of life in Jesus Christ. The new life revealed in our reproduction is sacred just as freewill is sacred, but overpopulation is a sign of the end times just as the universal corruption of freewill is a sign of the end times. The suffering caused by overpopulation reflects the suffering of the faithful. The bad prefiguring the good is not surprising. The bad necessarily always prefigures the good since everything in this life has been corrupted. The finite likewise always foreshadows the infinite since everything in this life is but a blurred image of the heavenly. Even the First Advent pointing to the Second Advent is the bad pointing to the good in the sense that the crucifixion represents the ultimate blasphemy against God.

The fear and dread of man falling upon all creatures after the Flood is a progressively negative image compared with man simply having dominion over lower creatures before the Flood, or at least before the Fall of Man (Gen 1:28). The increasing enmity between human flesh and animal flesh is an image of conflicted flesh foretelling the self-annihilation of flesh that proceeds from our sinful nature, the evil imagination of man's heart. The emphasis on fear and dread is part of the postdiluvian narrative, exemplified by the suffering of Job (Job 3:25) and lamented in the vanity of flesh (Eccl 12:13). The fear and dread of man falling upon all creatures finally portends the fear and dread of the man of sin falling upon all flesh (2 Thess 2:3). But fear precedes love just as law precedes grace just as this world precedes the next. The image of fear is always connected with the natural body, while the image of love is always connected with the spiritual, or glorified, body. The beginning of wisdom is fear (Ps 111:10), but the end of wisdom is love (1 John 4:16).[55]

---

[55] The new covenant with Noah appears to indicate a radical shift in the interaction between man and beast (Coffman 134; Gen 9:1–3). And likewise for all levels of reality,

Genesis 9:3–4 Every moving thing that liveth shall be meat for you; even as the green herb have I given you all things. 4 But flesh with the life thereof, [which is] the blood thereof, shall ye not eat.

The directive to eat the flesh of animals reflects the ceremonial animal sacrifice prescribed by the formal law, but all spilling of blood is ultimately a prophecy of the crucifixion. Christ would affirm that we must eat his flesh and drink his blood (John 6:53). Flesh and blood represent, respectively, death and life, likewise the natural and the spiritual, and likewise law and grace. The formal law condemns flesh to death but also testifies that the life is in the blood (Deut 12:23). The directive to eat the flesh of Christ is the call to submission under the curse of Adam in which man is called to live in the flesh and to die in the flesh, that is, man is called to repentance in the flesh. In contrast, the directive to drink the blood of Christ is a vision of our redemption by the blood of Christ, which is our redemption by grace through faith in Christ, specifically the life of Christ that is the life in Christ. Eating the flesh of Christ is the baptism in water, in the flesh, while drinking the blood of Christ is the baptism of fire, of the Holy Spirit. To eat flesh and drink blood is the death of the natural body and the resurrection of the spiritual, or glorified, body, whereby Christ commands us to first eat his flesh and second drink his blood just as the natural body precedes the spiritual body just as this world precedes the next just as the baptism in water precedes the baptism of the Holy Spirit. The admonition to not literally drink the blood of animals represents the delay of the resurrection of the dead until the last days, a promise sealed by the blood of Christ but not yet revealed (Acts 15:20).[56]

The green herbs originally given to Adam for food foreshadow the animal meat given to Noah just as the formation of Adam from the dust prefigures the incarnation of Jesus Christ in the flesh (Gen 1:29). The contrast between green herbs and animal meat is a vision of the relationship between the Covenants of Law and Grace. Green herbs grow in the ground just as Adam was formed from the dust of the ground, while animals are symbolic of the breath of life that proceeds from God just as Christ would come from heaven (1 Cor 15:47). Animals are a higher order of life than plants (animals consume plants) just as the Covenant of Grace is greater than the Covenant of Law (grace subsumes law). The life in Christ is likewise a higher order, actually the highest order, compared with the life of Adam. The threefold image of green herbs followed by the flesh and blood of animals reflects, respectively, the first man Adam followed by the First and Second Advents of Christ. Eating the flesh of animals prefigures eating the flesh of Christ, an act embodied by the First Advent, while the prohibition against literally drinking the blood of animals prefigures the

---

including a new relationship between man and the environment, also a new relationship between the daughters of men and the sons of God.

[56] "The world Noah entered from the ark was significantly different from the world he knew before. . . . [P]resumably before the flood, man had a completely different relationship with the animals" (Guzik 75; Gen 9:1–4). Likewise, a completely different relationship between God and man.

delay between the First and Second Advents. The faithful will not truly drink the blood of Christ, also expressed as being washed in the blood of Christ, until the resurrection in Christ (Rev 1:5). The distinction in the law between clean and unclean foods also testifies to the distinction between Adam and Christ, but the final commandment to not distinguish between clean and unclean foods is a vision of the redemption of Adam through Christ (Acts 10:13–15).[57]

Genesis 9:5–6 And surely your blood [H1818] of your lives [H5315] will I require; at the hand of every beast will I require it, and at the hand of man; at the hand of every man's brother will I require the life of man. 6 Whoso sheddeth [H8210] man's blood [H1818], by man shall his blood [H1818] be shed [H8210]: for in the image of God [H430] made he man.

The name *God* (Elohim) [H430] (image of God) evokes an image of "rulers" and "judges," which emphasizes justice in contrast to mercy. The prophecy that blood would be required for blood is a corresponding image of judgment. The seed of life is preserved after the Flood just as the seed of life had been preserved after the Fall of Man, but a progressive revelation of judgment is nevertheless evident just as an increase of sinfulness is evident. Sin had increased from the first disobedience to the first murder to a universal depravity that heralded the floodwaters. Now the formal law would be added, ultimately through and by Moses, but with the law our offense is actually magnified (Rom 5:20). The condemnation of man increases after the Flood with the addition of the formal law just as personal sinfulness is more disgraceful after the baptism in water just as faithlessness is unforgivable after the Passion of Jesus Christ—specifically after the baptism, or coming, of the Holy Spirit. The progressive condemnation of man points to a final judgment just as the incomplete destruction by water portends an utter destruction by fire. But the firstfruits of the grave also point to the harvest of mankind. Where sin abounded, grace did much more abound (Rom 5:20). The vision of man avenging the blood of man is, not a commandment to capital punishment, but rather a prophecy of the capital punishment of Jesus Christ under the law and finally the persecution of all flesh by the man of sin.[58]

The word *blood* [H1818] (man's blood) is synonymous with "life," whereby spilled blood implies a silence of the flesh, a silence in the flesh, specifically the silence concomitant with our separation from God (Ps 13:1). The word *sheddeth*, *shed* [H8210] (man's blood) means "to pour out," which is the fundamental image of the sacrificial altar, the pouring out of blood (Deut 12:27), while the

---

[57] "The blessings given to Noah are an unqualified reaffirmation of the original blessings in Gen 1. The only change in the original order is God's permitting the people to kill animals for food, a change introduced for the sake of human weakness rather than divine improvidence" (Clifford, *New Jerome* 15; Gen 6:9–9:29). The freedom of man to choose his diet is an affirmation of the freewill of man.

[58] Gen 8:20–9:17 shows a chiastic literary construction with 9:2–6 as the pivot (Waltke 127). The pivotal image of legislating blood in the time of Noah and the Flood points to the crucifixion of Christ under the law as the pivot of all history.

word *lives* [H5315] (blood of your lives) evokes an image "that which breathes," which recalls the original breath of life endued by God, the breath embodied by God (Acts 17:25). The emphasis on blood in the law points to the centrality of the death and resurrection of Jesus Christ, while the connection of blood and life represents our inheritance in life that comes only through the blood of Christ. The necessary reckoning of all life is a prophecy of the cross as the necessary recompense for all life, whereby the reckoning of life is finally our new genesis in the Body of Christ. The given reason for the requirement of the reckoning of all life is that man is the image of God—which recalls man originally made in the image of God, expressly Elohim in contrast to YHWH, reflecting justice in contrast to mercy. The death and resurrection of the perfect image of God embodied by Jesus Christ therefore represents the perfect reckoning of life, that is, the perfect fulfillment of the law (Col 1:15). The call to pick up our own cross and follow Christ is an affirmation of a corresponding condemnation of the natural body in the same prophecy that all blood will be reckoned (Mark 8:34).

Genesis 9:7 And you, be ye fruitful, and multiply; bring forth abundantly in the earth, and multiply therein.

The expansion of world populations is a prophecy of the multiplication of the faithful in the one Body of Christ. The fruitfulness in the earth prefigures a fruitfulness in the promised new heaven and new earth.

Genesis 9:8–10 And God spake unto Noah, and to his sons with him, saying, 9 And I, behold, I establish [H6965] my covenant [H1285] with you, and with your seed after you; 10 And with every living creature that [is] with you, of the fowl, of the cattle, and of every beast of the earth with you; from all that go out of the ark, to every beast of the earth.

The word *covenant* [H1285] (covenant of God) means "pact, compact" but has a connotation "alliance of friendship (between God and man)," reflecting the promise of God as the embodiment of the love of God. A covenant is a relationship between man and God established by God and through God and in God for the sake of man. The differences between men are great and myriad, but there is only one mankind and only one natural body, likewise only one fundamental covenant that governs the natural body and the original creation in which the natural body exists. The formal covenants established with Adam and Noah and Abraham and Moses and David are all the same covenant, the Covenant of Law. The law has also always been a prophecy of grace, but only in Jesus Christ is the law fulfilled and the ultimate grace revealed.

The essence of law is the punishment of sin and the reward of righteousness, but eternal salvation is not afforded since no mere man from Adam can keep the law, that is, no man can embody a perfection of the law except Christ (Gal 3:3). A man can almost keep the law in his body but never in his heart, a reality reflected in the emphasis of the law on the physical in contrast to the spiritual.

The natural body and the law embody the same finiteness of the original creation, but the finite goodness unattainable through the law points to the infinity of God Almighty. The law leads us to grace just as mortal life leads us to eternal life (Gal 3:24). The dichotomy of punishment and reward in the law is a vision, respectively, of the death of the natural body and the resurrection of the spiritual, or glorified, body.

God affirming a covenant relationship not only with mankind but also with the animal kingdom implies a kinship between man and animal. The relatively neutral kinship between man and earth, emphasized in our original formation from the dust, is now supplanted by an animalistic carnality, reflecting an internalization of the dominion of the serpent. The progressive degradation of the natural body reflects a shift in emphasis from our sinful acts to our sinful nature that is paralleled in the shift from law to grace. But where sin abounded, grace did much more abound (Rom 5:20). The image of both man and beast saved together in the ark is a prophecy that all creation is ultimately redeemed in Jesus Christ, while the implication that the covenant of God covers only those who come out of the wooden ark is a vision of our salvation coming only by faith in the wooden cross. The relationship between man and animal reflecting both our condemnation and our redemption testifies to the fundamental duality of death and resurrection.

The word *establish* [H6965] (establish my covenant) has a connotation "to arise, stand up" in the Hebrew, which foreshadows the resurrection in fulfillment of the covenant of God, that is, the fulfillment of law in grace. The strong emphasis after the Flood on possessing the promised land represents a call to return to an innocent, or blameless, existence—specifically a return to a covenantal relationship in the land, symbolically a covenantal relationship with the land, or creation, ultimately representing a relationship with the Creator. This covenant is the baptism in water heralding our new life. The land, the dust of the ground, represents the flesh that was taken from the dust, whereby the call to the land, to a covenant in the land, represents the call to repentance in the flesh. Our new life is a reflection of the image of God ultimately revealed in Christ. The faithful will possess the land just as the faithful will be resurrected in a true body, but only through faith and not by works. The progression from the garden of Eden to the promised land to the kingdom of God reflects the threefold call to faith, repentance in the natural body, and redemption in the spiritual, or glorified, body, whereby the kingdom is not simply a return to the garden but rather a fulfillment of the garden just as the spiritual body is not merely a purification of the natural body but rather something new.

Genesis 9:11–13 And I will establish my covenant with you; neither shall all flesh be cut off any more by the waters of a flood; neither shall there any more be a flood to destroy the earth. 12 And God said, This [is] the token [H226] of the covenant which I make between me and you and every living creature that [is] with you, for perpetual generations: 13 I do set my bow [H7198] in the cloud [H6051], and it shall be for a token of a covenant between me and the earth.

ADAM, NOAH, ABRAHAM

The word *bow* [H7198] (bow of God) means "rainbow" in similitude of an "archer's bow," having connotations of "hunting" and "battle." Images of hunting and killing reflect an utter condemnation of the natural body without hope of mercy. The inherent distance between an archer and his target, reflected in the distance between rainbows in the sky and mankind in the earth below, testifies to the separation between God and man. The Fall of Adam and the Flood of Noah both foreshadow the death of Christ in the First Advent, but the preservation of flesh after the Fall and again after the Flood foreshadows the preservation of flesh after the First Advent. The preservation after the Fall of Man is our preservation in sin, or in the natural; the preservation after the Flood is our preservation in repentance; and our eternal preservation, or redemption, sealed by the First Advent is our preservation by grace through faith. Our threefold preservation reflects the threefold Creator (of a creation lower than himself), Redeemer (in death and resurrection), and Sanctifier (received only through faith). God the Father, God the Son, and God the Holy Spirit.[59]

The word *token* [H226] (token of the covenant) is the same word used to describe the *mark* [H226] placed upon Cain (Gen 4:15). The sinful world would be preserved just as sinful Cain had been preserved. The token of the rainbow is a mark of life that represents the preservation of flesh, but the promise of the flesh is not immortality in the natural body. The bow of God also foreshadows judgment just as the destruction in the floodwaters foreshadows the death of all flesh. Obedience to the law is likewise connected with both long life in the flesh and also the condemnation of the flesh (Deut 11:26). The cross is likewise our hope of life and also our call to imitate Christ in death (Rom 8:2). The revelation of the token of the rainbow is an affirmation that spiritual meaning is reflected in the natural world, while the emphasis on God establishing his covenant with the earth is an affirmation of the redemption of all creation in Christ. The image of God establishing his covenant for perpetual generations reflects the promise of eternal life.[60]

The word *cloud* [H6051] (bow set in the cloud) has an association in the Hebrew "to practice soothsaying (sorcery)" [H6049], which portends a prevalence of the occult in the end times. Clouds literally represent a coming storm and figuratively represent the coming judgment of sin, whereby the bow of God is not only a symbol of the restraint of judgment (by force) but ironically also portends a final judgment (by force). The promise that the world would never again be destroyed by water is not a promise that the world would never again be destroyed but rather portends a final destruction that will come

---

[59] "The Orthodox Church believes that God the Father is the 'Creator of Heaven and earth and of all things visible and invisible' " (Hopko, *Orthodox Faith* 1:44); "God the Father created the world through the Son (Word) in the Holy Spirit" (Hopko, *Orthodox Faith* 1:143). The fatherhood of God the Father is naturally linked to the act of creation.
[60] ". . . 'A Gentile who occupies himself with the study of Torah is deserving of death' [*Sanhedrin*] . . . . 'When he [the Gentile proselyte] has immersed himself and ascended from the water he is an Israelite [to be accepted] in every respect' [*Jebamoth*]" (Cohen, *Rabbinic Sages* 63–65). The former is an ironic prophecy of the call to imitate Christ in death, while the latter foreshadows the one Body of Christ.

by fire in contrast to water. Water is a symbol of flesh and likewise the law that governs flesh and likewise the baptism of repentance in the flesh, whereby the emphasis that the final judgment will not come by water is a prophecy that Christ would die only once under the law just as the faithful in Christ would die only once in the natural body just as the world would be destroyed only once by water. The foretold destruction by fire will consume creation in fulfillment of the prophecy embodied by the destruction in the floodwaters just as the foretold lake of fire, or water of fire, will (eternally) consume all flesh in fulfillment of the prophecy embodied by the death in the baptismal waters. But the second death will have no dominion over the new creation of the faithful in Christ, for whom and in whom the foretold fire in fulfillment of water will be finally revealed as the baptism of the Spirit in fulfillment of the baptism of repentance (Rev 2:11).[61]

Genesis 9:14–17 And it shall come to pass, when I bring a cloud over the earth, that the bow shall be seen in the cloud: 15 And I will remember my covenant, which [is] between me and you and every living creature of all flesh; and the waters shall no more become a flood to destroy all flesh. 16 And the bow shall be in the cloud; and I will look upon it, that I may remember the everlasting covenant between God and every living creature of all flesh that [is] upon the earth. 17 And God said unto Noah, This [is] the token of the covenant, which I have established between me and all flesh that [is] upon the earth.

The natural relates the spiritual and, therein, testifies to the essential union of the natural and the spiritual.

Ω Ω Ω

The three primary events in the natural history of the earth are the original creation, the destruction in the floodwaters, and the foretold but not yet manifested new creation in the last days. This threefold progression represents birth, death, and rebirth. The three primary events in the natural history of man are our original creation in Adam through Christ, the sanctification of the flesh by the incarnation of Jesus Christ, and finally our foretold but not yet manifested resurrection in Christ in the last days. And this threefold progression also reflects birth, death, and rebirth. A comparison of the natural history of the earth with the natural history of man highlights the parallel between their respective threefold patterns. Adam is identified with creation. The First Advent is identified with the Flood. And the resurrection of the dead is identified with the renewal of physical creation. Adam is the embodiment of all creation as the

---

[61] "[T]he bow, seen upon the storm clouds of judgment [Gen 7:11], has been thought to speak of the cross where judgment, never to be repeated, has been visited upon the believer's sins [Gal 3:10–14, Heb 10:14–18]" (Scofield 17 n. b; Gen 9:13). The death and resurrection of the whole world in Jesus Christ.

physical father of all mankind. The condemnation of the Son is the condemnation of all creation. And the promised resurrection of all the dead is the rebirth of all creation, a new heaven and a new earth. The overarching birth, death, and rebirth—which demarcates the natural history of the earth, or physical creation as a whole in the macrocosm—reflects the transcendent threefold God the Father as our creator, God the Son as our redeemer, and finally the indwelling Holy Spirit as our sanctifier in the promised new creation. The more intimate birth, death, and rebirth embodied by Adam-kind in the microcosm also reflects the Father, Son, and Holy Spirit but is most closely related to the threefold progression of our birth in Adam recalling the original creation, the death with Christ revealed at the First Advent, and finally the promised resurrection in Christ to be fulfilled at the Second Advent.[62]

1	2	3
GOD THE FATHER	GOD THE SON	GOD THE HOLY SPIRIT
CREATION	FLOOD	NEW CREATION
ADAM	FIRST ADVENT	SECOND ADVENT

The parallel between the three events demarcating human creation and the three events demarcating the overall physical creation reflects the parallel between earth and heaven and likewise the parallel between the natural and the spiritual. The parallel between the earthly domain and the heavenly domain testifies that the Son of man is the man from heaven and likewise that the promise embodied by creation proceeds from heaven (1 Cor 15:47). The representation of the seven millennia of creation by three milestones represents a folding of the seven millennia of creation into three millennia. In this view, the fifth millennium is superimposed onto the second millennium, subsuming the intervening millennia. And the seventh millennium is superimposed onto the sixth millennium. The superimposition of the fifth millennium onto the second millennium is an identification of Passion of Christ with the Flood of Noah. The superimposition of the seventh millennium onto the sixth millennium is an identification of the foretold separation of the nations and the schism of the visible church (Matt 25:32). The folding of time in this fashion represents the sanctification of creation through recapitulation in Christ. The former things are subsumed by the First Advent, while the latter things are subsumed by the Second Advent. The First Advent is the fulfillment of the law, while the Second Advent is the fulfillment of grace. The number 7, enumerating the days of creation, is most closely connected with the original creation through Christ, while the number 3, enumerating the days of the interment of Christ, is most closely connected with our new creation in Christ. The three millennia of creation underlying the seven millennia represents the spiritual underlying the physical. The folding of seven into three represents the natural

---

[62] "Hence the Creed may be briefly comprised in these few words: 'I believe in God the Father, who created me; I believe in God the Son, who redeemed me; I believe in the Holy Spirit, who sanctifies me' " (Luther, *Large Catechism* 55). The Father of all creation, the Redeemer nailed to the cross, and the Holy Spirit who makes us holy.

body being superseded by the spiritual body and likewise the law being superseded by grace. The number 7 represents the fulfillment of the Old Testament, or Old Covenant, while the number 3 represents the fulfillment of the New Testament, or New Covenant. But the fulfillment of the New is simultaneously the fulfillment of the Old.[63]

The parallel between the First Advent and the Flood is unique in the threefold natural history of creation. For these two events alone are obviously and dramatically offset in time with respect to one another in the historical chronology. Thereby, it is the parallel between the Flood and the First Advent that most clearly implies a folding of the timeline. The folding implied by this asymmetry points to the incarnation of Jesus Christ being a recapitulation of all creation and, therein, a sanctification of all creation. For the death and resurrection of Christ is understood as the death and resurrection of all creation. The obvious nature of the offset between the Flood and First Advent is itself a reflection of the incarnation of Jesus Christ being the visible, or obvious, revelation of the very image of God. The life of Christ is finally and fully a recapitulation of all creation, but it is first of all a recapitulation of the call of the chosen people spanning this specific period between the Flood and the First Advent. Jesus Christ would be conceived of the Holy Spirit expressly as a Jew—representing the embodiment of the chosen people of God and, thereby, recalling the entire history of the Jews beginning with the call of father Abraham after the Flood. And the dramatically increased density of narration between the Flood and the First Advent is itself a reflection of the central importance of the incarnation of the Son.

The coming of the Son is finally the embodiment of the revelation of the fullness of the Trinity, wherein the folding of the sevenfold creation into the threefold creation testifies to the Trinity being the singular font of all creation. When Jesus Christ as the spiritual man is specifically compared to the transcendent three persons of the Trinity, then Adam as the natural man can be compared to the visible sign of the Trinity, namely, the formation of Adam followed by the First and Second Advents of Christ. The parallel between the threefold natural history of man and the overarching threefold natural history of the earth likewise reflects the parallel between the natural and the spiritual. The twofold parallel between the sevenfold creation and the threefold creation is a synergy embodied by the twofold natures of Christ, who is fully man and fully God. The sevenfold is the literal and therefore represents flesh, while the threefold is the spiritual, or sublime, representing spirit.

---

[63] The three millennia from the incarnation of Christ compared with the seven millennia from the creation of Adam can also be viewed as three millennia superseding seven millennia, but this perspective is not unique, in that the same fundamental sanctification through recapitulation is still comprehended.

ADAM, NOAH, ABRAHAM

1	2
THE NATURAL MAN ADAM	THE SPIRITUAL MAN CHRIST
SEVEN MILLENNIA OF THE ORIGINAL CREATION	THREE MILLENNIA OF THE NEW CREATION
THREEFOLD NATURAL HISTORY OF MAN	THREEFOLD NATURAL HISTORY OF THE EARTH
ADAM, FIRST ADVENT, SECOND ADVENT	FATHER, SON, HOLY SPIRIT

The parallel between the threefold natural history of the earth and the threefold natural history of man implies a folding of the seven millennia of creation into three millennia, representing our new creation in Christ, while the fundamental oneness underlying all creation reflects the promised sanctification of creation as a whole. It is, however, the chiastic pattern evident in the sevenfold creation that is most closely identified with the Son and most clearly shows the recapitulation of history in the person of Christ. The mirror image defining the chiastic pivot represents the redemption of man in Christ, specifically as a reverse image of the corruption of man through Adam (Rom 5:19). The 1-2-3-4-5-6-7 millennia of creation are marked, respectively, by Adam, Noah, Abraham, the revelation of the kingship, the death and resurrection of Christ, the schism of the visible church, and finally the foretold second coming of Christ. A chiastic structure A-B-C-D-C'-B'-A' is evident with the fourth millennium as the pivot. The call of the faithful in the third millennium, manifest in the call of Abraham from his native country, parallels the call of all the faithful to repentance from sin, as embodied by the First Advent of Christ in the fifth millennium. The Flood of Noah in the second millennium and, correspondingly, the schism of the church in the sixth millennium both represent death. Our original life through Adam in the first millennium and, correspondingly, our promised rebirth in Jesus Christ in the seventh millennium both represent divine acts of creation. The wooden ark of Noah heralds the call of the children of Abraham just as the wooden cross of Christ heralds the call of all the children of God. The fourth-millennium pivot then climactically marks the central importance of the kingdom, ultimately fulfilled in the conception of Jesus Christ.[64]

---

[64] Per Ussher's chronology, Adam was formed in 4004 BC (Ussher 17), Noah was born in 2948 BC (Ibid. 18), Abraham, or Abram, was born in 1996 BC (Ibid. 22), David was born in 1085 BC (Ibid. 58), and Jesus Christ was born in 5 BC (Ibid. 779); The East–West Schism of AD 1054, also called the Great Schism, which distinguished Eastern Orthodoxy and Roman Catholicism, was the first major rupture of the earthly church (*The World Book Encyclopedia*, 1967 ed., s.vv. "Christianity," "Eastern Orthodox Churches"). Key dates not aligning perfectly with the millennia of creation reflects the corruption of the image of God, the image of the creator, being the corruption of creation itself, while the aligning of the millennia still being manifest reflects the singular will of God being undeniable, or relentless, despite the manifold sins of Adam-kind. It is presumably also true that there are unknown events identified with each personage or corresponding watershed that are perfectly aligned with the changing millennia.

NOAH

1	2	3	4	5	6	7
				THE CALL OF THE FAITHFUL	DEATH	NEW CREATION
				∧	∧	∧
ADAM	NOAH	ABRAHAM	KINGDOM	HEAD	SCHISM	BODY
∨	∨	∨				
CREATION	DEATH	THE CALL OF THE FAITHFUL				

    When viewed as a whole, the natural history of the earth, together with the natural history of man, represents the totality of creation and, therein, God the Father as the Creator. The pattern is complex and shows nonuniform intervals in time but is analogous to the serial, or simple repeating, 1-2-3, 1-2-3 pattern also identified with God the Father, though the repeated 1-2-3 pattern is in parallel and not in series. The threefold creation testifies to the coming of the Son as the incarnation of God, the embodiment of the Trinity, but the oneness of the Son, reflecting the oneness of God, implies a further folding of the threefold creation into a singularity that, in turn, emphasizes the sanctification of creation as a whole. This ultimate folding is also implied in the parallel between the natural histories of man and earth, but it is most obvious in the chiastic structure of creation. Specifically, the folding of time into a singularity is represented by the pivot defining the chiastic structure of the seven-millennium timeline. The mirroring about the pivot points to the pivot as a representation of the whole, a culmination of everything around it, that in turn implies a telescoping of the entire chronology into the pivot.

    The chiastic structure is most closely identified with God the Son, wherein the singularity implied by the pivot reflects the oneness of the Son, embodying the oneness of Godhood. A singularity is another unique, or independent, example of a complex pattern showing a type of nonuniformity in time. A telescoping of the chiastic structure of the original seven days of creation is also practicable, similar to that of the seven millennia of creation, but such a reduction would most directly represent the totality of the act of creation as the one will of God, in contrast to the totality of the whole of creation being the one Body of Christ. Finally, the complex, nonuniform analogue of the chiastic pattern is not only the singularity represented by Christ and the Body of Christ but, ultimately, all individual believers throughout all time. Every individual believer points to the one man Jesus Christ just as every individual is a microcosm of all creation. This is the call to imitate Christ and the promise that the sanctity of the individual is inviolable in the Body of Christ.

ADAM, NOAH, ABRAHAM

CHAPTER THREE OUTLINE

Key Images

PRIME IMAGES		
Material	Abstract	Spiritual
Noah.	A new father of humanity.	Jesus Christ as a new Adam.
The wooden ark.	One salvation.	The wooden cross.
The Flood.	The destruction and renewal of the original creation.	The death and resurrection of Christ and likewise our death and resurrection in Christ.

TWOFOLD IMAGES		
Material	Abstract	Spiritual
Unclean and clean animals.	Unacceptable and acceptable. Flesh and spirit.	Adam and Christ.
Raven and dove.	First and second. Unclean and clean animals. Flesh and spirit.	Adam and Christ. First and Second Advents.
Green herbs and meat.	First and second. Lifelessness and life. Flesh and spirit.	The Covenants of Law and Grace.
Flesh and blood.	Allowed and forbidden food. Flesh and spirit.	The body and blood of Christ and likewise the First and Second Advents of Christ.

THREEFOLD IMAGES		
Material	Abstract	Spiritual
The flight of the raven, the first and second flights of the dove.	Separation, repentance linked with redemption.	Adam, First and Second Advents of Christ.
Green herbs, meat, blood.	Promise, death, life.	Adam, First and Second Advents of Christ.
Noah, sons, wives.	Father, son, progeny.	Father, Christ, Bride of Christ. Father, Christ, Body of Christ. Father, Son, and Holy Spirit.

Synopsis

PROMISE		
	Material	Spiritual
5:1–20	The book of the generations of Adam.	A prophecy of all creation moving inexorably unto the last days, when the redemption of the individual, the family, and the generations of man will be finally realized.
5:21–27	And Enoch walked with God, and he was not. For God took him.	God taking the one antediluvian man Enoch prefigures the resurrection and rapture of the one Body of Christ in the end times.
	And all the days of Methuselah were nine hundred sixty and nine years, and he died.	The long life of Methuselah, surpassing even Adam, prefigures a covenant with death being attempted in opposition to the life in Christ.
5:28–31	Noah is born.	Recalls the creation of Adam and also prefigures the incarnation of Jesus Christ.
	Noah will be our comfort from the curse.	Recalls our rest in the garden of Eden and also prefigures our peace in the kingdom of God.

NOAH

5:32		And Noah begat Shem, Ham, and Japheth.	The three sons of Noah, the new Adam, reflect the triunity of God and likewise the threefold totality of creation formed in the image of God.
	JUSTICE AND MERCY		
		Material	Spiritual
6:1–4		There were giants in the earth in those days and also afterward, when the sons of God came in unto the daughters of men and they bear children to them.	The unholy offspring of the sons of God would be seen even after the baptism in the floodwaters just as sin would continue in the world after the baptism of the cross.
6:5–6		The heart of man is continually evil.	The spirit of disobedience (Eph 2:2).
		It repented the Lord.	God himself is our repentance in the incarnation of Jesus Christ.
6:7–10		The Lord will destroy man and beast and creeping thing and the fowls of the air.	A vision of the end of the natural body that recalls the death of the first man Adam and also foreshadows the death of all creation in the end times.
		But Noah found grace in the eyes of the Lord.	The preservation of Noah and his family by the Lord prefigures the blessing of the Son, likewise the faithful in the Son, by the Father.
	THE ARK		
		Material	Spiritual
6:11–16		The Lord instructs Noah to build the ark.	The call of man to repentance and likewise the call of the faithful to Jesus Christ.
6:17–18		And, behold, I, even I, do bring a flood of waters upon the earth, to destroy all flesh wherein is the breath of life.	God taking full responsibility is God humbly condescending to allow the freewill of man in both the acts of creation and new creation.
6:19–7:3		The Lord instructs Noah to save both clean and unclean animals.	Sin will continue after the Flood, but the clean (Christ) will save the unclean (Adam).
7:4–6		And Noah was six hundred years old when the flood of waters was upon the earth.	The sixth and seventh millennia will be connected by the tribulation period.
	RENEWAL		
		Material	Spiritual
7:7–24		Noah is saved through the floodwaters.	The baptism in water representing the death of the natural body and the resurrection of the glorified body, which is ultimately embodied by the death and resurrection of Jesus Christ and likewise the faithful in the Body of Christ.
8:1–6		God remembers Noah in the ark.	The Father remembers the Son on the cross.
8:7–12		The raven and the dove.	A vision of Adam and Jesus Christ.
8:13–14		In the six hundredth and first year of Noah's life, the waters were dried up.	The year of the Flood points to the Day of the Lord (2 Pet 3:10).
	COVENANT		
		Material	Spiritual
8:15–19		Noah is called forth from (the side of) the ark.	Recalls Eve taken from the side of Adam (Gen 2:21) and foreshadows water and blood flowing from the side of Christ (John 19:34).
8:20–22		Noah offers burnt offerings.	Marks the end of the overt dominion of the serpent and prefigures the corresponding victory of Christ over death.
9:1–2		Noah blessed to be fruitful and multiply.	Recalls the blessing of Adam and foreshadows the blessing of the faithful in Jesus Christ.
9:3–4		Flesh given as food.	Foreshadows the flesh of Christ that we are commanded to eat (John 6:53).
		But blood is forbidden.	The fullness of the blood of Christ will not be revealed until the resurrection of the dead in the last days.

9:5–6	And surely your blood of your lives will I require.	A vision of the bloody cross as the necessary propitiation for sin.
9:7	And you, be ye fruitful and multiply and bring forth abundantly in the earth.	The fruitfulness in the earth prefigures a fruitfulness in the promised new creation.
9:8–13	Never again will floodwaters destroy the earth.	There is only one life in the natural body and likewise only one crucifixion of Jesus Christ (Heb 9:25–27).
9:14–17	And God said unto Noah: the bow in the cloud shall be the token of the covenant, which I have established between me and all flesh that is upon the earth.	The natural relates the spiritual and, therein, testifies to the essential union of the natural and the spiritual.

CHAPTER FOUR

Ham, Shem, Japheth

The prime images emphasized in the account of the dispersion of mankind after the Flood are the one language of mankind, the migration to the east, and the building of the tower of Babel. The original unity of language in the world reflects the universal corruption of creation after the Fall of Man (Matt 15:18) but ironically also foreshadows the promised unity of the Holy Spirit (Acts 2:6). The fall through the one man Adam likewise foreshadows the exaltation in the one man Jesus Christ (Rom 5:12). The migration of mankind to the east after the Flood recalls the exile of Adam from the east of Eden but also foreshadows the foretold glorious reappearing of the Son of man in the east (Matt 24:27). The city of Babel is a microcosm of a sinful world, but the cities of men foreshadow the city of God just as the natural body foreshadows the spiritual body. The striving to raise the tower of Babel recalls Adam coveting the tree of knowledge, while the confounding of the tower of Babel recalls the denial of the tree of life. The meaning of the tower of Babel shifts from the tree of knowledge to the tree of life just as the tree of knowledge points to the tree of life just as the Covenant of Law leads us to the Covenant of Grace.

The key twofold images emphasized in the account of the dispersion of postdiluvian mankind are the cursing and blessing of Noah's sons, also the first and second descents of the Lord to Babel. The curse of Ham reflects the condemnation of the natural body, while the blessing of Shem and likewise the blessing of Japheth with Shem reflect the promise of the spiritual, or glorified, body. The cursing and blessing of Noah's sons reflect the same dichotomy of death and life as manifested in the law and fulfilled in grace (Deut 11:26). The two descents of the Lord to Babel foreshadow the First and Second Advents of Christ. The first and second descents of the Lord to Babel, like the cursing and blessing of Noah's sons, reflect the first and second covenants, the Covenants of Law and Grace. The Lord descends to Babel the first time not to judge the city but to see the city, which is an image of the First Advent of Christ, coming not to judge humanity but to save humanity (John 12:47). The Lord descends to Babel a second time to confound language in an act of judgment, which is an image of the Second Advent heralding the judgment of the world (2 Tim 4:1).

The traditions of men, representing the perspective of the flesh, connect the First Advent of Christ most closely with salvation by grace, while the same traditions connect the Second Advent with the destruction of the world under the law. According to the Scriptures, however, the law is manifested on the cross in the First Advent while grace will not be fully manifested until the resurrection of the Body of Christ in the Second Advent.

The three emergent postdiluvian sons Ham, Shem, and Japheth recall the three antediluvian sons Cain, Abel, and Seth, while both sets of three sons reflect Adam and the First and Second Advents of Christ, also God the Father, God the Son, and God the Holy Spirit. The firstborn Cain, paralleled by Ham, both embody fallen man and, thereby, both recall the first man Adam. But they both also reflect God the Father, the first person of the Trinity, in that the first man Adam was originally formed in the image of God, with Adam's firstborn, Cain, being the foremost heir of that image. The death of Abel prefigures the death of Christ, while the blessing of Shem by Noah prefigures the blessing of the Son by the Father. The birth of Seth was a figurative resurrection of Abel, prefiguring the resurrection of the faithful in Christ by the power of the Holy Spirit in the last days, while the blessing of Japheth with Shem prefigures the blessing of the faithful in Christ according to the fullness of the indwelling Holy Spirit, also in the last days.

The Vineyard

Genesis 9:18–19 And the sons of Noah, that went forth of the ark, were Shem, and Ham, and Japheth: and Ham [is] the father of Canaan. 19 These [are] the three sons of Noah: and of them was the whole earth overspread [H5310].

The three sons Ham, Shem, and Japheth recall the three sons Cain, Abel, and Seth just as Noah recalls Adam just as the Flood recalls the Creation. The identification of the original creation with the one man Adam reflects the oneness of God. The identification of the renewal of creation with the one man Noah is an affirmation of the oneness of God. The repeating identification of three sons with the acts of creation and new creation reflects the threefold God the Father, God the Son, and God the Holy Spirit as being both the original font of life and also the fulfillment of the promise of new life. The word *overspread* [H5310] (Noah's sons overspread the whole earth) has a connotation "to dash to pieces," which does portend an utter corruption of all creation, but the preservation of mankind despite sin reflects the undeniable, or relentless, nature of the will of God for the welfare of humanity.

The common ordering of the names of the sons of Noah (Shem, Ham, Japheth) does not necessarily reflect the literal birth order, but Shem placed ahead of his brothers definitely reflects Jesus Christ superseding Adam. The ambiguity of the birth order of Noah's sons reflects the mystery of the ordering of Adam and Jesus, namely, that Adam is both created through Christ (John 1:3) and is simultaneously the physical progenitor of Christ (Luke 3:23–38). And

Christ himself points out the paradox of his lineage from David (Matt 22:43). The ambiguity of the birth order of Noah's sons also echoes the account of Abel and Seth supplanting the firstborn Cain. The brotherhood of Cain and Abel specifically reflects the intimate juxtaposition of our separation from God and our kinship with God, likewise our condemnation under the law in contrast to our exaltation by grace. The paradox of creation is the fundamental tension between flesh and spirit, likewise between law and grace—a tension that can only be resolved in the Body of Christ just as creation could only emerge through Christ in the first place.

Genesis 9:20 And Noah began [H2490] [to be] an husbandman [H376, H127], and he planted [H5193] a vineyard:

The occupation of Noah in the ground recalls the occupation of Adam in the ground just as the preservation of Noah after the Flood recalls the preservation of Adam after the Fall of Man. The rendering *husbandman* [H376, H127] (Noah began to be an husbandman) connotes "man as husband," which recalls the marriage between spirit and dust as related by the original formation of man from the dust of the ground (Gen 2:7). The imperfect union of flesh and spirit in the natural body prefigures the perfect union of flesh and spirit, likewise law and grace, in the Body of Christ just as the natural man Adam prefigures the spiritual man Jesus Christ.

The word *began* [H2490] (to be an husbandman) has associations "to pierce" [H2490] and also "to profane" [H2490], which portend the crucifixion of Christ (Lev 19:12). The word *began* [H2490] is also the same word used to describe antediluvian man originally *beginning* (profanely) [H2490] to call upon the name of the Lord at the time of the birth of Enos (Gen 4:26). The birth of Enos is an affirmation of the Messianic bloodline through Seth after the death of Abel that points to the incarnation of Christ, whereas antediluvian man profaning the name of the Lord at the time of the birth of Enos prefigures postdiluvian man defiling the person of Jesus Christ. Noah beginning to be a husbandman has an ironic undertone of beginning to profane the land, which finally points to the end times. The seemingly common and unspecific nature of the word *began* [H2490] reflects the universal apostasy of man. The relative subtlety of lexical connotations reflects intangible spiritual meaning underlying tangible literal meaning, also the spiritual body being dimly perceived in the natural body.[1]

The word *planted* [H5193] (planted a vineyard) means "to plant" with a connotation "to establish, usually people" and is the same word used to describe God *planting* the garden of Eden, representing creation and likewise covenant (Gen 2:8). The emphasis on the image of a vineyard points to Jesus Christ being a vine in which the faithful are the branches (John 15:1), while the

---

[1] The apologists of the second century—Aristides, Justin Martyr, Athenagoras, Tatian, and Theophilus of Antioch—emphasized the Father and the Son but simultaneously testified to the Father, Son, and Holy Spirit (Rusch 5). God the Holy Spirit is the most subtle person of the Trinity.

wine of the vineyard is the essential blood of Christ (Luke 22:20). The image of Noah planting a vineyard, closely connected with the destruction by water, finally points to the harvest of mankind in the last days, which is closely connected with the foretold destruction by fire (Matt 13:30).[2]

Genesis 9:21 And he drank [H8354] of the wine, and was drunken [H7943]; and he was uncovered [H1540] within his tent [H168].

The word *drank* [H8354] (drank wine) has connotations "to drink blood (of slaughter)" and also "of drinking cup of Yahweh's [Jehovah's] wrath," prefiguring Christ drinking the cup of wrath in his passion (John 18:11). The conflict between our horror at the cross and our hope in the cross is the fundamental tension between flesh and spirit, which is finally resolved in the death of the natural body heralding the rebirth in the spiritual, or glorified, body. The word *drunken* [H7943] (Noah was drunken) is derived from the root "to be or become drunk" [H7937], which has a connotation "of nations staggering helplessly under calamity," prefiguring the great and dreadful Day of the Lord (Mal 4:5). The horror and hope represented by the coming Day of the Lord is the same paradox of death and life. The suffering of Jesus Christ is imitated in the suffering of the faithful in Christ.

The nature of drunkenness is a type of unconsciousness representing death, whereby the drunkenness of Noah prefigures the suffering and death of the promised Messiah. Jesus Christ would be beaten figuratively into a stupor. Comparing the suffering of Christ to drunkenness is not blasphemy but rather reflects the essential paradox in the blessed Christ becoming accursed on the cross. The drunkenness of Noah prefigures Christ drinking the cup of wrath, also the harlot drunk on the blood of the saints, just as the humble condescension of Christ embodies, not only the exaltation of the spiritual body, but also the condemnation of the natural body (Rev 17:6). Jesus Christ would quite literally become a curse, all curses, on the tree of the cross. Any rejection of the essential condescension of Christ in the incarnation is a rejection of the redemption in Christ through the Holy Spirit (Gal 3:13).[3]

The word *tent* [H168] (uncovered within his tent) denotes simply a "dwelling, habitation" but connotes "tent of the testimony." The tabernacle (tent) is to the temple (house) as the natural body (perishable) is to the spiritual, or glorified, body (imperishable), whereby Noah being unconscious expressly within his tent reinforces the image of the death of the natural body. The nakedness of Noah

---

[2] "When Noah left the ark he planted a vineyard, drank thereof, and was drunken. Christ also, born in the flesh, planted the Church and suffered [Jerome, *Dialogue Against the Luciferians*]" (Schaff and Wace, *Nicene and Post-Nicene Fathers: Second Series* 6:331). The prophecy and the reality of the new Adam.

[3] ". . . Noah, foreshadowing the future reality, drank, not water, but wine, and thus showed forth our Lord's passion [Augustine, *On Christian Doctrine*]" (Schaff, *Nicene and Post-Nicene Fathers: First Series* 2:590). Noah actually came by floodwaters and by wine, or by water and by blood, just as Jesus Christ would be marked by a flow of blood and water on the cross, John 19:34.

also reinforces the image of death. Clothing recalls our original nakedness in the garden, whereby clothing is a symbol of sin, or shame, closely related to corrupted flesh. To be unclothed is literally the exposure of flesh and symbolically the exposure of sin, again pointing to the condemnation of the natural body. The nakedness of Adam and also the nakedness of Noah both prefigure the nakedness of Christ on the cross just as the curse incurred by Adam and affirmed by Noah prefigures Christ becoming a curse for the sake of Adam. Noah becoming unconscious is an image of the death of Christ, also the destruction of the harlot, and finally the destruction of the world, but the wine of Noah is also a symbol of blood and the life in the blood, which is ultimately received only in the spilled blood of Jesus Christ.[4]

The word *uncovered* [H1540] (Noah uncovered) means "to uncover" and "to remove" and has a connotation "to carry away into exile," recalling the original nakedness of Adam as a primordial sign of our sinful nature and the closely connected exile from the garden (Gen 3:11). Our exile from the garden is an exile from the presence of God, whereby our nakedness is not only a physical nakedness but also a spiritual nakedness. But the faithful are not called to return to a state of nakedness and immaturity just as the kingdom of God is not simply a return to the garden of Eden. If the kingdom were simply a return to the garden, the saints in heaven would be depicted as naked, in contrast to being clothed in white robes (Rev 6:11). On the contrary, it is the harlot who is depicted as naked in her final destruction, a shameful exposure reflecting the hopeless nakedness outside of grace (Rev 17:16). The disobedient man is stripped of his dominion, while the faithful man is clothed in righteousness.

The Flood in the time of Noah is a vision of the death and resurrection of Jesus Christ and likewise the death and resurrection of all creation in Christ, that is, the Body of Christ. The repetition of imagery from the First Creation and the Fall of Man in the subsequent but closely connected account of the Flood affirms that sin would continue in the world after the Flood just as sin had continued after the Fall of Man. But the progressive clarity of the redemption of man through suffering and death, represented by the advent of the floodwaters, points to a progressive sanctification of the faithful in Christ that will be finally fulfilled in the Body of Christ in the last days.

NAKEDNESS

Genesis 9:22–23 And Ham, the father of Canaan, saw the nakedness [H6172] of his father, and told his two brethren without. 23 And Shem and Japheth took a garment, and laid [it] upon both their shoulders, and

---

[4] "And when to the expression 'he [Noah] was naked' Scripture adds 'in his house,' it elegantly intimates that Jesus was to suffer the cross and death at the hands of His own household, His own kith and kin, the Jews" (Augustine, *City of God* 523). The nakedness of Adam is the nakedness of Noah is the nakedness of Jesus Christ is the nakedness of the Body of Christ.

went backward, and covered [H3680] the nakedness of their father; and their faces [were] backward, and they saw not their father's nakedness.

The one man Noah recalls the one man Adam and likewise the one humanity formed in the image of the one God, whereby Ham violating his father Noah reflects mankind corrupting the image of God. The word *nakedness* [H6172] (of his father) has connotations of "shameful exposure" and "shameful punishment," which recalls the physical and spiritual nakedness of Adam and also portends the nakedness of Christ on the cross for the sake of Adam. All corruptions of the image of God are ultimately visions of the scourging and crucifixion of Jesus Christ. Man is merely the image of God, while Jesus Christ is the invisible God made visible (Col 1:15).

The nakedness of Noah being exposed by Ham recalls the nakedness of Adam being exposed by the serpent, whereby Ham is identified with the same spirit of disobedience originally revealed in the garden and first affirmed in Cain. Adam personifies freewill as the father of both wicked Cain and righteous Abel, whereby Cain represents corrupted freewill (choosing the bad) while Abel represents uncorrupted freewill (choosing the good). Noah is likewise the father of both wicked and righteous sons. Cain and Ham are the spiritual offspring of sin, the serpent, and thereby they embody death. But Abel and Seth, also Shem and Japheth, embody the promise of life in Christ, in the Body of Christ. The progression from brother against brother in the time of Adam to son against father in the time of Noah reflects an increasing apostasy in the world that will be finally revealed in the end times.[5]

The word *covered* [H3680] (Shem covered his father) has a connotation "to cover transgressions," which points to the sins of mankind being hidden from God through the person of Jesus Christ (Jas 5:20). Shem covering his father is a vision of our reconciliation with the Father through the Son, while Japheth assisting Shem is a vision of the faithful in Christ being buried and resurrected with Christ (Rom 6:4). Shem covering the nakedness of Noah recalls God covering Adam (Gen 3:21), while both images foreshadow Christ clothing the faithful in righteousness (Rev 7:14). Shem and Japheth walking backward, not looking upon the nakedness of their father, is also an affirmation that man in the natural body cannot look upon God, relating both the normal frailty of man represented by Japheth and the surprising condescension of the Son represented by Shem (Exod 33:20). The fluid comparisons of Noah to both God the Son and God the Father reflect the unity of God the Holy Spirit, while the ambiguity between Christ and the faithful in Christ reflects the unity of the Body of Christ. The brotherhood of Japheth and Shem foreshadows the literal blessing of the Gentile nations through the one nation Israel but is ultimately a

---

[5] Many have supposed that Ham did more than just look upon the nakedness of Noah, a suspicion that seems confirmed by Gen 9:24 (Gill 1:54; Gen 9:22). This suspicion is related to the purposeful ambiguity of the account, pointing to a larger reality, namely, the humiliation of Jesus Christ on the cross.

prophecy of the essential brotherhood of the faithful, Jew and Gentile, in Christ and with Christ (Matt 12:50).

Curse and Blessing

Genesis 9:24–27 And Noah awoke from his wine, and knew what his younger son had done unto him. 25 And he said, Cursed [be] Canaan [H3667]; a servant of servants shall he be unto his brethren. 26 And he said, Blessed [be] the LORD God of Shem [H8035]; and Canaan [H3667] shall be his servant. 27 God shall enlarge Japheth [H3315], and he shall dwell in the tents of Shem [H8035]; and Canaan [H3667] shall be his servant.

The name *Shem* [H8035] literally means "name" [H8034], which recalls the emphasis on the name of Noah (Gen 5:29). Noah awakening foreshadows the resurrection of Jesus Christ, while Noah knowing what Ham had done reflects the divine omniscience of Christ revealed in his glorification. The blessing of Shem by Noah would ultimately be fulfilled in the Son receiving honor and glory from the Father (2 Pet 1:17). The true comfort from the curse of Adam foretold in the original blessing of Noah would likewise be embodied by Christ. The fluid comparisons of Noah to both the Father and the Son again reflect the unity of the Holy Spirit. The comparison of both the father Noah and the son Shem to the person of Christ testifies to Christ being the incarnation of God. The close connection of the blessing of the Lord with the blessing of Shem again points to the incarnation of God in the person of Jesus Christ. The focus on individual names foreshadows the singular name of Jesus given unto mankind for our salvation (Acts 4:12). The persistent placement of Shem's name ahead of his brothers' names in the Scriptures represents the second born usurping the birthright and blessing of the firstborn. The ubiquitous image of an older brother serving a younger brother is a prophecy of the second son Jesus Christ redeeming the first son Adam.[6]

The name *Ham* [H2526] literally means "warm, hot" [H2525], which recalls man originally cursed to eat bread in the sweat of his face, while the name *Canaan* [H3667] has a connotation "merchants" and is derived from the root "to be humble (humbled)" [H3665], which again reflects the curse and the consequent economy of suffering after the exile from the garden (Gen 3:19). The name *Canaan* [H3667] connoting "merchants" finally foreshadows the merchants identified with Babylon in the end times (Rev 18:11). The ambiguity around the names *Ham* and *Canaan* implied by their unexplained interchange portends the dark unity of the anti-trinity, represented by the dragon, beast, and

---

[6] The blessing of the Lord God of Shem is a prophecy of the Messianic bloodline coming through Shem, while the blessing of Japheth in Shem is a prophecy of Gentiles being brought into the church (Henry 1:63–64; Gen 9:24–27). The two blessing are one blessing just as Jesus Christ, though fully God and fully man, is one person just as the Body of Christ, though many, are united with Christ, the Head.

false prophet (Rev 16:13). The condemnation of Canaan by Noah finally points to the foretold destruction of Babylon in the end times (Rev 18:11), a region closely identified with the offspring of Ham (Gen 10:10). The foretold destruction in the end times is prefigured by the destruction of Sodom and Gomorrah (Luke 17:28), a region closely identified with the Canaanites (Gen 10:19) and also with the conflict between the Canaanites and the Israelites after the Exodus (Exod 23:23). Canaan being punished, at least figuratively, for the sin of Ham recalls our inheritance in original sin from Adam, but the law stipulating that a child shall not be punished for the sins of his father points to our promised redemption from original sin (2 Chr 25:4). The image of Canaan cursed to be a servant of servants represents an utter annihilation of freewill, the complete enslavement to sin, but the servitude of Canaan to Shem and Japheth, specifically to Japheth through Shem, also represents the hope of the natural body in the resurrection of the spiritual, or glorified, body.[7]

The name *Japheth* [H3315] is derived from the root "to be spacious, wide, open" [H6601], which foreshadows the vastness of the promised kingdom of God, the house with many mansions (John 14:2). The blessing of Japheth, emphasizing the enlargement of Japheth expressly in the tents of Shem, is a corresponding vision of the multitude of the faithful in Christ, in the Body of Christ. The image of Japheth living in the tents of Shem is also an affirmation that the blessing of the nations would proceed only through the one nation of Israel (Gen 22:18), whereby the genealogies of Japheth's descendents recorded in the Scriptures point to the Gentile nations that would receive the Gospel through Israel (Gen 10:5, Isa 49:1). But the blessing through the one nation of Israel is ultimately fulfilled in our redemption in the one man Jesus Christ. The curse of Ham embodies the condemnation of the natural body under the law, while the blessing of Shem and the blessing of Japheth through Shem embody the blessing of Christ and likewise the blessing of the faithful in Christ.[8]

The ordering Ham, Shem, and Japheth in their cursing and blessing by Noah is a spiritual ordering that recalls the ordering serpent, woman, and man in the original cursing in the garden. The implied comparison of Ham to the serpent reflects a spiritual lineage of Ham from the serpent through Cain. The comparison of Shem to Eve reflects the prophecy that Jesus Christ would appear as the Seed of woman in the virgin birth. The comparison of Japheth to Adam reflects the promised redemption of mankind in Christ represented by Japheth being blessed through Shem. Further, the spiritual ordering Ham, Shem, and Japheth in their cursing and blessing by Noah parallels the literal ordering Cain, Abel, and Seth as born of Adam. The implied equality between the spiritual ordering Ham, Shem, and Japheth and the literal ordering Cain,

---

[7] "And Ham (*i.e.*, hot) ... what does he signify but the tribe of heretics, hot with the spirit, not of patience, but of impatience, with which the breasts of heretics are wont to blaze, and with which they disturb the peace of the saints?" (Augustine, *City of God* 522). The spirit of anti-christ snaking its way through history.

[8] "Is it not also in the houses of Christ, that is, in the churches, that the 'enlargement' of the nations dwells? For *Japheth* means 'enlargement' " (Augustine, *City of God* 522). The Judeo–Christian expansion identified with the Roman West.

Abel, and Seth is a testimony to the simultaneous literal and spiritual reality of the fundamental ordering of Adam followed by the First and Second Advents of Christ. The literal ordering Cain, Abel, and Seth precedes the spiritual ordering Ham, Shem, and Japheth just as the natural body precedes the spiritual, or glorified, body.[9]

Genesis 9:28–29 And Noah lived after the flood three hundred and fifty years. 29 And all the days of Noah were nine hundred and fifty years: and he died.

Adam and also Noah as the new Adam both living very nearly but not exceeding one thousand years reflects the relationship between the days of the Lord as creator and the millennia of creation tracing the image of God (Gen 2:17, 5:5). The ark being lifted up in the midst of the natural life of the one man Noah foreshadows the cross being lifted up in the midst of natural creation as a whole. And the relationship between days and millennia, between individuals and creation, points to the fulfillment of all creation in the Day of the Lord, corresponding to the seventh, or Sabbath, day, or millennium, from Adam.

Three Sons

Genesis 10:1 Now these [are] the generations of the sons of Noah, Shem, Ham, and Japheth: and unto them were sons born after the flood.

The traditional rendering of Genesis 10:21 places Japheth as the oldest son, while, according to the context, Genesis 9:24 presumably refers to Canaan and not Ham as the youngest son, literally grandson. A birth order of Japheth, Ham, Shem is finally implied by the subsequent ordering of the genealogies of the descendants of the three sons. The order of the listing of clan genealogies is like the birth order of their respective patriarchs but on a different level of reality. In contrast, the ordering Ham, Shem, and Japheth according to their received cursing and blessing is a spiritual ordering reflecting the curse followed by our redemption from the curse. Ham occupying the prime position in this ordering places an emphasis on the curse that reflects the present world under the dominion of the devil. The common Scriptural ordering Shem, Ham, and Japheth is a spiritual ordering reflecting the preeminence of Shem. And Shem

---

[9] "[R]emember that it was so from the beginning, the devil always setting up error by the side of truth. . . . Cain and Abel . . . the sons of Seth and the daughters of men . . . Ham and Japhet [Ham and Japheth], Abraham and Pharaoh, Jacob and Esau . . . Moses and the magicians, the Prophets and the false prophets, the Apostles and the false apostles, Christ and Antichrist [Chrysostom, *Homilies on 2 Timothy*]" (Schaff, *Nicene and Post-Nicene Fathers: First Series* 13:504). Ye thought evil against me, but God meant it unto good, Gen 50:20.

occupying the prime position in this ordering places the emphasis on our redemption from the curse that is our new creation.[10]

The different orderings of the names of Noah's sons represents a timeline tracing the literal, or natural, to the spiritual, specifically the first man Adam being supplanted by the second man Jesus Christ. The ordering Japheth, Ham, Shem (birth order) being followed by the ordering Ham, Shem, Japheth (present accursed order in this world) reflects the original corruption of creation, while the final ordering Shem, Ham, Japheth (blessed new order) reflects the redemption of creation. The ordering by birth—Cain, Abel, Seth—reflects the same fallen world order as the ordering by cursing and blessing—Ham, Shem, Japheth—which is an identification of the direct offspring of Adam with the death that originally entered the world through the first sin (Rom 5:12). The varied ordering of the names of Noah's sons as compared with the static ordering of the names of Adam's sons reflects the increasing specificity that characterizes progressive revelation.

There being three different orderings of Noah's sons implies a threefold set of interpretations, but the ordering Ham, Shem, Japheth—parallel to the ordering Cain, Abel, Seth—is the most relatable and manifest since it is a reflection of the present fallen order of the world. Not how we should have been exalted in the garden, but how we will be exalted given the reality of our exile. The image of God is evident in the present order of the world despite our corruption just as the will of God for the sanctification of his children is undeniable, or relentless, despite our disobedience. The three postdiluvian sons Ham, Shem, and Japheth and also the three antediluvian sons Cain, Abel, and Seth directly reflect Adam and the First and Second Advents of Christ, while Adam and the First and Second Advents finally reflect the Father, Son, and Holy Spirit. Cain and Ham are both explicitly marked by sin and, thereby, represent embodiments of the original curse of Adam. The Fall of Man. The firstborn Cain murdering the second born Abel is a vision of the first man Adam spiritually murdering the second man Jesus Christ, while the blessing of Shem compared with the cursing of Ham is a vision of the second man Jesus Christ supplanting the first man Adam. The First Advent. The reassertion of the Messianic bloodline in Seth after the murder of Abel is finally a vision of the resurrection of the faithful in Christ, while the close identification of Japheth with Shem in the act of covering the nakedness of Noah is a vision of the faithful reborn in the Body of Christ. The Second Advent.

The history of creation encapsulated by Adam and the First and Second Advents of Christ reflects the one will of God in the threefold revelation of God the Father as creator, God the Son as redeemer, and God the Holy Spirit as sanctifier. The image of our Father, our creator, or spiritual progenitor, is

---

[10] Understanding Canaan and not Ham to be the younger son, or offspring, that defiled Noah is consistent with Ham always being named second in the listing of Noah's sons and also with the subsequent curse being pronounced upon Canaan and not Ham (Gill 1:54–55; Gen 9:24). The ambiguity of the Scriptures reflects the subtlety of the Holy Spirit moving providentially and yet at no time violating freewill.

reflected in the first man Adam created in the image of God and also in Adam's firstborn, Cain, even though the image had been profoundly corrupted in all Adam-kind. The Son, our redeemer in death and resurrection, is reflected in the death of righteous Abel followed by the exaltation of righteous Shem. The Holy Spirit, our sanctifier in our promised new creation, is reflected in the figurative resurrection of Abel, embodied by Seth but finally fulfilled, or completed, in the totality of new life represented by the progeny of Shem. The blessing of Japheth in Shem is a further vision of the promised fullness of the Holy Spirit animating and indwelling the Body of Christ. The will of the Trinity is singular just as creation, redemption, and sanctification are all acts of the one same creation. The acts of redemption and sanctification follow the original creation just as the Son and the Spirit proceed from the Father.[11]

Genesis 10:2–5 The sons of Japheth; Gomer, and Magog, and Madai, and Javan, and Tubal, and Meshech, and Tiras. 3 And the sons of Gomer; Ashkenaz, and Riphath, and Togarmah. 4 And the sons of Javan; Elishah, and Tarshish, Kittim, and Dodanim. 5 By these were the isles of the Gentiles [H1471] divided in their lands; every one after his tongue, after their families, in their nations.

Listing the physical descendants of Japheth first, before those of his brothers, reflects Japheth as the physical firstborn son of Noah. The name *Gentiles* [H1471] (isles of the Gentiles) ultimately points to the western nations to which Christianity would migrate and, thereby, identifies Japheth expressly with the Gentile nations to which Israel would be a light of salvation (Isa 49:6). The nations would be blessed through Israel just as Japheth would be blessed through Shem.[12]

Genesis 10:6–20 And the sons of Ham; Cush, and Mizraim, and Phut, and Canaan. 7 And the sons of Cush; Seba, and Havilah, and Sabtah, and Raamah, and Sabtecha: and the sons of Raamah; Sheba, and Dedan. 8 And Cush begat Nimrod: he began to be a mighty one in the earth. 9 He was a mighty hunter before the Lord: wherefore it is said, Even as Nimrod the mighty hunter before the Lord. 10 And the beginning of his kingdom was Babel [H894], and Erech, and Accad, and Calneh, in the land of Shinar. 11 Out of that land went forth Asshur, and builded Nineveh, and the city Rehoboth, and Calah, 12 And Resen between Nineveh and Calah: the same [is] a great city. 13 And Mizraim begat

---

[11] Augustine compares the Trinity to three aspects of the individual, or self: being, knowing, and willing (Augustine, *Confessions* 279–80). Augustine's ordering implies a concurrent comparison of the Father, Son, and Spirit to the three respective aspects of creation (procreative being), redemption (knowing the Son), and sanctification (the indwelling Holy Spirit relating the will of God).

[12] The geographic area peopled by the descendants of Japheth is primarily to the north and west of Canaan (Sarna 68; Gen 10:1–32). A prefiguring of the Judeo–Christian expansion.

ADAM, NOAH, ABRAHAM

Ludim, and Anamim, and Lehabim, and Naphtuhim, 14 And Pathrusim, and Casluhim, (out of whom came Philistim,) and Caphtorim. 15 And Canaan begat Sidon his firstborn, and Heth, 16 And the Jebusite, and the Amorite, and the Girgasite, 17 And the Hivite, and the Arkite, and the Sinite, 18 And the Arvadite, and the Zemarite, and the Hamathite: and afterward were the families of the Canaanites [H3669] spread abroad. 19 And the border of the Canaanites [H3669] was from Sidon, as thou comest to Gerar, unto Gaza; as thou goest, unto Sodom [H5467], and Gomorrah [H6017], and Admah, and Zeboim, even unto Lasha. 20 These [are] the sons of Ham, after their families, after their tongues, in their countries, [and] in their nations.

Listing the physical descendants of Ham second reflects Ham as the physical second born son of Noah. The genealogy of Ham's offspring is larger than the corresponding records of Japheth and Shem combined, which portends a prevalence of apostasy in the end times.[13] Ham is identified with the evil *Canaanites* [H3669] and also with evil *Babel* (Babylon) [H894], which is an identification of Ham with death and destruction.[14] The highlighting of *Sodom* [H5467] and *Gomorrah* [H6017] in the genealogy of Ham's offspring specifically points to the foretold destruction by fire (Luke 17:28). The identification of the offspring of Ham with hunting is an identification with the shedding of blood. That animal blood signifies human blood is clearly established in the fulfillment of the sacrificial law in the crucifixion of Jesus Christ. The image of Nimrod being a mighty hunter before the Lord is not an image of Nimrod's majesty but rather his arrogance.[15]

Genesis 10:21–31 Unto Shem also, the father of all the children of Eber, the brother of Japheth the elder, even to him were [children] born. 22 The children of Shem; Elam, and Asshur, and Arphaxad, and Lud, and Aram. 23 And the children of Aram; Uz, and Hul, and Gether, and Mash. 24 And Arphaxad begat Salah; and Salah begat Eber. 25 And unto Eber were born two sons: the name of one [was] Peleg; for in his days was the earth divided; and his brother's name [was] Joktan. 26 And Joktan begat Almodad, and Sheleph, and Hazarmaveth, and Jerah, 27 And Hadoram, and Uzal, and Diklah, 28 And Obal, and Abimael, and Sheba, 29 And

---

[13] The geographic area peopled by the descendants of Ham, compared with Shem and Japheth, is by far the most extensive and includes the great river civilizations of the Nile and the Euphrates (Sarna 68; Gen 10:1–32). Wide is the gate and broad is the way that leadeth to destruction, Matt 7:13.

[14] "[T]here are uniquely no sevens in the structuring of the Canaanite genealogy. The representation of the Canaanites in the Table of Nations [Gen 10] stands apart by its asymmetry to match their chaos" (Waltke 165). The number 7 signifies creation and life and completeness, whereby its absence signifies death and annihilation.

[15] "[T]he godless cities Nimrod builds, Babylon and Nineveh, are the cities that eventually bring the northern and southern kingdoms of Israel to their knees" (Waltke 175). The shared origin of Babylon and Assyria points to a single anti-spirit.

Ophir, and Havilah, and Jobab: all these [were] the sons of Joktan. 30 And their dwelling was from Mesha, as thou goest unto Sephar a mount of the east [H6924]. 31 These [are] the sons of Shem, after their families, after their tongues, in their lands, after their nations.

Listing the physical descendants of Shem last, after even Ham, reflects Shem as the physical third born son of Noah. The brotherhood of Shem and Japheth is emphasized only in the genealogy of Shem's offspring just as the redemption of the faithful comes, not of ourselves, but rather only through a brotherhood with Jesus Christ. The division of the earth being connected with the genealogy of Shem portends the judgment of the earth in the end times that is connected with the Second Advent. The offspring of Shem are finally identified with the *east* [H6924] just as we look to the east for the glorious reappearing of Jesus Christ (Matt 24:27).

Genesis 10:32 These [are] the families of the sons of Noah, after their generations, in their nations: and by these were the nations divided in the earth after the flood.

The Table of Nations is set. The division of the nations between the three brothers Ham, Shem, and Japheth is literally the division of the earth but spiritually the division of all creation. This division signifies the separation of curse and blessing embodied by the separation of the children of the devil and the children of God. Japheth and Shem are divided just as man is exiled from God, but the foretold blessing of Japheth being in Shem despite their separation represents the promised redemption of the faithful being in accord with Christ in the Body of Christ despite our original rebellion.[16]

Oneness

Genesis 11:1 And the whole earth was of one language [H8193], and of one speech [H1697].

The word *language* [H8193] (one language) evokes an image of the body part "lip" in the Hebrew. The inherent connection between the tangible body and the intangible utterances of the body reflects the duality of flesh and spirit. The unity of language, after both the original creation and the renewal of creation in the floodwaters, also reflects the unity of flesh and spirit, the preordained unity of flesh and spirit. But the singular voice of mankind, both before and after the Flood, was raised in opposition to God. The inseparable reality of flesh and spirit had been corrupted together. The freewill choice between the bad and the

---

[16] The seventy souls belonging to Abraham in Egypt, Gen 46:27, parallel the seventy nations proceeding from Noah, Gen 10, which relates Israel as a microcosm of all the nations (Waltke 164, 175). The one and same image of God, the I AM, is evident on all the different layers of reality, or being.

good had been corrupted. In the corruption of freewill, the singular language of humanity, originally reflecting the one will of God, becomes an emblem of the singular heart of mankind, continually evil (Gen 6:5). The corruption of the unity of language in profaning the name of God would be manifested as a confounding of a singular language into many languages, spiritually a confusion representing the broad way that leads to destruction (Matt 7:13).[17]

The word *speech* [H1697] (one speech) means "speech, word," recalling the *Logos* (the Word) [G3056], ironically, given the context. This is the original creation by and through the *Logos* (John 1:3). The unity of speech after the Flood recalls the original unity of Adam and Eve, the twofold man and woman, created in the image of the one God (Gen 1:27). But the one speech raised in universal apostasy recalls the one serpent. The unity of the Holy Spirit implies one and only one anti-spirit, or anti-logos, because any other hypothetical spirit could not both agree and disagree with the Spirit of God. Any such hypothetical gray spirit, somewhere between harmony and conflict with the Holy Spirit, would represent some compromise with the Spirit of God. But there can be no fellowship between the light and the darkness and, therefore, no such gray spirit (2 Cor 6:14). The one anti-spirit is the spirit of disobedience, the spirit of lawlessness (Eph 2:2). The physical manifestations of the spirit of disobedience are innumerable, but the utterance of the one anti-spirit is always a singular rejection of God. The repeating image of the condemnation of apostate mankind is an affirmation of the irreconcilable nature of apostasy and likewise the absolute and essential separation of evil and good.[18]

Genesis 11:2 And it came to pass, as they journeyed [H5265] from the east [H6924], that they found a plain [H1237] in the land of Shinar [H8152]; and they dwelt there.

The word *east* [H6924] (journeyed eastward) has connotations of "beginning" and "ancient time" and also has an association "to come in front, meet" [H6923], recalling the presence of God in the primordial garden and specifically entrance to the garden of God in the east (Gen 3:24). Cain, representing apostate antediluvian mankind, journeying east of Eden to settle in Nod portends Ham, representing apostate postdiluvian mankind, journeying eastward to settle in Shinar, ultimately Babel in Shinar (Gen 4:16). The former journey after the murder of Abel, the latter after the violation of Noah. The journey of postdiluvian man eastward also echoes the exit from Noah's ark just

---

[17] The account of the city and tower of Babel, Gen 11:1–9, parallels the account of the sons of God taking the daughters of men, 6:1–4, within an overall alternating literary construction (Waltke 19–20). The primeval consummation of evil in an unholy union of flesh and spirit that is in manifest opposition to the law.

[18] "The history of Babel ('confusion') strikingly parallels that of the professing Church. (1) Unity [Gen 11:1]—the Apostolic Church [Acts 4:32–33]; (2) Ambition [Gen 11:4], using worldly, not spiritual, means [Gen 11:3], ending in a man-made unity—the papacy; (3) the confusion of tongues [Gen 11:7]—Protestantism, with its innumerable sects" (Scofield 18 n. 1; Gen 11:1). The garden, the cross, and the final judgment.

as the journey of antediluvian man eastward echoes the exile from the garden of God. The name *Nod* [H5113], literally meaning "wandering (of aimless fugitive)" [H5112], portends the name *Babel* [H894], synonymous with "confusion, confoundedness." Man wandering the land is an image of man searching the flesh, symbolically the dust of the ground, but man, of himself, finds only dens of confusion. The word *journeyed* [H5265] (journeyed eastward) means "to pull out, set out," not to arrive, which emphasizes man of his own freewill departing from the presence of God. Our self-determined separation from God is not some destination representing self-actualization but a sad departing representing self-annihilation. Nod at the time of Cain and also Shinar at the time of Ham both represent the cities of men in conflict with the city of God, but the detailed description of the apostasy of Babel compared with that of Nod typifies the increasing clarity of progressive revelation that finally points to the foretold Babylon of the end times (Rev 14:8).

The name *Shinar* [H8152] corresponds to "Babylonia," while the name *Babel* [H894] corresponds to "Babylon," which is specifically connected with the foretold destruction in the end times (Rev 18:21). The word *plain* [H1237] (plain in Shinar) is derived from the root "to cleave, break open or through" [H1234], which reflects the fundamental image of cutting a covenant (Gen 15:10) and finally prefigures the foretold splitting of the Mount of Olives at the Second Advent (Zech 14:4). The plain of Shinar is to the east of the altar of Noah just as the Mount of Olives is to the east of the temple. The connection of the east with both the final destruction and also the glorious reappearing of Christ reflects the fundamental dichotomy of death and life. The Flood recalls the Fall of Man but ultimately points to the First Advent and finally to the Second Advent. The progression from the Covenant of Law to the Covenant of Grace points to the fulfillment of all things in the Second Advent. The east is the place of the rising sun, representing our foretold rebirth, whereby the faithful look to the east for the reappearing of the Son of man (Matt 24:27).[19]

The Name

Genesis 11:3 And they said one to another, Go to, let us make brick [H3835], and burn [H8313] them throughly. And they had brick [H3843] for stone [H68], and slime [H2564] had they for morter [H2563].

The words *slime* [H2564] and *morter* (mortar) [H2563] (had slime for morter) are both derived from the root "to ferment, foam up (as water or wine)" [H2560], which has a connotation "of distress at calamities," foreshadowing the blood of Christ spilled in violence, as would be marked by both blood and water (John 19:34). The word *slime* [H2564] means "bitumen, asphalt," which recalls the *pitch* [H3724] used to seal Noah's ark, though distinct Hebrew words are used in each case (Gen 6:14). The former word *pitch* [H3724] (pitched the

---

[19] "Shinar is an ancient name for Babylon (Babel)" (Viviano, *Collegeville* 51; Gen 11:1–9). Many names, but only one reality.

ark with pitch) has a connotation "the price of a life, ransom," which foreshadows the life of Jesus Christ as a ransom for many. The ark of Noah was figuratively pitched with the blood of Christ and, thereby, represents a preservation through death by the blood of Christ. The Passion of Christ truly embodies the renewal of all creation, as prefigured by the Flood. Now man seeks his own redemption through the tower of Babel, figuratively with his own blood as signified by the employed pitch. But the differentiation between the words *slime* [H2564] (used to pitch Babel) and *pitch* [H3724] (used to pitch the ark) affirms the distinction between death and life, between curse and blessing, and between the way of man and the way of God.

The word *brick* [H3843] (brick for stone) is derived from the root "to be white" [H3835] (make brick), which has a connotation "to purify," while the word *burn* [H8313] (burn bricks) has a connotation "of burning red heifer (to produce ashes for purification)." The attempted purification and elevation by the tower recalls the attempted self-deification by the tree but, ironically, also prefigures the guaranteed sanctification by the cross. The tower of Babel is raised into the sky in a testimony to the sin of pride, likewise the curse of pride, just as Christ would be raised on the cross, spiritually the tree of knowledge, as the embodiment of sin, in which Christ would become a curse for the sake of us sinners (Gal 3:13). God himself in the person of Christ being falsely accused of the ultimate pride is the divine perspective, or reality, of lowly man attempting to elevate himself to the heavenly throne. The tree of knowledge stood as the primal representation of original sin at the opening of the antediluvian era just as the tower of Babel stands in affirmation of the apostasy of man at the opening of the postdiluvian era just as the cross would stand as the embodiment of the curse at the opening of the present era, our promised new creation and new song in the Body of Christ.

The word *stone* [H68] (brick for stone) is closely connected with building altars (Deut 27:6) and also sacred pillars (Gen 28:18) and heaps (Gen 31:46), whereby specifically using brick in the place of stone implies a counterfeit altar (Exod 20:25). The tower is an abstract altar that portends the crucifixion, but the faithlessness embodied by raising Babel is a reverse image of the faithfulness of Christ ascending the cross. Likewise, the fall through the one man Adam is a reverse image of our exaltation through the one man Jesus Christ. Death is a reverse image of resurrection. The counterfeit salvation represented by the tower portends a final counterfeit religion in the end times. The defilements represented by the tree of knowledge and the tower of Babel culminating in the defilement of the person of Christ on the cross even now points to a final abomination in the end times, a final desecration of the altar of God proceeding directly from the primordial serpent (Matt 24:15). The repeating pattern of faithlessness is itself an affirmation of the irrevocable condemnation of the natural body, while the increasing intensity of the Biblical narrative progressing from the disobedience of the one man Adam to the universal apostasy of all Adam-kind points to a final condemnation of all flesh. The account of the tower of Babel, however, represents not only the faithlessness of man but also

HAM, SHEM, JAPHETH

the faithfulness of God just as the cross represents both the curse of the natural body and also our promised blessing in the spiritual, or glorified, body.

Genesis 11:4 And they said, Go to, let us build [H1129] us a city [H5892] and a tower [H4026], whose top [H7218] [may reach] unto heaven [H8064]; and let us make us a name [H8034], lest we be scattered abroad upon the face [H6440] of the whole earth [H776].

The city of Babel in Shinar is identified with Ham in the genealogy through Nimrod (Gen 10:1–10), while the word *build* [H1129] (let us build a city) recalls the same word used to describe Cain *building* the city of Enoch in Nod (Gen 4:17). The building of Babel succeeded Ham defiling Noah just as the building of Enoch succeeded Cain murdering Abel. The defilement of Noah recalls the condemnation in the floodwaters, while the murder of Abel recalls the condemnation of Adam in death and exile. The word *build* [H1129] used to describe both Cain and Ham *building* [H1129] cities has a connotation "to be established, made permanent" and is also the same word used to describe God *making* [H1129] a woman from the rib (side) of Adam (Gen 2:22) and also Noah *building* [H1129] an altar (Gen 8:20). To build is to make some covenant. The image of man establishing himself in cities implies not only a new physical order but also a new spiritual order in some covenant. The covenant of Babel, however, proceeds not from the hand of God but rather from the hand of man. And the only covenant that can proceed from man is the covenant of death. This is a counterfeit of the covenant of life that proceeds from God and as such testifies that the condemnation of man is a self-condemnation. The covenant of death that proceeds from the flesh is the covenant of Cain and also of Ham, namely, the Covenant of Law.[20]

The word *city* [H5892] (let us build a city) has a connotation of "excitement (of terror)," portending the death of the prophets and ultimately the death of Jesus Christ in the city of Jerusalem (Luke 13:33). And this is finally the death of all flesh in the end times, marking the Body of Christ, and is closely linked with the destruction of the city of Babylon (Rev 16:19). Also, however, the word *city* [H5892] is derived from the root "to rouse oneself, awake" [H5782], foreshadowing the promised resurrection of the dead that is heralded by the death of the natural body (1 Cor 15:36). The faithless build cities as monuments to the flesh, but the faithful are nomadic, waiting for a future city of God (Heb 11:9–10). Nonetheless, the cities of men foreshadow the city of God just as the one man Adam foreshadows the one man Jesus Christ just as the natural body foreshadows the spiritual, or glorified, body just as the Covenant of Law foreshadows the Covenant of Grace.

---

[20] "The great city which Cain first built and called after his son must be taken to represent this world, which the devil, that accuser of his brethren, that fratricide who is doomed to perish, has built of vice, cemented with crime, and filled with iniquity [Jerome, *Paula and Eustochium to Marcella*]" (Schaff and Wace, *Nicene and Post-Nicene Fathers: Second Series* 6:63). The mortar of sin has built up the cities of men, but it is also what will cause them to finally crumble.

ADAM, NOAH, ABRAHAM

The word *tower* [H4026] (let us build a tower) has a connotation "elevated stage, pulpit (of wood)" and is derived from the root "to grow up, become great (be magnified)" [H1431]. The profane self-magnification of the men of Babel foreshadows, in reverse, the sacred glorification of the Son by the Father just as the fall through the one man Adam foreshadows our exaltation in the one man Jesus Christ (Rom 5:19). The word *heaven* [H8064] (build a tower unto heaven) literally means "sky" but has a spiritual connotation "abode of God," while the word *top* [H7218] (top unto heaven) has a connotation "chief (man)" and is the same word used to describe the *head* [H7218] identified with the serpent (Gen 3:15). The men of Babel seeking to elevate themselves to the abode of God represents an opposition to God, whereby the men of Babel raising the tower foreshadows mankind raising the cross. The account of Babel is a microcosm of the world just as every man is an Adam unto himself—that is, every man recapitulates the original disobedience of Adam as consummated in the murder of righteous Abel. Men seek to elevate themselves to the throne of God through the tower of Babel just as Adam had sought to become like a god through the tree of knowledge (Gen 3:5), but the tower of Babel will be denied just as the tree of life was denied (Gen 3:22–23). Only in Jesus Christ does the tree of knowledge become the tree of life, likewise the cross of suffering becomes the staff of life. The tree of knowledge becomes the tree of life just as the Covenant of Law leads us to the Covenant of Grace just as the death of the natural body heralds the rebirth in the spiritual, or glorified, body.[21]

The word *name* [H8034] (let us make us a name) corresponds to the name *Shem* [H8035], which evokes an image of the Messianic bloodline. The men of Babel do not, however, seek the name of the Lord, but rather they seek to substitute their own names for the one name of Jesus Christ. Only the one name of Jesus Christ is given for our salvation (Acts 4:12), whereby all the other names of men are figuratively forgotten in the absence of grace (Rev 20:15). The men of Babel would inevitably remain nameless, in stark contrast to the detailed genealogies of the line of Christ. Antediluvian man began to call upon, profane, the name of the Lord at the time of the birth of Enos, which was an affirmation of the murder of Abel that presaged the judgment in the floodwaters (Gen 4:26). Postdiluvian man now seeks to make a name for himself, which portends the rejection of the name of Jesus Christ and the corresponding embrace of the name of anti-christ (Rev 13:17). The progression from profaning the name of the Lord to elevating one's own name reflects the primordial psychology of the dragon, that old serpent, which is hopelessly imitated by his children.[22]

---

[21] The rebellion of the men of Babel represents man putting himself in the position of adoration and praise that is reserved for God and God alone (Coffman 160; Gen 11:4). The original sin of man is the pride of the serpent.

[22] "Before Christ's second coming the Church must pass through a final trial that will shake the faith of many believers. The persecution . . . will unveil . . . a religious deception offering men an apparent solution to their problems at the price of apostasy

HAM, SHEM, JAPHETH

The image of postdiluvian mankind scattered abroad upon the *face* [H6440] of the *earth* [H776] also reinforces the theme of names being forgotten outside of grace and specifically recalls the curse of Cain to be a fugitive and a vagabond (Gen 4:14). To wander hopelessly is to be a forgotten name. Mankind was dispersed after the Flood just as mankind was originally exiled after the Fall of Man, but our dispersion in this life foreshadows, in reverse, our foretold unity in the Body of Christ just as our fall through the one man Adam foreshadows our promised elevation in the one man Christ.[23]

SON OF MAN

Genesis 11:5 And the LORD [H3068] came down [H3381] to see [H7200] the city and the tower, which the children [H1121] of men [H120] builded.

The name *Lord* [H3068] (the Lord came down) is the proper name of God *Jehovah* (YHWH) and literally means "the Self-Existent." The emphasis on the proper name of God is an emphasis on the tangible reality of God that, particularly in context, foreshadows the person of Jesus Christ, the invisible God made visible (Col 1:15). The word *came down* [H3381] (the Lord came down) means "to come or go down, descend," which additionally foreshadows the incarnation of Jesus Christ, specifically as the man who would come from heaven (1 Cor 15:47). The Lord God is the God of Abraham, Isaac, and Jacob—that is, the God of the living and not the dead—of itself implying an eternal body and, thereby, the resurrection of the body, whereby the Lord himself must exist in spirit and flesh because God, the self-existent one, also lives eternally (Matt 22:32). To say, as most do, that God is life but does not literally live is a sophisticated, though fundamentally incoherent, way of saying that God is a dead thing.

The word *see* [H7200] (came down to see) has connotations "to discern" and "to distinguish" and "to consider," reflecting the passive, not coerced or compelled, call to repentance in the flesh that is embodied by the passive, not coerced or compelled, call to accept the incarnation of Christ in the flesh. This is an image specifically of the First Advent. The Son of man coming not to judge but to save mankind in the First Advent was a passive appearing (John 12:47), while the foretold coming of the Son of God to judge all mankind in the

---

... The supreme religious deception is that of the Antichrist, a pseudo-messianism by which man glorifies himself in place of God . . . ." (Rom. Catholic Church, *Catechism* 193–94). Not the church in isolation, but all creation, earth and heaven.

[23] "Their [the peoples of Babel's] pride-filled sin is threefold. [1] They disobey the divine command to fill the earth . . . [2] They also scheme . . . seeking their significance [name] independently from God . . . [3] [T]hey transgress the boundaries of heaven and earth . . . ." (Waltke 161). The first aspect recalls the dispersion from the garden, the second opposes the one name *Jesus* [G2424←H3091], "YHWH is salvation," and the third points to the last days. And the actual ordering of this threefold sin in Gen 11:4 being the reverse reinforces the image of Adam-kind rejecting, or reversing, the law of God.

Second Advent will be an active appearing (2 Tim 4:1). But the image of the *children* [H1121] of *men* [H120] building Babel is an emphasis on the flesh in contrast to spirit. The city and tower are built by the children of men in contrast to the children of God just as the condemnation of flesh is ultimately a self-condemnation proceeding from the hand of man and not from the hand of the Lord God. The faithless finally condemn themselves with their own mouths (2 Sam 1:16). The call to repentance precedes the call to redemption just as the baptism in water precedes the baptism of the Holy Spirit just as the First Advent of Christ precedes the Second Advent just as the natural body precedes the spiritual, or glorified, resurrection body.[24]

Genesis 11:6 And the LORD said, Behold, the people [H5971] [is] one [H259], and they have all one [H259] language; and this they begin [H2490] to do [H6213]: and now nothing [H3808, H3605] will be restrained [H1219] from them, which they have imagined to do [H6213].

The word *people* [H5971] (people is one) has a connotation "one's own people" and also an association "to darken, dim" [H6004], reflecting the inherited darkness of flesh in contrast to the unmerited light of the Spirit. The inherent separation of darkness and light is itself a prophecy of the inevitable separation between evil and good and likewise between the natural and the spiritual. The word *one* [H259] (one people, one language) reflects our unique human freewill created in the image of the one God. Uncorrupted freewill in contrast to corrupted freewill also reflects the fundamental separation between light and darkness. The utterances of the mouth are the overflow of the heart (Matt 15:18), whereby the emphasis on the language of man points to the intangible word as the intangible spirit of disobedience (Eph 2:2). The one language of the one people of Babel is, not the Word of God, but rather the word of man that is continually evil (Gen 6:5). The emphasis on the unity of language reflects the universal condemnation of flesh, while the emphasis expressly on the language of man reflects the curse as a self-condemnation proceeding ultimately from the flesh itself and not from the Spirit.[25]

The word *do* [H6213] (people begin to do) recalls the same word used to describe God *making* [H6213] the original creation, which is a contrast reflecting the hand of man attempting to displace the hand of God (Gen 1:31). The word *begin* [H2490] (people begin to build) has an association "to profane" [H2490], which recalls antediluvian man originally *beginning* (profanely) [H2490] to call upon the name of the Lord at the time of the birth of Enos (Gen 4:26). The birth of Enos represents a reassertion of the line of Christ that recalls the

---

[24] Gen 11:1–9 shows a simultaneous alternating and chiastic literary construction (Waltke 176). The alternating construction reflects the will of the Spirit supplanting the will of the flesh, while the chiastic pivot marking the descent of the Lord reflects the centrality of the cross.

[25] "[E]ven in the worst conditions, no person can be [demonically] Possessed [*sic*] without some degree of cooperation on his or her part" (Martin xx). The faithful in Christ are free indeed, whereas the faithless of the devil are slaves to sin.

original creation and also foreshadows our new creation in the Body of Christ. The account of the building of the city of Enoch is followed by the birth of Enos just as the account of the building of the city of Babel is followed by the call of Abraham. The offspring of Abraham, like the offspring of Seth, point to Jesus Christ, who would be faithful unto death, even the death of the cross, for the sake of a sinful world (Phil 2:8). The people of Babel exercise the dominion of freewill, the embodiment of our creation in the image of God, but the building of Babel is a corruption of freewill and likewise a corruption of the image of God that ultimately prefigures the defilement of the image of God on the cross and finally the defilement of the Body of Christ in the end times.[26]

The rendering *nothing* [H3808, H3605] (nothing restrained from man) overlaps with the word used to describe Abraham withholding *not* [H3808] his son Isaac from God, whereby the unrestrained imagination for evil of the people of Babel ironically portends the death of Christ for the sins of the world (Gen 22:12).[27] The tower of Babel recalls the tree of knowledge to which Christ would be spiritually nailed, while the denial of the tower of Babel recalls the denial of the tree of life in which the hope of the faithful would rest until the last days (Gen 3:22, Rev 2:7). The word *restrained* [H1219] (nothing restrained from man) has a connotation of "secrets, mysteries," reflecting both the restrained mystery of lawlessness (2 Thess 2:7) and also the hidden mystery of salvation in the Son of man (Eph 3:8–9). The nature of freewill allows the emergence of good and also evil, whereby the unrestraint of the people of Babel, or Adam-kind, prefigures both Christ and anti-christ (Rom 5:20). The people of Babel rising up and thereby proving both the desire and potential for a complete unrestraint, a reality explicitly affirmed in the text, is finally a prophecy of the Restrainer being removed. The image of the unrestrained potential of the men of Babel recalls men becoming like God, knowing good and evil, after eating from the tree of knowledge (Gen 3:22–23), and this image also presages the abomination of desolation standing in the holy place (Matt 24:15). The unrestrained potential of Babel—that is, the freewill of the people of Babel—foreshadows an explosion of technology in the end times for both good and bad (Dan 12:4). The apostate unity of Babel portends a modern globalism and ecumenism in opposition to the one true God. But the ultimate restraint of the people of Babel affirms the original preservation of mankind, despite the curse, until the appointed time of our redemption (Heb 9:27).[28]

---

[26] Some Rabbinical traditions link the tower of Babel with mankind seeking to wage war with God (*Jewish Encyclopedia*, s.v. "Babel, tower of"). Waging war against God is seeking to kill God.

[27] The Hebrew word *not* = H3808 in Gen 22:12 is listed in the appendix to *Strong's* with the Greek under 3808, 3756—i.e., H3808, G3756—and also in *Green's Interlinear* in parallel with the Hebrew text.

[28] The descendants of Cain are identified with the arts and sciences, Gen 4:17–24, while the descendants of Seth are identified with long and full lives, 5:1–32 (Waltke 113), whereby the postdiluvian manufacturers and builders of Babel are taken to be the spiritual heirs of Cain and not Seth (Waltke 177–78). A fullness and completeness of life being identified with the Messianic bloodline reflects an essential adherence unto God

ADAM, NOAH, ABRAHAM

Son of God

Genesis 11:7 Go to, let us go down [H3381], and there confound [H1101] their language [H8193], that they may not understand [H8085] one another's speech.

The word *go down* [H3381] (let us go down) means "to come or go down, descend," which marks a distinct second descent of the Lord to Babel, compared with 11:5, and prefigures a distinct reappearing of Jesus Christ in the Second Advent. The Lord now descends to Babel a second time to judge the people because of the tower of Babel just as the Second Advent of Christ will herald the judgment of the world in a final fulfillment of the curse originally incurred through the tree of knowledge. Again, the tower of Babel is related to the tree of knowledge. The first descent of the Lord to the city of Babel is to see the sins of men, which is an image of the incarnation in the flesh of man (John 12:47), while the second descent of the Lord is to confound the language of flesh, which is an image of the destruction of flesh (2 Tim 4:1). The first descent is singular (the Lord came down), while the second descent is plural (let us come down). The former descent is a vision of the incarnation of the one man Jesus Christ. The latter foreshadows the fullness of the revelation of the Trinity in the Second Advent of Christ, in which the Son will present his faithful to the Father in the unity of the Holy Spirit. And the importance of the two distinct descents of the Lord to Babel is affirmed in the two distinct descents to Sodom and Gomorrah (Gen 19:1, 19:15).[29]

The word *language* [H8193] (confound their language) evokes an image of the body part "lip," which is a metaphor for flesh in general, while the word *understand* [H8085] (that they may not understand) means "to hear" and has a connotation "to obey," which, in context, is an image of flesh obeying flesh, following the way of flesh. The dark unity of language at Babel portends a universal apostasy in the end times, the enslavement of all flesh to the one spirit of disobedience in the body of anti-christ. The subsequent multiplication of languages does not, however, represent the true and eternal will of God but rather testifies to the curse of the flesh. The multiplication of languages, the languages of the flesh, reflects the broad road to destruction (Matt 7:13–14). In contrast, the one will of the one God is revealed in the unity of language represented by Pentecost, which would be a deposit on the promised unity of the Body of Christ (Acts 2:6). God causing the people of Babel to not understand one another, not to follow the way of flesh, was a mercy just as denying the tree of life to apostate man is a mercy, but the curse of the flesh will

---

under the law, Deut 31:12–13, whereas the arts and sciences ultimately being twisted into a humanistic, apostate religion is despite the fact, actually because of the fact, that they reflect the mind and nature of God.

[29] "He [God] speaketh, as though he took counsel with his own wisdom and power: to wit, with the Son and holy Ghost . . . ." (Whittingham et al., *Geneva Bible* 6L n. h#1; Gen 11:7). The Trinity has one unified will, namely, the welfare of the faithful.

ultimately be affirmed in a curse of the spirit if the call to repentance is finally rejected. The delay of judgment is the call to repentance, but the chaos of language at Babel finally presages the inevitable and earth-shattering fall of the house of satan (Mark 3:26).

The word *confound* [H1101] (confound their language) means "to mix, confuse, confound" but also has a connotation "to anoint" (Ps 92:10), which reflects the paradox of curse and blessing in the anointing of Jesus Christ for burial (John 12:7). The confounding of language at Babel after the advent of the floodwaters is a reverse image of the unity of language in the first Pentecost after the death and resurrection of Christ (Acts 2:6) just as our original condemnation through the one man Adam is a reverse image of our promised exaltation in the one man Jesus Christ (Rom 5:19). Death is likewise a reverse image of life. The anointing of the Holy Spirit in the first Pentecost would, however, be only a deposit on the promised fullness of the Spirit, a deposit pointing to the end times (2 Cor 5:5). The resurrection of Christ as and with the firstfruits of the grave likewise points to the harvest of the faithful in the end times (1 Cor 15:23, Matt 27:52–53). The first foreshadows the second, while the second fulfills the first. The confusion at Babel likewise points to an utter chaos in the end times. The overlapping of images of the confusion of the flesh and the clarity of the Spirit represents the condemnation of the natural body heralding the exaltation of the spiritual, or glorified, body.[30]

Genesis 11:8 So the LORD scattered [H6327] them abroad from thence upon the face of all the earth: and they left off [H2308] to build the city.

The word *scattered* [H6327] (the Lord scattered them abroad) means "to be dispersed, scattered" and has connotations "to break asunder" and also "to overflow." The former connotation reflects the utter condemnation of flesh under the law, while the latter foreshadows burgeoning world populations and a concomitant overflow of the human heart (Luke 6:45). The scattering of mankind is a separation of flesh from flesh representing the curse of flesh and likewise the death of flesh. But the death of the natural body heralds the rebirth in the spiritual, or glorified, body (1 Cor 15:36) just as the curse under the law leads us to the blessing that comes only by grace (Gal 3:24). The dispersion from Babel recalls the exile of Adam from the garden (Gen 3:23) and also the curse of Cain to wander the earth (Gen 4:11–12) and also foreshadows the many repeated dispersions of the Israelites (Deut 28:64). But a remnant is always preserved, representing our promised rebirth in the Body of Christ (Rom 11:5). Flesh of itself cannot inherit the kingdom of God (1 Cor 15:50), but in

---

[30] "By the name 'Christ' is connoted one who anoints, the one who is anointed, and the ointment itself with which he is anointed. Now, in point of fact, the Father has anointed, but the Son has been anointed—in the Spirit who is the ointment. This is why the Logos says through Isaiah, 'The Spirit of God is upon me because he has anointed me' [Isa 61:1], referring at once to the anointing Father, the anointed Son, and the ointment, which is the Spirit [Irenaeus of Lyon, *Against Heresies*]" (Norris 51). Salvation is a Trinitarian event.

Christ the faithful become kings and priests (Rev 1:5–6). The peoples of the world would be called out of the dispersion from the tower of Babel to the one true faith in Jesus Christ just as the apostles scattered by the horror of the cross of Calvary would be called back to the risen Christ (Mark 14:27–28).

The word *left off* [H2308] (left off to build) means "to cease" and has a connotation "to leave (forsake)" (Judg 9:11), presaging Christ forsaken on the cross (Matt 27:46). The tower of Babel recalls the tree of knowledge to which Jesus Christ would be figuratively nailed, whereby the tower left unfinished ironically foreshadows the harvest of mankind left undone at the time of the First Advent. The faithful are thereby forsaken with Christ on the cross in imitation of Christ. The Son was forsaken awaiting his resurrection as (and with) the firstfruits, while the faithful in Christ are now forsaken awaiting the resurrection of the Body of Christ. Our transitory preservation in this life points to our eternal redemption in the next just as the tree of knowledge points to the tree of life just as the First Advent points to the Second Advent. The Father would remember the Son on the cross just as the city of man would not be left undone forever, but the true city of man is the city of God (John 18:36). And the faithful even now sojourn in a strange land in submission to the righteous curse of dispersion (Heb 11:9–10). The shifting significance of the tower of Babel from condemnation to hope is the same shift in emphasis from the Covenant of Law to the Covenant of Grace. The dispersion of mankind portends a final condemnation from the point of view of the faithless but represents the call to repentance and redemption from the point of view of the faithful. The cities of men, even Babel, foreshadow the city of God just as Adam foreshadows Christ, but the futility of the cities of men, affirmed in the dispersion from Babel, foreshadows the faithless being forbidden from entering the gates of the New Jerusalem (Rev 22:14–15).

Babel

Genesis 11:9 Therefore is the name of it called Babel [H894]; because the LORD did there confound the language of all the earth: and from thence did the LORD scatter them abroad upon the face of all the earth.

The name *Babel* [H894] is synonymous with "confusion, confoundedness" in the Hebrew. The emphasis on confusion does not portend an end of reason but rather a substitution of human reason in place of true religion, knowledge in place of wisdom, flesh in place of spirit. But the understanding of the prudent will be brought to nothing (1 Cor 1:19). The confusion of religion is not an end of religion but rather a corrupting of true religion, a counterfeiting of worship, that will culminate in the abomination of desolation standing in the holy place

(Matt 24:15–16). The Jews require a sign, the Greeks seek wisdom, but the faithful preach Christ crucified (1 Cor 1:22–23).[31]

The ancient Babel should be contrasted with the ancient Salem. The former antecedent to Babylon, the latter to Jerusalem. The account of Babel precedes the account of Salem just as the natural man Adam precedes the spiritual man Jesus Christ. The mighty hunter Nimrod identified with Babylon prefigures the son of perdition (Gen 10:8–10), while the king and priest Melchizedek identified with Jerusalem prefigures Christ as king of kings and high priest (Gen 14:18). The progenitor of Nimrod is Ham and spiritually Cain, reflecting the anti-christ proceeding directly from the serpent (Rev 13:2), but the genealogy of Melchizedek is hidden, reflecting the true descent of Christ being by the Spirit in contrast to flesh (Heb 7:3).[32]

The tower of Babel is denied just as the tree of life is denied, but the imagination of the hearts of Adam-kind will not be denied forever (Gen 6:3). God will not violate freewill (Rom 1:24). The Restrainer will be removed (2 Thess 2:7). God answers all prayers, but the prayers of the flesh are ironically a petition of self-condemnation (Job 9:20). God will not be mocked (Gal 6:7). The paradox of judgment being undeniable and delayed reflects the essential union of justice and mercy embodied by all creation, while the delay of the coming reality of our promised perfection in Christ reflects the call to repentance that must precede redemption.[33]

Genesis 11:10–25 These [are] the generations of Shem: Shem [was] an hundred years old, and begat Arphaxad two years after the flood: 11 And Shem lived after he begat Arphaxad five hundred years, and begat sons and daughters. 12 And Arphaxad lived five and thirty years, and begat Salah: 13 And Arphaxad lived after he begat Salah four hundred and three years, and begat sons and daughters. 14 And Salah lived thirty years, and begat Eber: 15 And Salah lived after he begat Eber four hundred and three years, and begat sons and daughters. 16 And Eber lived four and thirty years, and begat Peleg: 17 And Eber lived after he begat Peleg four hundred and thirty years, and begat sons and daughters. 18 And Peleg lived thirty years, and begat Reu: 19 And Peleg lived after he begat Reu two hundred and nine years, and begat sons and daughters. 20 And Reu lived two and thirty years, and begat Serug: 21 And Reu lived after he begat Serug two hundred and seven years, and begat sons and daughters.

---

[31] Demonic possession is like an "inrushing babel . . . . [strangely] neutral . . . baleful" (Martin 155). In accordance with the sanctity of freewill, men are given over to their desires, physically and spiritually.

[32] "[T]he most judicious interpreters allow that by Salem, *Jerusalem* is meant. That it bore this name anciently is evident from [Ps 76:1–2] . . . ." (Clarke 1:102; Gen 14:18). The changing of the names of people and places is a ubiquitous sign in the Bible, reflecting the transformation of man and correspondingly the progressive revelation of God.

[33] God partitioning mankind at the tower of Babel was a great mercy in that the reach and influence of our sinful nature has been greatly curtailed (Guzik 86; Gen 11:5–9). God calls us to grace and forgiveness, but man chooses to condemn himself.

22 And Serug lived thirty years, and begat Nahor: 23 And Serug lived after he begat Nahor two hundred years, and begat sons and daughters. 24 And Nahor lived nine and twenty years, and begat Terah: 25 And Nahor lived after he begat Terah an hundred and nineteen years, and begat sons and daughters.

The Messianic bloodline will not be confounded by the rebellion of the multitudes. The clear Word of God stands in diametric opposition to the babel of fallen mankind just as the singular Messianic bloodline stands in stark contrast to the divers nations of Adam-kind. Accordingly the Word of God humbly goes out to all the nations, not vice versa, in testimony to the essential condescension of the Lord God in the act of creation and likewise new creation. Lord God have mercy.[34]

Ω Ω Ω

The 1-2-3 pattern evident in the account of Ham, Shem, and Japheth is specifically an overlapping 1-2, 1-2 pattern, reflecting the twofold natures of the Son, who is fully man and fully God. The structuring of the narrative deals, first, with the twofold relationship between Ham and his collective brothers and, second, with the twofold relationship between Shem and Japheth. Ham personifies unrighteousness in the defilement of his father, whereas his brothers personify righteousness in the honoring of their father. Shem and Japheth are both blessed, but Japheth is blessed expressly in Shem, representing the redemption of the faithful in the Body of Christ. Ham reflects Adam; Shem reflects Jesus Christ; and Japheth reflects the faithful in Christ. Shem honoring his father specifically reflects the First Advent of Christ, while the blessing of Japheth in Shem points to the Second Advent. The 1-2-3 pattern realized in the Biblical narrative reflects the Trinity, while the edifying, literally constructing, 1-2, 1-2 pattern reflects the twofold natures of the Son. The singularity implied by the unity of the pattern reflects the oneness of God. The primordial image of God is oneness, testifying to the one God being the one font of all life. Our personal experience of reality is, however, twofold just as the twofold natures of Christ relate the visible image of God (Col 1:15). And the fullness of progressive revelation is finally threefold, reflecting the wholeness of truth in the Father, Son, and Holy Spirit (Matt 28:19).

1	2	3
ADAM	FIRST ADVENT	SECOND ADVENT
1	2	
HAM	SHEM	
(UNRIGHTEOUS)	(RIGHTEOUS)	
	1	2
	SHEM	JAPHETH
	(BLESSED)	(BLESSED IN SHEM)

---

[34] Translating the Bible, the Word of God, into all languages, in contrast to making all peoples learn Greek and Hebrew, is an essential distinctive of Biblical Christianity.

HAM, SHEM, JAPHETH

The account of the sons of Noah, like the account of the sons of Adam, is a kind of refrain, echoing the main chorus of the fundamental bloodline proceeding from Adam through Seth and Shem to Jesus Christ. The account of the sons of Adam is closely linked with the Fall of Adam and the corresponding prophecy of the death of all mankind in Adam, a prophecy of death entering the world first realized in the exile from the garden and first affirmed in the murder of Abel by Cain (Gen 2:17). In contrast, the account of the sons of Noah is closely linked with the Flood and the corresponding prophecy of the comfort of mankind from the curse incurred by Adam, a prophecy first realized in the preservation of Noah's family through the Flood and first affirmed by the blessing of Shem and the corresponding blessing of Japheth in Shem (Gen 5:29). The figurative resurrection of Abel in Seth and also the blessing of Japheth in Shem prefigure the redemption of the faithful in Christ, but the blessing of Shem, compared with the death of Abel, is a shift of emphasis from death to life that represents an increasing clarity, an increasing presence, of the Body of Christ. The blessing of Japheth in Shem represents the blessing of the faithful in Christ, not simply by Christ. An increasing clarity is also evident in the progression from Cain defiling Abel, brother against brother, to Ham defiling Noah, son against father, reflecting an ever-increasing awareness of the defilement of Adam-kind being a defilement of the image of God in which Adam was originally made (Rom 6:4).[35]

1	2	3
ADAM	FIRST ADVENT	SECOND ADVENT
CAIN	ABEL	SETH
HAM	SHEM	JAPHETH

The refrains manifested according to the accounts of the sons of Adam and the sons of Noah are an echoing of the main chorus represented by the account of Adam and Jesus Christ just as the song we sing in this life is an echoing of the harmony in heaven (Rev 5:9). The resounding of salvation in both the natural order and our personal lives affirms the undeniable nature of the will of God. The promise of redemption being manifested in the personal lives of the patriarchs reflects the will of God for the sanctification of the very essence of our persons as individuals with freewill. The promise of redemption being manifested in the natural order of the physical world specifically affirms that the spiritual body will be a true body concomitant with individual freewill. The progression of the Biblical narrative pointing to the last days reflects the movement of God the Holy Spirit leading us to grace (Gal 3:24). The story, or song, of salvation impressed upon all creation is our sanctification by the Holy Spirit in the Body of Christ to be finally revealed in the Second Advent. God

---

[35] In an alternating literary construction, the account of Abel being cut off without offspring, Gen 4:1–16, parallels the account of Japheth's offspring, 10:1–5, while Cain's offspring, 4:17–26, parallels Ham's offspring, 10:6–20 (Waltke 19–20). Wicked Cain is the spiritual antecedent of Ham, whereas the death of Abel points to the blessing of Japheth in Shem just as the First Advent of Christ points to the Second Advent.

ADAM, NOAH, ABRAHAM

the Son proceeding from God the Father is related in the humble incarnation of God, that is, the condescension of God for the sake of the faithful.

1	2	3
GOD THE FATHER	GOD THE SON	GOD THE HOLY SPIRIT
CREATOR	REDEEMER	SANCTIFIER
ADAM	FIRST ADVENT	SECOND ADVENT
IMAGE OF GOD	HEAD OF THE BODY	BODY OF CHRIST

HAM, SHEM, JAPHETH

CHAPTER FOUR OUTLINE

Key Images

	PRIME IMAGES	
Material	Abstract	Spiritual
The east.	The place of the rising sun.	A symbol of our new creation.
One language.	One "lip."	The universal apostasy of flesh.
The city of Babel.	The city of man.	The way of flesh.
The tower of Babel.	An attempted self-elevation.	The tree of knowledge.
	TWOFOLD IMAGES	
Material	Abstract	Spiritual
The cursing and blessing of Noah's sons.	Slavery and freedom. Flesh and spirit.	The Covenants of Law and Grace.
The first and second descents of the Lord to Babel.	First to see, second to confound. Test the flesh, judge by the Spirit. Flesh and spirit.	The First and Second Advents of Christ.
	THREEFOLD IMAGES	
Material	Abstract	Spiritual
Japheth, Ham, Shem.	The order of the genealogies.	The Trinity in original creation.
Ham, Shem, Japheth.	The order of cursing and blessing.	The Trinity in fallen creation.
Shem, Ham, Japheth.	The common (inspired) order.	The Trinity in our new creation.

Synopsis

	THE VINEYARD	
	Material	Spiritual
9:18–19	The three sons of Noah go forth of the ark.	Echoes the three sons of Adam.
	The offspring of Noah's three sons overspread the whole earth.	The undeniable presence of the Trinity in the unfolding of world history.
9:20	Noah began to be an husbandman.	Recalls the occupation of Adam in the ground, also the original formation of man from the dust of the ground.
9:21	Noah becomes drunk on wine.	Drunkenness represents death, while wine is a corresponding symbol of spilled blood.
	NAKEDNESS	
	Material	Spiritual
9:22–23	Ham violates the nakedness of Noah.	The nakedness of Noah exposed by Ham recalls the nakedness of Adam exposed by the serpent, while both foreshadow the nakedness of Christ exposed on the cross.
	But Shem and Japheth cover Noah.	An image of the Son with the faithful, the Body of Christ, approaching the Father.
	CURSE AND BLESSING	
	Material	Spiritual
9:24–27	Ham (Canaan) is cursed.	Adam.
	Shem is blessed.	Jesus Christ.
	Japheth is blessed in Shem.	The Body of Christ.

ADAM, NOAH, ABRAHAM

9:28–29	Noah lived after the Flood three hundred and fifty years, and all the days of Noah were nine hundred and fifty years.	The Flood came in the midst of the natural life of Noah just as the Cross would be lifted up in the midst of natural creation as a whole.
	THREE SONS	
	Material	Spiritual
10:1–32	The generations of the sons of Noah.	The division of the earth, representing the separation between the faithful in Christ and the faithless outside of Christ.
	ONENESS	
	Material	Spiritual
11:1	The whole earth was of one language and one speech.	The unity of the Holy Spirit rejected in favor of a universal spirit of disobedience.
11:2	Journey from the east (eastward).	Recalls Adam exiled east of Eden (Gen 3:24), but also foreshadows the Son of man, the new Adam, appearing in the east (Matt 24:27).
	THE NAME	
	Material	Spiritual
11:3–4	Let us build us a city and a tower that reaches unto heaven.	The tower is an abstract altar that recalls the tree of knowledge and portends the cross.
	Let us make us a name, lest we be scattered abroad.	A rejection of the one name of Jesus Christ.
	SON OF MAN	
	Material	Spiritual
11:5	And the Lord came down to see the city and the tower.	Foreshadows the incarnation of Jesus Christ in the First Advent.
11:6	Now nothing that they have imagined will be restrained from the people of Babel.	The unrestraint of the evil one in the end times (2 Thess 2:7).
	SON OF GOD	
	Material	Spiritual
11:7–8	The Lord descends to Babel a second time.	Foreshadows the foretold Second Advent.
	Language is confounded.	Foreshadows the chaos of the end times, but also, though in reverse, the unity and peace of the Holy Spirit.
	And mankind is scattered abroad.	Foreshadows the rejection of the faithless, but also, though in reverse, the faithful entering the city of God.
	BABEL	
	Material	Spiritual
11:9	Therefore is the name of it called Babel.	The faithless condemn themselves with their own mouths (2 Sam 1:16).
11:10–25	The generations of Shem.	The one bloodline of Christ stands in contrast to the nations of Adam just as the singular Word of God stands in contrast to the babel of Adam-kind.

ABRAHAM

יהוה

CHAPTER FIVE

Abraham and Sarah

The singular faith of Abraham, the land of Canaan, and the sign of circumcision are the prime images emphasized in the account of Abraham and Sarah. The call of Abraham out of the east is a reverse image of the exile of Adam from the east of Eden and the eastern gateway to the garden (Gen 3:24) just as our glorification in the one man Jesus Christ is a reverse image of our condemnation in the one man Adam (1 Cor 15:22). The nation of Israel born through the faithfulness of the one man Abraham foreshadows the rebirth of the entire world through the faithfulness of the one man Christ. The promise of the land of Canaan recalls the lost garden of Eden and foreshadows the promised kingdom of God. The intimate connection between the promise of life and the promise of land recalls the original formation of man from the dust of the ground and foreshadows the resurrection of man in a true body (Matt 22:32). Circumcision is a mark in the flesh and, thereby, represents flesh and likewise the law that governs flesh. The mark of circumcision required by the law foreshadows the affliction of the flesh of Jesus Christ under the law. But the circumcision in the flesh also foreshadows the circumcision of the heart (Rom 2:28–29) just as the baptism of repentance in water foreshadows the baptism of redemption that comes by the Holy Spirit (John 3:5–7).

The pairwise relationships emphasized in the account of Abraham and Sarah are those of Abraham and Sarah themselves, Hagar and Sarah, Ishmael and Isaac, Eliezer and Isaac, Lot and Abraham, and also the kings of Sodom and Salem. Abraham and Sarah reflect the union of law and grace, while the promised birth of Isaac reflects the fulfillment of the promise of new life in the Body of Christ. Hagar and Sarah embody slavery and freedom and, thereby, reflect the Covenants of Law and Grace (Gal 4:22–24). Ishmael is the son of a bondwoman, while Isaac is the son of a freewoman. Accordingly, the promise of Isaac supplanting the reality of Ishmael reflects the promise in Christ supplanting the curse of Adam. The promised son Isaac, not the eldest servant Eliezer, would be the heir of Abraham just as God the Son, not God the Holy Spirit, would embody the inheritance of Adam—that is, the curse of Adam—on the cross (Gal 3:13). Abraham taking care of Lot, at least figuratively adopting him, reflects the Father redeeming Adam—that is, the Father adopting sons (Rom 8:23). Abraham saving Lot first from captivity and second from destruction by fire specifically prefigures the First and Second Advents of Christ. Abraham rejecting the king of Sodom but accepting the king of Salem reflects the curse of Adam contrasted with the blessing in Christ.

The three sons Nahor, Haran, and Abram reflect Adam and the First and Second Advents of Christ. Nahor not being called into the promised land recalls the exile of Adam. The death of Haran prefigures the death of Christ in the First Advent, while Abram taking care of Lot, Haran's offspring, prefigures the resurrection of the dead in Christ at the Second Advent. The threefold call of Abram to leave his country, his kindred, and finally his father's house reflects the call to reject the corrupted world, the corrupted flesh, and finally the corrupted spirit embodied expressly by the father of lies. The threefold call of Abram also reflects a parallel call to recognize the Father, Son, and Holy Spirit as creator, redeemer, and sanctifier. The threefold journey from Ur of the Chaldees to the land of Haran to the land of Canaan represents birth, death, and rebirth but ultimately points to the Father, Son, and Holy Spirit, again as creator, redeemer, and sanctifier. Ur is the native country of Abram (birth); Abram's father, Terah, dies in the land of Haran (death); and Canaan is the new country of Abram (rebirth). Birth reflects creation; death reflects the suffering of the Son; and rebirth reflects the promised sanctification by the Holy Spirit. The three angels promising Abraham the birth of Isaac but also warning of the destruction of Sodom and Gomorrah is a vision of the dichotomy of life and death proceeding from the Trinity and ultimately revealed in the Son. Only two angels proceeding to Sodom reflects God the Holy Spirit and God the Son proceeding from God the Father.

THE CALL

Genesis 11:26 And Terah lived seventy years, and begat Abram [H87], Nahor, and Haran.

The name *Abram* [H87] means "exalted father," which reflects the faithful being exalted not of themselves but only in Christ. Abram is the figurative father of the faithful just as Adam was the literal father of all humanity. Abram does not exalt himself in a new creation just as Adam did not form himself in the original creation. Not even Christ exalts himself, but rather Christ is exalted by the Father (John 17:5). Man is made in the image of God, whereby Adam could not exalt himself through the tree of knowledge just as Christ would not exalt himself, or crucify himself, on the cross. Christ submitted to the cross willingly, but he did not crucify himself, he did not commit suicide. The defilement of Christ by humanity is the rejection of God by Adam, but Abram represents a new Adam, a new creation in Christ.

The exaltation of the faithful in Christ is foremost on the cross but finally in the promised resurrection unto eternal life. The work of the cross is the perfect fulfillment of the law. The work of the cross is the long-suffering of God made

ABRAHAM AND SARAH

visible just as Christ is God made visible (Col 1:15). In the person of Christ and only in the person of Christ do works and faith converge in a perfect unity. The incarnation of Christ represents the perfect union of flesh and spirit. The life of Christ embodies the perfect union of works and faith. The promise of Christ is the perfect union of law and grace. The Old Testament actually does teach that we are saved by works, but not by our own works, rather only by the works of Jesus Christ. And the work of Christ is not merely the fulfillment of the law but rather the fulfillment of law in grace. The work of the cross is literally the perfect faithfulness of God. The faithful are called to imitate Christ, but not of ourselves, rather only in the Body of Christ.[1]

Genesis 11:27–28 Now these [are] the generations of Terah: Terah begat Abram, Nahor, and Haran; and Haran begat Lot. 28 And Haran died before his father Terah in the land of his nativity, in Ur of the Chaldees.

The three sons of Terah recall the three sons of Adam and the three sons of Noah and also foreshadow Abram's threefold offspring through Hagar, Sarah, and Keturah. The premature death of Haran recalls the murder of Abel, while Abram subsequently looking after Haran's son Lot, at least symbolically adopting Lot, recalls the figurative resurrection of Abel in Seth (Gen 4:25) and also recalls the blessing through Shem of Japheth (Gen 9:27). Abram represents a figurative resurrection of Haran as a new father figure to Haran's son Lot, whereby Abram is also symbolically blessed through Haran as a figurative fulfillment of the life of Haran just as the faithful are blessed through the death and resurrection of Christ. The ordering Cain, Abel, Seth and likewise Ham, Shem, Japheth are thereby reflected in the rearranged ordering Nahor, Haran, Abram, which is a pattern representing the present world order of fallen creation and likewise the unfolding history of our redemption.

The three sons of Noah can be organized by order of physical birth, reflecting the original creation before our fall (Japheth, Ham, Shem), also by order of the cursing and blessing by Noah, reflecting fallen creation (Ham, Shem, Japheth), and finally by the common Scriptural order, reflecting our promised new creation (Shem, Ham, Japheth). A comparison with the three ordering patterns of the three sons of Noah confirms that the common Scriptural ordering Abram, Nahor, Haran is the order of physical birth, again reflecting the original creation before the Fall of Man. Abram being understood as the firstborn in the common Scriptural ordering is a testimony to Christ and not Adam being the true progenitor of the original uncorrupted creation. The spiritual ordering Nahor, Haran, and Abram again reflects fallen creation and likewise reflects the unfolding history of our redemption, whereby Abram being

---

[1] A king of this world may or may not obey his own temporal edicts, but God is always the first to obey his own divine edicts, *Leviticus Rabbah* (Cohen, *Rabbinic Sages* 210). The obvious necessity of God himself keeping all of his own edicts in order to be perfectly righteous points to the absolute necessity of the incarnation of God as a literal man in real flesh in order to perfectly, or wholly, fulfill the law.

shifted to the third position in this ordering prefigures the promised restoration, or re-creation, of creation in the Second Advent.²

The common Scriptural ordering Cain, Abel, and Seth reflects both the order of physical birth and also the order of fallen creation, in an alignment reflecting the undeniable condemnation of all flesh under the original curse of Adam, a condemnation closely identified with antediluvian mankind. In contrast, the succeeding common Scriptural ordering Shem, Ham, and Japheth reflects a new order of creation that is closely identified with the death and resurrection of all creation through the floodwaters in the time of Noah, a death and resurrection prefiguring the death and resurrection of Christ. But the sons of the first major patriarch, Adam, and those of the second major patriarch, Noah, compare most symmetrically to the sons of the third major patriarch, Abram, not to Abram and his brothers, the sons of Terah. Abram, when compared with Adam and Noah, is most closely identified with the second appearing of Christ in the last days, whereby the threefold Abram, Nahor, and Haran—the ordering by birth aligned with the common Scriptural ordering—points to the recapitulation of history in the person of Christ and likewise to the restoration, or re-creation, of creation in the Body of Christ. The heaping of threefold patterns specifically in the genealogy of the third major patriarch in the opening of the third millennium from the first Adam points to the fulfillment of all things in the Trinity in the dawn of the third millennium from the incarnation of Jesus Christ, the last Adam.³

Genesis 11:29–30 And Abram and Nahor took them wives: the name of Abram's wife [was] Sarai; and the name of Nahor's wife, Milcah, the daughter of Haran, the father of Milcah, and the father of Iscah. 30 But Sarai was barren; she [had] no child.

Abram reflects Jesus Christ, the Head of the Body, while Sarai reflects the faithful, the Body of Christ, called to be the bride of the Lamb, one flesh (Rev

---

² "Perhaps in the proper order of things, Abraham should have been the first man created, not Adam. God, however, foresaw the fall of the first man, and if Abraham had been the first man and had fallen, there would have been no one after him to restore righteousness to the world; whereas after Adam's fall came Abraham, who established in the world the knowledge of God. As a builder puts the strongest beam in the centre of the building, so as to support the structure at both ends, so Abraham was the strong beam carrying the burden of the generations that existed before him and that came after him [*Genesis Rabbah*]" (Rapaport, *Midrash* 67). Adam preceding Christ testifies to the inviolable sanctity of freewill, whereby the strongest beam should be recognized as the cross and the decision whether to accept or reject it.

³ "For the cosmos, Revelation affirms the profound common destiny of the material world and man . . . . The visible universe, then, is itself destined to be transformed . . . sharing their glorification [red earth with ruddy man] in the risen Jesus Christ" (Rom. Catholic Church, *Catechism* 295–96). Man is necessarily a microcosm of creation as a whole because creation, representing the dominion of freewill, is the essential extension of the natural body and likewise of the resurrection body.

21:9). The barrenness of Sarai represents the spiritual barrenness and concomitant material barrenness of fallen humanity outside of grace. The implied fertility of Milcah, later confirmed, is identified through Nahor with Cain and Ham since the ordering Nahor, Haran, Abram parallels Cain, Abel, Seth and also parallels Ham, Shem, Japheth (Gen 22:20). The identification of the fertility of Milcah with Cain, Ham, and Nahor represents the transitory preservation of fallen creation and the concomitant fleeting prosperity of the faithless. The lineage of Sarai, in contrast to that of Milcah, not being listed in the present passage reflects the mystery of the invisible Body of Christ, in contrast to the seeming nearness of the visible, earthly church.

Genesis 11:31–32 And Terah took Abram his son, and Lot the son of Haran his son's son, and Sarai his daughter in law, his son Abram's wife; and they went forth with them from Ur of the Chaldees, to go into the land of Canaan; and they came unto Haran, and dwelt there. 32 And the days of Terah were two hundred and five years: and Terah died in Haran.

The native origin of Abram's family in the east represents our physical birth in the natural body. Nahor staying in Ur of the Chaldees is an image of our primal apostasy, reinforcing the identification of Nahor with Cain and Ham. The death of Terah in the land of Haran followed by his surviving family proceeding to the land of Canaan represents the (figurative) death and resurrection in the repentance of sins that must precede redemption.[4] Entering the land of Canaan represents the (literal) death of the natural body and the resurrection of the spiritual, or glorified, body in the Body of Christ. The call to repentance is in the flesh, in the natural body, but the call to redemption is from the flesh, that is, from the way of flesh. The threefold progression from physical birth (Ur of the Chaldees) to death (land of Haran) to rebirth (land of Canaan) is the promise of life embodied by physical birth (creation), the death and resurrection represented by the baptism in water (repentance), and finally our promised new creation in the baptism of the Holy Spirit (redemption). The threefold image of promise, repentance, and redemption reflects the Father, Son, and Holy Spirit as our creator, redeemer, and sanctifier.[5]

Genesis 12:1 Now the LORD had said unto Abram, Get thee out of thy country [H776], and from thy kindred [H4138], and from thy father's [H1] house, unto a land [H776] that I will shew thee:

---

[4] The name *Haran* [H2039], Abram's brother and Lot's father, is a distinct Hebrew word compared with the place *Haran* [H2771], where Terah died.

[5] "... 'By three things is the world preserved: by truth, by judgment, and by peace' [*Pirke Aboth*] ... 'The three are really one; if judgment is executed, truth is vindicated and peace results' [*Palestinian Taanith*]" (Cohen, *Rabbinic Sages* 206). The faithful in Christ recognize the unity that is the truth of the Father, the judgment of the Son on the cross, and the peace of the Holy Spirit.

ADAM, NOAH, ABRAHAM

The word *country* [H776] (get thee out of thy country) means "land," specifically Abram's native land in context, but also has a connotation "whole earth," whereby the call to figuratively get out of the whole earth is a reverse image of the original dispersion from the garden. Our exaltation in Christ is a reverse image of our condemnation from Adam. The use of the same Hebrew word *country*, *land* [H776] to denote both the *land* of Abram's nativity and also the *land* promised to Abram prefigures the restoration, or re-creation, of creation in Christ. The spiritual, or glorified, body is a true body, a body previewed in the resurrection of Christ.[6]

The word *kindred* [H4138] (get thee out from thy kindred) is derived from the root "to bear, bring forth, beget" [H3205], which has a connotation "to travail," reflecting the suffering in the flesh inherited from the first man and woman and ultimately embodied by Jesus Christ on the cross. The emphasis on kindred is an emphasis on blood relationship, pointing to the blood of Christ, while the image of children being brought forth in suffering prefigures our rebirth in Christ through the cross. The Lord calls Abram out from his kindred just as Christ calls the faithful out from the curse inherited from Adam.

The word *father* [H1] (get thee out from thy father's house) means "father" with a connotation of "ruler, chief," which is an image of a son being ruled by his father, symbolically ruled by a common nature inherited from his father. The call of father Abram out of his own father's house is figuratively the call to reject the nature of flesh, to reject the way of disobedience. The name *Abram* [H87] is derived in part from the word *father* [H1] just as the nature of man descends from, or is begotten of, our father Adam.[7] Abram represents all mankind in the call, but Abram embodies only the faithful in his obedience to the call. Abram represents the Second Advent when compared with Adam and Noah, while the land of Canaan represents the promised body when compared with Ur of the Chaldees and the land of Haran. Accordingly, Abram's entry into the promised land specifically represents the third person of the Trinity, the Holy Spirit, indwelling our new creation in the Body of Christ.[8]

The threefold call of Abram to leave his country, his kindred, and his father's house reflects, respectively, the call to be separate from a corrupted world, the call to reject our inheritance in original sin from Adam, and finally the call to renounce the father of lies. The threefold rejection of the world, the rejection of the inheritance in Adam, and finally the rejection of the father of lies is a telescoping threefold condemnation of the corrupted creation all around us, the condemnation of our own corrupted flesh, and finally the condemnation of the internal spirit of rebellion. The microcosm reflects the macrocosm. The concurrent restoration of creation, restoration of flesh, and restoration of spirit

---

[6] "This call of Abraham is an emblem of the call of men by the grace of God out of the world . . . ." (Gill 1:74; Gen 12:1). The call to walk not by sight but by faith.

[7] Etymology per *Strong's*, but the relationship is clear in *Brown-Driver-Briggs*.

[8] The seven promises of Gen 12:2–3 given to Abraham—to be made a great nation, to be blessed, and so forth—relate to three expanding horizons: to come out from family, to become a blessed nation, and finally to become a blessing for the whole earth (Waltke 203). The seven days of creation likewise translate to the three days of Christ.

is a reflection of the Father, Son, and Holy Spirit, respectively, as our creator, redeemer, and sanctifier. The promised threefold restoration, or re-creation, is also reflected in the threefold sequence represented by the original creation, the destruction by water, and finally the foretold destruction by fire and likewise in the threefold sequence represented by the formation of Adam, the incarnation of Jesus Christ at the First Advent, and finally the glorification of the Body of Christ in the Second Advent.[9]

Genesis 12:2–3 And I will make [H6213] of thee a great nation, and I will bless [H1288] thee, and make thy name [H8034] great [H1431]; and thou shalt be a blessing: 3 And I will bless [H1288] them that bless [H1288] thee, and curse [H779] him that curseth [H7043] thee: and in thee shall all families of the earth [H127] be blessed [H1288].

The word *bless, blessed* [H1288] (bless thee, bless them that bless) has a connotation "to kneel," which emphasizes our exaltation in submission to God, in contrast to the inevitable degradation of the faithless standing against God. But the Lord needs no attendants to either his person or his ego. God is infinite. Our submission to the will of God is our salvation by grace in contrast to works. The connection between submission and salvation testifies to our freewill choice to either accept or reject Jesus Christ. The image of submission to God is not slavery, not in any way an annihilation of freewill, but rather reflects an understanding to choose the good and reject the bad, an understanding the faithful receive from the Father through the Son by the indwelling Holy Spirit. The faithful are obedient to the Son just as the Son is obedient to the Father (John 17:21).

The word *curseth* [H7043] (him that curseth) has a connotation "to be trifling (of little account)," which is the degradation of the faithless that always proceeds from the dismissal of Christ. To trifle with Abram, to dishonor Abram, is to reject God and likewise to reject the person of Christ. To reject the messenger is to reject the message. Abram would be blessed just as Jesus Christ would be blessed, while Abram would be a blessing just as the faithful are blessed through Christ. The blessing of those that bless Abram and the cursing of those that curse Abram is an affirmation of our freewill choice to either accept or reject Christ, specifically our freewill choice to either accept or reject the call to repentance in Christ. The choice between blessing and cursing Abram is also a testimony that our promised redemption comes only through

---

[9] "There is an *order* in the Trinity. There is even a *hierarchy* if we do not take this term to mean some difference in nature between the Father, Son and Holy Spirit, but merely the *way* in which the Divine Persons relate to One Another and to man and the world. For in the Trinity Itself the Father Alone is the 'Source of divinity.' The Son is the expression of the Father and is 'subject' to Him. And the Holy Spirit, of one essence and fully equal with the Father and the Son, is the 'third' Person who fulfills the will of the Father and the Son" (Hopko, *Orthodox Faith* 1:57). To reject the order and hierarchy of the Trinity requires a fundamental rejection of the threefold names *Father, Son*, and *Spirit*, which is nothing less than a rejection of God himself.

Christ. Faith is by grace just as our redemption is by grace. Our redemption is by grace through faith. Our faith in Christ is the mark of the Holy Spirit, a mark placed upon all the children of God. The resolution of the tension between our inviolable freewill and our promised salvation is our promised perfection of understanding in unity with the Holy Spirit.[10]

The same word is used to denote those that *bless* [H1288] Abram and those that are *blessed* [H1288] by God, while distinct words are used to denote those that *curse* [H7043] Abram and those that are *cursed* [H779] by God. The former unity reflects the oneness of the faithful and God—the one Body of Christ, the anointing of all the faithful in the one Spirit of God. The latter difference reflects the utter separation between the faithless and God and likewise the fundamental distinction between the faithless and the faithful.[11]

The word *make* [H6213] (thee a great nation) means simply "to do, make" but recalls the same word used to describe the original act of *making* [H6213] creation and, thereby, prefigures our new creation in Christ (Gen 1:31). The prophecy that Abram would be made into a great nation literally refers to his physical progeny and the nation of Israel but spiritually refers to the faithful in Christ and the kingdom of God (Gal 3:7). The word *great* [H1431] (make thy name great) means "to grow up, become great (be magnified)," which reflects our promised exaltation in the Body of Christ (2 Thess 1:12), while the word *name* [H8034] corresponds to the name *Shem* [H8035], which recalls the blessing of Japheth through Shem, representing the redemption of all nations through the one nation Israel (Gen 9:27). The prophecy that the name of Abram would be made great literally refers to the greatness of the name of Israel but spiritually refers to the one name of Jesus Christ (Acts 4:12).[12]

The word *earth* [H127] (all in the earth will be blessed) is related to the name *Adam* [H121], which points to our redemption in Christ from the curse of Adam. All in the earth will be blessed, all in Adam will be blessed. The peoples of the earth would be materially blessed through Israel by the revelation of the law and the prophets but spiritually blessed in the person of Christ. The former in the natural body, the latter in the spiritual, or glorified, body. The literal and spiritual levels of prophecy are both correct and both reflect the same fundamental truth, but the literal, or physical, meaning is only a shadow of the

---

[10] "[T]he call of Abraham, the Friend of God, the Father of the Faithful . . . a type of Almighty God himself. All the saved of all ages are in a specific and genuine sense 'the children of Abraham' [Gal 3:29]" (Coffman 167; Gen 12). Our father Abraham being simultaneously the friend of God and a type of God prefigures the Body of Christ.
[11] *Them that bless* is plural, referring to many, while *him that curseth* is singular (Gill 1:74; Gen 12:3). In the human body, there is one head but two, or plural, heels, Gen 3:15.
[12] "And as he himself [Christ], hallowing all, says again to the Father, 'On our behalf he hallows himself' [John 17:19]—not that the Word may become holy, but that he himself in himself might hallow all of us—thus the present statement 'he will highly exalt him' is to be taken, not in order that he himself might be exalted, for he is the highest, but in order that he himself on our behalf 'might become righteousness' [1 Cor. 1:30] . . . . [Athanasius, *Orations Against the Arians*]" (Rusch 105). The resurrection of Christ will be fulfilled in the resurrection and rapture of the faithful in Christ.

spiritual meaning just as everything in this life is only a shadow of eternal life (1 Cor 13:12). Even the Scriptures are a shadow of the will of God in the sense that not all the times and manners of events have been revealed. Even the incarnation of Christ, particularly before the glorification and ascension, is a shadow of God in the sense that the incarnation is a condescension of God.[13]

Genesis 12:4–5 So Abram departed, as the LORD had spoken unto him; and Lot went with him: and Abram [was] seventy and five years old when he departed out of Haran. 5 And Abram took Sarai [H8297] his wife, and Lot his brother's son, and all their substance that they had gathered, and the souls [H5315] that they had gotten in Haran; and they went forth to go into the land of Canaan [H3667]; and into the land of Canaan [H3667] they came.

The word *souls* [H5315] (souls they had gotten in Haran) means "living being" and evokes an image "that which breathes," which recalls God breathing the breath of life into mankind (Gen 2:7). The emphasis on having gotten souls in the land of Haran points to the connection of the land of Haran with the baptism of repentance. The emphasis on Abram taking souls to the land of Canaan, the promised land, testifies to the promised redemption of the faithful in Christ and reinforces the connection between Canaan and the baptism of the Holy Spirit. The faithful along with tangible creation is, collectively, the bride of the Lamb (Rev 21:9). The matriarch Sarai embodies all the souls in the camp of Abram just as Eve was the mother of all humanity (Gen 3:20).

The name *Sarai* [H8297] is derived from the word "ruler, prince" [H8269] just as the word *woman* [H802] is derived from the word "man" [H376].[14] Abram and Sarai recall Adam and Eve, but the image of prince and princess is exalted compared with the image of man and woman. Adam and Eve primarily evoke an image of flesh, while Abram and Sarah primarily evoke an image of faith. Humanity is exalted in royalty just as flesh is transcended by faith. The progression from Adam to Abram prefigures the fulfillment of law in grace and likewise the redemption of Adam in Christ. The image of Eve being taken from the flesh of Adam in the preordained order of creation reflects grace proceeding from law, while the union of Abram and Sarai in the faithful expectation of the promise of life reflects the exaltation of the faithful in the kingdom of God. The emphasis in the account of the formation of Eve from Adam is companionship, while the emphasis in the account of the union of Abram and Sarai is producing offspring. The fundamental union of man and woman represents the fulfillment of law in grace, but the new life that proceeds through procreation is something new. A child proceeding from the union of man and woman transcends the

---

[13] In order to emphasize that the Father and the Son are of the same substance and nature, the Son did not say the Father is "better" than himself but rather "greater," John 14:28—Athanasius, *Orations Against the Arians* (Rusch 123). The faithfulness of the Son to the will of the Father in no way diminishes the Son.

[14] Etymologies per *Strong's*, but the relationships are clear in *Brown-Driver-Briggs*.

simple sum of man and woman and, thereby, prefigures the promised new creation of the faithful in Christ.

The name *Canaan* [H3667] is derived from the root "to be humble (humbled)" [H3665], which foreshadows the rejection of the Canaanites and finally the rejection of all flesh. But the land of Canaan becoming the land of Israel is a vision of the renewal of the world, likewise a vision of the resurrection of the body. Abram already being an old man at the beginning of the Scriptural account of his life represents an emphasis on spiritual (supernatural) rebirth in contrast to physical (natural) birth. The implication is that true life, or the fullness of life, begins in our response to the call to repentance. The call of Abram in his old age reflects the individual passing through death into eternal life and likewise the promised renewal of all creation in the end times. The entry of Abram into the land of Canaan in his old age prefigures the appearance of Christ in the last days.[15]

Two Altars

Genesis 12:6–7 And Abram passed through the land unto the place of Sichem [H7927], unto the plain [H436] of Moreh [H4176]. And the Canaanite [was] then in the land. 7 And the LORD appeared unto Abram, and said, Unto thy seed [H2233] will I give this land: and there builded [H1129] he an altar [H4196] unto the LORD, who appeared unto him.

This first altar built by Abram in Canaan is closely linked with the promised seed of Abram and, thereby, represents the law that governs flesh and ultimately the crucifixion in fulfillment of the law. The First Covenant and the First Advent. Abram's first altar in Canaan recalls Noah's first altar after the Flood (Gen 8:20) just as the Passion of Christ recalls the Flood (1 Pet 3:21). The First Destruction and the First Advent. The word *altar* [H4196] (altar unto the Lord) is derived from the root "to slaughter for sacrifice" [H2076], which is the literal sacrifice of animals but ultimately portends the crucifixion of Christ.[16] The word *builded* [H1129] (builded an altar) has a connotation "to be established, made permanent," which reflects the eternal covenant relationship established by God with man in the person of Jesus Christ.[17]

---

[15] "Abraham's journey to the center of the land . . . is duplicated in Jacob's journeys . . . and in the general route of the conquest under Joshua . . . 'Scripture intends to present us here, through the symbolic conquest of Abraham, with a kind of foretaste of what would happen to his descendants later' [U. Cassuto]" (Clifford, *New Jerome* 20; Gen 12:5–9). The conquest of the promised land by Joshua then points to the yet future Second Advent of Yeshua, Rev 11:15.

[16] H4196 is coded incorrectly as H4096 on page 258 of *Brown-Driver-Briggs*, per *Green's Interlinear* and also *Strong's*.

[17] "God reveals Himself and his favors by degrees; before, He had promised to *show* Abram this land, now, to *give* it him: as grace is growing, so is comfort" (Henry 1:72; Gen 12:6–9). There is a ubiquitous parallel between the progressive revelation of our

ABRAHAM AND SARAH

The name *Sichem* (Shechem) [H7927] (through the land unto Sichem) literally means "shoulder (probably shoulder of mountain)" [H7926], which imminently foreshadows Isaac carrying the wood for his own sacrifice (Gen 22:6) but ultimately Christ carrying his own cross (John 19:17). The burden shouldered in this life is the enslavement of flesh to sin and the corresponding condemnation of the natural body under the law. Sichem is again connected with the law when the men of Sichem are marked for death by the sign of circumcision (Gen 34:24–25). The tree of Moreh recalls the tree of knowledge and foreshadows the wooden cross. The name *Moreh* [H4176] (there builded he an altar) means "teacher" [H4175], which is a reflection of the law leading us to grace (Gal 3:24).[18] The word *plain* [H436] (of Moreh), or "trees," has an association "ram (male lamb)" [H352], which imminently foreshadows the ram that would replace Isaac in his figurative sacrifice (Gen 22:13) but ultimately foreshadows the Lamb of God (John 1:29).[19]

The altar of Abram at Sichem is explicitly marked by the promise that the seed of Abram would inherit the land. The word *seed* [H2233] (unto thy seed will I give) recalls the same word used to describe the promised *Seed* of woman, whereby the emphasis on the seed of Abram being given the land points to the one Seed Jesus Christ and also to the singular Body of Christ. The word *seed* [H2233] is used to denote both the *seed* of the serpent and the *Seed* of the woman, reflecting the dichotomy of death and life (Gen 3:15). The promise of the land applies to both the physical descendants of Abram and also the spiritual descendants of Abram just as there is always a correspondence between the physical and the spiritual. But the rightful descendants of Abram are the faithful (Gal 3:7) just as the kingdom of God is not of this world but the next (John 18:36). The physical and spiritual meanings are both true, but the spiritual meaning is ironically more true than the physical meaning. The physical descendents of Abram can only take partial control of the land, while the spiritual descendent of Abram, Jesus Christ, will take complete control of all creation. The inheritance of the Israelites being expressly through Abram is then a vision of our own inheritance through faith in Christ. Abram is a symbol, or prophecy, of faith; Christ is the embodiment of faith; and our new creation in Christ is the fulfillment of faith (Heb 12:2).[20]

Genesis 12:8 And he removed from thence unto a mountain on the east of Beth-el [H1008], and pitched his tent, [having] Beth-el [H1008] on the

---

salvation, or sanctification, and the progressive revelation of God himself, which is not surprising since God himself is our salvation.

[18] *Strong's* incorrectly codes *Moreh* = H4170 in the main concordance but correctly *Moreh* = H4176 in the accompanying *Strong's Dictionary of the Hebrew*, per *Green's Interlinear* and also *Brown-Driver-Briggs*.

[19] Abram proceeded first to Sichem, the physical center of the country, Gen 12:6 (Sarna 90; Gen 12:6–9). The center of the land representing the beating heart of the land.

[20] "All good people must consider themselves strangers and sojourners in this world, and by faith sit loose to it as a strange country" (Henry 1:72; Gen 12:6–9). The kingdom of God is not of this world, which is a good thing given that this world is fallen.

west, and Hai [H5857] on the east: and there he built an altar unto the LORD, and called upon the name of the LORD.

The name *Bethel* [H1008] (on the west) literally means "house of God," while the name *Hai* (Ai) [H5857] (on the east) has an association "ruin, heap of ruins" [H5856]. The contrast between Bethel and Hai is the contrast between life and death and likewise between spirit and flesh. The altar of Abram being specifically on the east side of Bethel prefigures the brazen (brasen) altar being positioned in front of the holy place as prescribed by and through Moses (Exod 40:6, Ezek 8:16). The image of ruins represented by Hai standing before the altar of Abram is the uncleanness of the world outside the sanctification of the altar of God. The altar of sacrifice points to the sacrifice of the cross through which the life of Christ would be the fulfillment of the law (Matt 5:17). The altar is built opposing a heap of ruins just as Christ would die for the sake of corrupted humanity. Since the sun rises in the east, a timeline can be applied from east to west such that a state of ruin precedes a union with the holy place. The expanse of space and time that then separates our ruination from our reunion with the holy place is the sacrificial altar of the cross. A state of ruin always exists outside the holy place, that is, outside the presence of God.

This second altar in Canaan, built by Abram at Bethel, recalls the first altar built at Sichem just as the birth of Christ recalls the formation of Adam just as the resurrection of the Body of Christ will recall the resurrection of Christ. But the two altars of Abram are not the same just as the Body of Christ is not merely a restoration of Adam just as the kingdom of God is not merely a return to the garden of Eden. A mere restoration of the original state of man would imply an endlessly repeating cycle of fall and ascension, but our promised redemption is eternal (Rom 6:9). The Body of Christ is something new. The promised sanctification of our whole body, soul, and spirit (1 Thess 5:23). In a progression from the promise of Christ to the reality of Christ that embodies the fulfillment of law in grace, the promise of the seed of Abram is emphasized in the first altar while the name of the Lord is emphasized in the second altar. The second altar transcends the first altar just as the image of the house of God (Bethel) transcends the image of teaching (Moreh) just as the image of a mountain transcends the image of a plain (tree) just as the reality of the name of the Lord transcends the original promise of the unnamed Seed of woman. The image of Abram calling upon the name of the Lord is a prophetic revelation of the name of the Lord that prefigures the fullness of the revelation of God in the end times. The emphasis on the name of the Lord, in contrast to animal sacrifice, testifies to salvation being by grace through faith in Jesus Christ, the only name given unto mankind for our salvation (Acts 4:12). The Body of Christ is something new. A new body, a new heart, a new song.[21]

---

[21] The Orthodox Church believes that at the deepest level the book of Psalms, in its entirety, should be understood as a spiritual telling of the life of Jesus Christ and our corresponding life, or salvation, in Christ (Hopko, *Orthodox Faith* 3:20–21). Singing a

ABRAHAM AND SARAH

Famine

Genesis 12:9–10 And Abram journeyed, going on still toward the south. 10 And there was a famine in the land: and Abram went down into Egypt to sojourn there; for the famine [was] grievous in the land.

Abram's descendants would sojourn in Egypt until the time of Moses just as Abram sojourned in Egypt (Gen 15:13). Jesus would also sojourn in Egypt and retrace the steps of Abram and also the steps of Moses and, thereby, sanctify their steps and our steps (Matt 2:14–15). The life of Christ is a recapitulation and, therein, a sanctification of all creation. Famine is literally a deprivation of the body caused by a lack of food and is naturally connected with leaving the land, but famine is also a metaphor for a deprivation of the spirit caused by leaving the presence of God. The deprivation of the body is a symbol of the death of the body, ultimately the death of Christ and likewise our shared death in Christ (Rom 6:3). Connecting famine and death specifically with Egypt and generally with the nations of the world is an identification of physical and also spiritual death with the apostasy of the nations.[22]

The repeating image in the Scriptures of leaving the promised land is a reflection of the original fall and the corresponding exile from the garden, which is the condemnation of all flesh in the person of Adam. Returning to the promised land represents entering into the kingdom of God, which is our salvation by grace through faith in Jesus Christ. The image of being dispersed but then collected, likewise the image of the preservation and multiplication of a remnant, is a vision of death and resurrection. The meaning of repetition itself is an affirmation of both the fundamental corruption of man and also the undeniable will of God for the exaltation of man. The macrocosm being reflected in the microcosm testifies to the universality of the image of God and specifically to man being created in the image of God.[23]

Genesis 12:11–13 And it came to pass, when he was come near to enter into Egypt, that he said unto Sarai his wife, Behold now, I know that thou [art] a fair woman to look upon: 12 Therefore it shall come to pass, when the Egyptians shall see thee, that they shall say, This [is] his wife:

---

psalm, or sacred song, is a kind of exaltation of the act of speaking and, yet more fundamentally, of the act of breathing.

[22] "Their [Abraham and Sarah's] going to Egypt and encounter with Pharaoh foreshadow their descendants' experience in Egypt, suggesting constant divine protection, in which Israel later must learn to trust" (Clifford, *New Jerome* 20; Gen 12:10–13:1). Not merely national Israel or the Jewish people, but Jew and Gentile together in the promised Body of Christ.

[23] "The resort to Egypt (the world) is typical of the tendency to substitute for lost spiritual power the fleshly resources of the world . . . ." (Scofield 21 n. 2; Gen 12:10). The constant tension between flesh and spirit is the universal dichotomy of law and grace, likewise justice and mercy.

and they will kill me, but they will save thee alive. 13 Say, I pray thee, thou [art] my sister: that it may be well with me for thy sake; and my soul shall live because of thee.

Abram's prediction that the Egyptians would kill him because of Sarai is not only a literal statement, which presumably would have been fulfilled and therefore was figuratively fulfilled, but it is also a spiritual prophecy that Christ would die for the faithful, his bride, which would be literally and spiritually fulfilled. Sarai being taken by Pharaoh but then given back by Pharaoh is an image of Christ laying down his life in the place of humanity but then taking his life back up again. The union of Sarai and Abram would be recognized not at first but only later just as the union of the faithful and Christ will not be fully revealed until the last days. Pharaoh is tormented just as the devil will be condemned, while Sarai is returned to Abram just as the faithful will be redeemed in Christ. The beauty of Sarai represents the value of humanity to God, while the old age of Sarai represents the advents of Christ occurring in the latter days of creation. The paradox of beauty and old age again points to the resurrection of the new body in the end times.

Sarai is both the wife and half sister of Abram, but Abram creates a mystery by introducing his wife Sarai as only his sister (Gen 20:12). The mystery surrounding the relationship between Sarai and Abram reflects the mystery surrounding the church and Christ, namely, that the faithful are the bride of the Lamb (Rev 19:7). The mystery of marriage is the mystery of one flesh, which is our redemption in the Body of Christ (Eph 3:4–6, 5:31–32). Christ is like the half brother of humanity just as Abram was the half brother of Sarai. Christ and Adam are likewise both the sons of God but not full siblings, since Adam was formed while Christ is begotten. Our surprise at Abram and Sarai embodying the union of half siblings represents our shock at the condescension of Christ in the humble incarnation in the flesh of man.

Genesis 12:14–15 And it came to pass, that, when Abram was come into Egypt, the Egyptians beheld the woman that she [was] very fair. 15 The princes also of Pharaoh [H6547] saw her, and commended her before Pharaoh [H6547]: and the woman was taken into Pharaoh's [H6547] house.

The word *Pharaoh* [H6547] (took Sarai) means "great house," which is an image of the dominion of the prince of this world (Eph 2:2). That old serpent, called the devil and also satan, with his angels with him (Rev 12:9). The emphasis on the princes of Pharaoh commending the fairness of Sarai recalls the sons of God taking the daughters of men being a central issue underlying the condemnation of the antediluvian world (Gen 6:2). Pharaoh took Sarai without any real consent of Abram and likewise without a holy fear of God just as the serpent corrupted Eve contrary to the birthright of Adam and likewise contrary to the will of God. Abram is the embodiment of faith and represents a fulfillment of both the promise embodied by Adam and also the repentance embodied by Noah. Abram represents a new man, a new Adam, prefiguring the fullness of revelation in Christ.

Pharaoh taking Sarai directly prefigures Pharaoh enslaving Israel, while the Lord afflicting the house of Pharaoh in the time of Abram prefigures the Lord afflicting all Egypt in the time of Moses. Abram ultimately receiving Sarai back from Pharaoh prefigures Moses receiving the Israelites back from Pharaoh. The redemption of the Israelites from slavery in Egypt is a figurative death and resurrection that prefigures the death and resurrection of Jesus Christ for the sake of the faithful. The redemption of Israel prefigures the blessing of the nations through Israel just as the death and resurrection of Jesus Christ prefigures the death and resurrection of the faithful in Christ.[24]

Genesis 12:16 And he entreated Abram well for her sake: and he had sheep [H6629], and oxen, and he asses, and menservants [H5650], and maidservants [H8198], and she asses, and camels.

The preservation of Abram for the sake of Sarai reflects the preservation of the natural body in expectation of the spiritual, or glorified, body, originally represented by the preservation of Adam in anticipation of the promised Seed of woman (Gen 3:15). The masculine is most closely identified with flesh, while the feminine is most closely identified with spirit. The enrichment of Abram by Pharaoh immediately prefigures the plundering of the Egyptians by the Israelites in the Exodus but ultimately prefigures the glorification of Jesus Christ in death and resurrection (Exod 3:22). The enrichment of Abram by Pharaoh in the land of Egypt prefigures the enrichment of Abraham by Abimelech in the promised land just as the glorification of Jesus Christ prefigures the glorification of the faithful in Christ (Gen 20:16). The first and second altars in Canaan at, respectively, Sichem and Bethel herald the first and second accounts of the abduction and return of the wife of Abraham by, respectively, Pharaoh and Abimelech just as the first and second sonships represented by Adam and Christ herald the First and Second Advents of Christ.

The six offerings of Pharaoh to Abram for the sake of Sarai are sheep, oxen, he asses, servants, she asses, and camels, reflecting the original six days of creation and likewise the six millennia of creation from the time of Adam. The word *sheep* [H6629] (first offering of Pharaoh), for example, has a connotation "multitude (of children)," which recalls the migrations of all mankind in exiled Adam at the opening of the first millennium. The words *menservants* [H5650] and *maidservants* [H8198] (fourth offering) reflect the servitude of humanity under the law, which foreshadows the kingship first revealed in David at the opening of the fourth millennium and finally fulfilled in the line of David in the conception of the king of kings, Jesus Christ, at the close of the fourth

---

[24] "Thus the children of God may look for no rest in this world, but must wait for the heavenly rest and quietness" (Whittingham et al., *Geneva Bible* 6L n. k#2; Gen 12:9). The promised rest in the Lord is not only a heavenly or spiritual rest or peace, but also a natural, physical, and moral strength, which itself is a form of rest.

millennium (Matt 2:2). The law precedes grace just as the kingship precedes the high priesthood just as birthright precedes blessing just as the incarnation precedes the glorification just as the First Advent precedes the Second Advent. The subsequent three living offerings of Abimelech to Abraham for the sake of Sarah would be sheep, oxen, and servants, which represents our new creation in the three days of Christ and likewise the three millennia from the incarnation of Christ (Gen 20:14). The three offerings of Abimelech in the promised land follow the six offerings of Pharaoh in Egypt just as our new creation in Christ supersedes our original creation in Adam.

Genesis 12:17–20 And the LORD plagued [H5060] Pharaoh and his house with great plagues because of Sarai Abram's wife. 18 And Pharaoh called Abram, and said, What [is] this [that] thou hast done unto me? why didst thou not tell me that she [was] thy wife? 19 Why saidst thou, She [is] my sister? so I might have taken her to me to wife: now therefore behold thy wife, take [her], and go thy way. 20 And Pharaoh commanded [his] men concerning him: and they sent him away, and his wife, and all that he had.

The word *plagued* [H5060] (the Lord plagued Pharaoh) means "to touch, strike," which recalls the prophecy that the Seed of woman would *bruise* [H7779] the head of the serpent, even though distinct Hebrew words are used in each case. Abram not telling Pharaoh that Sarai is his wife is no excuse for the dealings of Pharaoh. The serpent was likewise held accountable for tempting Eve just as all men are expected to know God through creation and ultimately recognize Jesus Christ as the incarnation of God (Rom 1:20). The restraint of Pharaoh and his princes recalls the condemnation of the sons of God in the Flood and prefigures the victory of Christ over death in the First Advent (Gen 6:4–6). The Lord plaguing Pharaoh in the time of Abram and again in the time of Moses recalls the original curse of the serpent and the corresponding condemnation of the natural body corrupted by original sin. Abram points to Moses. The first man Adam points to the second man Jesus Christ. The curse of Adam—affirmed in the curse of all mankind and embodied by the life of Abram as a stranger in a strange land (Heb 11:9) and ultimately by the life of Moses (Exod 2:22)—prefigures Christ becoming a curse for the sake of Adam-kind (Gal 3:13). The Fall of Man points to the Passion of Christ.[25]

Genesis 13:1–4 And Abram went up out of Egypt, he, and his wife, and all that he had, and Lot with him, into the south. 2 And Abram [was] very rich [H3513] in cattle, in silver, and in gold. 3 And he went on his journeys from the south even to Beth-el [H1008], unto the place [H4725]

---

[25] ". . . 'As the red heifer brought atonement for sins, similarly does the death of the righteous bring atonement for sins' [*Moed Katan*]" (Cohen, *Rabbinic Sages* 118). The blood of amoral animals cannot be efficacious but rather must be pointing to truly innocent blood. And no one is truly, perfectly, and wholly innocent except the Lord himself.

where his tent had been at the beginning [H8462], between Beth-el [H1008] and Hai; 4 Unto the place of the altar, which he had made there at the first: and there Abram called on the name of the LORD.

The word *rich* [H3513] (Abram was rich) means "to be honoured (honourable)" but has a connotation "to be heavy, burdensome," reflecting the paradox of the burden of the Messianic kingship, the suffering king, our suffering savior. The word *beginning* [H8462] (even at the beginning), as the word *beginning* [H2490], has associations "to profane" [H2490] and "to pierce" [H2490], which recalls the primordial rejection of the bloodline of Christ embodied by the original sin (Gen 4:26). The word *place* [H4725] (place at the beginning) means "standing-place, place" and is derived from the root "to arise, stand up" [H6965], which reflects the resurrection of the body in fulfillment of the promise of the Seed of woman proclaimed at the beginning of human history (Gen 3:15). The word *Bethel* [H1008] (as at the beginning) literally means "house of God," which reflects Christ ascending back to the Father after his death and resurrection and finally points to the exaltation of the faithful in Christ (John 14:2–3). The emphasis on Abram returning to Bethel after his sojourn in Egypt likewise points to the fulfillment of the glorification of Christ (First Advent) in the glorification of the Body of Christ (Second Advent).

The altars at Sichem and Bethel reflect, respectively, Adam and Jesus Christ and likewise, respectively, the First and Second Advents of Christ, whereby the altar at Bethel reflects both the glorification of Christ and the glorification of the faithful in Christ. The Head and the Body are one Body (Col 1:18). Abram does not return to his first altar at Sichem, but rather he returns to his second altar at Bethel. Likewise, Jesus Christ is not merely a new Adam. Jesus Christ is our great God (Titus 2:13). The Body of Christ is our new creation. The connection of the second altar at Bethel with the first taking and returning of Sarai in Egypt, in contrast to the second taking and returning of Sarah in the promised land, is a testimony to the First Advent of Christ being the necessary foundation of the Second Advent (Gen 20:2). The twofold revelation of Christ in the First and Second Advents reflects the twofold natures of Christ as simultaneously true man and true God and likewise the promised twofold union of the faithful with God.[26]

DIVISION

Genesis 13:5–7 And Lot also, which went with Abram, had flocks, and herds, and tents. 6 And the land was not able to bear [H5375] them, that they might dwell together [H3162]: for their substance [H7399] was great, so that they could not dwell together [H3162]. 7 And there was a strife

---

[26] ". . . Abram's use of the term Yahweh (Jehovah) [Gen 13:4, 14:22, etc.] at a time long prior to the event in [Exod 6:3]; revealing that it was of a *more complete knowledge* of that name that God spoke to Moses" (Coffman 202; Gen 14:18–20). God, who is triune, exists by nature simultaneously in time and outside time.

ADAM, NOAH, ABRAHAM

[H7379] between the herdmen [H7462] of Abram's cattle and the herdmen [H7462] of Lot's cattle: and the Canaanite and the Perizzite dwelled then in the land.

The word *substance* [H7399] (their substance was great) means "property, goods," which recalls the original dominion of man in the garden, our possession of the garden. The word *strife* [H7379] (between the herdmen of Lot and Abram) means "strife, dispute" and has a connotation "case at law," which are images of the condemnation of man and the corresponding condemnation of the land under the law. The word *bear* [H5375] (the land could not bear them) means "to lift, carry, take," which reflects the inability of the law to yield salvation, the inability of the law of itself to exalt even the faithful (1 Cor 15:56). The word *together* [H3162] (could not dwell together) has a connotation of "unitedness," which recalls not only our lost communion with God in the garden but also points to our promised unity in the Body of Christ. The *herdmen* (herdsmen) [H7462] (of Lot and Abram) represent spiritual guidance embodied by the act of herding, whereby the discord between the herdsmen of Lot and those of Abram reflects the conflict inspired by the spirit of disobedience, the conflict between the dragon and the angels of the Lord, the conflict between the children of the devil and the children of God, the conflict between flesh and spirit. The emphasis on the strife existing between the herdsmen of Lot and Abram, in contrast to Lot and Abram themselves, is a testimony to the spiritual nature of our warfare (Eph 6:12).

Abram is a spiritual man, an image of God, while Lot is a natural man, an image of fallen man. The division between the camp of Lot and the camp of Abram recalls the exile of man from the garden, which was the original division between the camp of man and the camp of God. The corruption of our original dominion by our disobedience to God is the origin of our separation from God just as the corruption of the substance of Lot through his strife with Abram is the origin of his separation from his father figure Abram. Since the Canaanites are closely linked with evil, the emphasis on their presence in the land casts a dark shadow across the relationship between Lot and Abram that recalls the serpent encouraging the discord between Eve and Adam and likewise between humanity and God. The separation of Lot and Abram reflects the fall of all mankind in Adam. Abram subsequently rescuing the enslaved Lot from the four kings reflects the baptism of repentance in the flesh under the law (Gen 14:18, 14:20). And the intervention of Abraham on behalf of Lot being connected with the destruction of Sodom and Gomorrah reflects the baptism of redemption by the Holy Spirit that is the grace of the Father unto the faithful in Christ (Gen 19:24). One, two, three.

Genesis 13:8–9 And Abram said unto Lot, Let there be no strife, I pray thee, between me and thee, and between my herdmen and thy herdmen; for we [be] brethren. 9 [Is] not the whole land before thee? separate thyself, I pray thee, from me: if [thou wilt take] the left hand, then I will

ABRAHAM AND SARAH

go to the right; or if [thou depart] to the right hand, then I will go to the left.

Abram establishing a peace with Lot through a separation from Lot recalls God preserving the lives of Adam and Eve in exile after their fall. Abram establishing Lot among the cities of the plain foreshadows his saving Lot out of the cities of the plain just as the Lord preserving fallen man in this life prefigures our promised redemption in eternal life (Gen 18:23). Lot is like an adopted son of Abram just as Adam is like an adopted son of God. Adam was not begotten but rather formed from the dust. The blood kinship between Lot and Abram represents the kinship between Adam and God through the person of Jesus Christ (Matt 12:50).

Genesis 13:10–11 And Lot lifted up his eyes, and beheld all the plain of Jordan, that it [was] well watered every where, before the LORD destroyed Sodom and Gomorrah, [even] as the garden of the LORD, like the land of Egypt, as thou comest unto Zoar. 11 Then Lot chose him all the plain of Jordan; and Lot journeyed east: and they separated themselves the one from the other.

The comparison of Sodom and Gomorrah to the garden of Eden reinforces the parallel between the account of Abram and Lot and the account of the Fall of Man. The imminent devastation looming over Sodom and Gomorrah represents the defilement of the garden of Eden that came through the original sin. Abram giving Lot first choice of the land is an affirmation of our freewill, which God will never violate, while Lot ultimately choosing to dwell in the cities of men recalls Adam effectively choosing to leave the garden through his rejection of the original commandment. Lot journeying east recalls Adam being expelled from the garden entrance on the east (Gen 3:24), Cain settling east of Eden (Gen 4:16), and also the descendants of Ham settling in the east in Babylonia, the land of Shinar (Gen 10:10).

Genesis 13:12–13 Abram dwelled in the land of Canaan, and Lot dwelled in the cities of the plain, and pitched [his] tent toward Sodom. 13 But the men of Sodom [were] wicked and sinners before the LORD exceedingly.

Lot chooses the fleeting cities of men, while Abram remains nomadic, awaiting the promised eternal city of God (Heb 11:9–10). A tent is a symbol of flesh since both are transitory habitations, whereby the emphasis on Lot pitching his tent toward Sodom reflects the strong preference of flesh in seeking sin. The separation of the natural man Lot and the spiritual man Abram is a corresponding image of the separation between flesh and spirit.

Genesis 13:14–17 And the LORD said unto Abram, after that Lot was separated from him, Lift up now thine eyes, and look from the place where thou art northward, and southward, and eastward, and westward:

15 For all the land which thou seest, to thee will I give it, and to thy seed for ever. 16 And I will make thy seed as the dust of the earth: so that if a man can number the dust of the earth, [then] shall thy seed also be numbered. 17 Arise, walk through the land in the length [H753] of it and in the breadth [H7341] of it; for I will give it unto thee.

The emphasis on Abram being blessed after his separation from Lot testifies to the blessing in the spiritual, or glorified, body following the condemnation of the natural body. The spiritual cannot be named greater unless the natural is named lesser (1 Cor 15:36). The promise of the seed of Abram is closely linked with the separation of Lot from Abram just as the original promise of the Seed of woman is closely linked with our primordial exile from the garden. The concomitant linking of the seed of Abram with the dust of the ground recalls the original formation of Adam from the dust and, thereby, points to creation itself, the dust of the ground, being a prophecy of our new creation (Rom 1:20). The Lord giving Abram the land in contrast to Abram earning the land reflects our redemption proceeding only from grace and not by works. The commandment to look upon the land is the fundamental call to see the spiritual reality in physical creation, which will ultimately be fulfilled in our promised new creation (Matt 13:10).[27]

The word *length* [H753] (of the land) has a connotation of "forbearance, self-restraint" (Prov 25:15), while the word *breadth* [H7341] (of the land) has a connotation of "largeness (of inner man, mind, will, heart)" (1 Kgs 4:29), which reflects the delayed judgment of creation (forbearance) and the corresponding multiplication of humanity in both knowledge and numbers (largeness). Our restriction to the length and the breadth of the land—in contrast to the length, breadth, and height of the land—is an emphasis on the explicitly twofold experience of the natural body, tangible flesh and soul in contrast to intangible spirit, but we nonetheless perceive our threefold creation—length, breadth, and height—just as the natural body points to the fullness of the spiritual body, a simultaneously distinct and unified spirit, soul, and body (1 Thess 5:23). Simply put, the natural body cannot fly, or transcend physicality, but the spiritual, or glorified, body can. The commandment to arise and walk through the land finally prefigures the resurrection of the dead, while the emphasis on inheriting the land is itself an affirmation that the spiritual body is a true body. The emphasis on Abram receiving all that he sees points to the restoration, or re-creation, of all creation. The image of a multitude proceeding from Abram is a prophecy of the multitude of faithful in Christ. The image of a man numbering the dust does not merely reflect an abstract large number but rather prefigures the one man Jesus Christ literally numbering every single faithful soul.[28]

---

[27] "The Word of God is present in all that exists, making it to exist by the power of the Spirit. Thus, according to Orthodox doctrine, the universe itself is a revelation of God in the Word and the Spirit" (Hopko, *Orthodox Faith* 1:143). The Trinity is the paradigm of creation.

[28] Abram taking spiritual ownership of the promised land prefigures Moses taking spiritual ownership of the same land, Deut 3:27, 34:4 (Clifford, *New Jerome* 20; Gen

ABRAHAM AND SARAH

Melchizedek

Genesis 13:18 Then Abram removed [his] tent, and came and dwelt in the plain [H436] of Mamre, which [is] in Hebron [H2275], and built there an altar unto the LORD.

The connection of the altar at *Hebron* [H2275] with the *plain* [H436], or "trees," of Mamre portends the tree of the crucifixion as a sacrificial altar, which is an emphasis on the First Advent that announces a repetition of the imagery of the previous two altars at Sichem and Bethel. The word *Hebron* [H2275] (altar at Hebron) means "association, league," which foreshadows the incarnation of Christ in the association, or community, of men. The relatively understated altar unto the Lord at Hebron is fulfilled, or completed, in the vivid Messianic image of Melchizedek offering bread and wine at Salem. The altar at Sichem was likewise fulfilled in the altar at Bethel. The altar at Hebron is fulfilled in the altar represented by the offering at Salem just as the original Davidic capital at Hebron would be fulfilled in, transferred to, Jerusalem just as the First Advent will be fulfilled in the Second Advent (1 Chr 3:4).

The two altars at Sichem and Bethel herald the two accounts of Sarah being abducted and then returned—first by Pharaoh and later by Abimelech (Gen 12:10)—just as the two altars at Hebron and Salem herald the two accounts of Lot being saved by Abraham—first in the war of the four kings and the five kings and finally from the destruction by fire (Gen 14:1). The personages of the two sons, or men, Adam and Jesus likewise prefigure the two advents of Christ. The progression from the more abstract to the more concrete reflects the fulfillment of prophecy in the world, that is, the progression of the promise of life. The progression from the wife of Abraham to the nephew (adopted son) of Abraham reflects the progression from the promise of the Seed of woman to the reality of the new creation of the children of God (Gen 3:15). The intense layering of prophecy in the account of the third major patriarch, Abraham, points to the fulfillment of all things in the Second Advent of Christ in the form of a yet future third man in the dawn of the third millennium from the First Advent of Jesus Christ. Adam, Christ, Body of Christ. The Body of Christ represents a third man, something new, animated by the fullness of God the Holy Spirit, the third person of the Trinity.

Genesis 14:1–11 And it came to pass in the days of Amraphel king of Shinar [H8152], Arioch king of Ellasar, Chedorlaomer king of Elam, and Tidal king of nations; 2 [That these] made war with Bera king of Sodom [H5467], and with Birsha king of Gomorrah [H6017], Shinab king of Admah, and Shemeber king of Zeboiim, and the king of Bela, which is Zoar. 3 All these were joined together in the vale of Siddim, which is the

---

13:14–18). Moses's spiritual possession of the promised land, seeing but not touching, then points to the First Advent of Jesus Christ, John 20:17.

salt [H4417] sea [H3220]. 4 Twelve years they served Chedorlaomer, and in the thirteenth year they rebelled. 5 And in the fourteenth year came Chedorlaomer, and the kings that [were] with him, and smote the Rephaims in Ashteroth Karnaim, and the Zuzims in Ham, and the Emims in Shaveh Kiriathaim, 6 And the Horites in their mount Seir, unto El-paran, which [is] by the wilderness. 7 And they returned, and came to En-mishpat, which [is] Kadesh, and smote all the country of the Amalekites, and also the Amorites, that dwelt in Hazezon-tamar. 8 And there went out the king of Sodom [H5467], and the king of Gomorrah [H6017], and the king of Admah, and the king of Zeboiim, and the king of Bela (the same [is] Zoar;) and they joined battle with them in the vale of Siddim; 9 With Chedorlaomer the king of Elam, and with Tidal king of nations, and Amraphel king of Shinar [H8152], and Arioch king of Ellasar; four kings with five. 10 And the vale of Siddim [was full of] slimepits [H875, H875, H2564]; and the kings of Sodom [H5467] and Gomorrah [H6017] fled, and fell there; and they that remained fled to the mountain. 11 And they took all the goods of Sodom [H5467] and Gomorrah [H6017], and all their victuals, and went their way.

The word *pits* [H875] (slimepits) has a connotation "grave (pit of)" (Ps 55:23) and is derived from the root "to make distinct, plain (expound)" [H874], which portends the judgment of flesh in death and the corresponding expounding, or revealing, of sins.[29] The word *salt* [H4417] (Salt Sea region of the five kings) has an association "to tear away, figuratively dissipate (disperse)" [H4414], which is literally a dispersion of salt but figuratively the dispersion of humanity because of sin, while the word *sea* [H3220] (Salt Sea) has a connotation "flood of invaders," which reinforces the motif of judgment and condemnation. Our present dispersion is the curse inherited from Adam, but our future unity is the blessing promised in Jesus Christ. Salt is connected with the utter desolation of warfare (Judg 9:45) and also with the covenant of salt representing the law (Num 18:19). Law and warfare are both condemnations of the natural body unto death (Rom 7:5). The law in its various forms is the covenant governing our separation from God, while grace through faith in Jesus Christ is the covenant governing our promised reunion with God. The promised internalization of the law in our new creation, having the law written on our hearts, is the promised indwelling Holy Spirit, which is the fulfillment of law in grace (Heb 10:16).

The kingdom of *Shinar* (Babylonia) [H8152] (of the coalition of four kings) and also the kingdoms of *Sodom* [H5467] and *Gomorrah* [H6017] (of the coalition of five kings) are all synonymous with evil, whereby neither coalition of kings prefigures the literal armies of God in the end times. The fundamental rejection of the authorities in the world is a rejection of the curse incurred by the first

---

[29] *Strong's* codes *slimepits* = H2564 in the main concordance, whereas *Green's Interlinear*, consistent with *Brown-Driver-Briggs*, codes *pits (was) full of asphalt* [was full of slimepits] = H875 + H875 + H2564.

man Adam, whereby the rebellion of the five kings against the four kings reflects a universal apostasy of mankind (Eph 6:5). The war of the four kings and the five kings is a conflict of man against man—a chaos inspired by the spirit of disobedience but not yet a vision of the last conflict, which will be man against God. Man against man is blasphemy against God the Son, but man against God is blasphemy against God the Holy Spirit. The rebellion of the five kings against the four kings precedes the final destruction of the cities of the plain by brimstone and fire just as wars and rumors of wars even now precede the foretold final destruction by fire of the natural body along with all of creation (Matt 24:6). The survivors of Sodom and Gomorrah fleeing from the four kings into the mountains likewise foreshadows the people of Judea fleeing into the mountains in the end times (Matt 24:15–16).[30]

Genesis 14:12 And they took Lot, Abram's brother's son, who dwelt in Sodom, and his goods, and departed.

The captivity of Lot is an image of the slavery of flesh to sin and the corresponding condemnation of the natural body under the law. Sodom and Gomorrah not being liberated apart from Abram reflects the hopelessness of humanity outside of salvation by grace through faith in Jesus Christ. The slavery of Lot follows his separation from Abram just as our slavery to sin followed, or resulted from, the original separation of Adam from God. But Lot will be preserved through the war of the four kings and the five kings and also through the final destruction of the cities of the plain by fire just as the faithful will be saved through the foretold wars and rumors of wars and also through the final destruction of creation by fire. The two tribulations of Lot reflect the two deaths (Rev 21:8). Lot is not a particularly sympathetic figure of the faithful since he chose to live in Sodom, but the faithful are neither saved by their own merit, rather only by grace. In our admission of our guilt before God, we should humbly identify with Lot and not with Abram. Only in our unmerited redemption in Christ should we identify with Abram.

Genesis 14:13–16 And there came one that had escaped, and told Abram the Hebrew [H5680]; for he dwelt in the plain of Mamre the Amorite, brother of Eshcol, and brother of Aner: and these [were] confederate [H1167, H1285] with Abram. 14 And when Abram heard that his brother was taken captive, he armed his trained [servants], born in his own house, three hundred and eighteen, and pursued [them] unto Dan [H1835]. 15 And he divided himself against them, he and his servants [H5650], by night, and smote them, and pursued them unto Hobah [H2327], which [is] on the left hand of Damascus. 16 And he brought

---

[30] We will see the Messiah only when the kingdoms of the world are making war with one another just as Abraham, Gen 14:18–20, received redemption when the kingdoms of the world were making war with one another, *Genesis Rabbah* (Cohen, *Rabbinic Sages* 350). The explicit structure of the Bible is implicit prophecy.

ADAM, NOAH, ABRAHAM

back all the goods, and also brought again his brother Lot, and his goods, and the women also, and the people.

The word *Hebrew* [H5680] (Abram the Hebrew) means "one from beyond (the river)," which literally reflects Abram originally migrating from the east but figuratively reflects God descending from heaven. The image of a river emphasizes the baptism in water, signifying death and resurrection. The east is the figurative birthplace of each new dawn and thereby an emblem of creation. The image of one who escaped reporting to Abram is an improbable event reflecting the supernatural omniscience of God. The emphasis on nighttime portends the death of Christ, while the emphasis on Abram dividing himself, his camp, portends the separation of the Father and Son (Matt 27:46) embodied by Christ becoming a curse on the cross (Gal 3:13). Abram literally divides his servants and not himself, but the separation between the Father and the Son reflects the same reality as the dispersion of fallen man. Abram redeeming Lot from captivity by force is a vision of the Father raising the Son from death through the power of the Holy Spirit.[31]

The rendering *confederate* [H1167, H1285] (with Abram) envelops the meanings "covenant" [H1285] and also "owner, lord" [H1167], with an additional connotation "husband," which reflects the host of heaven (represented by Abram's allies) in intimate communion with God (represented by Abram). The word *servants* [H5650] (Abram and his servants) means "slave, servant" but has a connotation "servants, worshipers (of God)," which reflects the faithful on the earth. The confederates of Abram fading into the background of the narrative, as compared with the servants of Abram, reflects the spiritual nature of our warfare in the present world (Eph 6:12). The wars of the plain portend the destruction of the plain just as the rejection of the Son of man portends the rejection of the Son of God, that is, the rejection of the incarnation at the First Advent portends the rejection of glorification in the Second Advent. The four kings are defeated in the normal way, but the final destruction of Sodom and Gomorrah by fire is supernatural. Likewise, wars and rumors of wars will precede the final destruction of all creation by fire.

The name *Dan* [H1835] (pursued them unto . . . and smote them) means "judge," which reflects the undeniable and incontrovertible judgments of God, while the name *Hobah* [H2327] (pursued them unto Hobah) literally means "hiding place," which reflects the wicked hiding from the face of God and likewise denying the righteousness of God.[32] But the redemption of Lot out of captivity and slavery prefigures the redemption of Lot out of death in the coming destruction of Sodom and Gomorrah just as the baptism in water prefigures the baptism of fire just as the First Advent prefigures the Second Advent. The emphasis on Abram restoring not only the people of the plain but

---

[31] The word *Hebrew* appears here in the Scriptures for the first time (Guzik 99; Gen 14:13–14). Abraham, not Moses, was the first father of the Hebrews, wherein the much later coming of Moses reflects the First Advent of Christ, not the first man Adam.

[32] Literal meaning of *Hobah* [H2327] per *Strong's*, not *Brown-Driver-Briggs*.

also their possessions is an affirmation of the resurrection, or glorification, of the body occurring together with the restoration, or re-creation, of creation.

Genesis 14:17 And the king of Sodom went out to meet him after his return from the slaughter of Chedorlaomer, and of the kings that [were] with him, at the valley of Shaveh [H7740], which [is] the king's dale.

The emphasis on Abram slaughtering Chedorlaomer testifies to the utter condemnation of the natural body, but the triumphal return of Abram prefigures the victorious resurrection of Jesus Christ in the conquest of death itself, specifically a conquest that is not finally fulfilled until the resurrection of the faithful in the end times. The word *Shaveh* [H7740] (meet Abram at Shaveh) is derived from the root "to agree with, be like, resemble" [H7737], which reflects the promised unity of the faithful in the Body of Christ and ultimately the unity of the Father and Son.[33]

Genesis 14:18 And Melchizedek [H4442] king [H4428] of Salem [H8004] brought forth bread [H3899] and wine [H3196]: and he [was] the priest [H3548] of the most high God.

The first name, or title, is *Melchizedek* [H4442], while the second name is *king* [H4428] of *Salem* [H8004]. The first name *Melchizedek* [H4442] is derived from the words "king" [H4428] and "rightness, righteousness" [H6664], whereby the first name *Melchizedek* [H4442] reflects an emphasis on justice. The word *Salem* [H8004] means "complete, safe, at peace" [H8003], whereby the second name *king* [H4428] of *Salem* [H8004] reflects a shift in emphasis from justice to mercy. Both names reflect kingship, but the emphasis shifts from justice to mercy. Adam and Jesus are likewise both true men, given kingships and dominions, but the former was governed by flesh while the latter is governed by the Spirit. The dominion of Adam (Gen 1:28) prefigures the dominion of Jesus Christ (John 16:33) just as creation reveals the Creator (Rom 1:20). The name *King of Righteousness* precedes the name *King of Peace* just as law precedes grace just as Adam precedes Jesus, while the two names together, *King of Righteousness* and *King of Peace*, imply a union of justice and mercy and likewise a union of law and grace. The unity of law and grace, likewise flesh and spirit, is the brotherhood of Adam and Jesus. The image of Melchizedek as the king of Salem likewise precedes the image of Melchizedek as the priest of the most high just as the kingship of Christ announced in the First Advent precedes the high priesthood of Christ that will be finally revealed in the Second Advent. The threefold sequence of the names, or titles, *Melchizedek*, *king of Salem*, and *high priest of God*

---

[33] "The Father is God, the Son is God, but by the same proclamation God is one, because neither in regard to nature nor activity [love] is any difference viewed [Gregory of Nyssa, *To Ablabius*]" (Rusch 159). One perfect love manifested in eternal life, one perfect unity manifested in the Body of Christ.

reflects, respectively, the threefold sequence of Adam and the First and Second Advents of Christ.[34]

The kingship of Christ is most closely identified with the First Advent, while the high priesthood of Christ is most closely identified with the Second Advent. Christ would be born of the tribe of Judah and not of the tribe of Levi, whereby his birthright under the law would proceed from David and not from Aaron. As the only begotten Son of God, Jesus Christ would be born king of kings, whereby the three magi from the east would testify at the manger to the kingship of Christ (Matt 2:1–2). Christ would persistently announce his kingdom in his earthly ministry (Matt 4:17) and would ultimately overcome the world as a conquering king (John 16:33), taking the keys of death from the prince of this world (Rev 1:18), the keys of death being the sting of death, the very power of sin, that is, the law (1 Cor 15:56). Even Pilate would mark his cross with the insignia "King of the Jews" (Matt 27:37). The traditional Jewish expectation for Messiah, according to the law of Moses, is also as a reigning king, which again connects the First Advent to kingship and to law (Mark 11:10). Kingship implies power and authority, which implies justice and likewise law, which implies flesh governed by law. The Jewish people are the formal custodians of the law and accordingly the embodiments of the law, whereby Christ would minister in the flesh only to the Jew and not to the Gentile (Matt 10:5–6). The flesh condemned under the law is embodied by the crucifixion of Jesus Christ at the First Advent, not by the glorification of Christ in the resurrection of the faithful in the Second Advent. The law governs flesh, even the incarnation of Christ in the flesh. The kingship is the birthright, while the high priesthood is the blessing.[35]

The word *priest* (kohen) [H3548] (priest of the most high) means "priest" but has a connotation "priest-king," which testifies to the union of kingship and priesthood in the person of Jesus Christ. The kingship is not simply replaced by the high priesthood, but rather the kingship is fulfilled in the high priesthood in a true union of law and grace. The resurrection of the Body of Christ in the Second Advent will likewise be the fulfillment of the resurrection of Jesus Christ as the Head of the Body in the First Advent. The Order of Aaron is the priesthood of the law, which governs the natural body, while the Order of Melchizedek is the union of kingship and priesthood in the fulfillment of law in grace, which governs the spiritual, or glorified, body. The Orders of Aaron and Melchizedek are both priesthoods, but the emphasis shifts from justice to mercy. The natural body and the spiritual body are both true bodies, but the

---

[34] "'After the order of Melchizedek' [Heb 6:20] refers to the royal *authority* and unending *duration* of Christ's high priesthood [Heb 7:23–24]" (Scofield 23 n. 1; Gen 14:18). King and high priest, birthright and blessing.

[35] "Jesus Christ, our great *Melchizedek*, is to be humbly acknowledged by every one of us as our king and priest . . . ." (Wesley 1:59; Gen 14:20). The person of Melchizedek prefigures the fullness of the revelation of Jesus Christ.

former is governed by flesh while the latter is governed by the Holy Spirit. Christ is both king and high priest. Christ is true man and true God.[36]

The birthright of Christ is the manifest kingship, while the blessing in Christ is the promised priesthood in which the faithful will enter into a full and eternal communion with God. The priesthood of Christ is the perpetual intercession for the faithful, the communion of Christ with the faithful, in which Christ is high priest forever in the Order of Melchizedek (Heb 7:25, Ps 110:4). Christ himself will be the temple in the kingdom of God in the fullness of the promised blessing (Rev 21:22). In imitation of Christ, the faithful will likewise enter into both the kingship and priesthood (Rev 1:6). The meaning of the Second Advent is the fulfillment of the First Advent just as the blessing in the priesthood is the fulfillment of the birthright of the kingship. Christ offers grace by virtue of his power and dominion under law. Priesthood implies atonement, which implies grace, which implies a spirit governed by grace. The promised exaltation of spirit by grace will be the revelation of the Body of Christ in the Second Advent, not the persecution of the faithful that marks the present world in the wake of the First Advent. The birthright inherited from Adam is death, but the blessing received by grace through faith in Jesus Christ is eternal life. The primal relationship between law and birthright is evident in the administration of the firstborn Adam under law even before our fall. The law precedes grace just as the birthright precedes the blessing just as the kingship of Christ precedes the priesthood of Christ.[37]

The bread and wine presented by Melchizedek is an image of the body and blood of Jesus Christ, who is the perfect union of flesh and spirit, likewise law and grace, and likewise kingship and priesthood. Melchizedek is a figure of Christ, while Abram, in the local context, is a figure of Levi, still in Abram at the time. Accordingly, Melchizedek presenting the body and blood to Abram prefigures the submission of Christ to the crucifixion under the law as represented by the tribe of Levi being custodians of the law (Heb 7:9–10). The word *bread* [H3899] (bread and wine) has a connotation "to fight, do battle" [H3898], which is an image of flesh, likewise of the death of the natural body. The word *wine* [H3196] (bread and wine) is derived from an unused root "to effervesce," which is literally the frothiness of wine but figuratively the uplifting intangible quality of the Spirit and likewise the uplifting resurrection of the

---

[36] "The episode [Abraham tithing to Melchizedek] is one of several allusions in the story to David, the later king of Jerusalem, who also exercised priestly functions (2 Sam 6:17)" (Clifford, *New Jerome* 21; Gen 14:18–20). The king-priest David then points to Jesus Christ as the king of kings and our high priest, Heb 7:17.

[37] " '[T]he cross makes kings of all those reborn in Christ and the anointing of the Holy Spirit consecrates them as priests ... What, indeed, is as royal for a soul as to govern the body in obedience to God? And what is as priestly as to dedicate a pure conscience to the Lord and to offer the spotless offerings of devotion on the altar of the heart?' [Leo the Great, *Sermons*]" (Rom. Catholic Church, *Catechism* 226). The kingship is as tangible as the flesh, while the priesthood is as ethereal as spirit.

spiritual, or glorified, body through the power of the Holy Spirit.[38] The relationship between body and flesh is direct, while the relationship between blood and spirit is perhaps less obvious but nonetheless clearly established by the received linking of blood and the vital, or life, force (Lev 17:11). Flesh embodies death, while spirit embodies life. Bread and wine also reflect, respectively, the Covenants of Law and Grace and likewise, respectively, the First and Second Advents, whereby eating the flesh of Christ (bread) represents the condemnation of the natural body under the law while drinking the blood of Christ (wine) represents our promised new creation in the Body of Christ (John 6:56). The revelation of both the bread and the wine in the First Advent is an affirmation that our promised redemption is guaranteed by the victory of Christ over death (Eph 1:13–14). This is the resurrection of Christ as the Head that points to the resurrection of all the faithful in the Body of Christ.[39]

Genesis 14:19–20 And he blessed him, and said, Blessed [be] Abram of the most high [H5945] God, possessor [H7069] of heaven and earth: 20 And blessed be the most high [H5945] God, which hath delivered thine enemies into thy hand. And he gave him tithes [H4643] of all.

The word *most high* [H5945] (Abram of the most high God) is derived from the root "to go up, ascend, climb" [H5927], which foreshadows the resurrection of Jesus Christ and likewise the resurrection of the faithful in Christ, the Body of Christ. The word *possessor* [H7069] (God is the possessor of heaven and earth) means "to get, acquire" and has connotations "to buy" and "of God as victoriously redeeming" and also "of acquiring knowledge, wisdom," recalling the original creation through God the Son and foreshadowing our new creation in God the Son (John 1:4).

Melchizedek (grace) blessing Abram (law) prefigures the Father (through the Spirit) blessing the Son (who fulfills the law in the flesh) and likewise the blessing of the faithful in the Son (the faithful in imitation of Christ). The juxtaposed comparisons of Melchizedek to both the Father and the Son reflect the unity of the Son and the Father (John 10:30), while the comparisons of Abram to both Levi and Christ reflect the fulfillment of the law in the person of Christ (Matt 5:17). The close connection of the blessing of the third major patriarch, Abram, with the blessing of God recalls the close connection of the blessing of the third son Shem with the blessing of God, while the ambiguity between man and God in each case points to our promised communion with God in the Body of Christ (Gen 9:26). The emphasis on God delivering

---

[38] Root per *Strong's*, not *Brown-Driver-Briggs*, but the significance of an uplifting, or upward, effervescence is clear regardless of exact etymology.

[39] "Also in the priest Melchizedek we see prefigured the sacrament of the sacrifice of the Lord, according to what divine Scripture testifies, and says, 'And Melchizedek, king of Salem, brought forth bread and wine' [Cyprian of Carthage, *Epistles*]" (Roberts et al., *Ante-Nicene Fathers* 5:359). The Old Testament prefiguring the New Testament—that is, the Old Covenant prefiguring the New Covenant—is the Covenant of Law pointing to and guaranteeing the Covenant of Grace.

Abram's enemies into his hands points to God the Father promising to make the enemies of God the Son his footstool in the end times of the present age (Acts 2:34–36, 1 Cor 15:25–26).

The word *tithes* [H4643] (Abram tithes) means "tenth part," which reflects the linking of the Covenant of Law with the number 10, epitomized by the Decalogue. Abram (Levi) tithing to Melchizedek (Christ) is an image of the submission of the law unto grace and likewise the fulfillment of the law in grace. The image of Levi tithing to Christ is a corresponding prophecy of the Order of Aaron being superseded by the Order of Melchizedek. The Order of Aaron is the priesthood of the first covenant, while the Order of Melchizedek is the priesthood of the second covenant (Heb 7:11). The blessing of Abram by Melchizedek (Christ submitting to the law) followed by the tithing of Abram to Melchizedek (Christ taking dominion over the law, likewise over death) is a vision of the death and resurrection of Christ at the First Advent heralding the death and resurrection of the Body of Christ in the Second Advent.[40]

Genesis 14:21–24 And the king of Sodom said unto Abram, Give me the persons, and take the goods to thyself. 22 And Abram said to the king of Sodom, I have lift up mine hand unto the LORD, the most high God, the possessor of heaven and earth, 23 That I will not [take] from a thread even to a shoelatchet, and that I will not take any thing that [is] thine, lest thou shouldest say, I have made Abram rich: 24 Save only that which the young men have eaten, and the portion of the men which went with me, Aner, Eshcol, and Mamre; let them take their portion.

Abram restoring the captives of war reflects the redemption of the faithful from slavery to sin, while Abram restoring their material possessions reflects the preservation of the faithful in the world and finally the restoration, or re-creation, of physical creation. Lot will remain in Sodom, but only for a time. The material goods of the people of Sodom represent physical creation, likewise the physical body, and likewise the works of the flesh. The king of Sodom presenting the goods of the people to Abram but claiming the people for himself is a vision of the devil presenting the works of man to God and claiming, or demanding, their condemnation. The king of Sodom seeks only the captives and not their material goods just as the devil finally seeks our spiritual corruption and not merely our physical corruption. But the captives and their possessions not being separated points to the promised union of spirit and flesh in the spiritual, or glorified, resurrection body. The king of Sodom offering the plunder to Abram is a corresponding offer to purchase the captives, whereby Abram not accepting any recompense is an affirmation that the redemption of life is only by grace and not by works. The people of Sodom, specifically Lot and his family, are not sympathetic figures of the faithful, but neither are any of

---

[40] "[N]ot only the tithe of all, but all we have, must be given up to him [Jesus Christ]" (Wesley 1:59; Gen 14:20). Yes, even our very lives also, for the present natural body must be supplanted by the spiritual, or glorified, resurrection body.

us, since we are in no way saved by our own merit, rather only by the grace of the Lord God.[41]

Firstborn

Genesis 15:1 After these things the word of the Lord came unto Abram in a vision, saying, Fear not, Abram: I [am] thy shield, [and] thy exceeding great reward.

Fear is the nature of flesh in the present fallen world, while love is the nature of spirit, at least for an uncorrupted soul. The image of the Lord as our shield reflects the preservation of the natural body. The image of the Lord as our reward is the promise of the indwelling Holy Spirit, the fullness of which will be finally revealed in the resurrection of the spiritual, or glorified, body.[42]

Genesis 15:2–5 And Abram said, Lord God, what wilt thou give me, seeing I go childless, and the steward [H1121, H4943] of my house [is] this Eliezer [H461] of Damascus? 3 And Abram said, Behold, to me thou hast given no seed: and, lo, one born in my house is mine heir [H3423]. 4 And, behold, the word of the Lord [came] unto him, saying, This shall not be thine heir [H3423]; but he that shall come forth out of thine own bowels [H4578] shall be thine heir [H3423]. 5 And he brought him forth abroad, and said, Look now toward heaven, and tell the stars, if thou be able to number them: and he said unto him, So shall thy seed be.

The image of Abram lamenting in his barrenness, wondering what he could possibly receive from the Lord, is a vision of the hopelessness of flesh outside of the grace that comes only through faith in the Son. Jesus Christ is the embodiment of the promised offspring of Abram that is the Body of Christ. The comparison of the promised descendants of Abram to the stars in the sky, in contrast to the previous comparison to the dust of the earth, is not only an

---

[41] Abram stating that he would not accept a thread even to a shoelatchet from the king of Sodom is a prophecy that a shoe—representing the walk, or works, of the old law and corrupted flesh—would not be accepted as payment for the redemption of the faithful, Ruth 4:7.

[42] Gen 11:27–22:24, termed the Abraham cycle, shows a concentric literary pattern centered upon the two elements 15:1–16:16 and 17:1–18:15 (Waltke 20). The Abraham cycle begins with the call of Abraham, 11:27–32, and ends with the bride of Isaac, 22:20–24, just as the call to faith leads us to the marriage of the Lamb. Gen 15:1–16:16 connects images of fear and captivity with the birth of Ishmael, while 17:1–18:15 connects images of new creation with the promise of Isaac. The former images connected with Ishmael look back to our death in Adam, while the latter images connected with Isaac look forward to our new life in Christ, in the Body of Christ. The blessing of Isaac and the blessing of Ishmael through Isaac being centered in the cycle reflects the cross standing in the crossroads of time between the original creation and the promised new creation.

affirmation of the multiplication of Abram but also points to the glorification of the resurrected body (Gen 13:16). The dust of the earth is to the stars of the sky as the natural body is to the spiritual, or glorified, body. The literal descendants of Abram prefigure the faithful as his true descendants just as the natural body prefigures the spiritual, or glorified, body (Gal 3:7).[43]

The name *Eliezer* [H461] (steward of my house) means "God is help" and is derived, in part, from the word *help meet* (helper) [H5828], describing Eve and closely identified with Eve being taken from the side (rib) of Adam (Gen 2:20–22).[44] The rendering *steward* [H1121, H4943] (Eliezer) envelops the meanings "son" [H1121] and "acquisition, possession (heir)" [H4943], which recalls the promised Seed of woman (Gen 3:15). Eliezer, as one who helps the house of Abram, has a feminine undertone that reflects the Holy Spirit, while the sonship also connected with Eliezer is an explicit masculine image of the Son. Images of the Spirit are commonly implicit, reflecting the relatively subtle and abstract nature and movement of the third person of the Trinity. The overlapping images of the Spirit and the Son marking the chief steward of Abram's house reflects the Spirit and the Son proceeding together from the Father and finally points to the unity of the Trinity. The Spirit and the Son proceeding from the Father is the breath of life embodied by Eve, the mother of all humanity, proceeding from the first man, Adam, in our original creation (Gen 2:23). The Son proceeding from the Spirit in the overshadowing of Mary by the Spirit is the call to repentance in the flesh (Luke 1:35). The Holy Spirit proceeding from the Son to indwell the faithful is our promised new creation in the resurrection (John 15:26). First, second, third. Father, Son, Spirit.[45]

The word *heir* [H3423] (heir of Abram) has connotations "to seize" and "to dispossess," which foreshadows the second son Jesus Christ seizing the discarded birthright of the first son Adam. Isaac would, at least figuratively, dispossess Eliezer, identifying Eliezer with Adam and Isaac with Christ. The parallel identification of Eliezer with both Adam and the Holy Spirit reflects Adam as the original embodiment of the breath of life (Gen 2:7). The parallel identification of Eliezer with both Adam and Christ reflects Christ as the new Adam (Eph 4:24). Eliezer would not be the heir of Abram just as Adam would

---

[43] Abraham's offspring being described first as the "dust of the earth" but later as the "stars of the heaven" implies a twofold distinction, namely, the literal descendents of Abraham in the flesh as compared with the spiritual children of Abraham by faith (Coffman 208; Gen 15:5). The natural must precede the spiritual.

[44] Etymology per *Strong's*, but the image, or meaning, "helper" being shared is clear in *Brown-Driver-Briggs*.

[45] "The Son is these things, who says, 'I am the life' [John 11:25] and 'I Wisdom have encamped with prudence' [Prov 8:12]. Therefore, is not the individual impious who says, 'There was once when the Son was not'? For this is the same thing as saying, 'There was once when the fountain was dry, without life and wisdom' [Athanasius, *Orations Against the Arians*]" (Rusch 82). The virgin birth is the procession of the Spirit and the Son from the Father made visible at a specific point, or pivot, in time, but the procession of the Trinity itself, viewed in isolation from creation, is necessarily without beginning or end.

not be the heir of the Father just as the Spirit of God, the embodiment of the primordial breath of life, is most closely identified with the original creation. The Son of God is most closely identified with our new creation in the Body of Christ. The primal image of creation in the Old Testament is the Spirit of God hovering over the waters (Gen 1:2), while the essential revelation of creation in the New Testament is the Son as the Word of God made flesh (John 1:3, 1:14). The progression of revelation from God the Spirit to God the Son reflects the Spirit and Son proceeding from God the Father, specifically in the overshadowing of Mary and generally in every act of creation. God the Son is begotten, not created, without beginning or end, but his nature, his very expression, is life, the embodiment of creation (John 1:4). The fundamental image of new creation in the New Testament is the Body of Christ, but the quickening of the Body is finally realized as the indwelling of God the Holy Spirit that is the fullness of the breath of life.[46]

The word *bowels* [H4578] (heir from the bowels of Abram) means "inward parts," which again recalls Eve and figuratively all humanity taken from the side of Adam (Gen 2:22). Isaac would proceed from the inward parts of Abram just as Christ is the only begotten Son of the Father (John 1:18). The promise is, not the natural body from Adam (original creation), but rather the spiritual, or glorified, body in Christ (new creation). Adam was formed, representing our original creation through the Son, but the Son is begotten as the embodiment of life itself, the font of our promised rebirth in the Son. Isaac and not Eliezer would be the heir of Abram just as Christ would follow Adam just as the Son and not the Spirit would redeem humanity through the cross (Matt 27:46). Father, Son, Spirit. Creator, redeemer, sanctifier.

Genesis 15:6 And he believed [H539] in the LORD; and he counted [H2803] it to him for righteousness [H6666].

The word *believed* [H539] (in the Lord) has connotations "to believe" and "to trust" and "to support, nourish" in the Hebrew, which reflects the fullness of the meaning of faith, in contrast to the popular conceptions of simple belief and blind faith.[47] Even the demons believe in God, but they deny the grace of God (Jas 2:19). The word *counted* [H2803] (counted for righteousness) has a connotation "to impute (righteousness or iniquity)," while the word *righteousness* [H6666] has a connotation of "judge, ruler, king." The Covenant of Law. The

---

[46] The life of God the Father is his own while the life of God the Son proceeds from the Father like the radiance of light from a source, but yet the light of God the Son is still the same light of God the Father—Athanasius, *Orations Against the Arians* (Norris 96). Jesus Christ is the way, the truth, and the life—the way of the Holy Spirit, the very embodiment of truth, and the life of the Father, John 14:6.

[47] "Some think his believing in the Lord respected, not only the Lord promising, but the Lord promised, the Lord Jesus, the Mediator of the new covenant. *He believed in Him*, that is, received and embraced the divine revelation concerning Him, and *rejoiced to see his day*, though at so great a distance, [John 8:56]" (Henry 1:82; Gen 15:2–6). The peoples of God throughout all time are redeemed according to the one cross.

faith of Abram being counted as righteousness, figuratively substituting faith in the place of justice, prefigures the faithful one, Jesus Christ, fulfilling the law and the prophets, substituting himself for the unrighteous.[48] The teaching that faith without works is dead (Jas 2:17) and likewise that the faith of Abram was made complete by what he did (Jas 2:22) are affirmations not of ourselves but rather the work of the cross (Gal 3:13–14). The call to be perfect under the law is a prophecy of the sinlessness of Christ and finally the perfection of the faithful in Christ by grace. The call to pick up our own crosses and follow Christ is finally a prophecy of our imitation of Christ in death and resurrection and likewise the incontestable condemnation of the natural body. We are saved only by faith and not by works. Our works are a manifestation of our salvation just as Jesus Christ is the visible image of the invisible God.[49]

Genesis 15:7–8 And he said unto him, I [am] the LORD that brought thee out of Ur of the Chaldees, to give thee this land to inherit [H3423] it. 8 And he said, Lord GOD, whereby shall I know that I shall inherit [H3423] it?

The emphasis on the Lord having brought Abram out of the east to inherit the promised land is an affirmation of the Lord being the God of creation and also the God of our new creation. The flowing continuity in the narrative from creation to new creation reflects the seamless unity of law and grace, likewise justice and mercy, and likewise flesh and spirit. Abram asks for a sign just as Israel would ask for a sign, in a universal supplication that would ultimately be answered in the sign of Jonah as the fulfillment of law in grace (Matt 12:39). The promise of Isaac, embodied by the sacrificial altars of Abram, precedes the birth of Ishmael just as the promise of life, embodied by physical creation, preceded the formation of Adam from the dust of the ground. Abram will *inherit* [H3423] the land of promise, but someone must die before an inheritance is received. And it seems that Abram knew full well that the required death would be the death of the Messiah and also the death of his own flesh in imitation, or anticipation, of the Messiah, John 8:56.

Genesis 15:9–10 And he said unto him, Take me an heifer [H5697] of three years old, and a she goat [H5795] of three years old, and a ram [H352] of three years old, and a turtledove [H8449], and a young pigeon [H1469]. 10 And he took unto him all these, and divided them in the midst, and laid each piece one against another: but the birds divided he not.

---

[48] "This is the first time we read of believing, and as early do we hear of imputed righteousness" (Gill 1:88; Gen 15:6). The Old and New Testaments are one Book.
[49] "This is urged in the New Testament to prove, that we are justified by faith without the works of the law, [Rom 4:3, Gal 3:6] . . . ." (Wesley 1:61; Gen 15:6). Actually by grace through faith in the work of the cross on our behalf.

ADAM, NOAH, ABRAHAM

The animal sacrifices appointed to Abram prefigure the enslavement and the emancipation of the Israelites in Egypt and ultimately the death and resurrection of Jesus Christ in the world. The repetition of three sacrifices, each three years old, points to the liberation of the seed of Abram at the end of four centuries and ultimately to the incarnation of the promised Seed of woman at the end of the fourth millennium (Gen 15:13, 15:16). A year represents an annual repetition of death and resurrection played out in the seasons, while each generation replacing the previous generation is also a figurative death and resurrection. Four generations comprise three repetitions, or figuratively three years. The three three-year-old sacrifices represent the passing of three generations, while the emphasis that each sacrifice must be three years old is an affirmation that the death and resurrection of each generation is a microcosm of the death and resurrection embodied by the overall enslavement and emancipation of the people of God.[50]

The three three-year-old sacrifices of Abram directly prefigure the passing of three generations of enslavement in Egypt, but ultimately the three threes point to the earthly ministry of Jesus Christ being finished in the three-day entombment and finally being fulfilled in the dawn of the third millennium from the incarnation. The three-year-old sacrifices compared to the four generations in Egypt thereby points to the sign of Jonah being fulfilled after the fourth millennium from Adam, likewise the three millennia from Christ following the four millennia from Adam. Three repetitions from the Davidic kingdom to the millennial kingdom. A total of seven millennia represents a total of six repetitions. The layering of symbolism reflects the universality of God as the Lord of all creation and likewise the certainty of the redemption of the faithful that is the will of God. The juxtaposition of revelations of specific and ambiguous time frames in the Scriptures reflects the paradox of the incontestable will of God contrasted with the inviolable freewill of man.[51]

The sequence of sacrifices being prescribed in the order of a *heifer* [H5697], a *she goat* [H5795], and a *ram* (male lamb) [H352] specifically represents the passing of the generations in Egypt and generally represents the passing of the generations of man until the kingdom of God as heralded by the kingship of David. The relationship to the overarching progression is evident in the varied Scriptural images connected with each sacrifice. A *heifer* [H5697] is identified with innocent blood spilled by an unknown assailant, which recalls the serpent encouraging Adam unto death, ultimately the death of all flesh in the Flood (Deut 21:1–9). A *she goat* [H5795] is identified with the rejection of the firstborn (of woman), which reflects the call of Abram as a new Adam after the Flood

---

[50] "[E]very animal allowed or commanded to be sacrificed under the Mosaic law is to be found in this list. And is it not a proof that God was now giving to Abram an *epitome* of that law and its sacrifices which he intended more fully to reveal to Moses;..." (Clarke 1:106; Gen 15:9). The law was proclaimed in the garden of Eden and, thereby, should be recognized as the very foundation of all creation, Gen 2:15–17.

[51] "God appointed that each of the beasts used for his service should be three years old, because then they were at their full growth and strength" (Wesley 1:62; Gen 15:9). The authority and power of Jesus Christ.

(Gen 27:9–10). The *ram* (male lamb) [H352] prefigures the Passover lamb of the fourth generation in Egypt and ultimately points to Christ as the Lamb of God in fulfillment of the Davidic kingdom of the fourth millennium.[52]

The pair of small birds is different in kind from the preceding animal sacrifices and, thereby, represents something new, specifically our new creation in the Holy Spirit. The *turtledove* [H8449] and *young pigeon* [H1469] prescribed to Abram prefigure the Holy Spirit descending upon the Lamb of God in the form of a dove (Matt 3:16). The law expressly allows the substitution of pairs of doves or pigeons for a lamb as a sacrifice, which represents the resurrection of Christ by the power of the Holy Spirit (Lev 5:7). The one ram sacrificed by Abram figuratively becomes two birds just as the one sacrifice of the Lamb of God heralds the resurrection of both the bridegroom and the bride. The one becoming two is also represented by the act of cleaving the sacrifices. The small birds not being cleft themselves is finally a sign of sinlessness, but the separation between the two small birds portends a separation between the bridegroom and bride, even after the sacrifice of the Lamb of God, that is, until the glorious reappearing.[53]

Genesis 15:11–16 And when the fowls came down upon the carcases, Abram drove them away. 12 And when the sun was going down, a deep sleep fell upon Abram; and, lo, an horror of great darkness fell upon him. 13 And he said unto Abram, Know of a surety that thy seed shall be a stranger in a land [that is] not theirs, and shall serve them; and they shall afflict them four hundred years; 14 And also that nation, whom they shall serve, will I judge: and afterward shall they come out with great substance. 15 And thou shalt go to thy fathers in peace; thou shalt be buried in a good old age. 16 But in the fourth generation they shall come hither again: for the iniquity of the Amorites [is] not yet full.

Abram driving away birds of prey reflects the preservation of humanity until the end times. Abram finally falling into a deep sleep and the concomitant setting of the sun represents death and destruction. The horror of darkness falling upon father Abram portends the judgment of God, the wrath of God. The collective seed of Abram would be strangers in Egypt just as the one Seed, Jesus Christ, would be a stranger in the world. The descendants of Abram would serve the Egyptians just as Christ would come to serve all humanity. And they would be afflicted just as Christ would be afflicted. But Egypt would be judged just as all creation will be judged. And the Israelites would come out of bondage with great wealth just as Christ would rise from the grave and be

---

[52] Some Rabbinical apocalyptic writers have viewed Abraham's four different kinds of sacrificed animals in Gen 15 as foreshadowing the four kingdoms in the book of Daniel (*Jewish Encyclopedia*, s.v. "Abraham"). The edifice of prophecy is motif.

[53] Christ sanctified himself in baptism not for his own sake but rather for our sake, for truly it was our body that he did bear—Athanasius, *Orations Against the Arians* (Rusch 110). Jesus is the prophesied new Adam, from whose side our promised resurrection bodies will proceed.

glorified.⁵⁴ The progression from the condemnation of the one nation of Egypt to the condemnation of the many nations of the Canaanites reflects the progression from the condemnation of the one man Adam to the final condemnation of all flesh, all creation. The foretold fullness of the iniquity of the Canaanites portends a universal apostasy in the end times.⁵⁵

Genesis 15:17 And it came to pass, that, when the sun went down, and it was dark, behold a smoking furnace [H8574], and a burning lamp [H3940] that passed between those pieces.

The word *furnace* [H8574] (smoking furnace) means "portable stove or fire pot," reflecting the wrath of God and likewise the justice of God as signified by baking bread, the bread of affliction (Lev 26:26). The word *lamp* [H3940] (burning lamp) means "torch," a light in the darkness symbolizing the promise of life and likewise the mercy of God (Isa 62:1). The furnace and lamp together represent the union of justice and mercy that is the fullness of the presence of God. The furnace is recounted before the lamp just as the law precedes the fulfillment of the law in grace. The sacrifices of Abram being cut in half is a fundamental image of covenant, reflecting the separation of evil and good embodied by the death and resurrection of Christ and likewise the death and resurrection of the faithful in Christ.⁵⁶ The emphasis on the smoking furnace and burning lamp passing between the pieces of the sacrifices is an affirmation of the essential separation of good and evil in the presence of God.⁵⁷

---

⁵⁴ "The future as unfolded here holds three successive stages of suffering: alienage, enslavement, and oppression, to be followed by three successive stages of redemption: judgment on the oppressor, the Exodus, and settlement in the promised land" (Sarna 115; Gen 15:13–16). The former stages of suffering reflect the original fall, the subsequent slavery to sin and death, and finally the wrath of God, while the latter stages of redemption reflect a sanctifying recapitulation of the former, specifically the victory of the cross, the call of the faithful, and finally the kingdom of God. Creation, redemption, sanctification.

⁵⁵ Gen 15:7–15:21 shows a chiastic literary pattern with 15:12–16 as the pivot (Waltke 36). The pivotal image of restoration from slavery being the sign of the promise of an inheritance in the land points to the death and resurrection of Christ being the seal of the promise of a restoration of and inheritance in all creation.

⁵⁶ In accordance with Jer 34:17–20, the cleaving of sacrifices is understood to have a retributive significance (Sarna 114; Gen 15:9–17). The cleaving of any flesh is the cleaving of all flesh.

⁵⁷ The smoking furnace and burning lamp parallel the presence of God as represented by the pillars of smoke and fire in the Exodus, while the sacrifices being cut into pieces can be compared to the broken body of Christ (Guzik 108; Gen 15:17–21). The analogy between the furnace and lamp as compared with the pillar of smoke and pillar of fire is unmistakable given the context of foretelling the Exodus, wherein cutting, or dividing, the sacrifices can further be connected with dividing the waters in the Exodus, which points to the fulfillment of the sign of circumcision in the baptism of Christ.

ABRAHAM AND SARAH

Genesis 15:18–21 In the same day the LORD made a covenant with Abram, saying, Unto thy seed have I given this land, from the river of Egypt unto the great river, the river Euphrates: 19 The Kenites, and the Kenizzites, and the Kadmonites, 20 And the Hittites, and the Perizzites, and the Rephaims, 21 And the Amorites, and the Canaanites, and the Girgashites, and the Jebusites.

The promised city of God to be set up in the midst of the nations of men during the millennial reign of Jesus Christ (Rev 20:7–9).

Genesis 16:1–3 Now Sarai Abram's wife bare him no children: and she had an handmaid, an Egyptian, whose name [was] Hagar. 2 And Sarai said unto Abram, Behold now, the LORD hath restrained me from bearing: I pray thee, go in unto my maid; it may be that I may obtain children by her. And Abram hearkened to the voice of Sarai. 3 And Sarai Abram's wife took Hagar her maid the Egyptian, after Abram had dwelt ten years in the land of Canaan, and gave her to her husband Abram to be his wife.

The Egyptian heritage of Hagar recalls the sojourn of Abram in Egypt because of a famine (Gen 12:10) and foreshadows the slavery of the offspring of Abram in Egypt that would also originate in a famine (Gen 41:57). Famine and exile are deprivations of the flesh that reflect the primordial exile of man from the garden and likewise the condemnation of the flesh under the law. Bondage is also a deprivation representing slavery to sin, the yoke of the law. The servitude of Hagar, as the Egyptian mother of Abram's firstborn, portends the enslavement to Pharaoh in Egypt, the nation of Israel being born in Egypt, of Egypt, just as Abram's firstborn would be born of Hagar (Gal 4:25). This is ultimately the enslavement of all humanity to sin. The number 10 is closely connected with the law and likewise the curse of the flesh under the law, whereby the linking of the servitude of Hagar with the ten years that Abram had lived in Canaan reinforces the connection between the law and slavery to sin. The emphasis on the long delay of the promised birth, specifically connected with a ten-year period, testifies to the long-suffering of God, expressly in the call to repentance proclaimed by the law.

Sarai giving Hagar to Abram recalls Eve giving of the forbidden tree to Adam, while Abram obeying Sarai recalls Adam obeying Eve (Gen 3:6). The promise of God does not satisfy Sarai just as the presence of God did not satisfy Eve. Sarai thinks that she can bear offspring—ultimately the promised Messiah, the Son of God—through Hagar just as Eve thought that she could become like God through the tree of knowledge—through the law of the flesh (Gen 3:5). The barrenness of Sarai apart from the promise of God reflects the barrenness of humanity apart from the presence of God. No overt image of the serpent marks the account of Sarai and Hagar, but rather their faithlessness itself is the manifestation of the spirit of disobedience, the wiles of the devil, the accuser (Eph 6:11–13). The degradation of the serpent from an explicit presence in the time of Adam to an implicit spirit of disobedience in the time of Abraham corresponds to a new world order having been established through the floodwaters in the baptism of the world (1 Pet 3:20–22).

Genesis 16:4–6 And he went in unto Hagar, and she conceived: and when she saw that she had conceived, her mistress was despised in her eyes. 5 And Sarai said unto Abram, My wrong [be] upon thee: I have given my maid into thy bosom; and when she saw that she had conceived, I was despised in her eyes: the LORD judge between me and thee. 6 But Abram said unto Sarai, Behold, thy maid [is] in thy hand; do to her as it pleaseth thee. And when Sarai dealt hardly with her, she fled from her face.

Abram obeying Sarai recalls Adam obeying Eve. The conception of Ishmael by the bondwoman Hagar reflects our inheritance of the original curse from Adam, while the offspring of Hagar ultimately being supplanted by the offspring of Sarai foreshadows our promised redemption in Christ. The flight of Hagar from Sarai reflects the flight of humanity from the presence of God. The haughtiness of Hagar recalls the primordial pride of humanity rebelling against the original commandment; the flight of Hagar recalls the original exile from the face of God; and the call to submission reflects the continuing call to repentance proclaimed by the law. Sarai laying the wrong she suffered from Hagar upon Abram prefigures the condemnation of the law being laid upon Jesus Christ. Sarai calling down the judgment of God between Abram and herself reflects the undeniable dominion of the law of God, the will of God, proceeding from God, ultimately resting upon God, and finally returning to God. Abram giving Hagar into the hand of Sarai, as well as Sarai dealing harshly with Hagar, reflects the undeniable condemnation of the natural body, ultimately realized in the Seed of woman being nailed to the cross.

Hagar and Sarai can be compared to the two covenants, respectively, the Covenant of Law and the Covenant of Grace (Gal 4:24). Hagar despising Sarai reflects the fundamental conflict between law and grace and likewise between flesh and spirit, while the servitude of Hagar to Sarai is an image of the law being superseded by grace and likewise the natural body being superseded by the spiritual, or glorified, body. Sarai's name would later be changed to Sarah as a sign of new creation in the second covenant, while Hagar's name would not be changed as a sign of our hopelessness in the first covenant. The one name *Hagar* is likewise an emblem of the one man Adam, while the two names *Sarai* and *Sarah* are emblems of the First and Second Advents of Christ.

Genesis 16:7–9 And the angel [H4397] of the LORD found her by a fountain of water in the wilderness, by the fountain in the way to Shur. 8 And he said, Hagar, Sarai's maid, whence camest thou? and whither wilt thou go? And she said, I flee from the face of my mistress Sarai. 9 And the angel [H4397] of the LORD said unto her, Return to thy mistress, and submit thyself under her hands.

ABRAHAM AND SARAH

The desolate wilderness of the desert is a reflection of a spiritually desolate world, while the fountain of water represents our cleansing from sin in the natural body. Water is a ubiquitous sign of flesh and likewise the law—exemplified by the ceremonial purification in water as prescribed by the formal law (Exod 29:4) that is the death and resurrection in fulfillment of the law as represented by the baptism in water (Rom 6:4). Ceremonial cleansing is a literal cleansing that emphasizes physical uncleanness, while the baptism in water is a symbolic death and resurrection that emphasizes spiritual uncleanness. Both water rituals represent the same call to repentance, but the progressive revelation of water baptism as compared with ceremonial cleansing reflects the reality of Christ compared with the promise of Adam. Likewise, water is the sign of the old covenant but blood is the sign of the new covenant (Luke 22:20). To be dipped in water is the baptism of repentance (Mark 1:4), but to be washed in the blood of Christ is the baptism of the Holy Spirit (Rev 1:5). The first baptism that is by water precedes the second baptism that is by the Spirit just as the first man Adam precedes the second man Jesus Christ just as the First Advent of Christ precedes the Second Advent.[58]

The word *angel* (Angel) [H4397] (angel of the Lord) means "messenger" in the Hebrew. God sending messengers into the world reflects our separation from God because of sin. The implicit call to recognize God not directly but rather in his messengers is the call to faith and finally the call to recognize Jesus Christ as the incarnation of God. The indirect representation of the will of God through messengers also reflects the revelation of the Creator in creation—including the physical world and the human mind and the human conscience—though again ultimately embodied by the humble condescension of Jesus Christ in the flesh (Rom 1:20). The angel asking where Hagar would go implies that Hagar has nowhere to go and likewise that humanity has nowhere to seek redemption except in Christ. The angel directing Hagar back to Sarai is a vision of the law guiding us to grace (Gal 3:24). The call of Hagar to submit to Sarai is the call to submit to the authorities of the world, likewise the call to submit to the law, and likewise the call to repentance in the flesh (Rom 13:1). The call to submit to the authorities of the world is the original curse of Adam.

Genesis 16:10–12 And the angel of the LORD said unto her, I will multiply thy seed exceedingly, that it shall not be numbered for multitude. 11 And the angel of the LORD said unto her, Behold, thou [art] with child, and shalt bear a son, and shalt call his name Ishmael [H3458]; because the LORD hath heard thy affliction. 12 And he will be a wild man; his hand [will be] against every man, and every man's hand against him; and he shall dwell in the presence of all his brethren.

---

[58] ". . . God's commandments and words and to speak, sing, and meditate on them. This, indeed, is the true holy water . . . ." (Luther, *Large Catechism* 4). Symbols, though static, represent doing, while doing, though impossible, represents becoming.

The name *Ishmael* [H3458] means "God will hear," which is specifically God hearing the suffering of Hagar in the desert, though finally God hearing the suffering of all humanity in the world. The wild man Ishmael would be a natural man, while Isaac would be a spiritual man. The firstborn Ishmael and the second born Isaac reflect the first man Adam and the second man Jesus (1 Cor 15:47). But the first man also prefigures the second man. The first foreshadows the second, while the second fulfills the first. The bondwoman Hagar reflects the law, whereby the multitude that would proceed from her represents all humanity enslaved under the law (Gal 4:24–25). Christ would likewise be condemned under the law. Ishmael being given to Hagar expressly because of her affliction points to Christ being afflicted for the sake of the world. The emphasis on Ishmael dwelling among his brothers points to the incarnation of Christ in the association of men. The universal conflict surrounding Ishmael, man striving against man, portends the death of all flesh decreed by the law and prefigures the crucifixion of Jesus Christ under the law. The condemnation of Adam likewise prefigures the condemnation of Christ and finally condemnation of the Body of Christ.

Genesis 16:13–16 And she called the name of the LORD **that spake unto her, Thou God seest me: for she said, Have I also here looked after him that seeth me? 14 Wherefore the well was called Beer-lahai-roi [H883]; behold, [it is] between Kadesh and Bered. 15 And Hagar bare Abram a son: and Abram called his son's name, which Hagar bare, Ishmael. 16 And Abram [was] fourscore and six years old, when Hagar bare Ishmael to Abram.**

The names *El* [H410] and *Elohim* [H430] are closely related in the Hebrew. Hagar using the name *El* [H410], in contrast to *Jehovah* (YHWH) [H3068], recalls Eve using the name *Elohim* [H430] in the context of the original commandment, which again identifies Hagar specifically with the law, in contrast to grace. The image of Hagar seeing God, implicitly under the Covenant of Law, is Hagar, at least figuratively, mistaking the angel of the Lord for God himself—that is, mistaking her perspective of God for the wholeness, or oneness, of the Godhead—which foreshadows the Israelites spiritually mistaking the formal law for the fullness of the promise of grace and finally preferring the rules of men to the mercy of God (Mark 7:7). No one has seen the Father, or knows the Father, except the Son (John 1:18). Hagar seeing God merely as One who sees her prefigures Moses seeing God but not the fullness of the Lord God (Exod 33:20).

Genesis 17:1–9 And when Abram [H87] was ninety years old and nine, the LORD **[H3068] appeared to Abram [H87], and said unto him, I [am] the Almighty [H7706] God [H410]; walk before me, and be thou perfect [H8549]. 2 And I will make my covenant between me and thee, and will multiply thee exceedingly. 3 And Abram [H87] fell on his face: and God [H430] talked with him, saying, 4 As for me, behold, my covenant [is]**

with thee, and thou shalt be a father of many nations. 5 Neither shall thy name any more be called Abram [H87], but thy name shall be Abraham [H85]; for a father of many nations have I made thee. 6 And I will make thee exceeding fruitful, and I will make nations of thee, and kings shall come out of thee. 7 And I will establish my covenant between me and thee and thy seed after thee in their generations for an everlasting covenant, to be a God [H430] unto thee, and to thy seed after thee. 8 And I will give unto thee, and to thy seed after thee, the land wherein thou art a stranger, all the land of Canaan, for an everlasting possession; and I will be their God [H430]. 9 And God [H430] said unto Abraham [H85], Thou shalt keep my covenant therefore, thou, and thy seed after thee in their generations.

The Lord presents himself in local context as the *Almighty* [H7706] *God* (El) [H410] and also *God* (Elohim) [H430], both of which emphasize justice, recalling our original creation, while the narrator uses the proper name *Lord* (YHWH) [H3068], which is an emphasis on mercy that foreshadows our new creation. The vantage point of the narrator transcends the local action just as the name *Jehovah* (YHWH) transcends the name *Elohim* just as the Covenant of Grace transcends the Covenant of Law. The covenant with Adam, like the covenant with Noah, like the covenant with Abraham, like the covenant with David, all emphasize justice and likewise physical creation, especially the natural body. The implicit foundation of all the covenants recorded in the Old Testament is the promise of prosperity in this life if one is obedient to the laws of God, while the new covenant, explicitly revealed in the New Testament, is the promise of eternal life by grace through faith in the Son. The old covenant foreshadows the new covenant just as mortal life foreshadows life eternal. The progressive clarification throughout the Old and New Testaments of the covenant in Christ, the covenant between God and man, reflects our physical and spiritual development, which is successive and simultaneous, embodied perhaps most tangibly by the development of every individual from childhood to adulthood (1 Cor 13:11). First milk, then meat (1 Cor 3:2). But the inherent mercy of the Lord God was not unknown to Adam or Noah or Abraham or David just as every child understands the difference between pleasure and pain. God has never desired sacrifice, but rather always mercy (Hos 6:6).

The word *perfect* [H8549] (be thou perfect) means "complete, sound" and has connotations of "innocent" and "entirely in accord with truth and fact," prefiguring the wholeness of our promised new creation. God commanding Abram to walk before him and be perfect is a prophecy of Christ and likewise the Body of Christ. The perfect obedience required by the law is ultimately fulfilled, not by our own good works, but rather by the perfect works of Jesus Christ. The new covenant in Christ is the fulfillment of the old covenant by Christ. The promised perfection of the faithful in the Body of Christ will be derived, not from our own merit, but rather from the indwelling Holy Spirit by grace through faith. The Holy Spirit indwelling the natural body in this life is only a foretaste of our rebirth in the spiritual, or glorified, body. The natural body cannot inherit the kingdom of God (1 Cor 15:50).[59]

The name *Abram* [H87] means "exalted father," which is an image of the exaltation (resurrection) of Christ at the First Advent, while the name *Abraham* [H85] means "father of a multitude," which is an image of the exaltation (resurrection) of the faithful in Christ in the Second Advent.[60] Changing the name *Abram* to *Abraham* is an image of the glorification of Christ and likewise our glorification in Christ. The image of a multitude proceeding from Abram is a prophecy of the faithful in Christ. The image of kings proceeding from Abraham is a vision of Christ as the king of kings (1 Tim 6:15) and finally the faithful in Christ as kings and priests (Rev 1:6). The emphasis on Abraham and his seed receiving the land in which they were, in the natural, strangers is a prophetic assurance of the restoration, or re-creation, of all creation through Christ, while the emphasis on the land being an everlasting possession is a testimony to the eternal life in Christ. The emphasis on the Lord being our God points to our promised communion with God in the Body of Christ.[61]

Genesis 17:10–14 This [is] my covenant [H1285], which ye shall keep, between me and you and thy seed after thee; Every man child among you shall be circumcised [H4135]. 11 And ye shall circumcise [H5243] the flesh of your foreskin; and it shall be a token [H226] of the covenant [H1285] betwixt me and you. 12 And he that is eight days old shall be circumcised [H4135] among you, every man child in your generations, he that is born in the house, or bought with money [H3701] of any stranger, which [is] not of thy seed. 13 He that is born in thy house, and he that is bought with thy money [H3701], must needs be circumcised [H4135]: and my covenant [H1285] shall be in your flesh for an everlasting covenant [H1285]. 14 And the uncircumcised [H6189] man child whose flesh of his foreskin is not circumcised [H4135], that soul shall be cut off [H3772] from his people; he hath broken my covenant [H1285].

The word *covenant* [H1285] (which ye shall keep) has an association "to eat (in the sense of cutting)" [H1262], which reflects the covenant of the Lord being our source of life, manna from heaven (John 6:32).[62] The image of cutting

---

[59] "This third Person is called, in technical language, the Holy Ghost or the 'spirit' of God. Do not be worried or surprised if you find it (or Him) rather vaguer or more shadowy in your mind than the other two. I think there is a reason why that must be so. In the Christian life you are not usually looking *at* Him: He is always acting through you" (Lewis, *Mere Christianity* 152). God the Holy Spirit is everywhere always, immanent and transcendent, throughout space-time and outside space-time.
[60] Literal meaning of *Abraham* [H85] per *Strong's*, but *Brown-Driver-Briggs* is similar.
[61] "Not only according to the flesh, but of a far greater multitude by faith, [Rom 4:17]" (Whittingham et al., *Geneva Bible* 7R n. a#2; Gen 17:4). It is utterly incomprehensible, but nonetheless the Word of God speaks of an innumerable multitude of faithful and, thereby, foretells an infinite multitude of faithful, Gen 22:17, Matt 3:9.
[62] Parenthetical "in the sense of cutting" per *Strong's*, not *Brown-Driver-Briggs*.

also recalls the three sacrifices of Abram being cut in half as a sign of the promised Seed (Gen 15:10). The animal and grain offerings required by the law are representations of food, which foreshadow the flesh of Christ as the bread of life, while the connection of death with both sacrificial offering and also ordinary eating reflects the condemnation of the natural body, which would ultimately be embodied by Christ on the cross. The words *circumcise* [H5243] (the flesh) and *circumcised* [H4135] (every man) both evoke an image "to cut off," which is literally cutting off the foreskin but again recalls the threefold sacrifices of Abram being cut in half.[63]

The act of circumcision represents a submission to the will of God, while the separation of the foreskin from the body represents a corresponding separation from the way of flesh. Circumcision is a mark of blood in the flesh that ultimately foreshadows the wounds in the flesh of Jesus Christ, whereby only men can be circumcised just as salvation comes only through the one man Jesus Christ. The emphasis on man, in contrast to woman, is an emphasis on justice that reflects the condemnation under the law, in contrast to our redemption by grace. The prophecy of man being cut off, represented by the sign of circumcision, is fully revealed on the cross in Christ being cut off from the land of the living (Isa 53:8). The warning that any uncircumcised man would be *cut off* [H3772] (from his people) is an affirmation that our redemption comes only by the cross. The word *uncircumcised* [H6189] is not related to either the word *circumcise* [H5243] or *circumcised* [H4135], which reflects an utter separateness between the faithful and the faithless.[64]

The mark of circumcision is specifically called a *token* [H226], whereby circumcision is a sign of the law just as the law is a prophecy of Christ. The circumcision of Adam, mankind, is imperfect in the sense that the works of man are imperfect, while the circumcision of Christ is imperfect in the sense that the First Advent is yet incomplete, awaiting the resurrection of the Body of Christ in the Second Advent. But circumcision in the flesh, as an imperfect obedience in the natural body, finally prefigures the circumcision of the heart, which will mark the perfect obedience of the spiritual, or glorified, body. Moses explicitly links circumcision with obedience to God ("Circumcise therefore the foreskin of your heart, and be no more stiffnecked") and, thereby, points to the perfect obedience of Christ under the law (Deut 10:16). The law written on stone tables (tablets) foreshadows the law written on our hearts (Heb 8:10). The distinction between those born in the house of Abraham in comparison with other servants bought with money foreshadows the Jews in comparison with the Gentiles. The emphasis on the money paid for the servants points to the death of Jesus as a ransom for many (Matt 20:28). The word *money* [H3701] specifically means "silver, money," which portends the thirty pieces of silver,

---

[63] The covenant between the pieces and the covenant of circumcision are intimately connected, sharing many elements and representing a clear progression of the promises of God (Sarna 123; Gen 16:1–27). Prophecy is pattern.

[64] "The *spirit* of this law [circumcision] extends to all ages, dispensations, and people; he whose heart is not purified from sin cannot enter into the kingdom of God" (Clarke 1:115; Gen 17:14). The circumcision of the cross transcends time and space.

the price set upon the life of Christ by the world (Matt 27:9). The circumcision of infants represents our inheritance in the original curse incurred by Adam. Circumcision being completed specifically on the eighth day of the newborn is an image of new creation, the first day of a new week, a new seven, that itself reinforces the emphasis on infant circumcision. We are born of Adam, but we are reborn in Jesus Christ. The seventh day is the Sabbath rest, which foreshadows the millennial reign of Christ, while the eighth day represents the opening of eternity after the close of the millennial kingdom.[65]

Genesis 17:15–16 And God said unto Abraham, As for Sarai [H8297] thy wife, thou shalt not call her name Sarai [H8297], but Sarah [H8283] [shall] her name [be]. 16 And I will bless her, and give thee a son also of her: yea, I will bless her, and she shall be [a mother] of nations; kings of people shall be of her.

The name *Sarah* [H8283] means "princess, noble lady (queen)" [H8282], which implies by the name change from *Sarai* to *Sarah* some exaltation in royalty, an exaltation that echoes the name change from *Abram* to *Abraham* (Gen 17:5). The names *Abram* [H87] and *Abraham* [H85] are both derived, in part, from the same root "father" [H1], which reflects God the Son proceeding from God the Father.[66] The change from *Abram* to *Abraham* reflects the glorification of Jesus Christ, God the Son, while the change from *Sarai* to *Sarah* reflects the glorification of the faithful in Christ, in the Body of Christ, the kingdom of God. The communication of the blessing of Sarah through Abraham reflects the redemption of the faithful only through Jesus Christ. The blessing of Sarah to be the mother of nations and kings affirms the blessing of Abraham to be the father of nations and kings just as the Covenant of Grace affirms the Covenant of Law just as the promised resurrection of all the dead affirms the resurrection of Jesus Christ.[67]

Abram's new name is given before Sarai's new name just as Adam was formed before Eve, implying that Sarah is named, figuratively reborn, through the faith of Abraham just as Eve was taken from the body of Adam and, thereby, named according to Adam (Gen 2:23). Man preceding woman represents law preceding grace, while the union of man and woman embodied by childbirth represents the fulfillment of law in grace in our new creation. Eve was literally the mother of all humanity, while Sarah is figuratively the mother of all the faithful. Eve prefigures Sarah just as the natural body prefigures the

---

[65] Before the eighth day, newborns were considered unclean just as the mothers were considered unclean for the same period, Lev 12:2–3 (Clarke 1:115; Gen 17:12). The unclean life that becomes clean life is the death and resurrection of the body.

[66] Etymologies per *Strong's*, but the relationships are clear in *Brown-Driver-Briggs*.

[67] "[T]here is nothing superfluous, nothing added at random in the Scriptures. For if these names had no use, they would not then have been added to the Epistle, nor would Paul have written what he has written [Chrysostom, *Homilies on Romans*]" (Schaff, *Nicene and Post-Nicene Fathers: First Series* 11:553). The Lord is perfect and complete in all his ways and, therefore, does not speak in vain as carnal men do.

spiritual, or glorified, body. Eve was taken from the side of Adam just as all creation proceeded through the Son (John 1:3), while Sarah, as the embodiment of the promised birth, is figuratively presented to Abraham just as the faithful will be presented as a bride to the Son (Rev 21:9).

Genesis 17:17–18 Then Abraham fell upon his face, and laughed, and said in his heart, Shall [a child] be born unto him that is an hundred years old? and shall Sarah, that is ninety years old, bear? 18 And Abraham said unto God, O that Ishmael might live before thee!

The laughter of father Abraham represents hope, not faithlessness, in that Abraham is not rebuked. The barrenness of Sarah reflects the hopelessness of humanity under the law, while the miraculous fertility of Sarah reflects the promise of life by grace. The emphasis on the old age of Abraham and Sarah testifies to the long-suffering of God in the call to repentance and the corresponding long delay until the final judgment. The love of Abraham for his firstborn son, Ishmael, reflects the love of God for his first son, Adam, and likewise all mankind in Adam. Abraham asking that Ishmael might live before God reflects the hope of life in God.[68]

Genesis 17:19–22 And God said, Sarah thy wife shall bear thee a son indeed; and thou shalt call his name Isaac [H3327]: and I will establish my covenant with him for an everlasting covenant, [and] with his seed after him. 20 And as for Ishmael [H3458], I have heard thee: Behold, I have blessed him, and will make him fruitful, and will multiply him exceedingly; twelve princes shall he beget, and I will make him a great nation. 21 But my covenant will I establish with Isaac [H3327], which Sarah shall bear unto thee at this set time in the next year. 22 And he left off talking with him, and God went up from Abraham.

The name *Ishmael* [H3458] means "God will hear," which directly recalls God hearing the suffering of Hagar in the desert but ultimately anticipates God hearing the suffering of Adam, all humanity, in the world. The name *Isaac* [H3327] means "he laugheth," which foreshadows our surprise and joy in the virgin birth of Jesus Christ, likewise our joy in the promise of redemption by grace through faith in Christ. Ishmael is the firstborn son of Abraham just as Adam was the first man formed by God, but Isaac is the only legitimate son of Abraham just as Jesus Christ is the only begotten Son of God (1 John 4:9). The emphasis that the son of the covenant must be born of the freewoman Sarah, not of the bondwoman Hagar, is an affirmation of the redemption of the

---

[68] "Abraham . . . asks God to consider the healthy teenager Ishmael as heir. God, however, insists on the literal interpretation of his earlier promise . . . ." (Clifford, *New Jerome* 22; Gen 17:17–19). The humble condescension of God in the act of creation, literally interpreted, is the promise, or prophecy, of creation realized as the essential incarnation of God.

faithful from slavery to sin. The emphasis that Isaac would be born at the appointed time is an affirmation of the undeniable will of God. The covenant would be established with Isaac and only with Isaac just as our redemption comes only through Jesus Christ, but Ishmael would also be blessed just as Adam, or Adam-kind, is even now preserved in the world, the faithful of which to be finally redeemed in Christ.[69]

The twelve princes that would proceed from Ishmael prefigure the twelve patriarchs that would proceed from Isaac just as the one man Adam prefigures the one man Jesus Christ (Rom 5:14). Ishmael himself begetting twelve princes reflects the multiplication of the kingdoms of the world proceeding directly from Adam, while the twelve patriarchs of Israel proceeding from Isaac through Jacob foreshadows the kingdom of God being established in the First Advent but not being finally fulfilled until the Second Advent. The offspring of the natural man Ishmael parallels the offspring of the spiritual man Isaac just as everything in the physical world is a blurred reflection of a spiritual reality (1 Cor 13:12). The emphasis on the one nation of Israel, likewise the one tribe of Judah, and likewise the one bloodline of David points to the one man Jesus Christ, who embodies the oneness of God and reflects the infinite importance of the individual to God.[70]

Genesis 17:23–27 And Abraham took Ishmael his son, and all that were born in his house, and all that were bought with his money, every male among the men of Abraham's house; and circumcised the flesh of their foreskin in the selfsame day, as God had said unto him. 24 And Abraham [was] ninety years old and nine, when he was circumcised in the flesh of his foreskin. 25 And Ishmael his son [was] thirteen years old, when he was circumcised in the flesh of his foreskin. 26 In the selfsame day was Abraham circumcised, and Ishmael his son. 27 And all the men of his house, born in the house, and bought with money of the stranger, were circumcised with him.

The circumcision in the flesh prefigures the circumcision of the heart just as the baptism of repentance prefigures the baptism of the Holy Spirit. Circumcision in the flesh and baptism in water are both representations of death and resurrection, but circumcision is a literal mark in the flesh while baptism in water is spiritual. The sign of circumcision prefigures the sign of baptism just as the natural body prefigures the spiritual, or glorified, body. The circumcision of the newborn Isaac represents the original death and

---

[69] "It was great condescension in the Divine Being to talk with a creature; it was wonderful grace and kindness to make such promises to him . . . ." (Gill 1:100; Gen 17:22). The condescension of God in the Old Testament is a prophecy of the incarnation of God in the New Testament.

[70] "God reveals the purposes of his good-will to his people by degrees. God had told *Abraham* long before, that he should have a son, but never 'till now that he should have a son by *Sarai*" (Wesley 1:70–71; Gen 17:10). The progressive revelation of the son of the promise is the progressive revelation of the Trinity.

resurrection of our inherited exile and preservation in Adam. The circumcision of Ishmael near the time of puberty represents the figurative death and resurrection in the call to repentance that corresponds to the age of accountability. The circumcision of Abraham in his old age represents the literal death and resurrection in Christ.[71]

The emphasis on Abraham and Ishmael being circumcised on the same day is an affirmation that our redemption begins with repentance and also that our redemption is guaranteed by our repentance. To be crucified with Christ is to be resurrected with Christ (Rom 6:5). Abraham in his old age and Ishmael in his adolescence being circumcised before Isaac is even born is a reversal of the natural timeline of birth and death prefiguring our rebirth in Christ and likewise our rejection of death in Adam. This reversal of the natural timeline also reflects the universality of the cross as the call of the peoples of all the ages to repentance, likewise the guarantee of the redemption of the faithful of all the ages. Circumcision is a sign of obedience, an obedience to the curse of Adam that prefigures an obedience to the Spirit in the Body of Christ, whereby the circumcision of newborns reflects not only the original sin of Adam but also the sinlessness of Christ, likewise the sinlessness of the faithful in Christ.[72]

Mystery

Genesis 18:1 And the LORD appeared unto him in the plains [H436] of Mamre: and he sat in the tent door in the heat of the day;

The appearance of the Lord to Abraham foreshadows the humble incarnation of Jesus Christ just as every condescension of God reflects the essential incarnation of God. The tent of Abraham is an emblem of the impermanent physical body and likewise the impermanent present world. The heat of the day recalls the curse incurred by Adam to eat bread in the sweat of his face, that is, in the natural body (Gen 3:19). In contrast, we see the Lord walking in the garden in the *cool* (ruwach) [H7307] of the day (Gen 3:8). The *plains* [H436], or "trees," of Mamre recall the forbidden tree in the garden and also portend the cross, the tree of the curse (Gal 3:13). The sign of the trees of Mamre previously preceded the account of the war of the four kings and the

---

[71] "[C]ircumcision did not contain the perfection of salvation, but signified it as to be achieved by Christ, Who was to be born of the Jewish nation. For this reason circumcision was given to that nation alone" (Aquinas, *Summa* 2:2417). The mandated circumcision of the one nation of Israel is a prophecy of the crucifixion of the one man Jesus Christ, while the propagation of circumcision to the nations of Ishmael is a prophecy of the redemption of Gentiles, representing the faithful from all Adam-kind, Gentiles and Jews, in Christ, Gen 17:26.

[72] "[H]e [Abraham] was not disobedient, nor dilatory to obey the command of God [to circumcise his household], but at once complied with it, not consulting flesh and blood, not regarding the pain he and his should endure, or the shame or danger they should be exposed unto . . . ." (Gill 1:100; Gen 17:23). Fear is the false counsel of the flesh, the way of all flesh, of all the earth, that leads unto death.

five kings (Gen 13:18), while the present sign of the trees of Mamre now precedes the destruction of Sodom and Gomorrah by fire (Gen 19:24). The account of the war of the four and five kings followed by the account of the destruction of Sodom and Gomorrah points to the foretold apocalypse, but the deliverance of Lot in each case is an affirmation of our promised salvation. The announcement of the birth of Isaac is closely linked with the destruction of the cities of the plain by fire just as the First Advent of Christ prefigures the destruction of all creation that is linked with the Second Advent.

Genesis 18:2–5 And he lift up his eyes and looked, and, lo, three men stood by him: and when he saw [them], he ran to meet them from the tent door, and bowed himself toward the ground, 3 And said, My Lord, if now I have found favour [H2580] in thy sight, pass not away, I pray thee, from thy servant: 4 Let a little water, I pray you, be fetched, and wash your feet, and rest yourselves under the tree: 5 And I will fetch a morsel of bread, and comfort ye your hearts; after that ye shall pass on: for therefore are ye come to your servant. And they said, So do, as thou hast said.

The word *favour* (favor) [H2580] (favour in thy sight) means "favour, grace" and has a connotation of "acceptance." Abraham seeking the favor of the three men is an image of salvation by grace through faith in Jesus Christ. Abraham bowing toward the ground recalls the origin of flesh from the dust of the ground (Gen 2:7) and also the curse of the ground incurred by Adam (Gen 3:17). The prostration of Abraham foreshadows the incarnation of Jesus Christ; the Fall of Man prefigures the Passion of Jesus Christ. Condemnation precedes justification just as repentance precedes redemption. The relationship between the door of Abraham's tent and his prostration before the theophany is an image of the human body as a tabernacle open to receiving the indwelling Holy Spirit. The expectation that the three strangers would continue on their journey after comforting their hearts reflects an acknowledgment of the righteousness of the curse of Adam and likewise the law that governs flesh. The three angels appearing as men is also an emphasis on justice, ultimately embodied by the one man Jesus Christ. The admonition to feed the hungry and take in the stranger is a reflection of God being a stranger in the world because of our sins and the corresponding hunger of God for our redemption (Matt 25:35).[73]

The emphasis on resting and eating beneath a tree recalls the forbidden tree in the garden and also foreshadows Christ nailed to a tree. The faithful are called to eat the flesh of the Son (John 6:51). The images of water and bread reinforce the emphasis on the Covenant of Law. The symbol of water evokes an image of ceremonial cleansing before the brazen altar and also the baptism in water in imitation of Christ, while the symbol of bread evokes an image of the

---

[73] The ambiguous depiction of God in the account of the three strangers may represent the mystery surrounding the presence of God in the world (Viviano, *Collegeville* 57; Gen 18:1–15). The very structuring of the Biblical narratives affirms that now we are seeing through a glass darkly, 1 Cor 13:12.

ABRAHAM AND SARAH

bread of affliction identified with the bondage in Egypt and also the crucifixion of Christ under the law. Abraham, at least figuratively, washing the feet of the three men foreshadows Christ, literally and spiritually, washing the feet of the apostles at the last supper. Christ humbly washing our feet reflects the essential condescension embodied in the First Advent (John 13:14). Christ washes our feet and we wash the feet of one another, reflecting our unity in the Body of Christ and likewise our participation in the death and resurrection of Christ (Rom 6:4). Abraham serving the three men portends the figurative sacrifice of Isaac just as the last supper would portend the crucifixion.[74]

Genesis 18:6–8 And Abraham hastened into the tent unto Sarah, and said, Make ready quickly three measures of fine meal, knead [it], and make cakes [H5692] upon the hearth. 7 And Abraham ran unto the herd, and fetcht a calf [H1121, H1241] tender and good, and gave [it] unto a young man; and he hasted to dress it. 8 And he took butter [H2529], and milk [H2461], and the calf [H1121, H1241] which he had dressed, and set [it] before them; and he stood by them under the tree [H6086], and they did eat.

Sarah quickly preparing *cakes* (bread) [H5692] for the three men foreshadows the Israelites preparing unleavened *cakes* (bread) [H5692] before leaving Egypt—prophetically the bread of the last supper before the crucifixion (Exod 12:39). The bread of affliction made in haste and identified with the death of the firstborn (Exod 12:12) prefigures the flesh of Christ cut off from the land of the living before the natural time of death, or figuratively cut off in haste (Deut 16:3). The transformation of fine meal into cakes foreshadows the resurrection of the body. The three measures of fine meal parallel the three men for whom the cakes (bread) are prepared, a correspondence that reflects the incarnation of Christ as the revelation of the Trinity. The contrast between *milk* [H2461] and *butter* (curds) [H2529] evokes an image of the transformation of milk into butter, which foreshadows the transformation of water into wine and likewise the fulfillment of the first covenant in the second covenant. The bread is the death and resurrection of Christ, while the wine is our death and resurrection in Christ. Eating the bread is the imitation of Christ, while drinking the wine is the participation in Christ.

The rendering *calf* [H1121, H1241] envelops the meaning "son" [H1121] in the Hebrew, whereby Abraham slaughtering the calf prefigures the world rejecting Christ. Abraham selecting a choice calf prefigures the sinlessness of Christ. Abraham serves bread before meat just as the promise of Christ declared by the law and the prophets precedes the reality of Christ in the fullness of grace. The veiled connotations of figures and events in the Scriptures, as well as

---

[74] The Orthodox Church believes that the three angels appearing to Abraham, recorded in Gen 18, foreshadows the explicit revelation of the Trinity in the First Advent of Jesus Christ (Hopko, *Orthodox Faith* 3:76). The Bible as a whole, the structure and the stream, locally and globally, is Trinitarian.

in life, reflect the mystery of Christ underpinning the law and the flesh. The word *tree* [H6086] connotes "gallows," whereby the three men eating beneath the tree foreshadows Jesus Christ being nailed to the wooden cross. Abraham standing by the men under the tree while they eat foreshadows Israel and ultimately the whole world standing as a witness to the crucifixion of Christ. The strangeness of angels sitting down to eat prefigures the scandalous incarnation of God in the flesh and likewise the shocking promise of salvation by grace through faith.

Genesis 18:9–15 And they said unto him, Where [is] Sarah thy wife? And he said, Behold, in the tent. 10 And he said, I will certainly return unto thee according to the time of life; and, lo, Sarah thy wife shall have a son. And Sarah heard [it] in the tent door, which [was] behind him. 11 Now Abraham and Sarah [were] old [and] well stricken in age; [and] it ceased to be with Sarah after the manner of women. 12 Therefore Sarah laughed within herself, saying, After I am waxed old shall I have pleasure [H5730], my lord being old also? 13 And the LORD said unto Abraham, Wherefore did Sarah laugh, saying, Shall I of a surety bear a child, which am old? 14 Is any thing too hard for the LORD? At the time appointed I will return unto thee, according to the time of life, and Sarah shall have a son. 15 Then Sarah denied, saying, I laughed not; for she was afraid. And he said, Nay; but thou didst laugh.

Abraham previously laughing is closely identified with his intercession with the Lord concerning Ishmael, but Sarah laughing is closely identified with her fearful response to the Lord concerning Isaac. The word *pleasure* [H5730] (shall I have pleasure) corresponds to the name *Eden* [H5731], which recalls the garden of Eden and also foreshadows the kingdom of God, whereby Sarah doubting pleasure in her old age figuratively represents doubting a restoration of creation in the last days. The Lord questioning why Sarah had laughed expresses an expectation that the faithful should know the ways of God. The commonplace absence of such understanding is a testimony to the corruption of the image of God embodied by humanity—our defilement through the spirit of disobedience, the spirit of anti-christ (Eph 2:2).

Abraham laughing in hope reflects the promise of life inherent in creation, while Sarah laughing in doubt recalls our original fall in Adam and portends the rejection of the promised Seed of woman. But the union of Abraham and Sarah as one flesh will produce Isaac as the embodiment of the faithful laughing in joy and surprise at the revelation of eternal life in the person of Jesus Christ. The threefold image of promise, rejection, and joy embodied by Abraham, Sarah, and Isaac reflects the threefold Adam and the First and Second Advents and likewise the threefold Father, Son, and Holy Spirit. The transformation of the barrenness of Sarah into fertility and likewise the transformation of her fear into love reflects the universal duality of flesh and spirit that is ultimately embodied by the death and resurrection of the foretold Seed of woman.[75]

Genesis 18:16   And the men rose up from thence, and looked toward Sodom: and Abraham went with them to bring them on the way.

The Lord communing with Abraham in the context of three men prefigures both the incarnation in the flesh and also the revelation of the Trinity just as the coming of the one man Jesus Christ embodies the revelation of the fullness of the Trinity (John 14:9). The partitioning of the threefold theophany into two plus one figures—the two figures that proceed to Sodom and Gomorrah compared with the one figure that stays with Abraham—reflects the Son and the Holy Spirit proceeding from the Father and, ultimately, the conception of Christ through the power of the overshadowing Holy Spirit (Luke 1:35). Abraham leading the two angels represents the actualization of the will of God in the flesh, not only via the law and the prophets, but ultimately in the incarnation of Jesus Christ and finally in our new creation in Christ.[76]

Abraham leading the angels further prefigures Jesus Christ leading the angelic host in the end times, while the subsequent deliverance of Abraham's blood kin Lot prefigures the gathering of God's elect (Matt 24:30–31). The comparison of both Abraham and the angelic presence to the incarnation of Jesus Christ reflects the reality of Christ as both the Son of man and the Son of God. The comparison of the angelic presence to both the Trinity and the literal angelic host reflects the unity of the Spirit. The angels of the Lord, also the prophets of the Lord, are commonly depicted as types of the Lord, giving the declarations of the Lord (Exod 7:1).

Genesis 18:17–19   And the LORD said, Shall I hide from Abraham that thing which I do; 18 Seeing that Abraham shall surely become a great and mighty nation, and all the nations of the earth shall be blessed in him? 19 For I know him, that he will command his children and his household after him, and they shall keep the way of the LORD, to do justice and

---

[75] "Sarah thinks this too good news to be true, and therefore cannot as yet find in her heart to believe it. *Sarah laughed within herself.* It was not a pleasing laughter of faith, like Abraham's, [Gen 17:17], but a laughter of doubting and mistrust. The same thing may be done from very different principles, which God only can judge of, who knows the heart" (Henry 1:93; Gen 18:9–15). The essential difference between Christ and antichrist is ever subtle because anti-christ puts itself forward in the place of Christ.
[76] "[T]he manifestation of God to the saints of the Old Testament . . . were manifestations of the Father, by, through and in his Son or Logos . . . [M]ediated by God's divine and uncreated Son" (Hopko, *Orthodox Faith* 1:68). It is completely normal for the Son to represent, or relate, the Father, whom only the Son has seen, John 6:46, just as it is completely normal for signs, types, and events to relate the Son, who is transcendent as well as immanent, John 6:48. The Holy Spirit points to the Son, the Son points to the Father.

ADAM, NOAH, ABRAHAM

judgment; that the Lord may bring upon Abraham that which he hath spoken of him.

The image of God hiding his will from Abraham reflects the mystery of the incarnation of Jesus Christ and likewise the mystery of our redemption in Christ. The emphasis on Abraham keeping the law preceding his being blessed by the Lord testifies to the law preceding grace, likewise repentance preceding redemption, and likewise the natural body preceding the spiritual, or glorified, body. The prophecy that the offspring of Abraham would keep the law foretells not only the law received by Moses but ironically the crucifixion of Christ under the law. The tension between the condemnation of Christ under the law and our hope in Christ through the fulfillment of the law reflects the universal tension between law and grace, likewise the tension between flesh and spirit, and likewise the tension between death and resurrection. The paradox of death and life is resolved only in the person of Jesus Christ, who is the perfect union of justice and mercy and likewise flesh and spirit.

Genesis 18:20–22 And the Lord said, Because the cry of Sodom and Gomorrah is great, and because their sin is very grievous; 21 I will go down now, and see whether they have done altogether according to the cry of it, which is come unto me; and if not, I will know. 22 And the men turned their faces from thence, and went toward Sodom: but Abraham stood yet before the Lord.

The image of the Lord descending to see the sins of Sodom and Gomorrah foreshadows the incarnation of Jesus Christ (First Advent), while the ultimate destruction of Sodom and Gomorrah by fire foreshadows the foretold destruction of all flesh by fire in the end times (Second Advent). The timing of the judgment of Sodom and Gomorrah corresponds to an overwhelming depravity in the cities, foreshadowing the corruption of the law at the time of the First Advent and finally the corruption of grace at the time of the Second Advent. The moral decline of creation has been prophesied by the debilitation and death of every living creature since the Fall of Man.[77]

Genesis 18:23–32 And Abraham drew near, and said, Wilt thou also destroy [H5595] the righteous [H6662] with the wicked [H7563]? 24 Peradventure there be fifty righteous [H6662] within the city: wilt thou also destroy [H5595] and not spare [H5375] the place for the fifty righteous [H6662] that [are] therein? 25 That be far from thee to do after this manner, to slay [H4191] the righteous [H6662] with the wicked [H7563]: and that the righteous [H6662] should be as the wicked

---

[77] The foretelling of the condemnation of the peoples of Sodom and Gomorrah is a cautionary tale regarding the final judgment of all the wicked (Coffman 242; Gen 18:16–18). A prophecy not only of the final judgment of the wicked but also a prophecy of a final warning of the final judgment of the wicked.

[H7563], that be far from thee: Shall not the Judge of all the earth do right? 26 And the LORD said, If I find in Sodom fifty righteous [H6662] within the city, then I will spare [H5375] all the place for their sakes. 27 And Abraham answered and said, Behold now, I have taken upon me to speak unto the Lord, which [am but] dust and ashes: 28 Peradventure there shall lack five of the fifty righteous [H6662]: wilt thou destroy [H7843] all the city for [lack of] five? And he said, If I find there forty and five, I will not destroy [H7843] [it]. 29 And he spake unto him yet again, and said, Peradventure there shall be forty found there. And he said, I will not do [it] for forty's sake. 30 And he said [unto him], Oh let not the Lord be angry, and I will speak: Peradventure there shall thirty be found there. And he said, I will not do [it], if I find thirty there. 31 And he said, Behold now, I have taken upon me to speak unto the Lord: Peradventure there shall be twenty found there. And he said, I will not destroy [H7843] [it] for twenty's sake. 32 And he said, Oh let not the Lord be angry, and I will speak yet but this once: Peradventure ten shall be found there. And he said, I will not destroy [H7843] [it] for ten's sake.

The word *wicked* [H7563] (destroy the wicked) connotes "guilty of crime," while the word *righteous* [H6662] (spare the righteous) connotes "lawful." The wicked and the righteous together testify to a universal law that governs flesh, affirming the undeniable nature of the will of God. The preservation of the wicked for the sake of the righteous reflects both the preservation of the world despite the wicked and also the preservation of individuals despite personal sins. The emphasis on the preservation of the wicked for only a small minority of righteous testifies to the profound corruption of even the faithful and finally points to a universal apostasy in the end times. But the preservation of the many wicked for the few righteous ultimately prefigures the redemption of the many by the one man Christ. The ubiquitous image of the preservation of a remnant through destruction is a corresponding vision of death and resurrection. The parallel between the corrupted creation and the condemned Christ reflects the essential condescension of Christ humbly becoming a curse for the sake of the children of God. The casual description of Abraham recognizing the Lord reflects an intimate and even familial communion between the faithful and God.

The word *destroy* [H5595] (the wicked) means "to sweep away (good and bad indiscriminately)," which foremost presages the utter destruction of Sodom and Gomorrah and finally portends the judgment of all flesh in the end times. The natural body is not inherently evil, but it must be utterly destroyed because it is fallen. The word *spare* [H5375] (the righteous) means "to lift, carry, take," which foreshadows the exaltation of the faithful in a redemption by grace, in contrast to vain works. Three different words *destroy* [H5595], *slay* [H4191], and *destroy* [H7843] are used to describe the judgment of Sodom and Gomorrah, while only one word *spare* [H5375] is used to describe the potential preservation of Sodom and Gomorrah. This reflects the path to destruction being broad in contrast to the road to salvation that is narrow (Matt 7:13–14). But God knows how to condemn the wicked and save the righteous (2 Pet 2:9). Abraham's intercession for Sodom and Gomorrah prefigures the perpetual intercession of Jesus Christ for the faithful, the communion of Christ with the faithful (Heb 7:25).

Genesis 18:33 And the LORD went his way, as soon as he had left communing with Abraham: and Abraham returned unto his place.

The emphasis on the separation between the Lord and Abraham, following the account of the intercession of Abraham, portends the destruction of the cities of the plain. Abraham returning to his place after communing with the Lord reflects the separation between man and God because of sin. The Son would likewise be separated from the Father, forsaken for the sake of us sinners (Matt 27:46). But Abraham returning to his place also foreshadows the restoration of all creation through Jesus Christ and likewise the restoration of the lost dominion of Adam in Christ. Abraham can reflect both Adam and Christ because Adam prefigures Christ. Man is the union of flesh and spirit, a living, breathing paradox.

Genesis 19:1 And there came two angels to Sodom at even; and Lot sat in the gate of Sodom: and Lot seeing [them] rose up to meet them; and he bowed himself with his face toward the ground;

The emphasis on the angels coming at evening portends the death of the individual and likewise the destruction of the world. Every sunset is a vision of death and destruction, but every sunrise is a prophecy of resurrection and renewal. The first visitation of the angels expressly to see the sins of the city of man prefigures the First Advent of Jesus Christ, while the subsequent movement of the angels to usher Lot and his family out of the city, before its destruction, prefigures the Second Advent of Christ. In their appearances to both Abraham and Lot, the angels initially seem to be men and only later appear as messengers of God. Christ would likewise reveal himself to his disciples first as the Son of man and second as the Son of God. The image of the Son of man precedes the Son of God just as the Covenant of Law precedes the Covenant of Grace just as Adam precedes Christ just as the First Advent of Christ precedes the Second Advent. The emphasis in the First Advent on the death and resurrection of Christ in the flesh is an emphasis on Christ as the Son of man. The emphasis in the Second Advent on the revelation of the glorified Christ to the whole world is an emphasis on Christ as the Son of God.

The greeting of the angels by Lot recalls the greeting of the angels by Abraham (Gen 18:2) just as the intercession of Lot for his family in Sodom recalls the intercession of Abraham for the faithful in Sodom (Gen 18:23). But the account of Abraham overshadows the account of Lot just as the overarching promise of eternal life in Christ overshadows the transitory preservation of Adam in the world. The account of Lot echoes the account of Abraham just as the suffering and death of every individual affirms the original curse of Adam. Abraham is the embodiment of faithfulness promised in Adam and sealed in Noah. But the first Hebrew, Abraham, the first man called into the promised land, is also the embodiment of the first Adam, the first man formed in the garden of Eden (Gen 14:13). The concurrent images of Adam and Christ prefigure the redemption of Adam in Christ.

Genesis 19:2–3 And he said, Behold now, my lords, turn in, I pray you, into your servant's house, and tarry all night, and wash your feet, and ye shall rise up early, and go on your ways. And they said, Nay; but we will abide in the street all night. 3 And he pressed upon them greatly; and they turned in unto him, and entered into his house; and he made them a feast, and did bake unleavened bread, and they did eat.

The original intention of the two angels to spend the night in the street reflects the preordained redemption of the faithful of all peoples in Christ. The angels ultimately spending the night in the one house of Lot prefigures Christ revealing himself first to the one nation of Israel (Matt 15:24). The image of all nations being saved through the one nation Israel reflects all humanity being saved through the one man Jesus Christ. Lot pressing the angels to stay with him foreshadows the angels pressing Lot to flee and escape the destruction by fire just as our imperfect righteousness under the law points to a perfection of righteousness by grace (Gal 3:24). The rebirth guaranteed by the First Advent is fulfilled in the Second Advent just as the redemption guaranteed by the baptism of repentance is fulfilled in the baptism of the Holy Spirit.

The image of Lot, at least figuratively, washing the feet of the visitors reflects the ceremonial cleansing required by the formal law and foreshadows the preparation of Jesus Christ for death and burial in fulfillment of the law (Luke 7:38). Lot preparing the bread of affliction in haste foreshadows the exodus from Egypt and finally the death and resurrection of Jesus Christ (Matt 26:26). The death of the Egyptian firstborn, separated from the blood of lambs, is a vision of the death of the natural body, while the redemption of the Israelite firstborn by the blood of lambs is a vision of the resurrection of the spiritual, or glorified, body (Exod 12:23).

Genesis 19:4–5 But before they lay down, the men of the city, [even] the men of Sodom, compassed the house round, both old and young, all the people from every quarter: 5 And they called unto Lot, and said unto him, Where [are] the men which came in to thee this night? bring them out unto us, that we may know them.

The men of Sodom coming for the angels at nighttime but before they could sleep prefigures the Sanhedrin taking Christ in the garden of Gethsemane (Matt 26:40). The short time the angels spend in Sodom prefigures the short life and short earthly ministry of Jesus Christ. The intended sexual attack is a graphic image of defiling the flesh that portends the defilement culminating in the crucifixion. The image of rape is a physical violation of flesh and a spiritual violation of freewill, in which the former reflects a blasphemy against the Son of man while the latter reflects the blasphemy against the Holy Spirit and likewise against the Son of God (Luke 12:10). The union of male and female is an image of God, reflecting the union of justice and mercy embodied by God, whereby the intended homosexual nature of the attack is innately a corruption of the image of God that represents justice in the absence of mercy. The emphasis on all the men of Sodom, the old and young from every quarter, seeking to defile the angels is a testimony to a universal rejection of Christ, not just by Israel but by the whole world, not just at the time of the earthly ministry of Christ but throughout all time. The rejection of Christ is not an accident of history but rather affirmed in every sin ever committed. The men of Sodom failing to recognize the power and authority of the two angels prefigures the world failing to recognize Jesus Christ as the incarnation of God.[78]

Genesis 19:6–8 And Lot went out at the door unto them, and shut the door after him, 7 And said, I pray you, brethren, do not so wickedly. 8 Behold now, I have two daughters which have not known man; let me, I pray you, bring them out unto you, and do ye to them as [is] good in your eyes: only unto these men do nothing; for therefore came they under the shadow of my roof.

Lot shutting his door represents both the separation between man and God because of sin and also the corresponding separation between the Son and the Father because of the curse of the cross (Mark 15:34). Lot standing in the breach between the men of Sodom and the angels of the Lord, pleading with the men of Sodom to not act so wickedly, is a vision of the incarnation of Jesus Christ and the corresponding call to repentance in the flesh. Lot offering his own daughters to the men of Sodom is a graphic image of Lot offering his own flesh, prefiguring Jesus Christ offering his own body on the cross, likewise the Father offering the Son. Our horror and disgust that Lot would offer his own daughters prefigures our horror and disgust at the unjust slaughter of Jesus Christ. Lot's willingness to accept the defilement of his daughters (flesh) but not the defilement of the angels (spirit) is an affirmation that blasphemy against the Son of man will be forgiven but not blasphemy against the Holy Spirit. The rejection of the First Advent will be forgiven but not the rejection of the Second Advent (Matt 12:31, Heb 6:4–6).

Genesis 19:9 And they said, Stand back. And they said [again], This one [fellow] came in to sojourn, and he will needs be a judge: now will we deal worse with thee, than with them. And they pressed sore upon the man, [even] Lot, and came near to break the door.

---

[78] The Arian profanation uses the language of the Bible in order to be disguised as the true faith in Christ and, thereby, represents a foreshadowing of the anti-christ—Athanasius, *Orations Against the Arians* (Rusch 63). The misrepresentation, or corruption, of the written Word is the rejection and defilement of the incarnate Word.

ABRAHAM AND SARAH

The image of Lot sojourning as a stranger in sinful Sodom prefigures the incarnation of Jesus Christ in a sinful world. The men of Sodom are outraged by the admonitions of the seemingly helpless Lot just as the world would scorn the forewarnings of the seemingly lowly Christ. The men of Sodom reject Lot as their judge (under law) just as the Israelites would reject Christ as their king (in fulfillment of the law and prophets). The kingship precedes the high priesthood just as law precedes grace. The men of Sodom intending to deal even more severely with Lot than with the angels portends the persecution of the Body of Christ in imitation of the crucifixion of the person of Christ. The Seed of woman will bruise the head of the seed of the serpent, while the seed of the serpent will bruise the Heel of the Seed of woman (Gen 3:15). But the sinful men of Sodom are finally unable to break down the door to the house of Lot just as the children of the devil will neither enter into the house of God. Christ is the door, the only door (John 10:9).

Genesis 19:10–11 But the men put forth their hand, and pulled Lot into the house to them, and shut to the door. 11 And they smote the men that [were] at the door of the house with blindness, both small and great: so that they wearied themselves to find the door.

Lot refusing to yield to the men of Sodom prefigures the obedience of Christ even unto death (Phil 2:8). The two angels putting forth their hand and pulling Lot back into his house prefigures Christ on the cross commending his spirit into the hands of the Father (Luke 23:46). The blinding of the men of Sodom reflects the spiritual blindness of the faithless, specifically a blindness to the reality of Jesus Christ as the incarnation of God. The emphasis that small and great men alike are blinded is an affirmation that no one can be saved outside of faith in Jesus Christ. The blinded men of Sodom wearying themselves trying to find a door reflects the hopelessness of the faithless groping around trying to save themselves. The image of God blinding the faithless does not mean that God is the origin of faithlessness but rather is a testimony to the sovereignty of God even in the administration of freewill. The men of Sodom are blind because they choose to walk in darkness (1 John 2:11).

Genesis 19:12–16 And the men said unto Lot, Hast thou here any besides? son in law, and thy sons, and thy daughters, and whatsoever thou hast in the city, bring [them] out of this place: 13 For we will destroy this place, because the cry of them is waxen great before the face of the LORD; and the LORD hath sent us to destroy it. 14 And Lot went out, and spake unto his sons in law, which married his daughters, and said, Up, get you out of this place; for the LORD will destroy this city. But he seemed as one that mocked unto his sons in law. 15 And when the morning arose, then the angels hastened Lot, saying, Arise, take thy wife, and thy two daughters, which are here; lest thou be consumed in the iniquity of the city. 16 And while he lingered, the men laid hold upon his hand, and upon the hand of his wife, and upon the hand of his two

daughters; the LORD **being merciful unto him: and they brought him forth, and set him without the city.**

Lot and his family saved through the destruction of Sodom foreshadows the faithful in Christ being saved through the final destruction of the world. The Lord sending angels to Lot followed by Lot being sent to his relatives reflects the Spirit and the Son proceeding from the Father into the world. The emphasis on Lot trying to save his relatives points to Christ seeking the children of God (Luke 20:36), while the emphasis on Lot specifically trying to save his sons-in-law testifies to a redemption of the faithful in Christ, in the Body of Christ, spiritually by adoption (Rom 8:15). But the failure of Lot to save the people of the city or even his own sons-in-law portends a universal apostasy in the end times. The warning of Lot appears as mocking to his sons-in-law just as the faithless are blind to the coming judgment.

Lot ultimately saving only his two daughters recalls Lot offering his own daughters, or spiritually his own flesh, as a sacrifice to the men of Sodom (Gen 19:8), in a progression that reflects the redemption of the faithful only through a participation in the death and resurrection of Jesus Christ (Rom 6:4). Lot lingering reflects the slowness of God to judgment, while the angels finally ushering Lot and his family out of Sodom in great haste reflects the eagerness of God to redeem the faithful. The judgment of Sodom and Gomorrah was delayed just as Adam was originally preserved just as the world is even now awaiting the appointed time of the end. But the delay of judgment is not boundless just as the natural body is not immortal. The delay of judgment is the embodiment of the call to repentance established by the mercy of God for the sake of his children.

Lot out of fear hesitates to leave Sodom just as he would subsequently express his fear of the mountains (Gen 19:19), but his disobedience is presumably encouraged by a knowledge of the mercy of the Lord God (Jonah 4:2). The image of Lot being a man afraid is not separate from the image of Lot as a harbinger of judgment, but rather fear is the nature of flesh, the way of flesh, reflecting the reality of the law that governs flesh. The foreboding of Lot for his own sake reflects the foreboding of Jesus Christ for the sake of the world. The angels can save Lot from his fear, but they cannot save the people of Sodom from their faithlessness.

The image of Lot being ushered from the city despite his hesitation is a profound vision of the undeniable will of God for the redemption of his children. The angels ushering Lot from the city is not a violation of his freewill, since Lot could have refused. The choice between death and life may not appear to be a real choice, but the commonplace choice of death over life demonstrates otherwise. The tension between our inviolable freewill and the incontrovertible will of God for our redemption is resolved by the gift of wisdom to choose the good and reject the bad, a wisdom that proceeds according to the Holy Spirit. The angels ushering Lot and his family from the city recalls Lot originally urging the angels to spend the night in his house, in a progression that reflects the magnification of our faith in our new creation. Lot emerging from the dying city of man is an image of death and resurrection, while the approaching dawn is a corresponding image of new creation.[79]

Genesis 19:17–22 And it came to pass, when they had brought them forth abroad, that he said, Escape for thy life; look not behind thee, neither stay thou in all the plain; escape to the mountain, lest thou be consumed. 18 And Lot said unto them, Oh, not so, my Lord: 19 Behold now, thy servant hath found grace in thy sight, and thou hast magnified thy mercy, which thou hast shewed unto me in saving my life; and I cannot escape to the mountain, lest some evil take me, and I die: 20 Behold now, this city [is] near to flee unto, and it [is] a little one: Oh, let me escape thither, ([is] it not a little one?) and my soul shall live. 21 And he said unto him, See, I have accepted thee concerning this thing also, that I will not overthrow this city, for the which thou hast spoken. 22 Haste thee, escape thither; for I cannot do any thing till thou be come thither. Therefore the name of the city was called Zoar.

The commandment to flee from the lowland of the plain to the heights of the mountain reflects the call from law to grace, from flesh to spirit, from death to life. The commandment to not look backward represents the end of evil desires and likewise the end of the dominion of flesh. Lot's fear that some evil would overtake him in a flight to the mountain portends the foretold flight into the mountains in the end times, the flight at the time of the great tribulation (Matt 24:16, 24:21). The angels being unable to destroy the cities of the plain until Lot reaches safety is a testimony to the promise that not a single child of God will be lost (Matt 18:14). The end will neither come until the fullness of sin manifests, namely, the abomination of desolation spoken of by the prophet Daniel (Matt 24:15). The preservation of a wicked remnant in Zoar from the judgment of God and the destruction by fire presages the preservation of the dragon until the conclusion of the millennial kingdom (Rev 20:2).[80]

Genesis 19:23–25 The sun was risen upon the earth when Lot entered into Zoar. 24 Then the LORD rained upon Sodom and upon Gomorrah brimstone [H1614] and fire [H784] from the LORD out of heaven; 25 And he overthrew those cities, and all the plain, and all the inhabitants of the cities, and that which grew upon the ground.

---

[79] "With what gracious violence Lot was brought out of Sodom . . . . Thus many, under some convictions about the misery of their spiritual state, and the necessity of a change, yet defer that needful work, and foolishly linger. . . . The salvation of the most righteous must be attributed to God's mercy, not their own merit" (Henry 1:98; Gen 19:15–23). The gracious violence of God is the work of the cross by which the faithful are saved by grace through faith in Jesus Christ.

[80] "Rest not in self and the world, for that is staying in the plain. Reach toward Christ and Heaven, for that is escaping to the mountain, short of which we must not rest" (Henry 1:98; Gen 19:15–23). The literal, the moral, the prophetic, and the spiritual levels of reality all testify to the one and sole image of the one and triune God.

The word *brimstone* [H1614] (rained out of heaven) has an association *gopher* [H1613] (gopher wood used to build Noah's ark), which implies a connection between the destruction of the antediluvian world by water and the destruction of Sodom and Gomorrah by fire, specifically a fulfillment of water by fire, the latter completing the former. But the destruction of the whole world by water is not fulfilled by the regional destruction of Sodom and Gomorrah. The destruction of the whole world by water, the first destruction, will be finally fulfilled in the foretold destruction of all flesh by fire, the second destruction. The prophecy of fire fulfilling water implies a symbolic conflagration of Noah's wooden ark, portending no safe haven for flesh being found in the final destruction by fire. The wooden ark of Noah foreshadows the wooden cross of Christ. For Jesus Christ himself is the sacrifice, or holocaust, and the cross is the altar, or specifically the burning wood of the altar fire.

The word *fire* [H784] (rained out of heaven) has a connotation "altar-fire," which evokes an image of condemnation, conflagration, under the law. Water is perhaps the most common symbol of the law that governs flesh, but the altar fire is also clearly linked with that same law. Fire is a symbol of spirit, whereby the altar fire prefigures grace just as the law itself prefigures grace. The images of *fire* [H784] and *brimstone* [H1614] not only portend the destruction by fire but also recall the destruction by water. The rain of floodwaters will be fulfilled in the rain of fire just as the law is fulfilled in grace just as the baptism in water is fulfilled in the baptism of fire, that is, the baptism of the Spirit. The images of water and fire are juxtaposed reflecting our inheritance in grace that is the fulfillment of the law. The natural body is condemned under the first covenant, the Covenant of Law, but the spiritual body is raised as a true living body in the second covenant, the Covenant of Grace. Two covenants, two baptisms, two destructions, two bodies.

Genesis 19:26   But his wife looked back from behind him, and she became a pillar [H5333] of salt [H4417].

The word *salt* [H4417] (pillar of salt) has an association "to tear away, figuratively dissipate (disperse)" [H4414], which reflects the dispersion of humanity in the world after the original condemnation of Adam under the law. Lot and his family being saved from the destruction by fire prefigures the redemption of the faithful from the final destruction in the end times, a redemption most closely identified with the Second Advent. But the disobedience of Lot's wife, also Lot's subsequent drunkenness, recalls the Fall of Man. The promised new creation recalls the original creation and the threefold pattern repeats, Adam followed by the First and Second Advents. The repetition itself affirms that the true fulfillment is yet incomplete, while the increasing clarity of progressive revelation points to the promised fullness of communion with God.

The word *pillar* [H5333] (pillar of salt) has a connotation "prefect," which again evokes an image of the law, while the emphasis on salt points specifically to the Covenant of Salt, which is the essence of the Covenant of Law. The

Covenant of Salt is closely identified with the redemption of the firstborn (Num 18:19) and is affirmed in the eternal kingship of David (2 Chr 13:5). The first man was Adam. But the firstfruits of the grave is (and belongs to) Jesus Christ, the king of kings (Matt 27:52–53, Lev 23:10–12). The prescription of the law to add salt to meat offerings further identifies salt with the incarnation (Lev 2:13), whereby the prophecy that everyone will be salted with fire is the call to share in the death and resurrection of Jesus Christ (Mark 9:49). Christ is the sacrifice; the faithful in Christ are the salt of the earth (Matt 5:11–13). The call to have salt in ourselves prefigures the law being written on our hearts (Mark 9:50).

Genesis 19:27–28 And Abraham gat up early in the morning to the place where he stood before the LORD: 28 And he looked toward Sodom and Gomorrah, and toward all the land of the plain, and beheld, and, lo, the smoke of the country went up as the smoke of a furnace.

Abraham standing before the place of the Lord foreshadows the twenty-four elders, with the slain Lamb, standing in the midst of the throne of God (Rev 5:6). The smoldering plain portends the judgment proceeding from the throne, likewise the altar burning before the throne (Rev 6:9). The emphasis on Abraham getting up early in the morning points to the haste of the resurrection of Jesus Christ (John 20:1) and finally the haste of the foretold return of Christ (Rev 22:7). Yet the faithful still await the glorious reappearing of Christ. The faithful naturally long for the fulfillment of all things, but the horror of the utter destruction of the cities of the plain reminds us not to long for the Day of the Lord (Amos 5:18). The faithful are rather called to intercede for the world for the sake of the righteous, in imitation of Abraham and ultimately in imitation of Jesus Christ (John 17:15). The juxtaposition of the patience of God and the haste of God is the same tension between flesh and spirit, between death and life, between law and grace. The death of the individual and the destruction of the world reflect the same reality of the law, whereby we should hope for the preservation of the world with the same passion that we hope for our own personal longevity. To long for the latter but to dread the former reflects a fundamental misconception of the curse of Adam—the curse embodied by Christ in his suffering and proclaimed in his calling us to repentance. To live is Christ, to die is gain (Phil 1:21).[81]

Genesis 19:29 And it came to pass, when God destroyed the cities of the plain, that God remembered Abraham, and sent Lot out of the midst of the overthrow, when he overthrew the cities in the which Lot dwelt.

---

[81] A single individual is equivalent to the sum of all creation, *Aboth d'Rabbi Nathan*, whereby killing even a single individual is like wiping out the entire world and saving even a single individual is like saving the entire world, *Sanhedrin* (Cohen, *Rabbinic Sages* 67). Each individual human being has infinite value to God, literally equal to creation as a whole, just as each person of the Trinity is fully divine.

ADAM, NOAH, ABRAHAM

God remembering Abraham in the land recalls God remembering Noah in the ark (Gen 8:1) and foreshadows the Father remembering the Son on the cross, or in the heart of the earth (Ps 22:1, 22:24). God preserving Abraham's blood relative Lot in remembrance of Abraham prefigures God resurrecting the faithful in Jesus Christ, the Body of Christ, in remembrance of the original resurrection of Christ the Head. Lot emerging from the destruction of the plain is an image of the death and resurrection of all creation as a whole, the individual together with physical creation.[82]

Genesis 19:30 And Lot went up out of Zoar, and dwelt in the mountain, and his two daughters with him; for he feared [H3372] to dwell in Zoar: and he dwelt in a cave [H4631], he and his two daughters.

The word *feared* [H3372] (Lot feared to dwell in Zoar) means "to fear" but has a connotation "to honour, reverence," reflecting the fear of God that marks flesh and foreshadows death. The word *cave* [H4631] (Lot dwelt in a cave) is derived from the root "to be exposed, bare (naked)" [H5783], which recalls the nakedness of Adam after the Fall of Man (Gen 3:7) and also the nakedness of Noah after the Flood (Gen 9:22) and now portends the nakedness of Lot after the destruction of the cities of the plain (Gen 19:32).[83] Abraham rescuing Lot from captivity in the war of the four kings and the five kings prefigures the First Advent of Christ (Gen 14:16), while Abraham interceding for Lot before the destruction of Sodom and Gomorrah by fire prefigures the Second Advent (Gen 18:23). But Lot now being driven from Zoar by fear recalls Adam originally being driven from the garden of Eden by the Lord God (Gen 3:24). The repetition of pairwise images of Adam and Jesus Christ, reflecting the twofold natures of Christ himself, is the basic building block of progressive revelation. Fear precedes love just as the natural precedes the spiritual just as law precedes grace.[84]

Genesis 19:31–32 And the firstborn said unto the younger, Our father [is] old, and [there is] not a man in the earth to come in unto us after the manner of all the earth: 32 Come, let us make our father drink wine, and we will lie with him, that we may preserve seed of our father.

---

[82] "Lot and his household are grasping and foolish, managing only to survive. Survive they do only because of Lot's relationship to the chosen Abraham" (Clifford, *New Jerome* 23; Gen 19:36–38). Our salvation is truly by grace alone.

[83] Etymology per *Strong's*, but a similar relationship is evident in *Brown-Driver-Briggs* via "to strip oneself (destroy)" [H6209].

[84] A parallel literary structure is evident in the three accounts of Lot, Gen 13:1–18, 14:1–24, and 18:1–19:38 (Waltke 218). The underlying literary unity of the superficially disjointed accounts of Lot reflects the preordained progression of the Spirit across the vast expanse of human history, wherein specifically the three accounts of Lot, viewed as a set, reflect the Fall of Man, the First Advent, and the Second Advent.

ABRAHAM AND SARAH

The emphasis on the old age of father Lot recalls the death of Adam near the end of the first millennium and, thereby, recalls the first millennium (Gen 5:5). The emphasis on old age finally portends an utter apostasy in the last days, figuratively the last millennium. The older daughter leading the younger astray reflects the inheritance of Eve passing through the generations. The drunkenness of Lot following the destruction of the cities of the plain recalls the drunkenness of Noah after the Flood. The image of there being no men in the earth recalls the antediluvian sons of God being destroyed in the floodwaters (Gen 6:4–7). Lot's two daughters lying with him recalls Ham and Canaan violating Noah (Gen 9:22, 9:25). The two daughters seeking to preserve the seed of their father reflects the preservation of man despite sin, also a corresponding preservation of the seed of the serpent. Nevertheless, the preservation of man despite sin is ultimately embodied by the promised Seed of woman and avowed by the rejection of the seed of the serpent (Gen 3:15).

Genesis 19:33–36 And they made their father drink wine that night: and the firstborn went in, and lay with her father; and he perceived not when she lay down, nor when she arose. 34 And it came to pass on the morrow, that the firstborn said unto the younger, Behold, I lay yesternight with my father: let us make him drink wine this night also; and go thou in, [and] lie with him, that we may preserve seed of our father. 35 And they made their father drink wine that night also: and the younger arose, and lay with him; and he perceived not when she lay down, nor when she arose. 36 Thus were both the daughters of Lot with child by their father.

The drunkenness of Lot after the destruction of the cities of the plain recalls the drunkenness of Noah after the destruction of the world, while both accounts prefigure the destruction of all creation, embodied by the crucifixion of Jesus Christ. Wine is a symbol of the blood of Christ, while drunkenness and unconsciousness are images of the death of Christ. Lot not perceiving his two daughters recalls Noah not perceiving Ham and Canaan, while both accounts prefigure Christ being blindfolded and beaten (Mark 14:65). The violation of Lot by his two daughters and also the violation of Noah by Ham and Canaan both foreshadow the humiliation of Jesus Christ by the Israelites and the Romans. Lot's older daughter encouraging his younger daughter foreshadows the Israelites demanding that the Romans crucify Christ (Mark 15:13). Lot's two daughters making him drunk two different times foreshadows the Jews abusing Christ followed by the Gentiles abusing Christ. To compare drunkenness and even sexual violation to the Passion of Christ represents the truly appalling sacrilege of Christ becoming a curse on the cross (Gal 3:13). Incest is a graphic image of flesh begetting flesh, flesh violating flesh, in the inheritance of original sin, but nonetheless the image of the childlessness, or figurative barrenness, of Lot's daughters being supplanted by fertility is a reflection of the preservation of mankind being despite our fall. Nations would arise out of incestuous origins in Lot just as the faithful will be saved despite our immeasurable sins. Such comparisons testify that our redemption is grossly undeserved.

Genesis 19:37–38 And the firstborn bare a son, and called his name Moab [H4124]: the same [is] the father of the Moabites [H4124] unto this day. 38 And the younger, she also bare a son, and called his name Ben-ammi [H1151]: the same [is] the father of the children of Ammon unto this day.

The name of the first son *Moab* [H4124] (father of the Moabites) means "from father," while the name of the second son *Benammi* [H1151] (father of the children of Ammon) means "son of my people."[85] Both names recall the incestuous origin of Lot's children and, thereby, emphasize the corruption of flesh, but the image of God is still evident in the flesh despite its corruption just as the will of God is undeniable, or relentless, despite our fall. The symbol of incest represents the way of flesh utterly separate from God the Holy Spirit, whereby our disgust at incest should not be directed at others but rather recognized as a graphic realization of our own personal uncleanness apart from the grace of the Lord God. Moab and Benammi would be preserved just as fallen man continues to be preserved, but the preservation of humanity is not boundless just as flesh is not immortal.

The first name *Moab* [H4124], "from father," reflects an emphasis on God the Father, while the second name *Benammi* [H1151], "son of my people," reflects an emphasis on God the Son. Moab and Benammi both proceed from Lot, but Benammi follows Moab and figuratively proceeds from Moab since Lot's older daughter encouraged her younger sister in the act of incest. The Spirit and Son would likewise proceed from the Father in the overshadowing of Mary (Luke 1:35). The Spirit (from Father) was manifested first; the Son (son of my people) was manifested second. The connection between the incarnation of Christ and the progeny of Lot is affirmed by the formal lineage of Christ proceeding through the Moabitess Ruth (Matt 1:5, Luke 3:32). The shocking image of Christ arising even symbolically from the incestuous origin of Moab is a graphic testimony to the humble condescension of sinless Jesus for the sake of sinful humanity, while the great faithfulness of Ruth to Naomi prefigures the exaltation of the faithful in Christ (Ruth 1:16–17).

Abimelech

Genesis 20:1–2 And Abraham journeyed from thence toward the south country, and dwelled between Kadesh and Shur, and sojourned in Gerar. 2 And Abraham said of Sarah his wife, She [is] my sister: and Abimelech king of Gerar sent, and took Sarah.

The account of Pharaoh taking and returning Sarai in Egypt prefigures Abimelech taking and returning Sarah in Gerar (Gen 12:15). The death and resurrection of Christ in the First Advent likewise prefigures the death and resurrection of the Body of Christ in the Second Advent. Egypt evokes an image of slavery to sin that foreshadows the death of Christ for the sins of the

---

[85] Literal meaning of *Moab* [H4124] per *Strong's*, not *Brown-Driver-Briggs*.

world, while the promised land (between the Nile and the Euphrates) represented by Gerar evokes an image of the promised kingdom of God (Gen 15:18). Christ would specifically come out of Egypt in the First Advent (Hos 11:1), while the promised land is most closely identified with the glorious reappearing in the Second Advent (Zech 14:4). Christ appearing only to Israel in the First Advent is, not primarily an image of Israel as the promised land, but rather Israel as a microcosm of a lost world, signified as the lost sheep of Israel (Matt 15:24). The new names of Abraham and Sarah being identified specifically with the second account in Gerar reflects the promised glorification of the faithful in Christ in the Second Advent. The mystery created by Abraham concerning the identity of his wife is the mystery of the salvation of the faithful by grace (Eph 5:32). The original mystery in Egypt concerning Sarai specifically reflects the mystery of Christ—namely, the incarnation through the Spirit—while the subsequent mystery in Gerar concerning Sarah reflects the mystery of the Body of Christ—namely, the unity of the faithful in the Spirit.[86]

Genesis 20:3–6 But God came to Abimelech in a dream by night, and said to him, Behold, thou [art but] a dead man, for the woman which thou hast taken; for she [is] a man's wife. 4 But Abimelech had not come near her: and he said, Lord, wilt thou slay also a righteous nation? 5 Said he not unto me, She [is] my sister? and she, even she herself said, He [is] my brother: in the integrity of my heart and innocency of my hands have I done this. 6 And God said unto him in a dream, Yea, I know that thou didst this in the integrity of thy heart; for I also withheld thee from sinning against me: therefore suffered I thee not to touch [H5060] her.

Abimelech is a king in the world, reflecting the dominion of flesh in conflict with the Spirit of God. Abimelech takes Sarah just as the serpent originally deceived the first woman, Eve. Abimelech does not recognize Sarah as the wife of Abraham just as satan does not acknowledge the rightful bride of the Lamb. Abimelech took Sarah without any real consent from Abraham, whereby Abimelech's claim of ignorance reflects an ignorance of the law that governs flesh and a corresponding spiritual separation from God. Abimelech proclaiming his own ignorance reflects the first man Adam effectively condemning himself in his own disobedience. Adultery and apostasy reflect the same primordial abomination.[87]

The word *touch* [H5060] (suffered I thee not to touch her) recalls the same word describing humanity not being allowed (in the words used by Eve) to *touch*

---

[86] A parallel literary construction is apparent in the three accounts of matriarch abduction, Gen 12:10–20, 20:1–18, and 26:1–17 (Waltke 210–11). The three accounts, viewed as a set, reflect the Fall of Adam, the First Advent of Christ, and the Second Advent, wherein the personages of Adam and Jesus Christ should be recognized as paralleling the First and Second Advents of Christ.
[87] The adulterer is identified with the atheist, *Numbers Rabbah* (Cohen, *Rabbinic Sages* 97–98). The persistent link between adultery and apostasy points to the marriage supper of the Lamb of God.

[H5060] the tree of knowledge, whereby the death identified with Abimelech touching Sarah recalls the death identified with touching the tree of knowledge (Gen 3:3). The foretold death of all flesh in the end times likewise recalls the original condemnation in Adam of all flesh, all Adam-kind. The image of God Almighty withholding the hand of Abimelech reflects the restraint of evil until the appointed time. The emphasis on nighttime portends the darkness preceding the glorious reappearing of Jesus Christ at the Second Advent, corresponding to the dawn of our promised new creation.

Genesis 20:7 Now therefore restore the man [his] wife; for he [is] a prophet, and he shall pray for thee, and thou shalt live: and if thou restore [her] not, know thou that thou shalt surely die, thou, and all that [are] thine.

The Lord God will not violate freewill, but the bride of the Lamb will be redeemed, though the lost oppose the will of God. The Lord is the God of history, leading the faithful by the law unto grace.[88]

Genesis 20:8–11 Therefore Abimelech rose early in the morning, and called all his servants, and told all these things in their ears: and the men were sore afraid. 9 Then Abimelech called Abraham, and said unto him, What hast thou done unto us? and what have I offended thee, that thou hast brought on me and on my kingdom a great sin? thou hast done deeds unto me that ought not to be done. 10 And Abimelech said unto Abraham, What sawest thou, that thou hast done this thing? 11 And Abraham said, Because I thought, Surely the fear of God [is] not in this place; and they will slay me for my wife's sake.

Abimelech not knowing why Abraham had hid the identity of Sarah represents an ignorance of the mystery of redemption. The refrain "I know not" is the byword of Cain, the way of the flesh unto dust (Gen 4:9). The implied predisposition of Abimelech to kill Abraham in order to possess Sarah reflects the desire of the serpent to destroy Christ in order to profane creation, even the throne of the Creator. The fear of God is the denial of God, but satan and his host take no responsibility for their apostasy (Jas 2:19).[89]

Genesis 20:12–13 And yet indeed [she is] my sister; she [is] the daughter of my father, but not the daughter of my mother; and she became my wife. 13 And it came to pass, when God caused me to wander from my father's house, that I said unto her, This [is] thy kindness which thou

---

[88] Abraham is the first person designated as a prophet in the Scriptures (Coffman 266; Gen 20:7). The father of the faithful comes by the spirit of prophecy.

[89] Gen 20:1–18 shows a chiastic literary construction with 20:8 as the pivot (Waltke 283). The pivotal image of being sore afraid portends the horror of the cross and the corresponding end of the natural body.

shalt shew unto me; at every place whither we shall come, say of me, He [is] my brother.

Our surprise at Abraham and Sarah being half siblings reflects our shock at Christ calling the faithful into a familial relationship with God (Matt 12:50). The relationship between God causing Abraham to wander and Abraham hiding the full identity of Sarah reflects the preservation of humanity in the world that in turn foreshadows the redemption of the faithful in the world to come. The mystery surrounding the relationship between Abraham and Sarah is the mystery of one flesh, that is, the mystery of the redemption of the faithful in the Body of Christ (Eph 5:32).

Genesis 20:14–18 **And Abimelech took sheep, and oxen, and menservants, and womenservants, and gave [them] unto Abraham, and restored him Sarah his wife. 15 And Abimelech said, Behold, my land [is] before thee: dwell where it pleaseth thee. 16 And unto Sarah he said, Behold, I have given thy brother a thousand [pieces] of silver: behold, he [is] to thee a covering of the eyes, unto all that [are] with thee, and with all [other]: thus she was reproved. 17 So Abraham prayed unto God: and God healed Abimelech, and his wife, and his maidservants; and they bare [children]. 18 For the LORD had fast closed up all the wombs of the house of Abimelech, because of Sarah Abraham's wife.**

The restoration of Sarah to Abraham is a vision of the redemption of the faithful in the Body of Christ—one flesh prefigured by Eve originally being taken out of Adam but then presented unto Adam (Gen 2:23). The enrichment of Abraham prefigures the glorification of the Body of Christ. Abraham reaping wealth, expressly without work, reflects salvation coming only by grace and not by works. The emphasis on the silver paid to restore Sarah points to the price of the life of Christ recompensed in the harvest of humanity (Matt 27:9). The emphasis on Abraham staying in the promised land points to the restoration, or re-creation, of creation in the kingdom of God. But the healing of Abimelech with his household portends the dragon and his host being preserved until the end of the millennial kingdom of Christ (Rev 20:2–3).[90]

Ω Ω Ω

The first three major patriarchs—Adam, Noah, and Abraham—each herald their respective millennia with great portent, but the account of Abraham in the opening of the third millennium from Adam represents a uniquely critical junction in the line of Christ. Abraham lived in an anticlimactic period

---

[90] The era of the Messiah is understood in much of Talmudic literature to be a time of transition between the present world and the world to come (Cohen, *Rabbinic Sages* 356). The end of the millennial kingdom of Christ will mark the opening of eternity in Christ, figuratively the eighth millennium.

ADAM, NOAH, ABRAHAM

compared with the dramatic creation of the first man Adam and the cataclysmic destruction of Noah's time, but yet the essential faith embodied by Abraham overshadows even the looming personages of Adam and Noah. The faith of Abraham specifically represents a fulfillment of the promise established in Adam and affirmed in Noah as a new Adam. The first man Adam embodies fallen man in the original curse of all flesh (Fall of Man) (Gen 2:15–17). Noah embodies the death and resurrection of Christ in the account of the Flood (First Advent) (Gen 5:29). And Abraham is finally the father, or first, of the faithful called out of the world and, thereby, prefigures the resurrection of all the faithful in Christ (Second Advent) (Gal 3:7). The first three major patriarchs—Adam, Noah, and Abraham—therefore reflect the same birth, death, and rebirth embodied, respectively, by the original creation followed by the First and Second Advents of Christ. And Adam, Noah, and Abraham finally reflect the Father, Son, and Holy Spirit as our creator, redeemer, and sanctifier.

1	2	3
ADAM	NOAH	ABRAHAM
CREATION, OR BIRTH	DEATH	REBIRTH
ORIGINAL CREATION OF ADAM	FIRST ADVENT OF CHRIST	SECOND ADVENT OF CHRIST
CREATOR	REDEEMER	SANCTIFIER
GOD THE FATHER	GOD THE SON	GOD THE HOLY SPIRIT

The faith of Abraham represents the fulfillment of the promise established according to Adam and sealed in Noah, but Abraham as the first father of the chosen people, the father of all the faithful, simultaneously hearkens back to the first man Adam as the father of all flesh, the first man formed in the very image of God. Abraham is a new Adam. Abraham simultaneously embodying both the original creation of Adam and also the foretold glorification of the faithful in Christ at the Second Advent represents the redemption in Christ of Adam, or all the faithful from Adam, likewise the redemption, or re-creation, of all creation.[91] Father Abraham embodying both our fall and our glorification is a reflection of the dichotomy of flesh and spirit as manifested in all mankind. This is the essential union of law and grace proclaimed by all creation. But the juxtaposition of Adam and Jesus Christ embodied by Abraham ultimately points to the nexus embodied by Christ himself, who is simultaneously and without contradiction fully man and fully God. Abraham represents the fulfillment of the promise embodied by Adam, but Abraham is not the final fulfillment of the promise. The personage of Abraham not only hearkens back to Adam but also points forward to the last days.

The 1-2-3 pattern evident in Adam, Noah, and Abraham is repeated in Abraham, David, and Jesus Christ, reflecting again the same birth, death, and rebirth embodied by the original creation in Adam followed by the First and Second Advents of Christ. The pattern repeats, but with increasing clarity. The call of Abraham to faith in the opening of the third millennium affirms the

---

[91] The redemption of all mankind? All mankind and likewise all creation are redeemed in Christ, but only the faithful will accept the gift of salvation. For many are called, but few are chosen, Matt 22:14.

ABRAHAM AND SARAH

original call of Adam to obedience. The Davidic kingship established in the opening of the fourth millennium heralds the conception of Jesus Christ as king of kings at the end of fourth millennium. The reality of Jesus Christ being publically revealed in the opening of the fifth millennium points to the resurrection of the Body of Christ in the end times. The First and Second Advents of Christ parallel the personages of David and Christ just as the First and Second Advents parallel the personages of Adam and Christ. The persistent duality underlying the Trinity testifies to the twofold natures of the Son, being true God and true man, through which all creation proceeds and subsists. The three millennia from the time of the First Advent through the millennial kingdom repeat again the fundamental threefold image of birth, death, and rebirth. Christ becoming the firstborn of the grave in the opening of the fifth millennium recalls the formation of the first man Adam. The silence and schism that mark the opening of the sixth millennium relate a degradation and destruction recalling the death of Christ. The yet future glorious reappearing of Christ in the dawn of the seventh millennium will encompass the promised resurrection and rapture of the faithful in Christ, in the Body of Christ.[92]

1	2	3	4	5	6	7
1 ADAM	2 NOAH	3 ABRAHAM				
		1 ABRAHAM	2 DAVID	3 CHRIST		
				1 HEAD	2 SCHISM	3 BODY

The repeating, overlapping 1-2-3, 1-2-3, 1-2-3 staircase pattern evident in the Biblical timeline points inexorably to the last days, specifically to the fulfillment of the promise of the fullness of the indwelling Holy Spirit, whereby this pattern is most closely identified with the Holy Spirit, specifically with the movement of the Spirit leading the faithful unto the fullness of grace. An analogous repeating, overlapping 1-2-3 staircase pattern that shows nonuniform time intervals is also evident in the same progression of generations. This nonuniform pattern departs from its uniform counterpart in the central interval between Abraham and the First Advent of Jesus Christ, wherein five principal 1-2-3 cycles are evident, making seven total 1-2-3 cycles from Adam to the Second Advent of Christ. These uniform and nonuniform patterns both point in parallel to the one and only Body of Christ being the fulfillment of the promised fullness of the indwelling Holy Spirit. The synergy between the uniform and nonuniform counterparts, being parallel yet simultaneously overlapping, then reflects the

---

[92] Per Ussher's chronology, Adam was formed in 4004 BC (Ussher 17), Noah was born in 2948 BC (Ibid. 18), Abraham, or Abram, was born in 1996 BC (Ibid. 22), David was born in 1085 BC (Ibid. 58), and Jesus Christ was born in 5 BC (Ibid. 779); The East–West Schism of AD 1054, also called the Great Schism, which distinguished Eastern Orthodoxy and Roman Catholicism, was the first major rupture of the earthly church (*The World Book Encyclopedia*, 1967 ed., s.vv. "Christianity," "Eastern Orthodox Churches"). The six days of man.

unity of the Holy Spirit, specifically the unity of God the Spirit and God the Son proceeding from God the Father.

A full discussion of nonuniform patterns is not the goal of the present work, but a few comments are appropriate for the purpose of establishing context. In the following graphic, focus on the 2-position in each cycle, which in each case is most closely related to the incarnation of Christ at the First Advent. Isaac is identified with the First Advent by his figurative sacrifice in Moriah (Gen 22:2). Moses is identified with the First Advent by the redemption of Israel out of slavery and the corresponding establishment of the Passover lamb (Exod 12:21). The time of Judges is identified with the First Advent by the recurring image of a single man being raised up in a time of universal apostasy (Judg 2:17–19). David being raised up to supplant Saul represents Christ raised up to supplant Adam (1 Sam 16:1). The exile of the Jewish people from the promised land represents Christ being cut off from the land of the living (Isa 53:8). The multiplication, or expansion, of cycles in the midst of the Biblical timeline is a kind of clarification that itself represents the incarnation of the visible image of God, likewise in the midst of the Biblical timeline. Such a time of clarification being defined specifically by the period between Abraham and the First Advent testifies to the life of Jesus Christ representing, first of all, a recapitulation of the call of the Jewish people. First the Jew, then the Gentile (Rom 1:16). The emphasis on the midst of the Biblical timeline, in contrast to the beginning or end, is a testimony to the central, or core, importance of the incarnation being our personal experience of Christ.[93]

---

[93] "And 6,000 years must needs be accomplished, in order that the Sabbath may come, the rest, the holy day 'on which God rested from all His works.' For the Sabbath is the type and emblem of the future kingdom of the saints, when they 'shall reign with Christ,' when He comes from heaven, as John says in his Apocalypse: for 'a day with the Lord is as a thousand years.' Since, then, in six days God made all things, it follows that 6,000 years must be fulfilled [Hippolytus of Rome, *On Daniel*]" (Roberts et al., *Ante-Nicene Fathers* 5:179). The structure of the Bible, being holy, is necessarily prophetic.

ABRAHAM AND SARAH

	SECOND CYCLE			THIRD CYCLE			FOURTH CYCLE			FIFTH CYCLE			SIXTH CYCLE		
1	2	3	1	2	3	1	2	3	1	2	3	1	2	3
ABRAHAM	ISAAC	JACOB	ISRAEL	MOSES	JOSHUA	JOSHUA & ELEAZAR	TIME OF JUDGES	TIME OF KINGS	SAUL	DAVID	SOLOMON	PROMISED LAND (FIRST TEMPLE)	NATIONAL EXILE (FIRST EXILE)	KINGDOM OF GOD (FIRST ADVENT)

ADAM, NOAH, ABRAHAM

CHAPTER FIVE OUTLINE

Key Images

	PRIME IMAGES	
Material	Abstract	Spiritual
Abraham.	One faithful man.	God is one.
The land of Canaan.	The promised land.	The kingdom of God.
Circumcision.	A mark of blood in the flesh. A requirement of the law.	The crucifixion of Christ.
	TWOFOLD IMAGES	
Material	Abstract	Spiritual
Abram renamed Abraham and Sarai renamed Sarah.	First and second. Flesh and spirit.	Original creation foreshadowing the promised new creation.
Abraham and Sarah.	Man and woman (one flesh). Justice and mercy. Flesh and spirit.	The Head and the Body of Christ.
Isaac and Eliezer.	Promised son and eldest servant. Flesh and spirit.	The Son and Spirit proceeding from the Father.
Hagar and Sarah.	Slave and freewoman. Flesh and spirit.	The Covenants of Law and Grace (Gal 4:24).
Lot and Abraham.	Lot saved by Abraham. Flesh and spirit.	Adam and Jesus Christ.
Kings of Sodom and Salem.	Genealogy, no genealogy. Rejected and accepted. Flesh and spirit.	A king followed by one that is both a king and a high priest. The First and Second Advents.
(1) Sarai taken and returned by Pharaoh, (2) Sarah taken and returned by Abimelech.	Egypt and Canaan. Exile and return. Flesh and spirit.	The First and Second Advents of Christ.
(1) Abram rescues Lot from captivity, (2) Abram intercedes for Lot in Sodom.	Rescue from slavery followed by rescue from death. Repentance and redemption. Flesh and spirit.	The First and Second Advents of Christ.
The first and second descents of the angels of God to Sodom and Gomorrah.	First to see, second to judge. Flesh and spirit.	The First and Second Advents of Christ.
	THREEFOLD IMAGES	
Material	Abstract	Spiritual
Nahor, Haran, Abram.	Cain, Abel, Seth. Ham, Shem, Japheth.	Adam, First Advent, Second Advent.
Get thee out from thy country, from thy kindred, and from thy father's house.	The call to reject the corrupted world, the corrupted flesh, and finally the corrupted spirit embodied by the father of lies.	The call to accept the Father, Son, and Holy Spirit that is reflected in our creation, redemption, and sanctification.
Ur, Haran, Canaan.	Birth, death, rebirth. Promise, repentance, redemption.	The Father, Son, Holy Spirit as creator, redeemer, sanctifier.
Three angels appear to Abraham.	Three appear to Abraham, but only two proceed to Sodom and Gomorrah.	The Holy Spirit and Son proceeding from the Father.

ABRAHAM AND SARAH

Synopsis

The Call

	Material	Spiritual
11:26–30	Terah begat Abram, Nahor, and Haran.	Recalls the three sons of Adam and the three sons of Noah and also foreshadows the threefold offspring of Abraham through Hagar, Sarah, and Keturah.
11:31–32	Terah takes Abram and Lot from Ur of the Chaldees to Canaan, but they stop to dwell in the land of Haran, where Terah dies.	The migration from Ur to Haran to Canaan reflects birth, death, and rebirth.
12:1	Get thee out of thy country.	The call to reject a corrupted world.
	And from thy kindred.	The call to reject corrupted flesh.
	And from thy father's house.	The call to reject the father of lies (John 8:44).
12:2–3	I will make of thee a great nation.	The kingdom of God.
	I will bless thee.	The blessing of the Son by the Father.
	I will make thy name great.	The one name (Acts 4:12).
	And thou shalt be a blessing.	The blessing of the faithful in the Son.
	I will bless them that bless thee, and curse him that curses thee.	Salvation is only by grace through faith in Jesus Christ.
	And in thee shall all families of the earth be blessed.	The promise of a universal redemption of all the faithful in Christ from all the nations.
12:4–5	Abram departs from the land of Haran.	The baptism of repentance.
	Abram enters the land of Canaan.	The baptism of the Holy Spirit.

Two Altars

	Material	Spiritual
12:6–8	The Lord foretells that the seed of Abram will inherit the land.	Jesus Christ, likewise the faithful in Christ, who will possess all creation.

Famine

	Material	Spiritual
12:9–13	Famine is in the land.	The original curse of the ground.
	A sojourn in Egypt.	The exile from the garden.
	The identity of Sarai is hidden.	The mystery of the bride of the Lamb.
12:14–20	Pharaoh takes Sarai.	Recalls the corruption of Eve and prefigures the defilement of Christ for the sake of all humanity that proceeded from Eve.
	Pharaoh returns Sarai.	Reflects the preservation of flesh in the world and prefigures the resurrection of Christ.
13:1–4	Abram is enriched.	The glorification of Christ.

Division

	Material	Spiritual
13:5–7	Strife between Lot and Abram.	Recalls the original strife in the garden between man and God.
13:8–17	Abram gives Lot the choice of the land.	God will not violate freewill.
	Lot chooses Sodom.	The way of the flesh.
	The Lord promises the land to Abram and also to his seed.	The promise of Jesus Christ and also the Body of Christ.

ADAM, NOAH, ABRAHAM

	MELCHIZEDEK	
	Material	Spiritual
13:18–14:11	Five kings rebel against four kings.	Wars and rumors of wars will precede the final destruction by fire.
14:12–16	Lot is taken captive.	Slavery to sin, likewise slavery to death.
	Abram rescues Lot by force.	The resurrection of Christ through the power of the Holy Spirit.
14:17–20	Melchizedek presents bread and wine to Abram.	The body and blood of Jesus Christ.
	Melchizedek blesses Abram.	The submission of Christ to the law.
	And Abram tithes to Melchizedek.	The law of death subjugated by Christ.
14:21–24	Abram refuses to be enriched by the king of Sodom.	Man is saved only by grace through faith in Christ and not by works.
	FIRSTBORN	
	Material	Spiritual
15:1–6	Not the steward Eliezer, but rather Abram's own son will be his heir.	Our promised inheritance is, not the original creation, but the foretold new creation.
15:7–21	The Lord instructs Abram to prepare a series of animal sacrifices.	Blood sacrifice is required by the law.
	The Lord foretells the slavery of Israel and also their ultimate emancipation.	Our redemption by grace through faith in Christ from the slavery of sin.
	A smoking furnace and a burning lamp.	A vision of the union of justice and mercy.
16:1–6	Abram obeys Sarai concerning Hagar.	Recalls Adam obeying Eve.
	And the slavewoman Hagar conceives Ishmael.	An image of our inheritance in original sin from Adam.
	Hagar despises Sarai.	Flesh contends against spirit.
	Hagar flees from Sarai.	Our separation from the Spirit of God.
16:7–16	The angel of the Lord instructs Hagar to submit to Sarai.	The call to submit to the authorities of the present world, which is the curse of the first son Adam (Rom 13:1).
	The seed of Hagar will become a multitude.	The preservation of flesh under the law.
	Ishmael will be a wild man.	The way of flesh.
17:1–9	God instructs Abram to walk before him and be perfect.	The perfection of Jesus Christ and also our new creation in Christ.
	God will make Abram into a multitude.	The faithful in Christ.
	Abram is renamed Abraham.	The glorification of Christ.
	Kings will come out of Abraham.	Christ and the faithful in Christ.
	The Lord will be God unto thee and thy seed.	Our promised communion with God in the Body of Christ.
	Abraham and his seed will be given the land in which they are strangers.	The restoration, or re-creation, of creation.
17:10–14	Circumcision will be the token of the covenant.	A prophecy of the crucifixion of Christ.
17:15–16	Sarai is renamed Sarah.	The glorification of the faithful in Christ.
17:17–18	Abraham laughs.	A laughter of hope.

ABRAHAM AND SARAH

17:19–22	The covenant will be established with Isaac, but Ishmael will also be blessed.		Adam will be redeemed in Jesus Christ.
17:23–27	Ishmael and Abraham are circumcised on the same day.		We are crucified with Christ (Rom 6:3–4).
		MYSTERY	
	Material		Spiritual
18:1–16	Three angels appear as men to Abraham.		A representation of the Trinity.
	The three men announce the birth of Isaac.		The promise of Jesus Christ.
	Two angels of God proceed to Sodom.		God the Spirit and God the Son proceeding from God the Father.
18:17–19	Shall the Lord hide from Abraham that thing which he does?		The mystery of Christ (Eph 1:9–10).
18:20–22	The Lord will go down to Sodom.		An image of the incarnation of Christ.
18:23–33	Abraham intercedes for the righteous.		Christ intercedes for the faithful.
	The Lord will not destroy the righteous with the wicked.		The preservation of the world for the sake of the righteous until the last days.
19:1–22	The two angels enter Sodom.		The First Advent of Jesus Christ.
	The men of Sodom seek to defile the two angels.		The defilement of the flesh of Christ in the crucifixion.
	Lot offers his own daughters to the mob.		Our disgust at the crucifixion of Christ.
	The two angels send Lot to bring his relatives out of Sodom.		The call of the faithful unto Christ.
	The two angels usher Lot out of Sodom.		The Second Advent of Christ.
19:23–29	The Lord rains brimstone and fire upon Sodom and Gomorrah.		A vision of the foretold second destruction of the world that will be by fire.
19:30–38	Lot driven from Zoar by fear.		Adam driven from the garden.
	Lot is made drunk by his daughters.		Drunkenness reflects the way of all flesh, all the earth, foreshadowing a universal death.
	Lot fathers Moab and Benammi.		The preservation of flesh despite sin.
		ABIMELECH	
	Material		Spiritual
20:1–18	The identity of Sarah is hidden a second time.		The mystery of the Body of Christ, specifically as identified with the Second Advent.
	Abimelech takes Sarah, then returns her.		The death and resurrection of the faithful.
	Abraham is again enriched.		The glorification of the Body of Christ.
	Abraham prays for the life of Abimelech.		The intercession of Christ for the world.
	Abraham stays in the land.		The kingdom of God.

CHAPTER SIX

Ishmael, Isaac, Keturah's Sons

The prime images emphasized in the account of Abraham's sons are the promise of Isaac, the sacrifice of Isaac, and the sole inheritance of Isaac. Abraham's first son, Ishmael, is the son of the bondwoman Hagar, reflecting our inheritance of original sin from the first man Adam. The love of Abraham for Ishmael reflects the love of the Father for Adam. The rejection of Ishmael corresponds to the admission of universal suffering through the sin of Adam. Abraham's second son, Isaac, is the son of the freewoman Sarah, reflecting our redemption in the second man Jesus. Abraham sacrificing in faithfulness his only son, Isaac, prefigures the Father giving his only begotten son, Jesus Christ, for the sake of the faithful (John 3:16). The figurative sacrifice of Isaac precedes the literal sacrifice of Christ just as the law precedes grace just as Adam precedes Christ just as Christ precedes the Body of Christ just as the promise of life precedes the reality of life. Isaac ultimately becoming the sole heir of Abraham reflects the Son receiving the singular blessing of the Father. Abraham's sons by Keturah are finally added to Isaac just as the Gentiles are added to the Jews. Abraham while he yet lived giving gifts to his sons by Keturah reflects the Creator bestowing the deposit of the Holy Spirit while the original creation yet endures.

The pairwise images emphasized in the account of Abraham's offspring are Abraham and Sarah as a primordial couple, Isaac and Rebekah as a promised union, and Ishmael and Isaac as first and second sons. Also emphasized are barrenness and fertility, the two flights of Hagar, and the two treaties with Abimelech. The union of Abraham and Sarah recalls the original creation, especially that of humanity, originally proceeding from God the Father. The union of Isaac and Rebekah reflects the incarnation of the Son being uniquely in Israel. The twelve tribes finally proceeding from Jacob prefigures the fullness of the Holy Spirit being revealed in the Body of Christ in the last days. The brotherhood of Ishmael and Isaac reflects the brotherhood of Adam and Jesus, while the ubiquitous image of barrenness being miraculously transformed into fertility reflects the redemption of Adam in Christ. The two flights of Hagar and also the two treaties between Abraham and Abimelech reflect the two covenants, law followed by grace, likewise the two baptisms, the baptism in water followed by the baptism of the Holy Spirit.

The threefold Abraham (man), Sarah (woman + implied offspring), and Isaac (Seed of woman) reflect, respectively, the Father, Son, and Holy Spirit, with an emphasis on the Spirit and the Son both proceeding from the Father but it being the Holy Spirit who finally indwells the one Body of Christ. The threefold Abraham (father), Isaac (son), and their descendants (sons) reflect, respectively, the Father, Son, and Holy Spirit, with emphasis on the Son being begotten of the Spirit but again it being the Holy Spirit who finally indwells the multitude of the faithful. Abraham sending his eldest servant on behalf of his son Isaac to call his bride reflects the Father sending the Holy Spirit to call the faithful unto the Son. Hagar, Sarah, and Keturah are a rejected concubine, a near-kin wife, and a concubine who becomes a wife; and thereby the three reflect, respectively, the slavery inherited from Adam, the freedom from sin established in the incarnation, and the resurrection of the dead in the last days. The threefold conception, birth (symbolized by circumcision), and weaning reflect, respectively, the promise of the Father manifested in the original creation, the incarnation of the Son, and the promised new creation by the Holy Spirit. The threefold sequence of Abraham laughing, Sarah laughing, and finally the foretelling of people laughing with Sarah reflects the promise, repentance, and redemption that is embodied by Adam and the First and Second Advents of Christ. The account of Abraham and Pharaoh followed by the two accounts of Abraham and Abimelech also reflects Adam followed by the First and Second Advents of Christ.

PROMISE

Genesis 21:1 And the LORD visited [H6485] Sarah as he had said [H559], and the LORD did [H6213] unto Sarah as he had spoken [H1696].

The word *said* [H559] (the Lord said) and the word *spoken* [H1696] (the Lord had spoken) both have a connotation "to promise," which reflects the promise of life, ultimately the promised Seed of woman, Jesus Christ (Gen 3:15). The word *visited* [H6485] (the Lord visited) has a connotation "to punish," which foreshadows the propitiation for sins embodied by the incarnation of God. The word *did* [H6213] (the Lord did) is the same word used to describe God originally *making* [H6213] man (Gen 1:26), which points to the fullness of the indwelling Holy Spirit as prefigured by the original breath of life (Gen 2:7). God speaking is an image of the promise of life embodied by the primordial Logos (John 1:1). God speaking is God promising, because God does not lie. The promise, our inheritance, proceeds uniquely from the Father. God visiting foreshadows the appearing of Jesus Christ at the First Advent, the ultimate recompense for sin, and finally our own repentance in Christ. The visitation of Christ in the incarnation under the law is the embodiment of repentance as the manifestation of perfect submission to the divine will, a repentance in which we participate by grace through faith. God doing (making) is finally our new creation—not by our own doing, or making—but rather by his grace, a gift that comes only by the indwelling Holy Spirit. The threefold *speak*, *visit*, and *do* represent promise, repentance, and redemption and finally God the Father, God the Son, and God the Holy Spirit. God promising is God repenting is God redeeming. The three are one, the one is three. Is the image of God repenting offensive? Yet God does repent (Gen 6:6).[1]

The threefold *speak*, *visit*, and *do* are organized in the narrative as a repeating pair: first, the Lord *said* [H559] and the Lord *visited* [H6485] followed, second, by the Lord *spoke* [H1696] and the Lord *did* [H6213]. Pairwise organization emphasizes the Father (speaking the promise) being the font of both the Son (visitation, or incarnation) and the Holy Spirit (doing, or animating, our new creation). Pairwise organization also emphasizes the parallel relationship between the incarnation (visit) and our new creation (do), that is, between the Son (Head) and the Holy Spirit (animation of the Body). The progression from the word *visited* [H6485] to the word *did* [H6213] represents increasing action, the promise of Christ becoming the reality of Christ, the fulfillment of the First Advent of Christ in the Second Advent. The incarnation (visit) precedes our new creation (do, or make) just as the Spirit proceeds from the Father (promise) through the Son (repentance) to indwell the faithful (redemption). The implied equality in the narrative construction between speaking and visiting and between speaking and doing represents the redemption of the children of God being expressly and certainly guaranteed by the promise of God. The ubiquitous organization of threefold reality as overlapping twofold pairs reflects the human condition itself embodying the tension between flesh and spirit, likewise the tension between law and grace.

Genesis 21:2 For Sarah conceived [H2029], and bare [H3205] Abraham a son in his old age [H2208], at the set time [H4150] of which God had spoken [H1696] to him.

The words *conceived* [H2029] (Sarah conceived Isaac) and *bare* [H3205] (Sarah bare Isaac) are the same words used to describe the *conception* [H2029] and *bringing forth* (birthing) [H3205] of Cain (Gen 4:1) and also of Ishmael (Gen 16:4, 16:15). The kinship between Ishmael and Isaac, likewise that between Cain and Abel, reflects an overarching kinship between Adam and Jesus Christ, a kinship that prefigures the oneness of the Body of Christ. Isaac born in the *old age* [H2208] of Abraham prefigures Jesus Christ being born in the latter days of Israel, after the revelation of the law and the prophets of old. The knowledge of youth is the way of flesh, while the wisdom of age is the way of spirit. The word *set* [H4150] (set time) has connotations "season" and "assembly," which recalls

---

[1] The apologists of the second century—Aristides, Justin Martyr, Athenagoras, Tatian, and Theophilus of Antioch—believed that the Son is the Logos, not in the sense that the Son originates with the Father, but rather that the Son is the expression of the Godhead (Rusch 5). The Son was not created but begotten, eternally begotten, existing before and after the visible incarnation.

the seasons (and days and years) established from the very beginning, a chorus throughout time testifying to the preordained will of God (Gen 1:14). The word *spoken* [H1696] (God had spoken) has connotations "to promise" and also "to command" and "to pronounce (sentence)," which are images of certainty that reflect an undeniable and unassailable divine authority. All prophecy relates the undeniable will of God as manifested for the welfare of mankind. All prophecy relates the unassailable reality of the incarnation of God as a true man.

The names *Abram* and *Sarai* being changed to *Abraham* and *Sarah* is a sign of new creation (Gen 17:5, 17:15), whereby Ishmael would proceed from Sarai but Isaac would proceed from Sarah (Gen 16:3). The barrenness of Sarai transformed into fertility by the Lord prefigures the bride prepared for her husband, the new Jerusalem (Rev 21:2). The barrenness of the bride is the barrenness of the bridegroom, whereby barrenness is ultimately an image of Christ cut off from the land of the living without any physical offspring (Isa 53:8). But the barren woman has more offspring than the fertile woman (Isa 54:1) because the husband of the barren woman is the Lord (Isa 54:5). The bondwoman Hagar giving birth to Ishmael reflects the Covenant of Law, while the freewoman Sarah giving birth to Isaac reflects the Covenant of Grace (Gal 4:22–24). Sin is not freedom but rather slavery to flesh. Obedience to God is not bondage but rather true freedom in the wisdom of the Spirit. The evil in the world is a resounding testimony that God will never violate freewill, while the misery that always courses from sin is a pathetic admission that freewill is inevitably renounced in the kingdom of satan.[2]

Genesis 21:3   And Abraham called the name of his son that was born [H3205] unto him, whom Sarah bare [H3205] to him, Isaac [H3327].

The word *born, bare* [H3205] (a son is born) recalls the same word originally used to describe the curse of woman to *bring forth* [H3205] children in sorrow (Gen 3:16). The pain of childbirth is closely identified with the promised Seed of woman, an identification that prefigures our rebirth through the suffering of the cross (Gen 3:15). The miraculous birth of Isaac proceeding from Abraham through the promise embodied by Sarah prefigures the virgin birth of Christ proceeding from the Father through the power of the Holy Spirit as embodied by Mary (Luke 1:35). The emphasis on Isaac being the only son of Abraham by Sarah points to Jesus Christ being the only begotten Son of God, conceived of the Spirit. The tension between the pain of childbirth and the promise of life is the paradox of flesh and spirit and likewise the paradox of law and grace. Isaac

---

[2] "Although one might anticipate the birth story [of Isaac] as the act's climax, this narrative of Abraham's walk with God and faith in a seed will not crest until Abraham has faced the ultimate challenge to his faith, the sacrifice of his son" (Waltke 291). The cross of Jesus Christ, not his birth, is likewise emphasized in the New Testament.

follows Ishmael just as the spiritual follows the natural just as grace follows law just as Christ follows Adam.³

The name *Isaac* [H3327] means "he laugheth," which foreshadows both our surprise at the birth of Christ and also our joy in salvation by grace through faith in Christ. Surprise is a reflection of flesh while joy is a reflection of spirit, whereby the name *Isaac* represents the union of flesh and spirit just as Jesus Christ is both the Son of man and the Son of God. Sarah previously laughed in surprise while Abraham laughed in joy, whereby the laughter embodied by Isaac also reflects the union of Abraham and Sarah as one flesh (Gen 17:17–18, 18:12–13). The previously discussed parallel between Sarah and the Holy Spirit does not now implicate any closeness between the Spirit proceeding from God and Sarah's unbelief but rather testifies to the corruption that comes through the spirit of disobedience in conflict with the Spirit of God. The identification of Isaac with not only the Spirit of faith that proceeds from God but also the nature of flesh corrupted by the spirit of disobedience portends Christ becoming a curse on the cross (Gal 3:13).⁴

Genesis 21:4 And Abraham circumcised [H4135] his son Isaac being eight days old, as God [H430] had commanded [H6680] him.

The name *God* (Elohim) [H430] evokes an image of "rulers" and "judges," which implies an emphasis on justice and law in contrast to mercy and grace. *Elohim* is the first name of God revealed in the Scriptures and, thereby, reflects a primal connection of justice and law with the original creation of flesh, a connection exemplified by the original commandment being given in the garden (Gen 2:17). The image of circumcision being *commanded* [H6680] by God also evokes an image of authority and power in contrast to mercy.⁵ However, the fullness of the revelation of God, the final revelation of God, is not merely justice but rather the perfect union of justice and mercy just as Christ is both the Son of man and the Son of God. The word *circumcised* [H4135] (Isaac circumcised) evokes images "to cut off" and also "to destroy," which imply separation, submission, and finally the death of the natural body. Circumcision is a mark of blood in the flesh that portends the baptism of crucifixion, while the God of creation commanding circumcision points to our promised new

---

³ ". . . Sarah was a type of the blessed *Virgin* . . . [and also without contradiction] a type of the *New Testament* and heavenly Jerusalem; . . ." (Clarke 1:115; Gen 17:16). A type of the Holy Spirit overshadowing the virgin Mary.

⁴ The freewoman Sarah represents a type of grace, the Jerusalem that is above, whereby Isaac represents a type of the true church, also Christ as the obedient son, also Christ as the bridegroom, and also the believer having a new nature reborn according to the Holy Spirit (Scofield 31 nn. 1–2; Gen 21:3). The life-giving grace that proceeds from God the Father by the indwelling of God the Holy Spirit is the mother of our new creation in God the Son, the Body of Christ.

⁵ The Strong's number H6680 = *commanded* is illegible in the author's copy of the thirty-eighth printing of *Strong's Concordance*, but the number has been confirmed using a copy of the forty-fourth printing.

creation in the death and resurrection of Christ. Circumcision is the primary sign of the first covenant, the law, which governs our separation from the Lord, but circumcision in the flesh prefigures circumcision of the heart (Rom 2:29). The Covenant of Law likewise foreshadows the Covenant of Grace just as the condemnation of Christ under the law foreshadows our freedom in Christ from death under the law. Circumcision expressly on the eighth day is a vision of the first day after the Sabbath—representing the dawn of a new creation, in accordance with circumcision being an external sign of a new nature.[6]

The Covenant of Grace will be embodied by the perpetual intercession of Christ as high priest, the communion of Christ with the faithful—ultimately fulfilled in the resurrection of the dead, specifically in the glorification of the Body of Christ in the Second Advent (Heb 7:25). The Covenant of Law is most closely identified with the kingship of Christ revealed at the time of the First Advent, not with the high priesthood in the Second Advent. The blood sacrifice embodied by Christ at the First Advent is commonly identified with the priesthood and the altar, but the law of the temple represents the Order of Aaron, not the Order of Melchizedek. The death of Christ is closely identified with the destruction of the temple, but this reflects the end of the altar, not the glory of the altar, and likewise the end of death, not the glory of life (Matt 26:61). The incarnation of Christ under the law at the First Advent is the birth of Christ as king (Matt 2:2) and his death as king (Matt 27:37). The nature of flesh expects the rule of law, but the nature of spirit looks for the anointing of grace. The priesthood of Aaron is not the priesthood of Christ but only points to the priesthood of Christ just as the first covenant points to the second covenant just as the First Advent points to the Second Advent. Christ would appear in the flesh at the First Advent to all Israel, but Christ would appear glorified unto only a very few. The appearance of Christ in glory unto only a few at the First Advent points to the Second Advent, when Christ will be revealed to the entire world. The resurrection of Jesus Christ as and with the firstfruits of the grave likewise points to the resurrection of all the dead in the last days (Matt 27:52–53, Lev 23:10–12).[7]

Genesis 21:5 And Abraham was an hundred years old, when his son Isaac was born unto him.

---

[6] Adam to the Flood is the first age (10 generations), the Flood to Abraham is the second age (10 generations), Abraham to David is the third age (14 generations), David to the Babylonian captivity is the fourth age (14 generations), the captivity to the First Advent is the fifth age (14 generations), the present time is the sixth age (unknowable generations), the Sabbath rest will be the seventh age, and eternity will be the eighth age (Augustine, *City of God* 867). The dispensations of the Lord God, correctly reckoned, are the eight millennial days, or prophetic days, of creation. For what are the dispensations of God, except each new day?

[7] " 'Wanton hatred is equal to the three transgressions of idolatry, unchastity, and bloodshed, and was the cause of the destruction of the Second Temple' [*Joma*]" (Cohen, *Rabbinic Sages* 99). Jesus Christ is the true temple, and the shedding of his blood is the wanton hatred of the flesh.

ADAM, NOAH, ABRAHAM

The miraculous birth of Isaac in the old age of Abraham prefigures the birth of Jesus Christ in the nation of Israel, long after the revelation of the law and prophets. The incarnation of Jesus Christ in Israel long after the revelation of the law likewise prefigures the yet future glorious reappearing of Christ in the end times of the world, long after the fulfillment of the law in the life, death, and resurrection of Christ. The miraculous birth of Isaac in the old age of Abraham is also a figurative resurrection of Abraham that reflects the exaltation of the Father through that of the Son and finally the exaltation of the faithful by the Holy Spirit in the Body of Christ (John 17:1). Each generation succeeding the previous is an image of death and resurrection that points to the inexorable fulfillment of all things in the last generation. Our miraculous death and resurrection in Christ is our impossible redemption through the undeniable, or relentless, will of God Almighty (Matt 19:26).[8]

Genesis 21:6–7 And Sarah said, God hath made me to laugh, [so that] all that hear will laugh with me. 7 And she said, Who would have said unto Abraham, that Sarah should have given children suck? for I have born [him] a son in his old age.

Sarah previously laughing in unbelief but now laughing in belief is a vision of the spirit of disobedience being supplanted by the Holy Spirit. The death of the natural body heralds the resurrection of the spiritual, or glorified, body. The image of Sarah laughing followed by all who hear laughing with her is a vision of the anointing of Christ by the Holy Spirit followed by the anointing of the faithful in Christ (John 16:7). The resurrection of Jesus Christ as and with the firstfruits of the grave points to the resurrection of all the faithful in Christ, in the Body of Christ, at the harvest of mankind (Matt 27:52–53, Lev 23:10–12). But only those who have ears can hear the laughter (Mark 8:18). Sarah contemplating who would have ever said that she would bear a son in the old age of Abraham reflects the mystery of our redemption, ultimately the mystery of the incarnation of Christ and finally the mystery of the Body of Christ.

Genesis 21:8 And the child grew, and was weaned [H1580]: and Abraham made a great feast the [same] day that Isaac was weaned.

The word *weaned* [H1580] (Isaac was weaned) has connotations "to ripen" and also "to recompense," which foreshadows the redemption of the faithful in the harvest of humanity (Matt 13:39). Weaning represents an end of infancy, emblematic of putting away childish ways in the ascent into adulthood, and

---

[8] "That the Church which before had been barren should have more children from among the Gentiles than what the synagogue had had before[:] . . . In Isaiah: 'Rejoice, thou barren, that barest not' . . . . Thus also to Abraham, when his former son was born of a bond-woman, Sarah remained long barren; and late in old age bare her son Isaac, of promise, who was the type of Christ [Cyprian of Carthage, *Treatises*]" (Roberts et al., *Ante-Nicene Fathers* 5:512). Not merely the Gentiles, but the Jews and the Gentiles together in the one Body of Christ.

foreshadows our rebirth by the Spirit, our maturity in Christ (1 Cor 13:11). The weaning of Isaac from Sarah naturally precedes the union of Isaac and Rebekah just as the spirit of disobedience is necessarily condemned before the anointing of the Holy Spirit. The union of male and female as one flesh is a vision of the union of justice and mercy, which is finally our redemption by grace, the promised resurrection of the spiritual, or glorified, body. The great feast celebrating the weaning of Isaac, the supernatural offspring, prefigures the marriage supper of the Lamb (Rev 19:9). Holding the feast the same day Isaac is weaned foreshadows the haste with which Christ will return at the appointed hour (1 Thess 5:2–3) and likewise the haste of our foretold transformation in the twinkling of an eye (1 Cor 15:52).

The progression of conception, birth, and weaning is a reflection of promise, repentance, and redemption. The threefold conception, birth, and weaning can be reformulated as conception, circumcision, and weaning since birth and circumcision are closely related according to a common mark of blood and, additionally, by circumcision being prescribed a mere eight days after being born. The miraculous conception of Isaac embodies the promise of God just as the original formation of Adam embodies the promise of life. The birth and circumcision of Isaac represents the inheritance of the flesh from Adam and also the submission of Christ in the flesh. The inheritance in the flesh is the law of the flesh and likewise the call to repentance in the flesh. The relationship between the curse and the blessing of the law reflects the brotherhood of Adam and Christ. Sin enslaves flesh under the law, but submission in the flesh foreshadows our rebirth by the Spirit just as birth is fulfilled by weaning just as the First Advent will be fulfilled by Second Advent. Weaning represents the first sign of maturity and, thereby, maturity itself. Our promised redemption. Circumcision precedes weaning just as the law precedes grace just as repentance precedes redemption. Conception precedes birth just as the promise of God is the font of life. The threefold image of promise, repentance, and redemption embodied by conception, circumcision, and weaning ultimately reflects the will of the Father, our death in the Son, and our rebirth by the Holy Spirit.[9]

Genesis 21:9 And Sarah saw the son of Hagar the Egyptian, which she had born unto Abraham, mocking [H6711].

The word *mocking* [H6711] (Ishmael mocking Isaac) is the same word used to describe Abraham *laughing* [H6711] (Gen 17:17) and also Sarah *laughing* [H6711] (Gen 18:12) and is the root word from which the name *Isaac* [H3327] is derived. The laughter of Abraham is linked in the narrative to Abraham yearning for the blessing of Ishmael, which reflects the promised redemption of Ishmael through Isaac, that is, our promised salvation by grace through faith in Jesus Christ (Gen 17:17–18). Sarah first laughed in disbelief at the promise of Isaac

---

[9] "For the old Israel, circumcision was not the covenant, but the sign of the covenant; but for Christians, circumcision (in the spiritual sense) is the union with Christ by means of being baptized *into him*" (Coffman 272; Gen 21:1–7). A baptism of blood, Rev 1:5.

but now laughs in joy at the reality of Isaac, which reflects our redemption proceeding only through the incarnation of Jesus Christ, only through the flesh. In stark contrast, Ishmael, the natural son, now laughs, or mocks, in derision at the reality of Isaac, the very person of Christ, which represents the irrepressible self-destructive contention between flesh and spirit and ultimately the undeniable self-condemnation of all flesh in the natural body.[10]

Genesis 21:10 Wherefore she said unto Abraham, Cast out [H1644] this bondwoman and her son: for the son of this bondwoman shall not be heir [H3423] with my son, [even] with Isaac.

The word *heir* [H3423] (Abraham's heir) has connotations "to seize" and "to dispossess," which is an image of the second son Jesus seizing the lost dominion of the first son Adam. The son of the bondwoman is displaced by the son of the freewoman just as the first man formed from the dust is displaced by the second man begotten of the Spirit. Sarah insists that Isaac would be the sole heir and, thereby, affirms that the natural man cannot enter the kingdom of God just as the law cannot yield eternal life (1 Cor 15:50). The word *cast out* [H1644] (cast out this bondwoman) has a connotation "divorced" and is the same word originally used to describe Adam and Eve being *driven out* [H1644] from the garden of Eden (Gen 3:24). Sarai commanded Abram to take Hagar just as Eve led Adam in the original disobedience—reflecting a continuing degradation, a progressive degradation, of humanity through the spirit of disobedience. But Sarah ultimately casts out Ishmael in favor of Isaac just as the natural is supplanted by the spiritual, which reflects the promised new creation of the Holy Spirit. Sarai sought offspring in the natural way, but Sarah bears supernaturally the son of the promise.

Genesis 21:11 And the thing was very grievous in Abraham's sight because of his son.

The agonizing image of casting out (the firstborn) Ishmael being very grievous to Abraham is a vision of the compassion of God for all mankind, figuratively (the first man) Adam. The terseness of the narrative reflects a terrible inevitability. Abraham is the father of both Ishmael and Isaac just as Noah is the father of both Ham and Shem just as Adam is the father of both Cain and Abel just as God is the Father of both Adam and Jesus Christ. Ishmael represents Adam, all humanity, called to repentance, while Isaac represents the one man Jesus Christ. We are not Jesus Christ. We are Adam. We are Cain. We are Ham. We are Ishmael. Every man is an Adam unto himself through participation in the original sin. Any prejudice against Ishmael or Isaac, against

---

[10] "He [Ishmael] derided God's promise made to Isaac, which the Apostle calls persecution, [Gal 4:29]" (Whittingham et al., *Geneva Bible* 9R n. c; Gen 21:9). The first man Adam not believing the promise of God and therein rejecting the presence of God is all Adam-kind persecuting Jesus Christ and likewise the faithful in Christ.

Arab or Jew, or against any peoples of the world represents an ironic and prophetic condemnation of ourselves. We are not redeemed by our own righteousness, but rather we are saved only by grace through faith in the one man Jesus Christ. A man identifies with Christ only by participating in the promise of God, that is, the Body of Christ.

Genesis 21:12 And God said unto Abraham, Let it not be grievous in thy sight because of the lad, and because of thy bondwoman; in all that Sarah hath said unto thee, hearken [H8085] unto her voice [H6963]; for in Isaac shall thy seed [H2233] be called.

The word *hearken* [H8085] (unto Sarah) means "to hear" and has a connotation "to obey" and is the same word used to describe Abram *hearkening* [H8085] unto Sarai concerning Hagar (Gen 16:2) and also Adam *hearkening* [H8085] unto Eve concerning the forbidden tree (Gen 3:17). The word *voice* [H6963] (of Sarah) is also the same *voice* [H6963] of Eve to which Adam hearkened. Sarai thought she could bear offspring through Hagar just as Eve thought she could become like God through the tree of knowledge (Gen 3:5). Abram hearkening to Sarai in taking Hagar reflects the spirit of disobedience, but Abraham hearkening to Sarah in casting out Hagar points to the Holy Spirit. The two women Hagar and Sarah embody the two covenants of law and grace and also the two spirits distinguished according to disobedience and faith, while their respective offspring represent the fruition of the two spirits as foretold by the two covenants (Gal 4:24). The firstborn Ishmael is a natural man, an image of Adam, while the second born Isaac is a spiritual man, an image of Jesus Christ. The offspring of Sarah supplants the offspring of Hagar just as grace supplants law. The wife Sarah originally preceded the concubine Hagar just as the promise of life preceded the law.

The account of the first flight of Hagar (Hagar fleeing from Sarai) is followed by the account of the covenant of circumcision (Gen 16:8, 17:10), while the second flight of Hagar (Sarah casting Hagar out) is followed by the figurative sacrifice of Isaac (Gen 21:14, 22:2). The sign of circumcision precedes the reality of the cross just as law precedes grace. The first flight is connected with Hagar rejecting the authority of Sarai just as Adam rejected the original commandment, while the second flight is connected with Ishmael mocking Isaac just as Jesus Christ would be mocked and rejected. The former is disobedience, while the latter is desolation and death. Disobedience precedes desolation just as exile precedes death just as the first death precedes the second death (Rev 20:14). But Ishmael is preserved in the land just as the world would be preserved even after the crucifixion of Christ. Hagar and Ishmael being saved from death is a figurative death and resurrection that prefigures the resurrection of the dead in the last days.[11]

---

[11] A parallel literary construction is evident between the two accounts of Hagar, Gen 16:1–16 and 21:1–21 (Waltke 250). The parallel between the two accounts of Hagar

ADAM, NOAH, ABRAHAM

Genesis 21:13 And also of the son of the bondwoman will I make a nation, because he [is] thy seed [H2233].

The word *seed* [H2233] (of Abraham) is used to describe both Isaac and Ishmael, which points to the brotherhood of Jesus and Adam. The preservation and multiplication of Ishmael reflects the preservation and multiplication of humanity in the present world. And no man should dare curse what the Lord God has blessed.

Genesis 21:14–16 And Abraham rose up early in the morning, and took bread [H3899], and a bottle of water [H4325], and gave [it] unto Hagar, putting [it] on her shoulder [H7926], and the child, and sent her away: and she departed, and wandered [H8582] in the wilderness [H4057] of Beer-sheba [H884]. 15 And the water was spent in the bottle, and she cast the child under one of the shrubs. 16 And she went, and sat her down over against [him] a good way off, as it were a bowshot: for she said, Let me not see the death of the child. And she sat over against [him], and lift up her voice, and wept.

The word *bread* [H3899] (given to Hagar) has contrasting connotations "to eat" [H3898] and "to fight" [H3898], a dichotomy reflecting bread as both the staff of life and the bread of affliction. The word *water* [H4325] (given to Hagar) likewise has connotations of both "refreshment" and also "distress," a dichotomy reflecting water as both the font of life and simultaneously the pit of destruction. Both bread and water are symbols of the natural body, likewise of the law that governs the natural body—specifically the duality of the body (flesh and spirit) as spoken of by Christ (Matt 26:41), likewise the dichotomy of the law (curse and blessing) as spoken of by the prophet Moses (Deut 11:26). Abraham placing water and bread upon the *shoulder* [H7926] of Hagar recalls the original curse of the law being placed upon the person of Eve and foreshadows the Seed of woman bearing the curse of the tree (Gen 3:15–16). Abraham put bread on Hagar before he put water on her just as the curse of Adam to eat bread in the sweat of his face would be affirmed in the floodwaters (Gen 2:17, 3:19, 6:13). The emphasis on the water being spent, in contrast to the bread, reflects the baptism in the floodwaters in the time of Noah pointing to the baptism of Jesus Christ on the cross—Christ being the manna, or bread, from heaven (John 6:41).

The word *wilderness* [H4057] (Hagar wandered in the wilderness) means "uninhabited land (in which is no man)" and has a connotation "desert," reflecting the solitude and isolation of the spiritual wilderness of the present world. The word *wandered* [H8582] (Hagar in the wilderness) has connotations "to be seduced (cause to morally err)" and "to stagger (of intoxication)," recalling the original fall and exile from the garden and also the confounding

---

reflects the intimate connection between the first man Adam and the second man Christ and likewise between the First and Second Advents of Christ.

and dispersing of the peoples of Babel. But the word *wandered* [H8582] is also used to describe Abram *wandering* from his father's house, which is closely linked with the mystery surrounding the identity of Sarah, representing the mystery of salvation (Gen 20:13). The faithful Abram shares the wandering of faithless Adam just as Jesus Christ would become a curse on the cross for the sake of sinners (Gal 3:13). Jesus Christ would be in the world but not of the world just as the faithful are likewise strangers in the world (John 17:15–18). The curse of the one man Adam is affirmed by the nomadic lifestyles of the three patriarchs Abraham, Isaac, and Jacob as a testimony to the unity of the Father, Son, and Holy Spirit in the proclamation of the curse. The rejection of the offspring of Hagar finally points to an utter condemnation of the natural body and a corresponding passing away of the law (Matt 5:18).[12]

Genesis 21:17 And God heard the voice of the lad; and the angel of God called to Hagar out of heaven, and said unto her, What aileth thee, Hagar? fear [H3372] not; for God hath heard the voice of the lad where he [is].

The word *fear* [H3372] (fear not) means "to fear" but has a connotation "to honour, reverence," which is an image of obedience in the flesh. But fear is only the beginning of wisdom (Ps 111:10). Love is the fulfillment of wisdom (1 John 4:18). God telling Hagar not to *fear* [H3372] represents the call from the flesh to the Spirit and likewise the call from law to grace.

Genesis 21:18 Arise [H6965], lift up [H5375] the lad, and hold [H2388] him in thine hand; for I will make him a great nation.

The word *arise* [H6965] (God commands Hagar) is the same word used to describe God *establishing* [H6965] his covenant with Noah (Gen 9:17) and also God *establishing* [H6965] his covenant with Abraham (Gen 17:7). The promise of God established in his covenants will finally be fulfilled in the call to arise in the resurrection of the dead, a progressive expectation reflected in the preservation of Ishmael in the hope of redemption through Isaac. The word *lift up* [H5375] (the lad) recalls Noah's ark *borne up* [H5375] above the earth upon the floodwaters (Gen 7:17) and foreshadows Jesus Christ *lifted up* [G5312] upon the cross (John 3:14). The image of being lifted up above the earth is a vision of exaltation from a sinful nature, from the dust of the ground signifying our sinful nature, and is closely identified with the baptism in water represented by the Flood (1 Pet 3:21) and ultimately with the baptism of Christ revealed in the Passion (Luke 12:50). The word *hold* [H2388] (hold the lad) has connotations "to strengthen" and "to encourage" and is the same word used to describe the

---

[12] "[T]hey [Hagar and Ishmael] got into the wilderness, wandered about and lost their way, and so became destitute of provisions; and this may be an emblem of the low, mean, and starving condition such are in who are under the law, and seek for happiness by the works of it . . . ." (Gill 1:118; Gen 21:14). The way of all the earth.

angels *laying hold* [H2388] upon Lot and ushering him from Sodom despite Lot's own hesitation (Gen 19:16). This is a vision of redemption by grace in the last days, the weakness of flesh overcome by the strength of the Spirit. The image of strengthening and encouraging prefigures the perpetual intercession of Christ for the faithful, the communion of Christ with the faithful (Heb 7:25). The threefold commandment to arise, lift up, and hold is a vision of promise (establishment), repentance (exaltation from the dust), and redemption (strengthening) that reflects the promise of God the Father, our repentance in God the Son, and finally our new creation by God the Holy Spirit. The promise to make Ishmael a great nation upon fulfilling the threefold commandment points to the one kingdom of God.

Genesis 21:19 And God opened her eyes, and she saw a well of water; and she went, and filled the bottle with water, and gave the lad drink.

The original flight of Hagar is connected with *Beerlahairoi* (well Lahairoi) [H883], which means "well of the living One that seeth me" (Gen 16:14), while the final flight of Hagar is connected with *Beersheba* [H884], which means "well of seven (as a place of swearing by seven)" (Gen 21:14). The first flight of Hagar connected with Beerlahairoi emphasizes seeing, or acknowledging, the will of God and submitting to the will of God. The call to repentance in the flesh. The second flight of Hagar connected with Beersheba emphasizes a salvation from physical death and the promise of blessing, which is a fulfillment of the repentance embodied by the first flight to Beerlahairoi. The promise of life by the Spirit. The first flight of Hagar prefigures the second flight just as the first man Adam prefigures the second man Christ just as the First Advent of Christ prefigures the Second Advent. Adam precedes Christ just as the natural precedes the spiritual. The First Advent precedes the Second Advent just as repentance precedes redemption.[13]

Hagar submitting to the commandment of God at Beerlahairoi is an image of submission to the law, whereby the waters of Beerlahairoi reflect the ceremonial cleansing of the law and also the figurative death and resurrection corresponding to the baptism of repentance in water. The waters of Beersheba represent, not foremost the water of repentance, but specifically the water of life, which is the baptism of the Holy Spirit. Hagar thirsting in the wilderness of Beersheba reflects humanity thirsting for redemption. God hearing the cry of Ishmael in Beersheba and saving Hagar with her son prefigures our redemption by grace through faith in Jesus Christ. Hagar could not see the waters of Beersheba by herself but only by the mercy of God just as our redemption comes only by grace and not by works. To see the water of life is to see the font of life, even God. To see God in this life is to recognize Jesus Christ as the incarnation of God; to see God in the next life is to be a new creature in Christ

---

[13] "Except God open our eyes, we can neither see, nor use the means which are before us" (Whittingham et al., *Geneva Bible* 9R n. h; Gen 21:19). We are not blind because God did not open our eyes but because we have willfully closed our own eyes to God.

(1 John 3:2). Further, the pregnancy of Hagar linked with Beerlahairoi reflects the promise, or guarantee, of life and life eternal just as the law is a prophecy of grace just as the water of repentance is a prophecy of the water of life. The symbol of water progressing, flowing, from repentance (Beerlahairoi) to redemption (Beersheba) reflects the death of the natural body heralding the rebirth in the spiritual, or glorified, body.[14]

Genesis 21:20–21 And God was with the lad; and he grew, and dwelt in the wilderness, and became an archer [H7198]. 21 And he dwelt in the wilderness of Paran [H6290]: and his mother took him a wife out of the land of Egypt.

The word *archer* [H7198] (Ishmael became an archer) has connotations of "hunting" and "battle." The preservation of Ishmael recalls the preservation of Adam. But the preservation of Ishmael is also identified with death and destruction, as signified by the archer's bow, and thereby reflects the irrevocable curse of mankind in Adam. The preservation of Ishmael prefigures the blessing of the faithful just as the mortal life of Adam prefigures eternal life in Christ. God being with Ishmael prefigures the indwelling Holy Spirit just as the transitory blessing of Adam under the law prefigures the eternal blessing in Jesus Christ by grace. A focus on the brotherhood of Ishmael and Isaac telescopes attention to the one nation of Israel, itself projecting outward as a microcosm of the world as a whole. The natural man Ishmael represents the earthly nation of Israel while the spiritual man Isaac represents the heavenly nation, whereby Ishmael prefigures Isaac just as the earthly Jerusalem prefigures the heavenly Jerusalem (Gal 4:25–26). Hagar taking an Egyptian wife for Ishmael specifically portends the bondage of the Israelites in Egypt. Ishmael dwelling in the region of *Paran* [H6290] portends the faithlessness of the Israelites at Kadesh in the wilderness of *Paran* [H6290] (Num 13:26).

Two Treaties

Genesis 21:22–23 And it came to pass at that time, that Abimelech and Phichol the chief captain of his host spake unto Abraham, saying, God [is] with thee in all that thou doest: 23 Now therefore swear [H7650] unto me here by God that thou wilt not deal falsely with me, nor with my son, nor with my son's son: [but] according to the kindness that I have done unto thee, thou shalt do unto me, and to the land wherein thou hast sojourned.

---

[14] "There is a well of water by them in the covenant of grace, but they are not aware of it; they have not the benefit of it, till God who opened their eyes to see their wound, opens them to see their remedy, [John 16:6–7]" (Henry 1:105; Gen 21:14–21). Salvation is, not by works, but by grace through faith in Jesus Christ.

ADAM, NOAH, ABRAHAM

The word *swear* [H7650] (swear by God) means "to bind oneself," probably "to seven oneself" or "to bind oneself by seven things," which reflects an acknowledgment of the rightful dominion of law over flesh, the law of creation, the law of sevens relating the seven millennia of creation. Abimelech seeks a quid pro quo agreement with Abraham, kindness according to kindness, which is the essence of the law, the way of all flesh, all the earth. Right action is exchanged for right action. Obedience is life, disobedience is death. In contrast, returning kindness for unkindness is the embodiment of grace, the way of the Spirit. Our redemption is fundamentally undeserved and cannot be negotiated. The clause for reciprocal kindness ironically turns the treaty into a curse, in accordance with the perpetual hostility between the Philistines and the Israelites. Abimelech curses himself just as Adam cursed himself. The offspring of Abimelech would affirm the curse in their aggression toward the offspring of Abraham just as all men affirm the curse of Adam in their individual sins.

Abimelech is a king of the world and ultimately reflects the prince of this world, the devil (John 14:30). The shift from an explicit spirit of disobedience, as embodied by the serpent in the Fall of Man, to an implicit spirit of disobedience after the Flood testifies to the condemnation of the serpent in the original curse being sealed by the floodwaters. The shift from explicit to implicit also reflects a corresponding internalization of the original sin in the ultimate revelation of our sinful nature, which is only evil continually. The singular serpent is the primary image of evil before the Flood, but the threefold Abimelech, his chief captain, and his host—now in the time of Abraham—represent an early glimpsing of a threefold anti-godhead, which is in imitation of the revelation of God as the God of Adam, Noah, and Abraham. In a dark counterfeit of progressive revelation, the threefold Abimelech, his chief captain, and his host (together) acknowledge that God is with Abraham, which is in anticipation of, or recognition of, the revelation of the triunity of God in terms of God being uniquely the God of the threefold Abraham, Isaac, and Jacob (Exod 3:6).[15] The emphasis on Abimelech, his son, and his son's son also reflects the shift from the singular serpent to the threefold Abimelech, which again anticipates Abraham, Isaac, and Jacob.[16]

The threefold Abimelech, his chief captain, and his collective host being contrasted with the threefold Abimelech, his sons, and his collective progeny implies that the devil has a detailed understanding, or knowledge, of the triunity of God. The same juxtaposition is evident in the relationship between Abraham and his eldest servant compared with the relationship between Abraham and his

---

[15] Other Trinitarian titles are "the God of Shadrach, Meshach, and Abednego," Dan 3:29, and "the God of Abraham, and the God of Nahor, the God of their father [Terah]," Gen 31:53. But these titles of deity are not emphasized beyond their local context and, not coincidentally, neither are they applied by God to himself, rather by the people of the world to God, Exod 3:6.

[16] Only the one true God—existing outside, inside, and throughout time and space—knows the end from the beginning, Isa 46:10. And thus the evil one in any way anticipating God must be understood as merely reflective of an intimate, or firsthand, knowledge of the triune nature of God, Luke 10:18.

offspring. This is the threefold man, woman, and child compared with the threefold father, son, and progeny. The threefold Abimelech portends the dragon, beast, and false prophet (Rev 16:13).

Genesis 21:24 And Abraham said, I will swear [H7650].

God will not violate freewill. Creation is condemned.

Genesis 21:25 And Abraham reproved [H3198] Abimelech because of a well [H875] of water [H4325], which Abimelech's servants had violently taken away.

Abimelech actually violating the treaty with Abraham before the treaty is even sworn reflects a horrible predictability and additionally reflects the foreknowledge of God. Abimelech figuratively violates the treaty in haste just as Adam disobeyed the original commandment in haste (before having offspring) just as Israel would reject Christ in haste (in his youth, or without offspring). The word *well* [H875] commonly means "well (of water)," which is a very positive image particularly in desert cultures, but the word *well* [H875] is also the same word describing the *pit* [H875] of destruction foretold through and by David (Ps 55:23). The word *water* [H4325] is likewise a positive image as the font of life, but word *water* [H4325] also has negative connotations of "distress" and "violence." The image of a well of water is therefore something good that has dark undertones just as the account of Abraham and Abimelech is outwardly peaceful but portends a continuing conflict between the Philistines and the Israelites. The law, the water of repentance, is our condemnation (Gal 3:10), but the law is also our guide to grace, the water of life (Gal 3:24).

Abimelech taking but then returning the well of water to Abraham recalls his house taking but then returning Sarah. Abimelech had previously *reproved* [H3198] Sarah because she presented herself as Abraham's sister (Gen 20:16), and now Abraham *reproves* [H3198] Abimelech concerning the violent taking of the well of water. The water of life recalls the water of repentance. The word *reproved* [H3198] can mean either "to justify" or "to rebuke," which reflects the dichotomy of the law that governs flesh, the choice between our being justified through the flesh of Christ (by the law) or our being rebuked in our own flesh (under the law) (Matt 21:44). In the former account, Sarah is justified, or recompensed, by Abimelech, while in the latter account, Abimelech is rebuked in an escalation portending the coming final judgment. The world would falsely rebuke the incarnation because of the virgin Mary, or the humanity of Mary, but in the end Christ will rightly rebuke the world because of the great whore (Rev 19:2). Abraham rebuking the one king Abimelech portends God judging all the kings of the earth, all flesh.

Genesis 21:26 And Abimelech said, I wot [H3045] not who hath done this thing: neither didst thou tell [H5046] me, neither yet heard [H8085] I [of it], but to day [H3117].

Abimelech denying any knowledge of Abraham's well recalls Adam and Eve hiding from God and therein denying God (Gen 3:8) and, like begetting like, Cain denying any knowledge of Abel (Gen 4:9). Abimelech does not know about Abraham's well of water just as flesh cannot comprehend the way of the Spirit (John 4:10). Abimelech's denial of any knowledge of the water is a figurative denial of any knowledge of creation, likewise any knowledge of the Creator. The word *day* [H3117] (to day) has connotations "heat of the day" and "working-day," recalling the curse of Adam to eat bread in the sweat of his face (Gen 3:19). Abimelech only now, or today, admits that Abraham's well of water had been violently taken just as the mystery of the Son of God will be fully revealed only in the end times, long after the Son of man is violently cut off. Abimelech's emphatic denial is expressly threefold, reflecting a threefold anti-godhead. Abimelech claimed to *wot* (know) [H3045] not (who hath), to not have been *told* [H5046] (about the well), and to not have *heard* [H8085] (about the well). To deny knowledge is to deny the font of knowledge, God the Father (who hath). To deny being told is to deny the incarnation of the Word of God, God the Son (who tells). To deny hearing, obeying, is to have ears but not hear, to have eyes but not see, that is, it is to deny any part in the Holy Spirit (by the power of whom we hear and obey).

Genesis 21:27 And Abraham took sheep and oxen, and gave them unto Abimelech; and both of them made a covenant.

The treaty acknowledging that Abraham had dug the well at Beersheba is a distinct treaty from the original nonaggression treaty presented by Abimelech. Abraham, at least symbolically, swore to reciprocal nonaggression before he rebuked Abimelech concerning the well of water. The grievance itself implies an expectation of nonaggression. Abimelech first seeks a treaty of equals with Abraham just as Adam originally sought equality with God (Gen 3:5). This quid pro quo contract presented by Abimelech represents the law condemning flesh (Rom 3:19), the law of death ironically being established by man through sin (1 Cor 15:56). But Abraham demands a second treaty affirming his possession of the well of water just as salvation proceeds only from God by grace and not from men under the law. The well of water being taken violently from Abraham is the way of flesh and reflects death entering the world through the first man Adam. The water being restored by the word of Abraham is the way of the Spirit and reflects the restoration of the faithful in the second man Jesus Christ. Abraham and Abimelech making distinct covenants of law and grace at the same time foreshadows the fulfillment of the Covenant of Law in the Covenant of Grace. Abraham takes back possession of the well from Abimelech just as Christ would take the keys of death from the prince of this world (Rev 1:18). Abimelech acknowledges Abraham as the originator and possessor of the well of water just as all the dead, small and great, will stand before the throne of God at the time of judging, or acknowledging (Rev 20:12). Abraham is the rightful owner of the well of water just as God is the true possessor of the water of life.

ISHMAEL, ISAAC, KETURAH'S SONS

Genesis 21:28–31 And Abraham set seven ewe lambs of the flock by themselves. 29 And Abimelech said unto Abraham, What [mean] these seven ewe lambs which thou hast set by themselves? 30 And he said, For [these] seven ewe lambs shalt thou take of my hand, that they may be a witness [H5713] unto me, that I have digged [H2658] this well. 31 Wherefore he called that place Beer-sheba; because there they sware both of them.

The word *digged* [H2658] (digged the well) has a connotation "to search out," which reflects the mystery of salvation. The dust of the ground is a metaphor for flesh since flesh was formed from the dust, whereby well water being drawn from the ground reflects the water of life proceeding from the flesh of Christ. The word *witness* [H5713] (seven lambs will be a witness) means "testimony, witness." The seven ewe lambs represent the original seven days of creation, likewise the seven millennia from Adam. The seven lambs are a witness that Abraham dug the well of water just as creation is a witness to the Creator (Rom 1:20). Each of the seven lambs reflects the one Lamb of God just as each day of creation and each millennium of creation prefigures the fulfillment of creation in Jesus Christ. The seven lambs are a witness that Abraham dug the well of water just as the Lamb of God testifies that the Father is the font of the water of life. The seven ewe lambs connect the seven days of creation with the one Lamb of God just as all creation originally proceeded through the Son (John 1:3). The seven ewe lambs finally prefigure the fulfillment of all things, law and grace, in the Body of Christ in the seventh millennium from Adam.

Genesis 21:32–34 Thus they made a covenant at Beer-sheba [H884]: then Abimelech rose up, and Phichol the chief captain of his host, and they returned into the land of the Philistines. 33 And [Abraham] planted a grove [H815] in Beer-sheba [H884], and called there on the name of the LORD, the everlasting [H5769] God. 34 And Abraham sojourned in the Philistines' land many days.

Abraham planting a *grove* (tamarisk tree) [H815] recalls the tree of knowledge and also prefigures the tree of life. The tree of knowledge represents not only the Fall of Man but also the Covenant of Law ultimately embodied at the First Advent of Christ. The tree of life represents not merely eternal life but also the Covenant of Grace finally revealed in the Second Advent. The two trees together represent the perfect union of flesh and spirit, likewise the perfect fulfillment of law in grace, embodied by the one man Jesus Christ. Abraham planting the grove specifically at *Beersheba* [H884], meaning "well of seven (as a place of swearing by seven)," points to the fulfillment of all things in the seventh millennium. The emphasis on Abraham staying in the land many days points to the millennial kingdom of Christ, while Abimelech departing from the presence of Abraham testifies to the final condemnation of the spirit of disobedience. The word *everlasting* [H5769] (everlasting God) has a connotation "to conceal" [H5956] and is the same word originally used to describe the *ever*

ADAM, NOAH, ABRAHAM

(for ever) [H5769] life identified with the tree of life (Gen 3:22). The everlasting tree of life will be concealed until the last days just as the everlasting face of God will be hidden until the last days. The way of flesh cannot perceive God or understand God (Exod 33:20).

The present account of Abraham and Abimelech is a second narrative compared with the previous account of Sarah being taken and returned by Abimelech (Gen 20:2) and is a third narrative compared with the yet earlier account of Sarai being taken and returned by Pharaoh (Gen 12:15). The first account of Sarai taken and returned by Pharaoh followed by the second account of Sarah taken and returned by Abimelech reflects, first, the condemnation and preservation of Adam followed, second, by the condemnation and exaltation of Christ. The three accounts (Pharaoh, Abimelech, Abimelech) together reflect Adam and the First and Second Advents of Christ. Sarah not being taken in the third and final account prefigures an assertion of the absolute dominion of Christ. Abimelech seeking a covenant of law in the third and final account generally portends the foretold condemnation of all flesh in the third millennium after the incarnation of Jesus Christ but specifically portends a threefold anti-godhead in the end times and the treaty, or anti-treaty, that will proceed from that anti-godhead.

The first and second abductions of Sarah, respectively, by Pharaoh and then by Abimelech compared with the subsequent near abduction of Rebekah by Abimelech also represents a series of three closely connected narratives (Gen 26:7). The account of the near abduction of Rebekah by Abimelech can then be directly compared to the account of the treaties with Abimelech, which in turn recalls the abduction of Sarah by Abimelech. The account of the treaties with Abimelech can also figuratively be considered a near abduction of Sarah. This comparison of the near abductions of Sarah and Rebekah, each representing the third narrative in the same progression, reveals a yet more detailed image of the overarching threefold progression of creation. From this viewpoint the account of the treaties with Abimelech does not prefigure the Second Advent directly but rather the period between the First and Second Advents as pointing to the Second Advent. The treaties thereby represent the delay of the time of judgment. The latter abduction accounts uniquely being connected by the person of Abimelech reflects the intimate connection between the First and Second Advents, separated from the original formation of Adam. The figurative third and final taking and returning of Rebekah finally represents the death and resurrection of the Body of Christ. Rebekah not literally being taken by Abimelech again prefigures an assertion of the absolute dominion of Christ.

BLOOD SACRIFICE

Genesis 22:1 And it came to pass after these things, that God did tempt [H5254] Abraham, and said unto him, Abraham: and he said, Behold, [here] I [am].

ISHMAEL, ISAAC, KETURAH'S SONS

The word *tempt* [H5254] (God did tempt) means "to prove" in the Hebrew, not "to try to disprove" as the common use in the English would imply.[17] The way of flesh is not the way of the Spirit (Jas 1:13). God tempts, or proves, us not to make us sin but to keep us from sin, not to make us afraid but to call us out of fear (Exod 20:20). The proving of God is the Covenant of Law that leads us to the Covenant of Grace (Gal 3:24). The paradox of our condemnation under the law and our redemption through the law is resolved only in Jesus Christ, in whom the faithful are justified not by works but by grace, a grace that comes by faith through the fulfillment of the law by Christ, the work of the cross. Our share in the temptation of Christ is a reflection of our share in the death and resurrection of Christ (Rom 6:4), but our imperfect righteousness is only a shadow of the perfect righteousness of Christ just as everything in the world is only a shadow of the heavenly reality (1 Cor 13:12).[18]

Genesis 22:2 And he said, Take now thy son, thine only [son] Isaac, whom thou lovest [H157], and get thee into the land of Moriah; and offer him there for a burnt offering [H5930] upon one of the mountains which I will tell thee of.

The word *burnt* [H5930] (burnt offering) evokes an image of "that which goes up to heaven" and is derived from the root "to go up, ascend, climb" [H5927], foreshadowing the elevation of Christ on the cross and also the ascension of Christ unto the Father. The blood sacrifice required by the law is a graphic testimony to the irrevocable condemnation of the natural body under the law. Abraham being sent to an unknown mountain within the land recalls his originally being called out of the east into an unknown land, in a succession that reflects the progressive revelation of the mystery of salvation in Christ (Gen 12:1). Isaac is the second son of Abraham compared with Ishmael just as Jesus Christ is the second son of God compared with Adam (1 Cor 15:47), but Isaac is the only legitimate son of Abraham just as Jesus Christ is the only begotten Son of God (John 3:16). Ishmael was conceived in the natural way just as Adam was formed from the dust of the ground. Ishmael was born of a bondwoman just as Adam became a living soul under the law. But Isaac was the child of promise just as the Son of God is conceived by the Holy Spirit.

The word *lovest* (love) [H157] (Abraham loves Isaac) appears here for the first time in the Scriptures, which reflects the singular love of the Father for the Son and likewise the love of the Father for the faithful in the Son (John 3:16). The word *kindness* [H2617] is previously used to describe the "goodness, kindness" shown between Abraham and Sarah, reflecting the relationship between God and creation expressly under the law (Gen 20:13). Goodness is to

---

[17] The translation should be "God did prove Abraham," not "God did tempt Abraham" (Coffman 285; Gen 22:1–2). The translation is not incorrect but rather our modern understanding of the translation.
[18] "*God did tempt Abraham*—Not to draw him to sin, so *Satan* tempts; but to discover his [the Lord's] graces . . . ." (Wesley 1:84; Gen 22:1). The providential movement of the Holy Spirit, working all things together for good to the faithful, Rom 8:28.

love as law is to grace. Abraham is the figurative father of the faithful, reflecting the perfect faithfulness of God the Father, whereby the love imparted to Isaac proceeds spiritually from the faithfulness of Abraham (Gal 3:17). The act of sacrificing his son identifies Abraham uniquely with faith among men (Heb 11:17). Abraham loves Isaac and likewise the offspring of Isaac just as the Father loves the Son and likewise the faithful in the Son. The love of Isaac proceeds from Abraham (figuratively) through Isaac to the offspring of Isaac just as the Holy Spirit proceeds from the Father (literally) through and in the Son unto the faithful. The triune virtues of faith, hope, and love likewise reflect the faith of the Father, the hope embodied by the Son, and the love finally revealed by the Holy Spirit, whereby we say that love is greater than faith and hope because love is the fulfillment of faith and hope (1 Cor 13:13).[19]

Genesis 22:3 And Abraham rose up early in the morning [H1242], and saddled his ass [H2543], and took two of his young men [H5288] with him, and Isaac his son, and clave [H1234] the wood [H6086] for the burnt offering, and rose up, and went unto the place of which God had told him.

The word *morning* [H1242] is derived from the root "to inquire, seek" [H1239], which reflects the faithful seeking God. Morning is the end of spiritual darkness and the dawn of spiritual awakening, foreshadowing the resurrection of the dead.[20] Abraham saddling an *ass* (donkey) [H2543] to take Isaac to Moriah prefigures the entry of Christ into Jerusalem sitting upon an ass (Matt 21:5). Traveling on a lowly donkey, a beast of burden, is a sign of humility that reflects the essential condescension of the incarnation of Christ and ultimately the crucifixion of Christ, the burden of the cross. The two *young men* [H5288] accompanying Isaac are at least figuratively slaves, prefiguring the two criminals, or slaves to sin, crucified with Christ. The two criminals crucified with Christ, one unrepentant and one repentant, are a microcosm of the totality of humanity, the faithless and the faithful (Luke 23:39–40). All men die, but the unfaithful die in vain (Gal 3:4) while the faithful die in Christ (Rom 6:4). The word *clave* [H1234] (clave the wood) means "to cleave, break open or through," which recalls Abraham dividing the threefold sacrifices and also the rite of circumcision (Gen 15:10). The word *wood* [H6086] (for the burnt offering) has a connotation "gallows," whereby the wood of the burnt offering is an emblem of the law, as implied by the prescription of burnt offerings, and also of the wooden cross of Christ, affirmed by the image of gallows. The cross is the

---

[19] The first use of the word *love* in the Old Testament describes the love of Abraham for Isaac, Gen 22:2, while the first use of the word *love* in the New Testament describes the love of the Father for the Son, Matt 3:17 (Coffman 285; Gen 22:1–2). The one true God names himself the God of Abraham, Isaac, and Jacob.

[20] "The fact that we awake from sleep is some evidence for the resurrection [*Genesis Rabbah*]" (Rapaport, *Midrash* 84). All creation testifies to the will of God.

sacrificial altar foretold by the law, while Christ cut off from the living is the circumcision foretold by the law.[21]

Genesis 22:4 Then on the third day Abraham lifted up his eyes, and saw the place afar off.

Abraham is not yet looking at the completed work of the sacrifice but rather at the place of the sacrifice just as the figurative sacrifice of Isaac points to the literal sacrifice of Jesus. The emphasis on Abraham initially seeing the place of elevation only from a distance testifies to the faithful seeing the promise of God only from a distance and, accordingly, points to the long delay between the crucifixion and the glorious reappearing (Heb 11:13). Abraham seeing the place of the sacrifice of Isaac on the third day of his journey presages the resurrection of Christ on the third day after the crucifixion. The arrival at the place of the sacrifice on the third day being connected with the promised resurrection after the sacrifice implies a parallel between the original commandment, or law, of sacrifice and the actual, or true, sacrifice—which is an equality between the commandment and the reality reflecting the undeniable nature of the will of God. To the same effect, the subsequent substitution of a ram for Isaac superimposes the image of death and the image of resurrection. The sacrifice of Isaac in the opening of the third millennium from Adam prefigures the sacrifice of Jesus Christ in the opening of the third millennium from Abraham just as the Covenant of Law prefigures the Covenant of Grace. We likewise now look for the glorious reappearing of Christ in the third millennium from the incarnation at the First Advent.[22]

Genesis 22:5 And Abraham said unto his young men, Abide ye here with the ass; and I and the lad will go yonder and worship [H7812], and come again to you.

The word *worship* [H7812] (Abraham and Isaac will worship) has connotations "to bow down, prostrate oneself," which reflects the fundamental condescension of Christ embodied by the incarnation and finally the crucifixion. Abraham and Isaac worshipping together reflects the unity of the Father and the Son, while the blessing that would proceed from the sacrifice of Isaac reflects the movement of the Holy Spirit, a blessing embodied by the progeny promised through Isaac. Abraham and Isaac proceed without their servants just

---

[21] "Abraham is trusting, even when he does not feel like it. There is not a line in this text about how Abraham felt, not because he didn't feel, but because he was walking by faith, not feelings" (Guzik 140; Gen 22:3). Even that which is not written has meaning.
[22] "[T]he deliverance of Isaac on this third day was doubtless typical of Christ's resurrection from the dead on the third day; for from the time that Abraham had the command to offer up his son, he was reckoned no other by him then as one dead, from whence he received him in a figure on this third day, [Heb 11:19]" (Gill 1:122; Gen 22:4). Implicit meaning prophesying an explicit reality unto the believer in God is a fundamental testimony of mortal life promising eternal life unto the faithful in Christ.

as the Father would raise the Son from the grave as (and with) the firstfruits of humanity (1 Cor 15:23, Lev 23:10–12). Abraham promises to return to his servants just as Christ would promise to rise from the dead (Matt 20:18–19) and also to return again in the end times (Matt 24:29–30). The emphasis on the servants remaining with the donkey, a beast of burden, affirms the continuation of the curse of Adam to toil in the ground, a curse that would remain even after the death and resurrection of Jesus Christ. The death and resurrection of Christ would not be a reprieve from the condemnation of the natural body but rather the ultimate testimony to the universal death sentence under the law. The two servants—representing the two criminals crucified with Christ and ultimately the totality of humanity in the subsequent church age—further reflect the ongoing slavery to sin that would persist even after the death and resurrection of Christ. The faithful are not saved from death but rather through death.

Genesis 22:6 And Abraham took the wood [H6086] of the burnt offering, and laid [H7760] [it] upon Isaac his son; and he took the fire [H784] in his hand, and a knife [H3979]; and they went both of them together.

The three symbols *knife* [H3979], *wood* [H6086], and *fire* [H784] reflect the Father, Son, and Holy Spirit. The knife and fire are linked together as the two symbols in the two hands of Abraham just as our experience of God the Father and God the Holy Spirit are both spiritual. The symbol of wood, placed upon the back of Isaac, is distinct from the symbols of the knife and fire, being in the hands of Abraham, just as God the Son is uniquely the incarnation of God. The knife carried by Abraham, the knife of circumcision, represents the birth and also the death of all flesh, all creation, under the law, whereby the knife of Abraham represents God as the font of creation under the law, God the Father, the father of creation. The fire of Abraham represents God the Holy Spirit, specifically the baptism of the Spirit symbolized as a baptism of fire (Matt 3:11). The purification connected with fire represents the sanctification by the Spirit, while the spontaneous ascension of fire points upward to God just as the indwelling Holy Spirit lifts up the faithful unto God. The symbol of wood portends Christ as a burnt offering nailed to the wooden cross. The symbols of fire and wood are also uniquely connected in the group of three symbols since the wood would be burned by the fire—a relationship reflecting the Spirit and Son both proceeding from the Father.[23]

The word *laid* [H7760] (laid wood upon Isaac) has connotations "to ordain" and "to appoint," reflecting the Father anointing the Son. Abraham himself identifies the symbol of wood with his son Isaac in the act of placing the wood upon Isaac—an act reflecting the undeniable and incontrovertible will of the Father, even the horrible certainty of the cross (Mark 8:31). The act of laying a

---

[23] "The rite of *circumcision* was *painful* and *humiliating*, to denote that *repentance, self-denial*, etc., are absolutely necessary to all who wish for redemption in the blood of the covenant; . . ." (Clarke 1:117; Gen 17). The circumcision of the flesh in the natural is finally a prophecy of the death of all flesh.

burden on someone is an image of birthright that reflects the anointing of a king, while someone taking up a burden is an image of blessing that reflects the anointing by a priest. Jesus Christ is both king of kings and high priest (Rev 5:10) just as he has the power to both lay down his life and pick it back up again (John 10:18). The First Advent of Jesus Christ, marked by the crucifixion under the law, is the embodiment of the kingship of Christ, while the Second Advent of Christ, marked by the resurrection of the faithful in Christ by grace, is the embodiment of the high priesthood. The First Advent of Christ points to the Second Advent. The resurrection of Christ as (and with) the firstfruits of the grave prefigures the resurrection of all the faithful in Christ, the Body of Christ, in the harvest of mankind (1 Cor 15:23, Matt 27:52–53, Lev 23:10–12).[24]

Genesis 22:7–8 And Isaac spake unto Abraham his father, and said, My father: and he said, Here [am] I, my son. And he said, Behold the fire and the wood: but where [is] the lamb for a burnt offering? 8 And Abraham said, My son, God will provide himself a lamb for a burnt offering: so they went both of them together.

Abraham is silently anticipating the resurrection of the dead in his expectation that God would raise Isaac back to life after his sacrifice (Heb 11:17–19). This expectation of Abraham not being explicitly revealed until the New Testament reflects the progressive revelation of the mystery of Christ. Isaac speaking to Abraham concerning the burnt offering prefigures the Son praying unto the Father concerning the cross (Matt 26:39). Isaac questioning his father expressly about the fire and wood but not about the knife reinforces the identification of the knife with God the Father and also reflects the Spirit and Son, represented by the fire and wood, proceeding from the Father. Abraham's response to Isaac foreshadows the substitution of a lamb for Isaac as the required burnt offering, a substitution that ultimately portends Jesus as the Lamb of God sacrificed on the cross. The emphasis on God himself providing the lamb points to Jesus Christ being the incarnation of God. Abraham is a child of God, with an understanding of the world that flows from faith, whereby death and resurrection, likewise law and grace, seem obvious to him. Faith is the mark of the Holy Spirit, whereby we become sons of Abraham, the sons of God, by faith and not by flesh (Gal 3:7).[25]

---

[24] "*Isaac's* carrying the wood was a type of Christ, who carried his own cross...." (Wesley 1:85; Gen 22:6). The tree of the knowledge of good and evil.

[25] "[T]he religion of Israel dates from Abraham rather than from Moses, in the sense that the unique relations of the chosen people with Jehovah began with Abraham. This is why the Israelites gloried in calling themselves the children of Abraham, and spoke of God as the God of Abraham, though Abraham does not refer in the same way to anyone before him" (*Catholic Encyclopedia*, s.v. "Abraham"). Abraham, the friend of God, reflects Adam, or Adam-kind, before the Fall of Man and simultaneously the Second Advent of Christ, whereby the name *God of Abraham* evokes an image of God as the God of creation and also new creation. The deliverer and lawgiver Moses is identified uniquely with the First Advent of Christ, whereby the notable absence of the name *God*

Genesis 22:9 And they came to the place which God had told him of; and Abraham built an altar there, and laid the wood in order [H6186], and bound Isaac his son, and laid [H7760] him on the altar upon the wood.

The word *laid in order* [H6186] (Abraham laid the wood in order) means "to arrange or set in order," which reflects the dominion of God even on the cross.[26] Abraham controls the scene just as the life of Jesus Christ would not be taken but rather freely laid down (John 10:18). The word *laid* [H7760] (Abraham laid his son on the altar) has connotations "to ordain" and "to appoint" and is the same word used to describe God originally *putting* [H7760] Adam in the garden (Gen 2:8). God appointed Adam and Adam-kind to the law just as God would appoint Jesus Christ to the cross, whereby our original creation in Adam prefigures our new creation in Jesus Christ. The binding of Isaac prefigures the binding of Christ, the ultimate embodiment of the bondage of sin, namely, Christ becoming a curse for our sakes (Gal 3:13). God foretold the place of the sacrifice of Isaac just as the law and the prophets foretold the death and resurrection of Jesus Christ. Abraham had not told anyone, at least in the formal account, of his intention to sacrifice Isaac just as the mystery of Christ would not be fully understood, not explicitly explained in the Scriptures, until after the crucifixion (Luke 9:44–45, Rom 11:25).[27]

Genesis 22:10–12 And Abraham stretched forth his hand, and took the knife to slay his son. 11 And the angel of the LORD [H3068] called unto him out of heaven, and said, Abraham, Abraham: and he said, Here [am] I. 12 And he said, Lay not thine hand upon the lad, neither do thou any thing unto him: for now I know that thou fearest [H3373] God [H430], seeing thou hast not [H3808] withheld thy son, thine only [son] from me.

The fear of Abraham is identified in the text with the name *God* (Elohim) [H430] (fear God), while the reprieve of Isaac is identified with the name *Lord* (YHWH) [H3068] (the Lord called out). The name *God* (Elohim) [H430] reflects the God of creation and likewise the original formation of man under the law, while the name *Lord* (YHWH) [H3068] reflects the God of redemption and likewise our promised new creation by grace. The word *fearest* [H3373] (fearest God) evokes a sense not only of "fear" but also "reverence," which reflects the justified condemnation of creation before the perfect righteousness of the Creator (Rom 9:21). Even Abraham, particularly Abraham, having to prove his fear of God reflects the undeniable condemnation of flesh, all flesh, under the law that governs flesh. But fear is only the beginning of wisdom just

---

of Moses in the Scriptures reflects the Passion of Christ being the visible image of the Fall of Man, not an image of the will of God per se.

[26] *Strong's* main concordance does not list *laid in order* (arranged) = H6186, but it is found in *Green's Interlinear* and also *Brown-Driver-Briggs*.

[27] "Yet it is necessary that a sacrifice be bound. The great Sacrifice [Jesus Christ] was, therefore so must Isaac be" (Henry 1:108; Gen 22:3–10). The binding of a sacrifice represents the curse of sin that is likewise a bondage, Gal 3:13.

as law is only the beginning of grace just as this creation is only the beginning of the promised new creation. The fulfillment of wisdom is love just as the law leads us to grace (Gal 3:24).

Abraham does not withhold Isaac just as the Father would not withhold the Son (John 3:16). Abraham taking the knife to slay his own son is a vision of the irrevocable condemnation of creation by God the Father, embodied by God the Son on the tree of the cross. The angel of God calling out "Abraham, Abraham" foreshadows Christ calling out "my God, my God" from the cross (Matt 27:46). The angel, in contrast to Isaac, calling out the name of Abraham prefigures Christ calling out the name of God, expressly from the spirit and not from the flesh, that is, prophetically. And represented here by the very sacrifice of Isaac is the question "Why have you forsaken me?" that is ultimately answered by the resurrection of Christ and finally the promised resurrection of the faithful in Christ (Ps 22:15, 22:24). Christ would become forsaken under the law so that we could be saved through him. The faithful in Christ are likewise forsaken under the law in order to be brought into grace. The drama of the last moment reprieve for Isaac represents our wonder at the death and resurrection of Jesus Christ. The reprieve coming swiftly but at the last moment presages Christ coming quickly but in the end times (Rev 22:20).

Genesis 22:13–14 And Abraham lifted up his eyes, and looked, and behold behind [him] a ram [H352] caught in a thicket by his horns: and Abraham went and took the ram, and offered him up for a burnt offering in the stead of his son. 14 And Abraham called the name of that place Jehovah-jireh: as it is said [to] this day, In the mount of the LORD it shall be seen [H7200].

The word *ram* (male lamb) [H352] has a connotation "leader, chief" in the Hebrew, which reflects the kingship of Jesus Christ being closely identified with the First Advent. The thicket prefigures the crown of thorns that would be placed on the head of Christ, while the ram caught by its own horns in the thicket prefigures Christ being condemned because of his birthright as king of kings (Matt 27:29). The horn of the house of David (Luke 1:69). God substitutes the ram for Isaac just as the Father raises the Son. The death of the ram is the death of the natural body, while the figurative resurrection of Isaac is the resurrection of the spiritual, or glorified, body. The emphasis on a continuing expectation that the ram will be *seen* [H7200] (to this day) on the mountain of the Lord points to the promised return of Jesus Christ in the end times. The figurative death and resurrection of Isaac directly represents the death and resurrection of Christ, likewise the faithful in Christ, since all Israel was yet in Isaac at the time.[28]

---

[28] Abraham is a type of the Father, Isaac a type of Jesus Christ, and the ram a type of substitutionary offering (Scofield 33 n. 1; Gen 22:9). The perceived emphasis on the Father and Son relationship in the Trinity is a testimony to the subtlety of providence

Genesis 22:15–18 And the angel of the LORD called unto Abraham out of heaven the second time, 16 And said, By myself have I sworn, saith the LORD, for because thou hast done this thing, and hast not withheld thy son, thine only [son]: 17 That in blessing I will bless thee, and in multiplying I will multiply thy seed as the stars of the heaven, and as the sand which [is] upon the sea shore; and thy seed shall possess the gate of his enemies; 18 And in thy seed shall all the nations of the earth be blessed; because thou hast obeyed my voice.

The angel of the Lord calls out two distinct times unto Abraham: the first time to ordain the sacrifice of Isaac, ultimately represented by the sacrifice of the ram, and now a second time to announce the blessing that will proceed from Abraham's faithful obedience to the call to sacrifice Isaac. The first call of the angel and the corresponding sacrifice of the ram is a vision of the First Advent of Jesus Christ, while the second call of the angel and the corresponding blessing is a vision of the Second Advent. The birthright first, the blessing second. Whoever seeks his life will lose it, but whoever loses his life for my sake will find it (Matt 16:25). The emphasis on the angel of the Lord calling out from heaven points to Jesus Christ being the embodiment of the Word of God (John 1:14). The emphasis on the obedience of Abraham points to the perfect obedience of Christ and in Christ.

The promised multiplication of Abraham being compared to both the stars in the heaven and the sand upon the sea shore reflects the duality of spirit and flesh embodied by Christ, also the Body of Christ.[29] The image of the stars preceding the image of the sand reflects the reality of the spiritual man supplanting the promise of the natural man. The seed of Abraham possessing the gate of his enemies is a prophecy of the victory of Christ over death (1 Cor 15:54). The promised blessing of all nations in the seed of Abraham is a prophecy of the redemption of both Jew and Gentile in the one Body of Christ (1 Cor 12:13). The Lord swearing by himself reflects God fulfilling the law himself in the person of Jesus Christ (Matt 5:17). Abraham reflecting aspects of both God the Father and God the Son also testifies to Jesus Christ being the incarnation of God.[30]

Genesis 22:19 So Abraham returned unto his young men, and they rose up and went together to Beer-sheba [H884]; and Abraham dwelt at Beer-sheba [H884].

---

and the movement of the Holy Spirit, which in turn is a testimony to the inviolable sanctity of freewill.

[29] The promise to multiply Abraham refers to both his natural seed according to the flesh and also his spiritual seed according to faith (Gill 1:125; Gen 22:17). The blood of Adam, or Adam-kind, points to the blood of Christ.

[30] The promise that the seed of Abraham would possess the gate of his enemies would be fulfilled literally by Joshua, David, and Solomon and fulfilled spiritually and literally by Christ in the victory over death and sin (Gill 1:125; Gen 22:17). David established the kingship, but Jesus Christ embodies the kingship.

ISHMAEL, ISAAC, KETURAH'S SONS

Isaac is, at least figuratively, still with Abraham, but his absence from the narrative after his symbolic death and resurrection foreshadows the ascension of the Son back unto the Father (Acts 1:9). An absence of the Son until the end times. The focus on Abraham is a corresponding subsuming of Isaac that reflects the unity of the Father and the Son in the glorification of the Son by the Holy Spirit (Matt 28:18–19). Isaac, as the offspring of Abraham, represents a part of Abraham. The name *Beersheba* [H884] (dwelt at Beersheba) means "well of seven (as a place of swearing by seven)," which recalls the original seven days of creation and also foreshadows our promised new creation in the dawn of the seventh millennium from Adam. An absence of the Son specifically until the seventh millennium. The two servants of Abraham recall the two criminals, one repentant and one unrepentant, that were crucified with Christ (Luke 23:39–40). The emphasis on the young men rising up and proceeding with Abraham to Beersheba points to the dead, the good and the evil, awaiting the foretold resurrections, either unto life or unto condemnation (John 5:28–29).[31]

Genesis 22:20–24 And it came to pass after these things, that it was told Abraham, saying, Behold, Milcah, she hath also born children unto thy brother Nahor; 21 Huz his firstborn, and Buz his brother, and Kemuel the father of Aram, 22 And Chesed, and Hazo, and Pildash, and Jidlaph, and Bethuel. 23 And Bethuel begat Rebekah: these eight Milcah did bear to Nahor, Abraham's brother. 24 And his concubine, whose name [was] Reumah, she bare also Tebah, and Gaham, and Thahash, and Maachah.

The news of the birth of Rebekah, the future wife of Isaac, reaches Abraham immediately after the symbolic death and resurrection of Isaac (Gen 24:67) just as the redemption of the faithful would be sealed by the death and resurrection of Jesus Christ (Gal 2:20). The delay between the symbolic sacrifice of Isaac and his subsequent marriage to Rebekah foreshadows the delay between the incarnation of Christ and the foretold marriage supper of the Lamb (Rev 19:9). Rebekah reflects all the faithful called as the bride of the Lamb just as all wives reflect the church (Eph 5:32). But Rebekah is most closely identified with the call of Israel just as Isaac is most closely identified with the First Advent. The Messiah in his earthly ministry would proclaim the kingdom exclusively to the Jews (Matt 15:24). Only in the new covenant, sealed by the blood of Jesus Christ, would both Jew and Gentile finally be called together unto the promised wedding supper (1 Cor 12:13).

---

[31] "All are raised from the dead into everlasting life . . . . For those who love God, resurrection from the dead and the presence of God will be paradise. For those who hate God, resurrection from the dead and the presence of God will be hell" (Hopko, *Orthodox Faith* 1:112). The present is prologue.

ADAM, NOAH, ABRAHAM

The Death of Sarah

Genesis 23:1–2 And Sarah was an hundred and seven and twenty years old: [these were] the years of the life of Sarah. 2 And Sarah died [H4191] in Kirjath-arba; the same [is] Hebron in the land of Canaan: and Abraham came to mourn for Sarah, and to weep for her.

Abraham, Isaac, and Jacob reflect the Father, Son, and Holy Spirit and likewise Adam and the First and Second Advents of Christ, whereby Sarah reflects all humanity in Eve, Rebekah reflects Israel called unto Christ, and the wives of Jacob reflect all nations finally redeemed in Christ. Sarah embodies the promise of life implied by creation itself. Rebekah reflects the call to repentance represented by the incarnation of Christ. The wives (free) and concubines (slave) of Jacob represent the Gentiles (grace) and Jews (law) called into the one Body of Christ.[32] The word *died* [H4191] (Sarah died) has a connotation "to die as a penalty, be put to death" and is the same word used to describe the *dying* [H4191] identified with the tree of knowledge (Gen 2:17). Every death is a fulfillment of the original curse, but the death of Sarah specifically recalls the original condemnation of creation through Eve (1 Tim 2:14). Abraham mourns the death of Sarah just as the Father mourns the curse of humanity in Eve. The physical separation between Abraham and Sarah implied by Abraham having to come to mourn for Sarah reflects the primordial separation between the Father and humanity because of sin. The account of the death of Sarah following closely behind the account of the sacrifice of Isaac reflects the condemnation of all flesh, all creation, embodied by Christ on the cross.[33]

Genesis 23:3–4 And Abraham stood up from before his dead, and spake unto the sons of Heth, saying, 4 I [am] a stranger [H1616] and a sojourner with you: give me a possession [H272] of a buryingplace with you, that I may bury my dead out of my sight [H6440].

The word *sight* [H6440] (out of my sight) is the same word used to describe Adam originally hiding from the *presence* [H6440] of the Lord (Gen 3:8) and later Cain being driven from the *face* [H6440] of the Lord (Gen 4:14). The lifeless remains of Sarah embody death, while death itself is the manifestation of sin

---

[32] "It is written [Isa 29:22]: 'Therefore thus hath said the Lord unto the house of Jacob, he who hath redeemed Abraham' [cf. JPS Tanakh, Isa 29:22]. Where do we find that Jacob redeemed Abraham? Said R. Jehudah: He redeemed him from the affliction of bringing up his children" (Rodkinson, *Talmud: Sanhedrin* 7[15]:50). Yes, a controversial rendering of Isa 29:22, yet the reading still indicates an instinctive understanding that father Abraham embodies the promise while Jacob, as the immediate father of the twelve tribes, embodies the fulfillment of the promise.

[33] "Sarah was . . . the only woman in Scripture whose age, death, and burial are mentioned . . . ." (Jamieson et al. 1:178; Gen 23:1). The time of the end appointed by the Father from the beginning.

and likewise of our separation from God (Rom 5:12). Accordingly, Abraham hiding the body of Sarah from his face reflects humanity hiding from the face of the Lord. But Abraham entombing the body of Sarah, in contrast to cremating or otherwise destroying her body, finally represents an anticipation of the resurrection of the dead. The account of the death and burial of Sarah, together with the connected expectation of the resurrection of Sarah, follows the figurative death and resurrection of Isaac just as the harvest of mankind follows the resurrection of Jesus Christ as (and with) the firstfruits of the grave (1 Cor 15:23, Lev 23:10–12). The death and resurrection of Sarah symbolically following the death and resurrection of Isaac likewise reflects the call to pick up our own cross and follow Christ—even through the veil of death, especially through the veil of death (Matt 16:24). The emphasis on Abraham standing up, rising up, from the dead body of Sarah testifies to the resurrection of the dead proceeding directly from the will of God.[34]

The word *stranger* [H1616] (Abraham a stranger) has a negative connotation of "no inherited rights," while the word *possession* [H272] (Abraham seeks a possession of a buryingplace) has a positive connotation of "possession by right of inheritance." The dichotomy of death and life. Abraham as a stranger in the land has no real possession of the land, but neither would the heralded kingdom of Jesus Christ be of this world (John 18:36). The buryingplace Abraham seeks is a token for the entire land, a token representing a deposit on his promised inheritance, but even the land in its entirety is itself a token for something more. This bespeaks of progressive revelation. The inheritance that Abraham seeks is not the city of man but rather the city of God, whereby the token of the land specifically as a place of burial is intimately connected to the end of the natural body (Heb 11:9–10). Our natural body is a deposit on our promised spiritual, or glorified, body. Our mortal life is a deposit on our promised eternal life. The body is sown in dishonor, but it is raised in glory. It is sown a natural body in the likeness of Adam, but it is raised a spiritual body in the likeness of Jesus Christ (1 Cor 15:43). Abraham while yet in the flesh was looking for a renewal of creation just as he was looking for the resurrection of Sarah. The promised body with the promised land, a true body, the Body of Christ.

Genesis 23:5–6 And the children of Heth answered Abraham, saying unto him, 6 Hear us, my lord: thou [art] a mighty [H430] prince [H5387] among us: in the choice of our sepulchres bury thy dead; none of us shall withhold from thee his sepulchre, but that thou mayest bury thy dead.

The word *mighty* [H430] (Abraham a mighty prince) corresponds to the word translated *God* (Elohim) [H430] in the original creation account, which reflects God the Father uniquely as the father of creation (Gen 1:1). The word *prince* [H5387] (mighty prince) has a connotation of "one lifted up" and evokes an image of a "rising mist, vapour (forming clouds and portending rain)," reflecting

---

[34] The burial of the dead is a form of prayer as are all physical enactments, but obviously all persons are resurrected regardless of what happens to their bodies after death.

the resurrection and ascension of God the Son and finally the promised glorification of the faithful in the Son. Abraham as a *mighty* [H430] *prince* [H5387] reflects the Father as the source of the Son and likewise the perfect unity of the Father and the Son, while Abraham speaking to the sons of Heth reflects the Word of God revealed to the world. The sons of Heth proclaiming Abraham to be a mighty prince reflects mankind honoring God with their lips but not with their hearts (Matt 15:8) and finally every tongue confessing to God before the judgment seat of Christ (Rom 14:10–12).

Genesis 23:7–18 And Abraham stood up, and bowed himself to the people of the land, [even] to the children of Heth. 8 And he communed with them, saying, If it be your mind [H5315] that I should bury my dead out of my sight; hear me, and intreat for me to Ephron the son of Zohar, 9 That he may give me the cave of Machpelah, which he hath, which [is] in the end of his field; for as much money as it is worth he shall give it me for a possession of a buryingplace amongst you. 10 And Ephron dwelt among the children of Heth: and Ephron the Hittite answered Abraham in the audience of the children of Heth, [even] of all that went in at the gate of his city, saying, 11 Nay, my lord, hear me: the field give I thee, and the cave that [is] therein, I give it thee; in the presence of the sons of my people give I it thee: bury thy dead. 12 And Abraham bowed down himself before the people of the land. 13 And he spake unto Ephron in the audience of the people of the land, saying, But if thou [wilt give it], I pray thee, hear me: I will give thee money for the field; take [it] of me, and I will bury my dead there. 14 And Ephron answered Abraham, saying unto him, 15 My lord, hearken unto me: the land [is worth] four hundred shekels of silver; what [is] that betwixt me and thee? bury therefore thy dead. 16 And Abraham hearkened unto Ephron; and Abraham weighed to Ephron the silver, which he had named in the audience of the sons of Heth, four hundred shekels of silver, current [money] with the merchant. 17 And the field of Ephron, which [was] in Machpelah, which [was] before Mamre, the field, and the cave which [was] therein, and all the trees that [were] in the field, that [were] in all the borders round about, were made sure 18 Unto Abraham for a possession in the presence of the children of Heth, before all that went in at the gate of his city.

The word *mind* [H5315] (if it be your mind that I should bury my dead) is the same word used to describe Adam originally becoming a living *soul* [H5315], a life derived from the very Spirit (breath) of God (Gen 2:7). Abraham calling upon the minds of the sons of Heth, calling upon their inner souls, to allow him to bury Sarah reflects the Father calling upon mankind, made in the very image of God, to faith in the promise of life. The emphasis on Abraham entreating (intreating) the whole community testifies to the call to faith in Christ being the call of all peoples to faith in Christ. Abraham bowing to the children of Heth and dealing with them according to their customs reflects the essential condescension of God. Christ would likewise humbly live among men, specifically in relation to the customs of men with regard to the law. Abraham strictly submits to the authority in the land just as the righteousness of God is in perfect accord with the law, even the law of the cross (Phil 2:8). The emphasis on Abraham purchasing the buryingplace (ground) affirms the redemption of our flesh (dust of the ground) (1 Cor 6:20). Ephron does not give the parcel to Abraham just as man cannot redeem himself. Our new creation proceeds solely from God just as our original creation proceeded solely from God. Ephron's original offer to freely give the land to Abraham was presumably disingenuous, which ironically reflects his personal inability to freely give the land.[35]

Abraham originally seeks to buy the cave of Machpelah, but Ephron sells him not only the cave but also the connected field, including the trees in the field. The cave of Machpelah being enlarged by the field, figuratively becoming the field, prefigures the resurrection of the dead, who will not be entombed forever (in the cave) but will rise to take possession of the land in Christ (into the field). Ephron's motivation for selling the cave and field together is presumably greed, which reflects the redemption of the faithful despite sin. Ephron ultimately sets the price for the land without any negotiation on the part of Abraham just as Israel would solely set the price for the life of Jesus just as Adam had solely incurred the curse outside the will of God (Matt 27:9). The trees of Machpelah represent the tree of knowledge and the tree of life, likewise law and grace, and likewise death and resurrection. The trees in Machpelah stand witness to the figurative death and resurrection of all flesh in Eve as embodied by Sarah just as the resurrection on the last day will be the fulfillment of law in grace. Sarah recalling the first woman Eve reflects the inheritance of all the faithful in the foretold Seed of woman.[36]

Genesis 23:19–20 And after this, Abraham buried Sarah his wife in the cave of the field of Machpelah before Mamre: the same [is] Hebron in the land of Canaan. 20 And the field, and the cave that [is] therein, were made sure unto Abraham for a possession of a buryingplace by the sons of Heth.

The field in Hebron is a small part of the promised land that represents the whole promised land just as Israel is a small part of the world that represents the whole world. Hebron specifically points to Jerusalem just as the city of man points to the city of God (1 King 2:11). Abraham preparing a place for the body of Sarah in the promised land reflects the preordained will of God for the exaltation of the faithful. Abraham having to purchase the field at Mamre reflects the undeniable righteousness of the law, while Abraham being publicly

---

[35] Ephron made a false show of generosity in adding the surrounding field to the cave, and Abraham would have understood that Ephron expected some valuable gift in return for that generosity (Jamieson et al. 1:179; Gen 23:11). The righteousness of the world is as a false piety before the Lord God.

[36] "... Abraham's possession of a portion of the land stands as a pledge of the future possession of the land in its entirety" (Viviano, *Collegeville* 61; Gen 23:1–19). Not merely the kingdom of Israel, but rather the kingdom of God.

deeded the field reflects the incontestable revelation of God in creation. Abraham, Isaac, and Jacob would finally all be buried in the cave in Hebron, testifying even in death to the unity of God the Father, God the Son, and God the Holy Spirit (Gen 49:29–33).[37]

The Eldest Servant

Genesis 24:1 And Abraham was old, [and] well stricken [H935] in age [H3117]: and the Lord had blessed Abraham in all things.

Abraham—particularly in the larger context of the threefold Abraham, Isaac, and Jacob—reflects God the Father and is closely identified with the original creation that proceeded from God the Father, the spiritual progenitor of creation. Adam is the primal embodiment of creation, whereby Abraham reflects both God the Father and the first man Adam just as Adam was originally formed in the very image of God. All creation proceeds from the Father just as all mankind proceeds from Adam. The word *stricken* [H935] (Abraham stricken) has a connotation "to come in, come, go in, go," which reflects the God of creation entering creation according to the person of the Son in the act of creation. The first man Adam points to the second man Jesus Christ. The same word *age* [H3117] (stricken in age) is used to describe the original *days* [H3117] of creation (Gen 1:5–2:4) and also Adam being cursed all the *days* [H3117] of his life (Gen 3:17). The image of Abraham aging does not, of course, reflect the aging of the God of creation but rather the aging of creation itself, a creation embodied by Adam and redeemed in Christ. The aging of Abraham thereby recalls the death of Adam and also prefigures the end of all flesh in the end times. The emphasis on the Lord blessing Abraham in all things affirms the multiplication of the first man Adam even after our fall—namely, the promise of life being embodied by our very existence and guaranteed by the incarnation of Jesus Christ, God the Son.[38]

Genesis 24:2 And Abraham said unto his eldest servant of his house, that ruled over [H4910] all that he had, Put, I pray thee, thy hand under my thigh [H3409]:

---

[37] "[W]hy should such care be taken of the body, if it be thrown away for ever, and must not rise again? . . . [Abraham] secures a place where, when he dies, his flesh may rest in hope" (Henry 1:112; Gen 23:16–20). The actions and prayers of men are all ultimately symbolic, being mere physical enactments that represent a larger spiritual reality, for the Lord knows perfectly well what we need, even before we do.

[38] In contrast to later theologians, the apologists of the second century—Aristides, Justin Martyr, Athenagoras, Tatian, and Theophilus of Antioch—understood the name *Father* to not singularly refer to the first person of the Trinity but rather to encompass the wholeness of the Godhead as the originator of all creation (Rusch 5). The oneness of God is uniquely identified with the Father, wherein God the Father as the spiritual progenitor of creation is always manifest just as the procession of God the Son and God the Spirit from the Father is always implied.

ISHMAEL, ISAAC, KETURAH'S SONS

Abraham reflects God the Father, while Abraham's eldest servant reflects the Holy Spirit. Accordingly, the eldest servant swearing by the thigh of Abraham represents God swearing by himself (Jer 22:5). The word *thigh* [H3409] (swear by my thigh) is used to describe the *loins* [H3409] in relation to procreation (Gen 46:26) and is also connected with the sword being strapped to a man's *side* [H3409] (Exod 32:27). The identification of the thigh with both procreation and the sword reflects the relationship between flesh and the law that governs flesh, between creation and the law that governs creation. The dichotomy of life and death. The oath of the eldest servant would specifically govern the procreation of the son, reflecting an essential binding of the nature of flesh under the rule of law, all flesh representing all creation. The word *ruled* [H4910] (ruled over) means "to rule, have dominion, reign." The complete dominion of the eldest servant over the affairs of Abraham reflects an absolute unity between the Holy Spirit and the Father while at the same time showing a procession of the Spirit from the Father. Images of God sending messengers to humanity are ubiquitous in the Scriptures, but no mere man or angel could ever claim a unique dominion over the affairs of the house of God just as no mere man or angel could claim the unique status of the only begotten Son (Heb 1:5).

Genesis 24:3–4 And I will make thee swear by the LORD [H3068], the God [H430] of heaven, and the God [H430] of the earth, that thou shalt not take a wife unto my son of the daughters of the Canaanites, among whom I dwell: 4 But thou shalt go unto my country, and to my kindred, and take a wife unto my son Isaac.

The implied equality between the one name *Lord* (YHWH) [H3068] and the two names *God* (Elohim) [H430] *of heaven* and *God* (Elohim) [H430] *of the earth* and reflects the perfect union of mercy and justice in the one self-existent being of God. The perfect union of justice and mercy is likewise evident in the perfect union of flesh and spirit embodied by the one person of Jesus Christ. The same dichotomy of justice and mercy is impressed upon all creation, in profession of the font of creation, the profession of the Spirit of truth (John 15:26). The name *God of heaven* preceding the name *God of the earth* reflects grace finally transcending law and likewise love finally supplanting fear. The wife of Isaac must come from among his kindred just as only the faithful in Christ can be united with Jesus Christ in the perfect union of law and grace. The wife of Isaac cannot come from among the Canaanites just as corruption cannot inherit incorruption (1 Cor 15:50).

Genesis 24:5 And the servant said unto him, Peradventure the woman will not be willing to follow me unto this land: must I needs bring thy son again unto the land from whence thou camest?

Abraham represents God the Father, the eldest servant represents the Holy Spirit, Isaac represents God the Son, and lastly the yet unknown bride of Isaac represents the faithful. The land of Canaan, specifically as the promised land, signifies the heavenly domain, while the land of Abraham's kindred in the east signifies the earthly domain.[39] Isaac after his symbolic sacrifice in Moriah represents the resurrected Christ ascended unto the Father, whereby Abraham forbidding Isaac—that is, the Father forbidding the Son—from leaving the promised land, the heavenly domain, represents the Son awaiting the time of the Second Advent as appointed by the Father (Acts 2:33–35). The eldest servant never considers securing a wife by force just as the Holy Spirit will never violate freewill. Finally, the servant asking Abraham whether Isaac, as a last recourse, should be brought back to the east anticipates the glorious reappearing of Christ in the east in the end times (Matt 24:27).[40]

Genesis 24:6 And Abraham said unto him, Beware [H8104] thou that thou bring not my son thither again.

The word *beware* [H8104] (that thou bring not my son) means "to keep" and "to watch" and "to preserve" and is the same word used to describe Adam being appointed to *keep* [H8104] the garden of Eden (Gen 2:15) and later the cherubim being appointed to *keep* [H8104] the way to the tree of life (Gen 3:24). The eldest servant of Abraham keeping and guarding Isaac thereby reflects the promise of life preserved even after the Fall of Adam, even after the Passion of Christ—a promise of life manifested in the Spirit calling our fallen world to faith in Jesus Christ, the new Adam.

Genesis 24:7 The LORD God of heaven, which took me from my father's house, and from the land of my kindred, and which spake unto me, and that sware unto me, saying, Unto thy seed will I give this land; he shall send his angel before thee, and thou shalt take a wife unto my son from thence.

The emphasis on the Lord as the God of heaven reinforces the image of Canaan, or the promised land, as the heavenly kingdom. Abraham announcing the intentions of the Lord God of heaven reflects the connection between Abraham and God the Father. The emphasis on the Lord sending his angel before Abraham's eldest servant reinforces the image of the eldest servant as a spiritual being, specifically the Holy Spirit. The angels are an image of God the Holy Spirit just as man, formed in the image of God, is an image of God the Father. The call of Abraham out of the east preceding the call of the bride of Isaac out of the east reflects the inheritance from Adam (the call to mortal life) preceding the inheritance in Christ (the call to eternal life) and likewise the

---

[39] Whether the land of Canaan represents the earthly domain or the heavenly domain depends entirely and always upon context.

[40] "Under no circumstances is Isaac to be allowed to return to Abraham's country [Gen 24:6]. Such a journey apparently was viewed as a turning back on God's promise of the land" (Viviano, *Collegeville* 61; Gen 24:1–67). The promise of the land is a prophecy of the resurrection of creation as a whole, including the physical body.

resurrection of Jesus Christ (as and with firstfruits) preceding the foretold resurrection of all the dead, specifically all the faithful (the harvest).

Genesis 24:8 And if the woman will not be willing to follow thee, then thou shalt be clear from this my oath: only bring not my son thither again.

When the land of Canaan, uniquely as the promised land, is compared with the land of the east, the land of Abraham's origin, then Isaac never leaving Canaan prefigures the ascendant Christ sitting at the right hand of the Father until the appointed time of the end. In this case, Canaan as the promised land represents the heavenly domain. This is specifically Isaac never leaving the land after his figurative sacrifice in the land. In contrast, when Canaan is viewed in relationship to the larger world, then Isaac never leaving Canaan prefigures the earthly ministry of Jesus Christ being only, or uniquely, unto Israel and not the nations (Matt 15:24). This is Isaac never leaving the land before his figurative sacrifice in the land. Context is critical. Christ was not rejected merely by the Jews but rather by the whole world just as Canaan is a microcosm of the world (John 15:18). Abraham hypothetically releasing his eldest servant from his oath if the called bride would not agree to return portends the rejection of Christ by Israel and finally a universal apostasy in the end times. Isaac staying in the land prefigures the First Advent and the subsequent age of the church, while Jacob finally going to the east for his wives points, with increasing clarity, to the promise of the Second Advent (Gen 28:2). The call of all nations through the one nation Israel reflects the call of the faithful through the one man Jesus Christ, while the long delay between the First and Second Advents of Christ reflects the long-suffering patience of God in the call to repentance.[41]

Genesis 24:9 And the servant put his hand under the thigh of Abraham his master, and sware to him concerning that matter.

Abraham's eldest servant, implicitly Isaac also, submitting to the will of Abraham reflects the Spirit and the Son proceeding from the Father. The initial emphasis on the eldest servant, in contrast to Abraham's only son, points to the procession of God the Holy Spirit (from God the Father through God the Son) in the sanctification of the faithful. In contrast, the Son proceeds by the Spirit in the incarnation, as related by the virgin birth being preceded by the Spirit overshadowing Mary (Luke 1:35). And the Word being the light of life likewise

---

[41] "Isaac, in his person and by his very presence in Canaan, symbolizes the fulfillment of both [the divine promises of posterity and territory]. That is why he alone of the patriarchs must never leave the land ... He also is the only one who sowed the soil ... If Isaac were to desert the land or intermarry with the local Canaanites, he would, in effect, be renouncing God's promises. His marriage is seen as part of the same divinely ordained historic process that commenced with Abraham's exodus from Ur" (Sarna 163; Gen 24:6–8). The promise embodied by Isaac points to the promise fulfilled in the First Advent of Jesus Christ.

precedes the Word becoming flesh (John 1:4, 1:14). The promise of life, embodied by creation and identified with the Spirit, proceeds from the Father through the Son (John 1:3). Yet Eve, reflecting the Spirit, was taken from the side of father Adam before the promised Seed of woman would proceed from Eve (Gen 2:24). The ambiguity between the Spirit and the Son reflects the oneness of God and the universality of the Spirit of God.

The Call of the Bride

Genesis 24:10 And the servant took ten camels of the camels of his master, and departed; for all the goods of his master [were] in his hand: and he arose, and went to Mesopotamia, unto the city of Nahor.

The material goods of Abraham taken by his eldest servant represent the gifts of the Holy Spirit proceeding from the Father. The Holy Spirit is most closely identified with the feminine, whereby Abraham's eldest servant being male specifically embodies the promise of the Son proclaimed by the Holy Spirit. The primal gift of the Spirit is the original creation through the Son, which is the breath of life, while the final gift of the Spirit is our promised new creation in the Son, which is the fullness of the indwelling Spirit. The ten camels of Abraham (God the Father) are figuratively equated to all his material goods (all creation), whereby the emphasis on the number 10 testifies to the close relationship between creation and the law governing creation as exemplified by the Ten Commandments. The city of Nahor is a microcosm of the cities of men, whereby the eldest servant of Abraham seeks the bride of Isaac in the city of Nahor just as the Holy Spirit calls the faithful out of the cities of men into the city of God. The long journey of the eldest servant to call the bride to Isaac and bring her back to Isaac reflects the long delay between the First and Second Advents of Christ.[42]

Genesis 24:11 And he made his camels to kneel down without the city by a well of water at the time of the evening, [even] the time that women go out to draw [water].

The ten camels of Abraham represent the law that governs creation, whereby Abraham's eldest servant driving the camels to the east and then making them kneel down reflects the submission to the law that heralds the subjugation of the law. The emphasis on evening points to the fulfillment of all things in the last days. Abraham's servant stopping outside the city reflects the separation

---

[42] Whenever God the Spirit is identified with the masculine—for example, masculine pronouns—an image of God the Holy Spirit administering the will of God the Father in God the Son should be understood, not a masculine characterization of God the Spirit. This reality is reflected in the prophetess Deborah, the wife of Lapidoth, emphasizing that as a judge of Israel she was performing a masculine role, like that of a man of war, Judg 4:6–8. Similarly emphasized is the judgment that a woman, in contrast to a man, would honor the Lord God in dispatching Sisera, Judg 4:9.

between God and man because of sin. The emphasis on drawing water points to the baptism in water necessarily preceding the baptism of the Holy Spirit.

Genesis 24:12–14 And he said, O LORD **God of my master Abraham, I pray thee, send me good speed this day, and shew kindness unto my master Abraham. 13 Behold, I stand [here] by the well of water; and the daughters of the men of the city come out to draw water: 14 And let it come to pass, that the damsel to whom I shall say, Let down thy pitcher, I pray thee, that I may drink; and she shall say, Drink, and I will give thy camels drink also: [let the same be] she [that] thou hast appointed for thy servant Isaac; and thereby shall I know that thou hast shewed kindness unto my master.**

The first sign marking the bride is the drawing of water, which reflects the baptism in water, while the second sign marking the bride is blood kinship, which reflects the baptism in the blood of the new covenant, that is, the baptism of the Holy Spirit. The baptism in water represents repentance in the natural body, a symbolic death and resurrection that prefigures a literal death and resurrection. The baptism of blood represents the kinship between humanity and Jesus Christ derived from the blood of Christ (Heb 2:10–11), that is, the life in the blood of Christ (Lev 17:11). The first sign is water, the second sign is blood. The natural body is condemned under the law, but the freewill death to sin in the act of repentance heralds a renewal in this life that prefigures the promised rebirth in the spiritual, or glorified, body. The kindness embodied by drawing water for a stranger reflects the essential righteousness of the law of repentance, a righteousness of the law that prefigures the mercy inherent in grace. The emphasis on the need to draw water for both the servant of Abraham and the ten camels of Abraham signals the fulfillment of all things—the baptism in water signified by the camels together with the baptism of the Spirit signified by the servant. This is the water of repentance that foreshadows the water of life, the water of redemption.[43]

The call to be washed in the blood of Jesus Christ is a baptism of blood that represents our new creation in Christ (Heb 9:22). The baptism of the Holy Spirit is both the baptism of fire and the baptism of blood. The image of fire emphasizes purification and destruction, while the image of blood, or life, emphasizes redemption and rebirth. The baptism in water precedes the baptism of blood just as repentance precedes redemption just as law precedes grace just as the natural body precedes the spiritual, or glorified, body. The blood sacrifice of the law prefigures salvation by grace through the blood of Christ just as the figurative death and resurrection in the baptism in water prefigures the literal

---

[43] "Though the sign is now changed from *circumcision* to *baptism*, each of them equally significant, yet the covenant is not changed in any part of its essential meaning. Faith in God through the great sacrifice, remission of sins, and sanctification of the heart, are required by the new covenant as well as by the old" (Clarke 1:117; Gen 17). The first foreshadows the second, while the second fulfills the first.

death and resurrection in the baptism of blood. Christ comes by water and blood just as Christ is the perfect union of flesh and spirit and likewise law and grace (1 John 5:6). No one comes to the Father except through the Son (John 14:6). The first man Adam points to the second man Jesus Christ. The First Advent of Christ points to the Second Advent.[44]

Genesis 24:15 And it came to pass, before he had done speaking, that, behold, Rebekah came out, who was born to Bethuel, son of Milcah, the wife of Nahor, Abraham's brother, with her pitcher upon her shoulder.

Rebekah appearing before Abraham's eldest servant has even finished praying is a vision of the haste of God to redeem humanity as soon as the time of harvest finally arrives.[45]

Genesis 24:16 And the damsel [was] very fair [H2896] to look upon, a virgin, neither had any man known her: and she went down to the well, and filled her pitcher, and came up.

The word *fair* [H2896] (Rebekah was fair) is the same word used to describe the original creation as very *good* [H2896], whereby the character of Rebekah recalls the promise of life embodied by creation (Gen 1:31). The virginity and beauty of Rebekah prefigure the purity and perfection of the resurrected body. Virginity is an image of faithfulness, while promiscuity is an image of faithlessness. Beauty represents an absence of corruption. The attributes of the natural body—whether beauty or wealth or even health or intelligence—cannot, of course, be used to judge the righteousness of any individual in the eyes of God. The wicked can absolutely be more beautiful or more educated or more prosperous or even have better health than the righteous. Only the Lord God can judge the heart of man (1 Cor 4:5). The person who receives faith will tend to be better off materially than they would have been otherwise, at least in the absence of overt persecution, but no one can boast of righteousness under the law (Eph 2:8–9). The positive attributes of the natural body are always a sign of the resurrected body—whether faith is accepted or rejected—while the failings of the natural body are always a sign of the curse. The time and chance of life is actually the essence of the curse (Eccl 9:11). The seeming arbitrariness of life expressly represents the irrational apostasy of mankind rejecting the clear truth of the Gospel. The arbitrariness of it all accentuates the sense of cruelty in the world that is a sign of the utter condemnation of the natural body. The

---

[44] "[T]here is surely also a water test for the Bride of Christ: 'Except a man be born of water and Spirit, he cannot enter the kingdom of God' [John 3:5]" (Coffman 307; Gen 24:10–14). A second test following that of water is according to the Spirit of life as represented by blood, or the life in the blood, Lev 17:11.

[45] The prophet Isaiah testifies to the graciousness of the Lord in answering the prayers of the faithful, Isa 65:24 (Guzik 148; Gen 24:15). In the end, God will answer all the prayers, all the innermost desires of the heart, of the faithless as well as the faithful, but unfortunately so for the faithless, whose desire, or prayer, is to be separated from God.

arbitrariness of life is, after all, not arbitrary at all. The will of the Creator is evident even in fallen creation (Rom 1:20).[46]

Genesis 24:17–20 And the servant ran to meet her, and said, Let me, I pray thee, drink a little water of thy pitcher. 18 And she said, Drink, my lord: and she hasted, and let down her pitcher upon her hand, and gave him drink. 19 And when she had done giving him drink, she said, I will draw [water] for thy camels also, until they have done drinking. 20 And she hasted, and emptied her pitcher into the trough, and ran again unto the well to draw [water], and drew for all his camels.

Abraham's eldest servant running to meet Rebekah reflects the haste of the Lord to redeem humanity. The haste of Rebekah to serve Abraham's eldest servant is an imitation of the original haste of the eldest servant that reflects an imitation of Christ and finally the fullness of the indwelling Holy Spirit.

Genesis 24:21 And the man wondering at her held his peace, to wit whether the LORD had made his journey [H1870] prosperous or not.

The word *journey* [H1870] (the journey to call Rebekah) is the same word used to describe the *way* [H1870] to the tree of life, which reflects the call to faith in Christ being the way to the tree of life (Gen 3:24). Rebekah immediately fulfills the sign of water by drawing water for Abraham's eldest servant, but the eldest servant must now wait for the final sign of her blood relationship to Abraham. The faithful must be marked by both signs, the sign of water and the sign of blood, figuratively turning water into wine (John 2:10) at the celebration of the marriage of the Lamb (Rev 19:7). The eldest servant waits for the final sign of blood kinship because the blood of the Lamb must mark the chosen people (1 Pet 1:18–19). The first sign of water reflects the original genesis of creation, the first destruction (by water) in the time of Noah, and ultimately the incarnation of Jesus Christ, while the second sign of blood reflects the glorious reappearing of Christ in the end times, the coming second destruction (by fire), and finally the promised new creation in the Body of Christ. The emphasis on Abraham's eldest servant wondering and waiting in silence points to the relative silence of God between the First and Second Advents.[47]

---

[46] "Biblical narrative rarely describes someone's appearance. Consequently, when it does it has a purpose, usually serving the plot" (Waltke 41). Everything has meaning, nothing is arbitrary, all that is written and all that is not written.

[47] "There was general agreement [among the rabbis] that prophecy, in its special connotation, ceased with the overthrow of the first Temple, although it lingered with a few men during the [Babylonian] exile" (Cohen, *Rabbinic Sages* 124). The reality is that miraculous signs and prophetic utterances are supernatural and therefore, by definition, have always been the exception, not the rule, throughout all of human history.

ADAM, NOAH, ABRAHAM

Genesis 24:22 And it came to pass, as the camels had done drinking, that the man took a golden earring of half a shekel weight, and two bracelets for her hands of ten [shekels] weight of gold;

Abraham's eldest servant placing gold jewelry on Rebekah reflects the Holy Spirit marking the faithful. The gold itself represents the corresponding gifts of the Spirit that proceed from faith. Abraham's eldest servant producing the gold jewelry for Rebekah, before she actually testifies to her blood kinship with Abraham, is an image of the Holy Spirit recognizing the faithful. Abraham's eldest servant waiting until his camels had finished drinking before marking Rebekah reflects the sign of water preceding the sign of blood. The law precedes grace just as repentance precedes redemption. Everything in its proper time according to the will of God, the way of God (Eccl 8:6).

Genesis 24:23 And said, Whose daughter [art] thou? tell me, I pray thee: is there room [in] thy father's house for us to lodge in?

The call to receive the indwelling Holy Spirit.

Genesis 24:24–25 And she said unto him, I [am] the daughter of Bethuel the son of Milcah, which she bare unto Nahor. 25 She said moreover unto him, We have both straw and provender enough, and room to lodge in.

The emphasis on Rebekah's lineage from Milcah recalls the premature death of Milcah's father, Haran (Gen 11:29). The lineage from Haran through Rebekah is a figurative death and resurrection that reflects the promised Seed of woman, through death and resurrection, striking, in the victory over death, the head identified with the seed of the serpent, which spiritually is the embodiment of death. The death and resurrection of Haran in the lineage of Rebekah parallels a death and resurrection of Haran in the personage of Abram just as the Passion of Christ recalls the Fall of Adam (Gen 11:27–28). The death and resurrection embodied by Rebekah echoes the sacrifice of Isaac just as the faithful are called to imitate Christ.

Genesis 24:26–27 And the man bowed down his head, and worshipped the LORD. 27 And he said, Blessed [be] the LORD God of my master Abraham, who hath not left destitute [H5800] my master of his mercy [H2617] and his truth [H571]: I [being] in the way, the LORD led me to the house of my master's brethren.

The emphasis on the Lord being the God of Abraham reinforces the identification of Abraham with God the Father. Abraham's eldest servant, identified with both the Spirit and the Son, bowing down and worshipping the Lord of his master reflects the unity of the Holy Spirit. The word *mercy* [H2617] (mercy of the Lord) means "goodness" and "kindness," while the word *truth* [H571] (truth of the Lord) means "firmness" and "faithfulness" and "truth."

The *mercy* [H2617] of God is the goodness of creation proceeding from the Father through the Son, while the *truth* [H571] of God is the promised indwelling Spirit of truth. The mercy and truth of God signifies the union of flesh and spirit embodied by the Son. The word *destitute* [H5800] (not left destitute of mercy and truth) means "to leave" and "to forsake" and is the same word used to foretell that a man should *leave* [H5800] his father and mother to become one flesh with his wife (Gen 2:24), a prophecy ultimately foreshadowing Jesus Christ being *forsaken* [G1459] on the cross (Matt 27:46). A man must leave his father and mother to be united with his wife just as Christ would become a curse on the cross, forsaken of the Father and of the Spirit, in order to be united with the faithful. But Isaac is not left destitute just as the Father would remember the Son. Isaac is not left without a bride just as the Father even now remembers the faithful in the Son. Everyone who has forsaken family—figuratively the original creation, or the natural body—for his name's sake, the Lord's, shall inherit eternal life, the promised new creation in the spiritual, or glorified, body (Matt 19:29).

Genesis 24:28 And the damsel ran, and told [them of] her mother's house these things.

The emphasis on Rebekah's mother again recalls the foretold Seed of woman and finally the Heel of the Seed of woman (Gen 3:15).

Genesis 24:29–31 And Rebekah had a brother, and his name [was] Laban: and Laban ran out unto the man, unto the well. 30 And it came to pass, when he saw the earring and bracelets upon his sister's hands, and when he heard the words of Rebekah his sister, saying, Thus spake the man unto me; that he came unto the man; and, behold, he stood by the camels at the well. 31 And he said, Come in, thou blessed of the LORD; wherefore standest thou without? for I have prepared the house, and room for the camels.

Laban's motivation is greed, at least figuratively, given the emphasis on his seeing the gold placed upon his daughter, Rebekah, and also his enthusiastic acknowledgment of the eldest servant being blessed. For both responses are seemingly based solely upon visible wealth. The character of Laban would also be confirmed in his subsequent corrupt dealings with Jacob (Gen 31:38–42). Nonetheless, Laban prophesies the blessing of Abraham in his personal acknowledgment of the blessing of the eldest servant just as every voice will finally acknowledge the blessing of the Lord in the last days. Prophecy proceeding from unlikely sources reflects the universal dominion of God. The ironic image of Laban being a prophet also reminds us that even the righteousness of the prophets is as filthy rags before the Lord (Isa 64:6).

Genesis 24:32 And the man came into the house: and he ungirded his camels, and gave straw and provender for the camels, and water to wash his feet, and the men's feet that [were] with him.

Ungirding and feeding the ten camels of Abraham represents the fulfillment of the Ten Commandments of God, while the image of washing feet represents a corresponding purification through the law. Not by the law but through the law. Abraham's eldest provides first for the beasts of burden and also for the servants just as law precedes grace just as repentance precedes redemption just as assent precedes marriage. Hungry camels and dirty feet both reflect a wandering through the wilderness just as the law guides us to grace through the moral wilderness of life (Gal 3:24).

Genesis 24:33 And there was set [meat] before him to eat: but he said, I will not eat, until I have told mine errand [H1697]. And he said, Speak on.

The word *errand* [H1697] (told my errand) means "speech, word," which is an image of the *Logos* (the Word) [G3056] (John 1:1). The implied physical hunger of Abraham's eldest servant reflects the impatient hunger of the Spirit of God to redeem mankind. But the marriage supper of the Lamb cannot proceed until the Word has been fulfilled (Rev 19:9).

Genesis 24:34–48 And he said, I [am] Abraham's servant. 35 And the LORD hath blessed my master greatly; and he is become great: and he hath given him flocks, and herds, and silver, and gold, and menservants, and maidservants, and camels, and asses. 36 And Sarah my master's wife bare a son to my master when she was old: and unto him hath he given all that he hath. 37 And my master made me swear, saying, Thou shalt not take a wife to my son of the daughters of the Canaanites, in whose land I dwell: 38 But thou shalt go unto my father's house, and to my kindred, and take a wife unto my son. 39 And I said unto my master, Peradventure the woman will not follow me. 40 And he said unto me, The LORD, before whom I walk, will send his angel with thee, and prosper thy way; and thou shalt take a wife for my son of my kindred, and of my father's house: 41 Then shalt thou be clear from [this] my oath, when thou comest to my kindred; and if they give not thee [one], thou shalt be clear from my oath. 42 And I came this day unto the well, and said, O LORD God of my master Abraham, if now thou do prosper my way which I go: 43 Behold, I stand by the well of water; and it shall come to pass, that when the virgin cometh forth to draw [water], and I say to her, Give me, I pray thee, a little water of thy pitcher to drink; 44 And she say to me, Both drink thou, and I will also draw for thy camels: [let] the same [be] the woman whom the LORD hath appointed out for my master's son. 45 And before I had done speaking in mine heart, behold, Rebekah came forth with her pitcher on her shoulder; and she went down unto the well, and drew [water]: and I said unto her, Let me drink, I pray thee. 46 And she made haste, and let down her pitcher from her [shoulder], and said, Drink, and I will give thy camels drink also: so I drank, and she made the camels drink also. 47 And I asked her, and said, Whose daughter [art] thou? And she said, The daughter of Bethuel, Nahor's son, whom Milcah bare unto him: and I put the earring upon her face, and the bracelets upon her hands. 48 And I bowed down my head, and worshipped the LORD, and blessed the LORD God of my master Abraham, which had led me in the right way to take my master's brother's daughter unto his son.

Abraham's eldest servant retelling the story of Abraham and Isaac reflects the law and prophets being revealed though God the Holy Spirit. The spreading of the Gospel to all nations, the call to imitate Christ, the Great Commission (Matt 28:19). The testimony of the person of the Spirit is repeated to every soul in every generation in every nation.[48]

Genesis 24:49 And now if ye will deal kindly and truly with my master, tell me: and if not, tell me; that I may turn to the right hand, or to the left.

God the Holy Spirit will not violate the sanctity of freewill, but the divine will for the welfare of the faithful will neither be denied.

Genesis 24:50 Then Laban and Bethuel answered and said, The thing [H1697] proceedeth from the LORD: we cannot speak unto thee bad [H7451] or good [H2896].

The word *thing* [H1697] (the thing proceedeth from the Lord), previously translated *errand* [H1697] (errand of the eldest servant), means "speech, word," which again reflects the *Logos* (the Word) [G3056] proceeding from God. The word of Abraham's eldest servant is Isaac signifying the one name of Jesus Christ (Acts 4:12). Laban not speaking bad or good concerning Isaac prefigures Laban not speaking good or bad concerning Jacob, a continuity that typifies the fulfillment of the First Advent of Jesus Christ in the Second Advent (Gen 31:24). The words *good* [H2896] and *bad* [H7451] (cannot speak bad or good) are the same words describing the *good* [H2896] and *evil* [H7451] connected with the tree of knowledge (Gen 2:17). The experiential knowledge of good and evil is the way of flesh, but the knowledge of flesh is ironically an ignorance of the Spirit. Laban not being able to speak bad or good concerning Isaac echoes the words of Cain concerning the fate of Abel, the mantra of the man without faith, the fruit of the tree of knowledge, namely, "I know not" (Gen 4:9). I would thou wert cold or hot (Rev 3:15).

---

[48] The principle of imitating God is a foundational tenet of Talmudic morality (Cohen, *Rabbinic Sages* 22). The call to imitate God, if it is to be truly and fully obeyed, must be followed to its logical conclusion, which is to be reborn in Christ.

Genesis 24:51–52 Behold, Rebekah [is] before thee, take [her], and go, and let her be thy master's son's wife, as the LORD hath spoken. 52 And it came to pass, that, when Abraham's servant heard their words, he worshipped the LORD, [bowing himself] to the earth.

The emphasis on no one being able to stop the Lord from taking Rebekah testifies to the promise that not a single sheep will be lost (Matt 18:14). The implication that Rebekah is given, at least initially, without her consent doesn't reflect the Lord violating freewill but rather reflects the Lord relentlessly calling the chosen from death unto life. Rebekah is later explicitly asked whether she will go with the eldest servant, which is an affirmation of the sanctity of freewill (Gen 24:58). Rebekah being initially given without consent is an image of death. Rebekah finally choosing Isaac is an image of our rebirth. The baptism in water precedes the baptism of the Spirit.[49]

Genesis 24:53 And the servant brought forth jewels of silver, and jewels of gold, and raiment, and gave [them] to Rebekah: he gave also to her brother and to her mother precious things.

The gifts of gold placed upon Rebekah at the well of water prefigured the vast wealth now bestowed on her at the banquet just as the anointing of the Holy Spirit in this life prefigures the fullness of the indwelling Holy Spirit in the next (Gen 24:22). The drink at the well is likewise completed by the drink and meat of the banquet just as the law is completed by grace. Abraham's eldest servant presenting precious gifts not only to Rebekah but also to her family reflects all the peoples of the world, even the faithless, benefiting from the presence of the visible church in the world.[50]

Genesis 24:54 And they did eat [H398] and drink [H8354], he and the men that [were] with him, and tarried all night; and they rose up in the morning, and he said, Send me away unto my master.

The great feast celebrating the betrothal of Rebekah to Isaac prefigures the wedding supper of the Lamb, but Isaac is notably absent, which is a sign that the call of the faithful, the betrothal, merely foreshadows the reality of our promised new creation, the promised union of law and grace (Rev 19:7). The call of Rebekah is most closely identified with the call of the faithful in the age of the church (not with the harvest of humanity in the end times) just as Isaac is most closely identified with the death and resurrection of Christ followed by the Holy Spirit being sent into the world (John 14:26). The word *eat* [H398] (they

---

[49] The undeniable, or relentless, nature of the will of God for the welfare of his faithful in Christ is exemplified by the call of Jonah unto Nineveh, Jonah 4:2, and affirmed in the sign of Jonah ultimately being received by the Gentiles, Matt 12:39.

[50] The house of Nahor was enriched because of Rebekah just as the world is enriched because of the church (Coffman 313; Gen 24:50–58). Those who choose to reject God are in reality rejecting all that is good, even the very font of life.

did eat) has a connotation "to be devoured by fire, consumed," while the word *drink* [H8354] (they did drink) has a connotation "of drinking cup of Yahweh's [Jehovah's] wrath." And both connotations are ominous portents of the end times. The call to eat the flesh of Christ and drink the blood of Christ is the call to imitate the death and resurrection of Christ (John 6:53). The emphasis on the men tarrying all night portends the darkness before the dawn of our promised new creation in the Body of Christ (Matt 24:29–31).

Genesis 24:55–56 And her brother and her mother said, Let the damsel abide with us [a few] days, at the least ten; after that she shall go. 56 And he said unto them, Hinder me not, seeing the LORD hath prospered my way; send me away that I may go to my master.

The call to abide for ten days reflects the present world under the law and likewise the call to repentance. This is the way of flesh. In contrast, the haste of Abraham's servant to return home reflects the haste of the Spirit to redeem the faithful. This is the way of the Spirit.

Genesis 24:57–59 And they said, We will call the damsel, and inquire at her mouth. 58 And they called Rebekah, and said unto her, Wilt thou go with this man? And she said, I will go. 59 And they sent away Rebekah their sister, and her nurse, and Abraham's servant, and his men.

The Lord will not violate freewill.[51]

Genesis 24:60 And they blessed Rebekah, and said unto her, Thou [art] our sister, be thou [the mother] of thousands of millions, and let thy seed possess the gate [H8179] of those which hate them.

The blessing of Rebekah and her seed reflects the blessing of the faithful in Christ. The *gate* [H8179] of those who hate the seed of Rebekah represents the *gates* [G4439] of hell (Matt 16:18).

Genesis 24:61 And Rebekah arose, and her damsels, and they rode upon the camels, and followed the man: and the servant took Rebekah, and went his way.

Rebekah, having accepted the call to Isaac, now follows Abraham's eldest servant through the wilderness, which reflects the faithful suffering in this life even after having accepted Jesus Christ (Matt 10:38). Sin would continue in the world after the death and resurrection of Christ just as sin continued in the

---

[51] "They [Christians] must, like Rebekah, *believe* the testimony of the 'Messenger,' which is the Holy Spirit, specifically, the Bible, which is the testimony of the 'Messenger' " (Coffman 313; Gen 24:50–58). The parallel between the written Word and the incarnate Word is God the Holy Spirit calling the faithful unto God the Son.

world after the destruction in the floodwaters just as the individual continues to sin after the baptism in water. The faithful do become new creatures in this life through the gifts of the Holy Spirit, but everything in this life is still only a foretaste of our promised new creation in the Body of Christ (1 Cor 13:12).[52]

Genesis 24:62–63 And Isaac came from the way of the well Lahai-roi; for he dwelt in the south country. 63 And Isaac went out to meditate in the field at the eventide: and he lifted up his eyes, and saw, and, behold, the camels [were] coming.

Isaac meditating at evening time and, at least symbolically, waiting for his bride prefigures the Son waiting for the faithful until the end times. The persistent emphasis on the ten camels of Abraham reflects the undeniable reality that is the dominion of the law. The journey of Rebekah from her natural relatives unto her promised husband Isaac, the spiritual son of the promise, is bracketed by the image of two wells, the well of Nahor and the well of Lahairoi, but both wells reflect the baptism in water, the natural baptism. The well outside the city of Nahor is connected with the call of Rebekah—reflecting the call to repentance—while the well of Lahairoi (Beerlahairoi) is connected with the submission of Hagar to Sarah, a submission concerning the firstborn Ishmael—reflecting obedience to the law (Gen 16:10, 16:14). But the first son Ishmael points to the second son Isaac just as the first man Adam points to the second man Jesus Christ, whereby Isaac coming from the way of the well of Lahairoi is an image of the submission of Jesus Christ to the cross for the sake of Adam, or Adam-kind. The journey of Rebekah from the well of Nahor to the well of Lahairoi in the caravan of the ten camels of Abraham reflects the baptism of the faithful in imitation of Christ, the baptism in water being ultimately fulfilled in the baptism of Christ.

In Christ, the baptism in water finally becomes the baptism of fire, the baptism of repentance becomes the baptism of redemption, and the baptism in the flesh becomes the baptism of the Spirit (Rev 21:6). This is an imminent transfiguration of all the faithful in the Body of Christ (Matt 17:2) as prefigured by the Holy Spirit immediately descending unto Christ upon the baptism in water administered by John (Matt 3:16). The Covenant of Law likewise becomes the Covenant of Grace just as mortal life becomes eternal life just as the natural man in Adam becomes the spiritual man, the new Adam. Abraham's eldest servant leads Rebekah from the waters of Nahor to the waters of Abraham just as the Holy Spirit leads the faithful from the baptism in water to the baptism of the Holy Spirit. The pregnancy of Hagar connected with Beerlahairoi reflects the promise of life just as the life of Adam points to the life in Christ, the Body of Christ, just as the First Advent of Jesus Christ prefigures the Second Advent.

---

[52] The Bible is silent concerning Isaac from the time of his figurative resurrection until his union with Rebekah and, therein, foreshadows the coming together of Jesus and the faithful (Guzik 149–50; Gen 24:61–67). The myriad nuances of the Scriptures reflect the subtlety of the Holy Spirit.

ISHMAEL, ISAAC, KETURAH'S SONS

The law is a prophecy of grace, but nevertheless the emphasis in the natural body is the baptism of repentance and the concomitant submission to the authority in the world (1 Tim 2:2).[53]

Genesis 24:64–65 And Rebekah lifted up her eyes, and when she saw Isaac, she lighted off the camel. 65 For she [had] said unto the servant, What man [is] this that walketh in the field to meet us? And the servant [had] said, It [is] my master: therefore she took a vail, and covered herself.

The camels of Abraham represent the law, whereby the image of Rebekah dismounting when she sees Isaac reflects the freedom of the faithful in Christ from the law. The servant of Abraham telling Rebekah the identity of Isaac is a corresponding image of the Holy Spirit revealing Jesus Christ unto the faithful. The eldest servant calling both Abraham and Isaac his master reflects the unity of the Holy Spirit. Rebekah veiling herself represents the faithful being separated from Christ until the marriage of the Lamb in the end times.[54]

Genesis 24:66 And the servant told Isaac all things that he had done.

Isaac being told all things by Abraham's eldest servant is an image of Jesus Christ as the embodiment of the fullness of the Holy Spirit, one with the Father (John 3:34). The eldest servant is sent by Abraham but returns to Isaac just as the faithful are called by the Father into the Body of Christ.

Genesis 24:67 And Isaac brought her into his mother Sarah's tent, and took Rebekah, and she became his wife; and he loved [H157] her: and Isaac was comforted [H5162] after his mother's [death].

Abraham, Isaac, and Jacob reflect Adam and the First and Second Advents of Christ, while their respective wives reflect corresponding dispensations. Sarah can be compared to the original creation, while Rebekah can be compared to Israel, or more generally to the faithful in the present world. The family of Jacob can be compared to the kingdom of God. The emphasis on Rebekah entering the tent of Sarah, comforting Isaac concerning the death of Sarah, testifies to the call of the faithful to Jesus Christ supplanting the original condemnation of all humanity through Eve (1 Tim 2:14). Rebekah figuratively replacing Sarah likewise represents our hope being embodied by the death and resurrection of Christ in the place of Adam. The word *comforted* [H5162]

---

[53] Jesus Christ did not need and was not seeking a spiritual cleansing for himself in the act of being baptized, but rather he was seeking and did accomplish through his own holiness the sanctification of the baptismal water itself—Gregory of Nazianzus, *Third Theological Oration* (Rusch 145). The faithful are one with Christ in the Body of Christ.

[54] Just as Isaac went forth to meet Rebekah, so will Jesus Christ meet us in the air, 1 Thess 4:17 (Coffman 315; Gen 24:61–67). The New Testament is to the Old Testament as the fullness of God is to man formed in the image of God.

(comforted after Sarah's death) has connotations "to suffer grief" and "to repent" and is the same word used in the prophecy that Noah would be a *comfort* [H5162] of man in the original curse of the ground (Gen 5:29). The connection of the death and resurrection of the world through the floodwaters and the death and resurrection of Sarah in Rebekah reflects the renewal of all creation through the death and resurrection of the promised Seed of woman.[55]

The word *love* [H157] is previously used for the first time in the Scriptures to describe the love of Abraham for Isaac (Gen 22:2). The word *love* [H157] is now used a second time to describe the love of Isaac for Rebekah. Abraham loves Isaac just as God the Father loves God the Son, while Isaac loves Rebekah just as the Son loves the faithful. Love proceeds from Abraham through Isaac to Rebekah just as the Holy Spirit proceeds from the Father through the Son to the faithful. The word *love* [H157] in the Scriptures is applied to divine love, familial love, romantic love, communal love, and even the appetites, such as the love of food (Gen 27:4). The universality of the word *love* [H157] reflects a multiplication of the one love flowing from the one God just as the multitude of all life, including plant and animal life, proceeds from the singular life of the one living God. But the first occurrences of the word *love* in the Scriptures are examples of spiritual love, not lower forms of love and desire, just as the source of love is sacred and not profane.[56]

East Country

Genesis 25:1 Then again Abraham took a wife, and her name [was] Keturah.

Hagar is described as a *maid* (maidservant) [H8198] and *wife* [H802] of Abraham (Gen 16:3). Sarah is the *sister* [H269] and *wife* [H802] of Abraham (Gen 20:12). And Keturah is the *concubine* [H6370] and *wife* [H802] of Abraham (Gen 25:1, 1 Chr 1:32). Since no other names of concubines are reported, Keturah is, at least figuratively, the mother of all Abraham's children through concubines. A threefold series is thus evident in the lives of Hagar, Sarah, and Keturah when ordered according to the accounts of the births of Abraham's children. Hagar is a bondwoman taken as a wife but is rejected. Sarah is a half sister and wife who dies and is mourned. Keturah is finally a concubine who becomes a wife, a second wife compared with Sarah. Hagar and Keturah also died, but only the death of Sarah is emphasized in the formal account. The bondwoman Hagar reflects humanity enslaved by original sin and condemned under the law. The kinswoman Sarah reflects the faithful in Christ called to

---

[55] Gen 21:8–28:4 shows a chiastic literary construction with 24:1–67 as the pivot (Waltke 290). The pivotal image of the call of Rebekah reflects the central importance of the call of the faithful as the very meaning of life.

[56] Gregory of Nazianzus and also Gregory of Nyssa believed that the acts of God originate with the Father and then progress through the Son and are finally finished in the Spirit (Rusch 24). The progressive unfolding of creation is necessarily the progressive revelation of God, for creation has been formed in the very image of God.

imitate the death and resurrection of Jesus Christ, while Keturah reflects the exaltation of the faithful from slavery under the law to freedom by grace.[57]

Genesis 25:2–4 And she bare him Zimran, and Jokshan, and Medan, and Midian, and Ishbak, and Shuah. 3 And Jokshan begat Sheba, and Dedan. And the sons of Dedan were Asshurim, and Letushim, and Leummim. 4 And the sons of Midian; Ephah, and Epher, and Hanoch, and Abida, and Eldaah. All these [were] the children of Keturah.

The offspring of Hagar, Sarah, and Keturah represent the fulfillment of the respective dispensations embodied by their mothers. The one son Ishmael reflects the bondage proceeding from the one man Adam, while the one son Isaac reflects the freedom of one man Jesus Christ. The multitude proceeding directly from Keturah reflects the multitude of nations called to faith in Christ. The fulfillment of fallen man under the curse is Israel under the law (Ishmael); the fulfillment of the blessing of Israel is the blessing of Jesus Christ (Isaac); and the fulfillment of the call of the faithful is the blessing in the Body of Christ (the multitude of Keturah). Ishmael reflects the earthly Jerusalem, while Isaac reflects the heavenly Jerusalem (Gal 4:24–26). The offspring of Hagar and Sarah point to the offspring of Keturah, relating a symbolic death and resurrection of Jew and Gentile together in one the Body of Christ.

Genesis 25:5–6 And Abraham gave all that he had unto Isaac. 6 But unto the sons of the concubines, which Abraham had, Abraham gave gifts, and sent them away [H7971] from Isaac his son, while he yet lived, eastward [H6924], unto the east [H6924] country.

The word *sent away* [H7971] (from Isaac) is the same Hebrew word used to describe Adam and Eve being *sent forth* [H7971] out of the garden (Gen 3:23), while the word *east* [H6924] has connotations of "beginning" and "ancient time" and recalls the original exile of man from the *east* [H6924] of Eden (Gen 3:24). The persistent echoes of the first man Adam portend the fulfillment of the curse of Adam in the person of Christ and finally the Body of Christ. The east is the place of exile but is also an emblem of our new birth, representing a dichotomy finally resolved in the death and resurrection of creation in the foretold harvest of mankind. Isaac is with his father, Abraham, just as the Son is with the Father, but we look for the sons of Keturah to be called back out of

---

[57] "The Church will enter the glory of the kingdom only through this final Passover, when she will follow her Lord in his death and Resurrection. The kingdom will be fulfilled, then, not by a historic triumph of the Church through a progressive ascendancy, but only by God's victory over the final unleashing of evil, which will cause his Bride to come down from heaven. God's triumph over the revolt of evil will take the form of the Last Judgment after the final cosmic upheaval of this passing world" (Rom. Catholic Church, *Catechism* 194). Yes, but not simply a repeat of the spring feasts, rather the fall feasts in fulfillment of the spring feasts.

the east just as we look for the appearance of Christ in the east, shining as far as the west (Matt 24:27).

Abraham giving all he has to Isaac is a vision of the Father giving all things to the Son (John 3:35), while Abraham giving gifts to the sons of his concubines reflects the gifts of the Holy Spirit specifically in the natural body (2 Cor 1:21–22). The gifts given to the sons of Keturah are not a full inheritance but rather only a token, or deposit, compared with the full inheritance of Isaac. The natural body is likewise only a foreshadowing of the spiritual, or glorified, body. The gifts given to the sons of Keturah necessarily proceed from the wealth of Abraham and therefore from the inheritance of Isaac just as the gifts of the Spirit proceed from the Father through the Son. The implication in the account that the gifts given to Keturah's sons do not diminish the inheritance of Isaac is a reflection of the infinite nature of God. The emphasis on Abraham giving gifts to the sons of his concubines while he is still alive affirms the administration of the law in the natural body, while Abraham sending his sons of concubines away from Isaac affirms the separation between the faithful and Christ, specifically during the age of the church (John 16:7).

Genesis 25:7–8 And these [are] the days of the years of Abraham's life which he lived, an hundred threescore and fifteen years. 8 Then Abraham gave up the ghost [H1478], and died [H4191] in a good [H2896] old age, an old man, and full [H7649] [of years]; and was gathered to his people [H5971].

Abraham is closely identified with God the Father and the creation proceeding from God the Father, while Isaac is closely identified with God the Son and the promise of new creation in the Son. The close relationship between God the Father and creation is reflected, for example, in Daniel's vision of God the Father as the Ancient of Days, in that the symbol of days is a reference to the temporal quality that defines creation (Dan 7:13). Creation proceeds from the Father through the Son just as the will of the Father proceeds through the Son (John 5:19). The emphasis on the old age of Abraham testifies to the passing ages from the time of Adam and points to the revelation of Christ in the last days. The word *ghost* [H1478] (gave up the ghost) is the same Hebrew word used to describe all flesh in the earth *dying* [H1478] in the floodwaters, which reflects a connection between the death of Abraham and the condemnation of creation (Gen 6:17). The word *died* [H4191] (Abraham died) has a connotation "to die as a penalty, be put to death" and is the same word used to describe the *death* that comes through the tree of knowledge, which also evokes an image of the condemnation of creation (Gen 2:17). But the word *people* [H5971] (Abraham gathered to his people) has a connotation "one's own people," which reflects the unity of the Holy Spirit in the Body of Christ (Matt 12:50).[58]

---

[58] It is only through the worth of Israel that the whole of creation was made, *Leviticus Rabbah* (Cohen, *Rabbinic Sages* 61). The merit of the one nation of Israel, representing

ISHMAEL, ISAAC, KETURAH'S SONS

The figurative death of God implied by the death of Abraham reflects God hiding his face because of sin and portends a final destruction of the original creation, but the preservation of creation foreshadows the redemption of creation just as the mortal life of Abraham foreshadows eternal life. God is eternal, whereby the death of the God of creation represents not the end of God but rather the end of the creation. The death and resurrection of the Son of God is likewise the embodiment of the death and resurrection of all creation. The word *good* [H2896] (good old age) is the same word used to describe the original creation as very *good* [H2896] (Gen 1:31). The good old age of Abraham is an image of the fullness of the days of creation, that is, a fulfillment of the days of creation in the promised renewal of creation in the last days. The word *full* [H7649] (full of years) means "sated, satisfied, surfeited," which reflects the fulfillment of all things in the fullness of time, both bad and good. But the decreased average lifetimes of humanity after the Flood portends the life of Christ cut off prematurely and also the approaching destruction in the end times. The natural death of the individual in old age reflects the appointed end of creation in the end times, while the premature death of some individuals reflects the cataclysmic events throughout the millennia and also the uncertainty of the appointed time of the end, a time known only by the Father, a time of new creation known only by the Father of creation (Mark 13:32).

Genesis 25:9–10 And his sons Isaac and Ishmael buried him in the cave of Machpelah, in the field of Ephron the son of Zohar the Hittite, which [is] before Mamre; 10 The field which Abraham purchased of the sons of Heth: there was Abraham buried, and Sarah his wife.

Abraham being buried with Sarah in the promised land is a prophecy of the Father reconciling creation unto himself, specifically through the sacrifice of the Son. The faithful burying their dead, in contrast to cremating their dead, reflects an expectation of a literal resurrection of the dead in a true body together with a literal renewal of physical (and spiritual) creation. Abraham being buried with Sarah, not with Hagar or Keturah, reflects the expectation of the fulfillment of the promise of life being expressly through the offspring of Sarah. The persistent emphasis on father Abraham having purchased the buryingplace from the Hittites prefigures the Father giving the Son for the salvation of the faithful in fulfillment of the law. The child of slavery, the firstborn Ishmael, and the child of freedom, the second born Isaac, are both witnesses to the burial of their father, Abraham, just as the Covenants of Law and Grace are both testimonies to the promise of the Lord God. Isaac buries Abraham with Sarah, in contrast to Sarah with Abraham, just as God humbly condescends to humanity and not vice versa. Isaac with Ishmael approaching Abraham reflects the Son presenting the faithful unto the Father. Ishmael approaching Abraham only in death reflects the undeniable condemnation of the natural body, while

---

the whole of creation, is ultimately embodied by the one man Jesus Christ, through whom all creation proceeds.

the absence of Keturah's sons reflects the faithful awaiting the resurrection of the spiritual, or glorified, body.[59]

Genesis 25:11 And it came to pass after the death of Abraham, that God blessed his son Isaac; and Isaac dwelt by the well Lahai-roi [H883].

The burial of Abraham in Machpelah, following the figurative death and resurrection of Isaac in Moriah, presages a relative silence between the ascension of Christ and the foretold glorious reappearing in the end times. The end of the era between Adam and Christ heralds a silence signifying the end of the natural body and calling the collective faithful to imitate the death and burial of the Lord. God blessing Isaac after the death of Abraham represents the Son sitting at the right hand of the Father after the ascension. *Beerlahairoi* (well Lahairoi) [H883] is closely connected with the baptism of repentance in the first flight of Hagar (Gen 16:14) and again in the call of Rebekah (Gen 24:62). Isaac staying at Beerlahairoi thereby reflects the baptism of repentance embodied by the call to imitate Jesus Christ in the age of the church between the First and Second Advents. The figurative sacrifice of Isaac in Moriah prefigures the First Advent of Jesus Christ, while the old age and literal death of Isaac prefigures the end of the church age culminating in the millennial kingdom of Christ. The subsequent multiplication of Jacob prefigures the Second Advent of Christ heralding the millennial kingdom.[60]

TWELVE PRINCES

Genesis 25:12 Now these [are] the generations of Ishmael, Abraham's son, whom Hagar the Egyptian, Sarah's handmaid, bare unto Abraham:

The emphasis on Ishmael being the son of Abraham testifies to the love of the Father for Adam, while the emphasis on Hagar being Sarah's handmaid testifies to the earthly Jerusalem being beneath the heavenly Jerusalem (Gal 4:24–26). The birth of Ishmael precedes the birth of Isaac just as the formation of Adam precedes the incarnation of Jesus Christ. Our offspring represent a fulfillment of our lives, either bad or good. The account of the offspring of Ishmael, figuratively the offspring of Adam, precedes the account of the offspring of Isaac, spiritually the offspring of Jesus Christ, just as the baptism in the floodwaters precedes the baptism of the cross. The true children of God are

---

[59] Every single living soul is translated, resurrected or raptured, either unto eternal life or unto eternal damnation, regardless of whether they were buried or cremated or killed in the womb or anything else, John 5:29.

[60] "According to the Lord, the present time [before his glorious reappearing] is the time of the Spirit and of witness, but also a time still marked by 'distress' and the trial of evil which does not spare the Church [1 Cor 7:26, 1 Pet 4:17, etc.] and ushers in the struggles of the last days. It is a time of waiting and watching [Matt 25:13, Mark 13:33–37, etc.]" (Rom. Catholic Church, *Catechism* 193). It is foremost the Lord who is waiting and watching for our repentance.

born of faith and not of flesh, but the faithful in this life should identify primarily with Ishmael, not with Isaac, since the spiritual, or glorified, body has not yet been fully revealed (Gal 3:7). Our redemption proceeds not according to the flesh, not by the death inherited from Adam, but only by grace through the Spirit, only in the promised resurrection of the Body of Christ.

The ordering of the accounts of the generations of the three groups of Abraham's sons (Keturah's sons, Ishmael, Isaac) (Gen 25:1, 25:12, 25:19) parallels the ordering of the generations of Noah's three sons (Japheth, Ham, Shem) (Gen 10:2, 10:6, 10:21). The ordering of both of these sets of generations places redeemed (opposite of fallen) man first and, thereby, reflects the Trinity in the original creation before the original sin. The ordering of the accounts of the births of Abraham's sons (Ishmael, Isaac, Keturah's sons) (Gen 16:15, 21:2, 25:2) parallels the ordering of the births of Adam's sons (Cain, Abel, Seth) (Gen 4:1, 4:2, 4:25) and also the ordering of the cursing and blessing of Noah's sons (Ham, Shem, Japheth) (Gen 9:25, 9:26, 9:27). The ordering of these two sets of births, specifically paralleling the ordering of the cursing and blessing of the nations, reflects the Trinity in fallen creation. The common ordering of Abraham's sons (Isaac, Ishmael, Keturah's sons) (1 Chr 1:28) parallels the common ordering of Noah's sons (Shem, Ham, Japheth) (Gen 6:10). The common orderings of both of these sets of names is according to prestige and, thereby, reflects the Trinity in the promised new creation.

Genesis 25:13–15 And these [are] the names of the sons of Ishmael, by their names, according to their generations: the firstborn of Ishmael, Nebajoth; and Kedar, and Adbeel, and Mibsam, 14 And Mishma, and Dumah, and Massa, 15 Hadar, and Tema, Jetur, Naphish, and Kedemah:

Ishmael was more prolific than Isaac in their day, in their bodies, even though Isaac received the blessing. The fertility of Ishmael reflects the prophecy that Adam would become a multitude (Gen 1:28), while the barrenness of Rebekah reflects the prophecy that the barren woman would have more children than she who has a husband (Gal 4:27). The Seed of woman would be cut off from life on the cross, but yet in him a multitude of spiritual children will enter into everlasting life. The barrenness of the wife of Isaac being miraculously transformed into fertility points to the nations that would proceed from the wives of Jacob just as the call of the nation of Israel in the First Advent of Christ points to the call of all nations in the Second Advent.

Genesis 25:16 These [are] the sons of Ishmael, and these [are] their names, by their towns, and by their castles; twelve princes according to their nations.

Hagar reflects the earthly Jerusalem, while Sarah reflects the heavenly Jerusalem (Gal 4:24–26). The twelve sons of Ishmael reflect the twelve earthly tribes of Israel, while the twelve sons of Jacob reflect the twelve heavenly thrones of Israel (Matt 19:28). Twelve sons are born unto Ishmael a generation before twelve sons would be born unto Isaac through Jacob just as the first generation represented by the time of the First Advent precedes the second generation represented by the time of the Second Advent. The offspring of Ishmael ultimately reflect not only the one nation of Israel but also all the nations of the world just as the one man Adam is the father of all mankind just as the one man Jesus Christ is the Head of the Body. The one city of Jerusalem is a microcosm for all the cities of the world just as one man Adam signifies all mankind just as the one man Christ sanctifies all the faithful. The earthly Jerusalem reflects the heavenly Jerusalem just as everything in this life reflects the true spiritual reality (1 Cor 13:12).

Genesis 25:17 And these [are] the years of the life of Ishmael, an hundred and thirty and seven years: and he gave up the ghost and died; and was gathered unto his people.

The account of the death of Ishmael echoes the account of the death of Abraham—the deaths of the first father of the faithful and his firstborn son both reflecting the end of the dispensation of the first man Adam.

Genesis 25:18 And they dwelt from Havilah unto Shur, that [is] before Egypt, as thou goest toward Assyria: [and] he died in the presence of all his brethren.

The sons of the firstborn Ishmael dwelling before Egypt toward Assyria foreshadows the first bondage of the Israelites in the land of Egypt and also the first conquest of the Israelites by the Assyrians (2 Kgs 17:6). Hagar and Ishmael are closely identified with images of bondage and exile, reflecting the enslavement of flesh to sin and reinforcing the parallel between the firstborn Ishmael and the first man Adam. Keturah's sons, in contrast, are sent to the east, the place of the rising sun, figuratively to await the dawn of the promised new creation. Ishmael precedes Isaac just as Adam precedes Jesus Christ, while Keturah's sons follow Isaac just as the faithful are added to the Body of Christ. Lord God have mercy.

Ω Ω Ω

The 1-2-3 pattern evident in the account of Abraham's sons is specifically an overlapping 1-2, 1-2 pattern reflecting the twofold natures of the Son, who is fully man and fully God. The structuring of the narrative deals, first, with the twofold relationship between Ishmael and Isaac and, second, with the twofold relationship between Isaac and Keturah's sons. Ishmael is the son of the bondwoman, ultimately rejected, while Isaac is the son of a freewoman, ultimately accepted. Isaac is the sole heir of Abraham, but Keturah's sons are given gifts. Ishmael was born after the flesh just as Adam was formed from the dust of the ground, whereas Isaac was born of a promise just as Christ Jesus is the embodiment of the promise of life (Gal 4:23). Isaac receiving the sole

ISHMAEL, ISAAC, KETURAH'S SONS

inheritance from Abraham reflects Christ receiving all things from the Father, while Keturah's sons receiving gifts out of the inheritance of Isaac reflects the faithful receiving the gifts of the Holy Spirit through the Son. Ishmael reflects Adam, while Isaac reflects Christ. Isaac specifically reflects the First Advent of Christ, as evident in the figurative sacrifice of Isaac by Abraham (Gen 22:2). Keturah's sons receiving gifts through Isaac points to the fullness of the indwelling Holy Spirit that will be manifested in the Second Advent. The 1-2-3 pattern evident in the Biblical narrative reflects the Trinity, while the underlying 1-2, 1-2 pattern reflects the twofold natures of the Son. The singularity implied by the unity of the pattern reflects the oneness of God. The primordial image of God is oneness, testifying to the one God being the one font of all life. Nevertheless, our personal experience of reality is twofold just as the twofold natures of Christ relate the visible image of God (Col 1:15). And the fullness of progressive revelation is finally threefold reflecting the wholeness of truth in the Father, Son, and Holy Spirit (Matt 28:19).

1	2	3
ADAM (IMAGE OF GOD)	FIRST ADVENT (HEAD)	SECOND ADVENT (BODY)
1	2	
ISHMAEL (SLAVE)	ISAAC (FREE)	
	1	2
	ISAAC (SOLE INHERITANCE)	KETURAH'S SONS (MANIFOLD GIFTS)

The accounts of the sons of Adam, the sons of Noah, and the sons of Abraham are a kind of refrain that echoes the main chorus of the fundamental Messianic bloodline from Adam through Noah and Abraham to Christ. The emphasis of the refrain, however, shifts from condemnation to redemption just as the main narrative shifts from death in the first man Adam to life in the second man Christ (Matt 5:38–39). Focusing on the curse becoming a blessing, the separation between man and God because of sin is affirmed in Cain being driven from the face of the Lord (Gen 4:14) but Noah subsequently cursing Ham, through Canaan, to be the servant of his brothers hints at the beginning of reconciliation (Gen 9:24–25). And Isaac and Ishmael together burying Abraham prefigures Christ Jesus finally restoring Adam unto the Father (Gen 25:9). Focusing on the blessing overshadowing the curse, a figurative resurrection is evident in Seth replacing Abel, even though the emphasis is on the shocking murder of Abel (Gen 4:25). And Japheth subsequently being blessed through Shem reflects the blessing of the faithful in Christ, even though the scene is darkened by the continuing servitude of Ham through his offspring Canaan (Gen 9:26–27). And the figurative sacrifice of Isaac is a vivid image of the Passion of Christ that specifically emphasizes the resurrection since Isaac doesn't literally die (Gen 22:12).

ADAM, NOAH, ABRAHAM

1	2	3
ADAM	FIRST ADVENT	SECOND ADVENT
CAIN	ABEL	SETH
HAM	SHEM	JAPHETH
ISHMAEL	ISAAC	KETURAH'S SONS

The refrain manifested in the accounts of the sons of Adam, the sons of Noah, and the sons of Abraham is an echo of the main chorus of the account of Adam and Christ Jesus just as the song we sing in this life is an echo of the harmony in heaven (Rev 5:9). The resounding of salvation in both the natural order and our personal lives affirms the undeniable nature of the will of God, while the ever-increasing intensity of the chorus of salvation revealed through progressive revelation heralds our glorification in the Body of Christ. The promise of redemption being manifested in the personal lives of the patriarchs reflects the will of God for the sanctification of the very essence of our persons as individuals with freewill. The promise of redemption being manifested in the natural order of the physical world expressly affirms that the spiritual body will be a true body, concomitant with individual freewill. The progression of the narrative pointing to the last days reflects the movement of the Holy Spirit leading us to grace (Gal 3:24). The story, or song, of salvation impressed upon all creation is our sanctification by the Holy Spirit in the Body of Christ to be finally revealed in the Second Advent. God the Holy Spirit proceeding from God the Father through God the Son represents our promised inheritance in the new creation, the Body of Christ.[61]

1	2	3
GOD THE FATHER	GOD THE SON	GOD THE HOLY SPIRIT
CREATOR	REDEEMER	SANCTIFIER
ADAM	FIRST ADVENT	SECOND ADVENT
IMAGE OF GOD	HEAD OF THE BODY	BODY OF CHRIST

---

[61] The two earliest known secular documents that mention Israel—a circa 1207 BC victory hymn of the Egyptian king Merneptah and a circa 830 BC victory inscription of the Moabite king Mesha—both prematurely celebrate the utter destruction of the Israelites (Sarna 227; Gen 32:28–29). The people of the world celebrated the day of the crucifixion, only to lament in horror the coming of the day of the resurrection.

ISHMAEL, ISAAC, KETURAH'S SONS

CHAPTER SIX OUTLINE

Key Images

PRIME IMAGES

Material	Abstract	Spiritual
The promise of Isaac.	A supernatural birth.	Jesus Christ is the man from heaven (1 Cor 15:47).
The sacrifice of Isaac.	The only son of the promise.	The Father gives his only begotten Son (John 3:16).
The sole inheritance of Isaac.	The one legitimate son, through the freewoman wife.	Our one and only redemption in the Son through the Spirit.

TWOFOLD IMAGES

Material	Abstract	Spiritual
Isaac and Rebekah.	Promised son and near-kin wife. Flesh and spirit.	Christ and Israel.
Ishmael and Isaac.	First and second sons. Natural and supernatural births. Illegitimate and legitimate sons. Son of slavery, son of freedom. Flesh and spirit.	Adam and Jesus Christ.
Barrenness and fertility.	Curse and blessing. Flesh and spirit.	Death of the natural body and resurrection of the spiritual body.
First and second flights of Hagar.	Submission and salvation. Flesh and spirit.	Law and Grace.
Two treaties with Abimelech.	By Abimelech, by Abraham. From man, from God. Flesh and spirit.	Covenants of Law and Grace.

THREEFOLD IMAGES

Material	Abstract	Spiritual
Abraham, Isaac, eldest servant.	Abraham sends his eldest servant on behalf of his only son to call the bride of his son.	Father, Son, Holy Spirit.
Abraham, Sarah, Isaac.	Man, woman (woman + implied Seed), child (offspring of woman).	Father, Son (Spirit and Son), and Holy Spirit (Body of Christ).
Abraham, Isaac, descendants.	Father, son, sons.	Father, Son (begotten of the Spirit), and Holy Spirit (indwelling the multitude of the faithful).
Hagar, Sarah, Keturah.	Rejected concubine, near-kin wife, concubine who becomes a wife.	Forsaken humanity in Eve, the one nation Israel, the redemption of the nations.
Conception, birth (circumcision), weaning.	Promise, law, grace.	Father, Son, Holy Spirit.
Abraham laughs, Sarah laughs, those who hear laugh with Sarah.	Promise, repentance, redemption.	Adam, First Advent of Christ, Second Advent of Christ.
Keturah's sons, Ishmael, Isaac.	The order of the genealogies.	The Trinity in original creation.
Ishmael, Isaac, Keturah's sons.	The order of births.	The Trinity in fallen creation.
Isaac, Ishmael, Keturah's sons.	The common order (by stature).	The Trinity in our new creation.

ADAM, NOAH, ABRAHAM

Synopsis

	PROMISE	
	Material	Spiritual
21:1–8	The promised birth of a son in the old age of Abraham.	The foretold incarnation of Christ in the latter days of Israel, after the law and prophets.
	Abraham names his son Isaac ("he laughs").	Our surprise and joy in the incarnation.
	Abraham circumcises Isaac.	A mark of blood that portends the crucifixion.
	God makes Sarah laugh, and all who hear will laugh with her.	The anointing of Christ in the Holy Spirit that is the anointing of the faithful.
	Isaac is weaned; Abraham makes a great feast.	The foretold great feast of the Lord.
21:9–11	Ishmael mocks Isaac.	Flesh contends against the Spirit.
	Sarah demands that Ishmael be cast out.	Flesh cannot inherit the kingdom of God.
	The thing is very grievous to Abraham.	The love of the Father for Adam.
21:12–13	In Isaac shall thy seed be called.	The promise of Christ.
	Ishmael will also be made a nation.	The preservation of Adam.
21:14–21	Abraham places bread and water on Hagar's shoulder and sends her and her child away.	The curse.
	Hagar and Ishmael wander in fear.	The world.
	But God opens Hagar's eyes. And she sees a well of water.	Our salvation by grace.
	And God was with Ishmael.	Prefigures the indwelling Holy Spirit.
	TWO TREATIES	
	Material	Spiritual
21:22–34	Abimelech calls upon Abraham to deal with him according to the kindness that he had done unto Abraham.	The Covenant of Law.
	Abraham reproves Abimelech concerning a well that had been taken violently. But Abraham then presents sheep and oxen to Abimelech as a seal of his ownership.	The Covenant of Grace.
	BLOOD SACRIFICE	
	Material	Spiritual
22:1–19	God tempts Abraham.	The Covenant of Law.
	The sacrifice of Isaac.	The crucifixion of Christ under the law.
	Isaac is spared.	The firstfruits of the grave.
22:20–24	The news of the birth of Rebekah reaches Abraham.	The faithful in Christ are sealed by the blood of Christ.
	THE DEATH OF SARAH	
	Material	Spiritual
23:1–20	Sarah dies.	The condemnation of all creation.
	Abraham mourns Sarah.	God longs for the redemption of humanity.
	Sarah is buried in the promised land.	The expectation of the resurrection of the dead, especially the faithful in Christ, and the corresponding renewal of creation.

ISHMAEL, ISAAC, KETURAH'S SONS

		THE ELDEST SERVANT	
		Material	Spiritual
24:1–9		Isaac not to leave the promised land.	The ascendant Jesus Christ sitting at the right hand of the Father until the appointed time (Acts 2:33–35).
		THE CALL OF THE BRIDE	
		Material	Spiritual
24:10–67		Abraham's eldest servant is sent by Abraham on behalf of Isaac to find the bride of Isaac.	The Holy Spirit proceeds from the Father through the Son to mark and seal the faithful.
		Abraham's eldest servant calls Rebekah to be the bride of Isaac.	The Holy Spirit calls the faithful unto Christ.
		Isaac and Rebekah are united as one flesh.	The church age.
		EAST COUNTRY	
		Material	Spiritual
25:1–6		The sons of Keturah.	The nations.
		Abraham gives everything he has to Isaac.	God the Father gives all things unto God the Son (John 3:35).
		Abraham, while he yet lives, gives gifts to the sons of Keturah.	The gifts of the Spirit in this life are a deposit on our inheritance in Christ (Eph 1:13–14).
		Abraham sends the sons of Keturah to the east country.	The nations await the new dawn of the promised new creation.
25:7–11		The death of Abraham.	The curse of Adam that is ultimately borne by God himself.
		Isaac and Ishmael bury Abraham.	Christ (Isaac) brings Adam (Ishmael) unto the Father (Abraham).
		God blesses Isaac.	The blessing of Jesus Christ and likewise the faithful in Christ.
		TWELVE PRINCES	
		Material	Spiritual
25:12–18		The twelve sons of Ishmael.	The twelve earthly tribes of Israel.
		Ishmael dies and is gathered unto his people.	The end of the dispensation of Adam.

AFTERWORD

The fundamental literary elements constructing the Scriptures are *prime*, *twofold*, and *threefold*, reflecting the essential oneness of God, the twofold natures of the Word of God, and finally the Trinitarian being of God. The oneness of God is uniquely identified with God the Father since the Son and the Spirit proceed from the Father. The twofold natures evident in the dichotomy of law and grace are uniquely identified with the Son, who is fully man and fully God. The threefold being of God is uniquely identified with God the Holy Spirit since the final revelation of the Body of Christ will be the fullness of the indwelling Spirit, through which the faithful are presented to the Father by and in the Son. The unity of the Spirit is the Trinity.

Our personal experience of reality is foremost twofold, reflecting the nearness of Jesus Christ and likewise our personal relationship with Jesus Christ. The oneness of objective reality reflects the oneness of the Father, likewise the oneness of the Son, and likewise the oneness of the Spirit that is the oneness of the Trinity; however, this is foremost the oneness of the Father since the Spirit and the Son, without beginning or end, eternally proceed from the Father. The movement of progressive revelation is the movement of the Holy Spirit, whereby the threefold progression in the Scriptures from the singular to the twofold to the threefold again expressly identifies the Spirit with the threefold. The singular, twofold, and threefold create a fundamentally interwoven whole, whereby the singular represents a primordial unity of the singular, twofold, and threefold. The twofold and threefold being subsumed by the singular testifies to the Son and the Spirit proceeding from the Father.[1]

GOD THE FATHER	GOD THE SON	GOD THE HOLY SPIRIT
PRIME	TWOFOLD	THREEFOLD

The three fundamental elements *prime*, *twofold*, and *threefold* build three complex pattern types *serial*, *chiastic*, and *staircase* that similarly reflect the God the Father, God the Son, and God the Holy Spirit. The serial pattern is most

---

[1] The essential core of the Christian catechism comprises the Ten Commandments, the Creed, and the Lord's Prayer (Luther, *Large Catechism* 6–7), respectively, what we are "to do," what we are "to believe," and finally what we are "to pray" (Ibid. 64). The original commandment that proceeds from the Father. The testimony, or creed, in the Son. And the new song of the indwelling Holy Spirit.

AFTERWORD

closely identified with the six days of creation and therefore with God the Father, from whom creation proceeds like an offspring. The chiastic pattern pointing to the incarnation at the center of creation is most closely identified with God the Son. The staircase pattern points to the final fulfillment of the law in grace in the last days and, therefore, is most closely identified with God the Holy Spirit, who leads the faithful by the law unto grace. The serial, chiastic, and staircase patterns follow an exactly repeating diurnal and likewise millennial cycle, reflecting the inviolable law of God Almighty. But analogues of these patterns, deviating from simple repeating time intervals, are similarly apparent, reflecting the transcendence of grace revealed in the Lord God.

The three nonuniform complex pattern types are manifested, respectively, in the natural history of creation as a whole, the individual as a microcosm of all creation, and finally the generations of the chosen people of God. And these three nonuniform patterns reflect the Father, Son, and Holy Spirit just as the corresponding uniform patterns reflect the Father, Son, and Holy Spirit just as the underlying fundamental elements reflect the Father, Son, and Holy Spirit. The natural history of creation, or simply the historical, reflects God the Father as the father of all creation. The faithful individual reflects the one man Jesus Christ, God the Son. The sequential and overlapping generations of the chosen people, pointing inexorably to the promised fulfillment of all things in the last days, reflects God the Holy Spirit leading the faithful to our promised inheritance in the Body of Christ.

GOD THE FATHER	GOD THE SON	GOD THE HOLY SPIRIT
PRIME	TWOFOLD	THREEFOLD
SERIAL	CHIASTIC	STAIRCASE
HISTORICAL	INDIVIDUAL	GENERATIONAL

The three increasingly complex sets, or layers, of elements and patterns—*prime, twofold,* and *threefold* followed by *serial, chiastic,* and *staircase* followed by *historical, individual,* and *generational*—also reflect, respectively, God the Father, God the Son, and God the Holy Spirit. The fundamental elements prime, twofold, and threefold represent a static viewpoint that reflects God the Father existing outside of time and space. The uniform complex patterns serial, chiastic, and staircase show an exact and specific structure in time that reflects the incarnation of God the Son occurring at a specific time and place. The nonuniform complex patterns historical, individual, and generational show a varying, or diverse, structure in time that reflects the movement of God the Holy Spirit, sweeping throughout all of creation, all time and space, in a progression of revelation leading all the faithful unto redemption.

GOD THE FATHER	GOD THE SON	GOD THE HOLY SPIRIT
PRIME, TWOFOLD, THREEFOLD	SERIAL, CHIASTIC, STAIRCASE	HISTORICAL, INDIVIDUAL, GENERATIONAL

The identification of each of the three layers of pattern types—elemental, uniform, and nonuniform—with a specific and different person of the Trinity finally implies different anthropological and eschatological contexts for the

AFTERWORD

narratives or aspects of the narratives encoded in each of the different layers. God the Father, God the Son, and God the Holy Spirit can be viewed, respectively, as creator, redeemer, and sanctifier. The Father, as the father of our creation, is uniquely identified with the original creation, particularly before sin entered the world. The Son, as our redeemer, is the person of the Trinity that was nailed to the cross and, therefore, is uniquely identified with fallen creation, that is, the world as we are now experiencing it. The Holy Spirit, as our sanctifier in the Body of Christ, is uniquely identified with the promised new creation, that is, the creation yet to be fully revealed.[2]

GOD THE FATHER	GOD THE SON	GOD THE HOLY SPIRIT
CREATOR	REDEEMER	SANCTIFIER
ORIGINAL CREATION	FALLEN CREATION	NEW CREATION

---

[2] "I therefore decided to give attention to the holy scriptures and to find out what they were like. And this is what met me: something neither open to the proud nor laid bare to mere children; a text lowly to the beginner but, on further reading, of mountainous difficulty and enveloped in mysteries. . . . Yet the Bible was composed in such a way that as beginners mature, its meaning grows with them" (Augustine, *Confessions* 40). The Scriptures are fundamentally supernatural and, therefore, cannot be properly described or explained in merely naturalistic terms.

EPILOGUE

The Lord's Prayer, Matthew 6:9–13, diagrammed by millennia and corresponding Biblical personages. The King James Bible standard English text is quoted, with editorial clarifications delimited in brackets and verbs in bold typeface.

	First Millennium	
After this manner therefore **pray** ye: Our Father which art in heaven, (Matt 6:9a).	ADAM	God the Father is our true father as our creator, but our heavenly Father is represented by our natural father Adam. Yet the emphasis on God the Father being in heaven testifies to the essential separation between the Holy Spirit and fallen flesh. Our physical father is a blurred reflection of our true spiritual Father just as everything in the present life is seen only through a glass darkly (1 Cor 13:12).
	Second Millennium	
Hallowed be thy name (6:9b).	NOAH	God does not proclaim the second day to be good (Gen 1:6–8). The emphasis on the name of God being hallowed recalls antediluvian man beginning to call upon, to profane, the name of the Lord (Gen 4:26). Mankind first beginning to overtly profane the Lord God is a watershed that culminates in the condemnation of the Flood. The word *hallowed* [G37] means "to separate from things profane" and "to purify," reflecting the setting apart of the righteous faithful that corresponds to the baptism in the floodwaters of Noah's day (1 Pet 3:20–21).

EPILOGUE

	THIRD MILLENNIUM	
Thy kingdom **come**. Thy will **be done** in earth, as [it is] in heaven (6:10).	ABRAHAM	Abraham is the first father of the kingdom of Israel that is yet to come—the promised earthly dominion of the spiritual body of the faithful. Abraham's faithfulness to the will of God on earth is exemplified by his sacrificing of Isaac—prefiguring the true nature of the kingship of Christ (Matt 27:37). God proclaims twice that the third day is good, reflecting the essential dichotomy of earth and heaven (Gen 1:9–13).
	FOURTH MILLENNIUM	
Give us this day our daily bread (6:11).	DAVID	The anointing of David as the king of Israel is fulfilled in the birth of Jesus Christ as the king of kings (1 Sam 16:13), wherein Jesus Christ is revealed to be our daily bread (Matt 26:26). Jesus Christ is the man from heaven, prefigured by the manna from heaven (John 6:58).
	FIFTH MILLENNIUM	
And **forgive** us our debts, as we **forgive** our debtors (6:12).	FIRST ADVENT	The debt paid in full by Christ on the cross. Our calling out for the forgiveness of our sins is a confession of our personal, or innate, guilt in the death of Christ, but this same calling out is also our certain hope, or expectation, for our redemption in Christ. And the concurrent call to forgive our own debtors is a profession of our participation in the Body of Christ, our literal union in the one Body.
	SIXTH MILLENNIUM	
And **lead** us not into temptation, but **deliver** us from evil: (6:13a).	SCHISM	The East–West Schism, or Great Schism, heralded a millennium marked to this very day by endless schism and conflict. This degradation of the earthly church recalls the defilement of Christ on the cross and portends the final persecution of the Body of Christ in the end times. We pray that the Lord leads us not into tribulation but delivers us from the evil one (Rev 3:10).

EPILOGUE

	SEVENTH MILLENNIUM	
For thine **is** the kingdom, and the power, and the glory, for ever (6:13b).	SECOND ADVENT	The seventh millennium is the Sabbath millennium, which corresponds to the millennial kingdom of Jesus Christ. The resurrection and rapture of the Body of Christ in the third millennium from the time of the First Advent will testify to the original firstfruits resurrection of Christ as the Head that was likewise on the third day (Matt 16:4). God blesses the seventh day (Gen 2:3).
	EIGHTH MILLENNIUM	
Amen (6:13c).	ETERNITY	And death and hell are cast into the lake of fire at the end of the millennial reign of Jesus Christ, heralding the opening of eternity in our sight (Rev 20:14). The eighth day is like the seventh day and is connected to the seventh day, wherein the Lord God not equating an evening and morning with the seventh day, as with the original six days, represents a looking forward from the seventh day into eternity (Gen 2:1–3).

SELECTED BIBLIOGRAPHY

Source materials are divided into subsections to highlight differences in genres and traditions as well as to facilitate referencing and to organize further reading. Not listed are original sources cited only via secondary sources, since in such cases the chief interest is in the secondary sources themselves, including their intrinsic filtering of the original sources. All such original sources are documented in the footnotes at least generally, along with complete citations for the secondary sources. Also not listed are a small number of general-purpose reference works.

SACRED TEXT

The Amplified Bible: Containing the Amplified Old Testament and the Amplified New Testament. Expanded edition. Grand Rapids: Zondervan, 1987.

The Holy Bible: Authorized King James Version. Pew Bible. Nashville: Holman Bible Publishers, 2014. Advocated by Bible Protector Ministries, Australia, as representing a pure presentation of the standard English text, first typeset circa 1900 and mass-produced by Bible and missionary societies in the twentieth century, ISBN 978-1-5864-0942-5.

The Holy Bible: The Catholic Bible, Douay-Rheims Version; Translated from the Latin Vulgate and Diligently Compared with the Hebrew, Greek and Other Editions; With Notes by Bishop [Richard] *Challoner and the Encyclical Letter "On the Study of the Holy Scriptures" by Pope Leo XIII, also a Presentation of the Essence of the Encyclical Letter "On Biblical Studies" by Pope Pius XII, and a Preface by Rev. William H. McClellan, S. J.; Also an Appendix Containing an Historical and Chronological Index, a Table of References and Maps.* New York: Benziger, 1941.

The Holy Bible: New International Version; Containing the Old Testament and the New Testament. Grand Rapids: Zondervan, 1984.

The New American Bible: Translated from the Original Languages with Critical Use of All the Ancient Sources; And the Revised New Testament Authorized by the Board of Trustees of the Confraternity of Christian Doctrine and Approved by the Administrative Committee/Board of the National Conference of Catholic Bishops and the U. S. Catholic Conference. Nashville: Catholic Bible Press, 1987.

Tanakh: A New Translation of the Holy Scriptures according to the Traditional Hebrew Text. First special-format edition. Philadelphia: Jewish Publication Society, 1985.

BIBLIOGRAPHY

Word Studies

Brown, Francis, S. R. Driver, and Charles A. Briggs. *The Brown-Driver-Briggs Hebrew and English Lexicon: With an Appendix Containing the Biblical Aramaic; Coded with the Numbering System from Strong's Exhaustive Concordance of the Bible; Based on the Lexicon of William Gesenius, as Translated by Edward Robinson, and Edited with Constant Reference to the Thesaurus of Gesenius as Completed by E. Rödiger, and with Authorized Use of the German Editions of Gesenius' Handwörterbuch über das Alte Testament.* Peabody: Hendrickson, 2007. Reprinted from the 1906 edition published by Houghton, Mifflin & Company. Strong's numbering added by Hendrickson.

Green, Jay P., Sr., ed. *The Interlinear Bible, Hebrew-Greek-English: With Strong's Concordance Numbers above Each Word.* Grand Rapids: Hendrickson, 1986. The Masoretic Text was type set in 1866 by the British and Foreign Bible Society. The Textus Receptus was type set in 1976 by Stephen Austin and Sons for the Trinitarian Bible Society and was based upon Scrivener's 1894–1902 *The New Testament in the Original Greek according to the Text Followed in the Authorized Version.*

Strong, James. *The Exhaustive Concordance of the Bible: Showing Every Word of the Text of the Common English Version of the Canonical Books, and Every Occurrence of Each Word in Regular Order; Together with a Key-Word Comparison of Selected Words and Phrases in the King James Version with Five Leading Contemporary Translations; Also Brief Dictionaries of the Hebrew and Greek Words of the Original, with References to the English Words.* Thirty-eighth printing. Nashville: Abingdon, 1980. Copyrighted 1890. Key-word comparison updated by Abingdon.

Thayer, Joseph H. *Thayer's Greek-English Lexicon of the New Testament: Coded with Strong's Concordance Numbers.* Peabody: Hendrickson, 2007. Reprinted from the 1896 fourth edition published by T&T Clark. Strong's numbering added by Hendrickson.

Talmudic Writings

Cohen, Abraham. *Everyman's Talmud: The Major Teachings of the Rabbinic Sages.* New York: Schocken, 1995. Reprinted from the 1949 edition published by E. P. Dutton.

Etheridge, J. W., ed. *The Targums of Onkelos and Jonathan ben Uzziel on the Pentateuch, with the Fragments of the Jerusalem Targum; From the Chaldee.* 2 vols. New York: KTAV, 1968. First published in 1862.

BIBLIOGRAPHY

Rapaport, Samuel., ed. *A Treasury of the Midrash*. New York: KTAV, 1968. First published in 1907 as *Tales and Maxims from the Midrash*.

Rodkinson, Michael Levi, Isaac Mayer Wise, and Godfrey Taubenhaus, eds. *New Edition of the Babylonian Talmud: Original Text, Edited, Corrected, Formulated, and Translated into English*. Bound in 10 vols. Boston: New Talmud, 1896–1903. Internal tract/volume, not bound volume, divisions are used in footnote citations.

PATRISTIC WRITINGS

Augustine of Hippo. *The City of God*. 1993 Modern Library edition. Translated by Marcus Dods. New York: Modern Library, 1994. Augustine lived 354–430.

Augustine of Hippo. *Confessions*. Oxford World's Classics. Translated by Henry Chadwick. New York: Oxford UP, 1998.

Norris, Richard A., Jr., ed. *The Christological Controversy*. Sources of Early Christian Thought. Series editor: William G. Rusch. Philadelphia: Fortress, 1982.

Roberts, Alexander, James Donaldson, A. Cleveland Coxe, and Allan Menzies, eds. *Ante-Nicene Fathers: The Writings of the Fathers down to AD 325*. Revised and chronologically arranged, with brief prefaces and occasional notes. 10 vols. Peabody: Hendrickson, 1995. Reprint edition of the American edition published 1885–1897 by Christian Literature Publishing.

Rusch, William G., ed. *The Trinitarian Controversy*. Sources of Early Christian Thought. Series editor: William G. Rusch. Philadelphia: Fortress, 1980.

Schaff, Philip, ed. *Nicene and Post-Nicene Fathers: A Select Library of the Christian Church; First Series*. 14 vols. Peabody: Hendrickson, 1995. Reprint edition of the American edition published 1886–1889 by Christian Literature Publishing.

Schaff, Philip, and Henry Wace, eds. *Nicene and Post-Nicene Fathers: A Select Library of the Christian Church; Second Series*. 14 vols. Peabody: Hendrickson, 1995. Reprint edition of the American editions published 1890–1898 by Christian Literature Publishing (vols. 1–8, 10–13) and 1899–1900 by Charles Scribner's Sons (vols. 9 and 14). Pagination of vols. 9 and 12 both subdivided.

BIBLIOGRAPHY

BIBLICAL COMMENTARIES

Clarke, Adam. *The Holy Bible Containing the Old and New Testaments: The Text Carefully Printed from the Most Correct Copies of the Present Authorized Translation, including the Marginal Readings and Parallel Texts; With a Commentary and Critical Notes Designed as a Help to a Better Understanding of the Sacred Writings.* A new edition, with the author's final corrections. 6 vols. New York: Abingdon-Cokesbury, [n.d.]. The first edition of Clarke's commentary was published in 1826.

Clifford, Richard J. Introduction and commentary on Genesis 1:1–25:18 in *The New Jerome Biblical Commentary*, 8–28. Edited by Raymond E. Brown, Joseph A. Fitzmyer, and Roland E. Murphy. Englewood Cliffs: Prentice-Hall, 1990. Previously published as *The Jerome Biblical Commentary*.

Coffman, James Burton. *Commentary on Genesis: The First Book of Moses.* James Burton Coffman Commentaries. Abilene: ACU Press, 1985.

Gill, John. *Gill's Commentary.* 6 vols. Grand Rapids: Baker, 1980. Reprinted from the 1852–1854 edition published by William Hill.

Guzik, David. *Verse-by-Verse Commentary on the Book of Genesis.* Enduring Word Commentary Series. Simi Valley: Enduring Word, 1998.

Henry, Matthew. Condensed commentary in *The Comprehensive Commentary on the Holy Bible: Containing the Text according to the Authorised Version; Scott's Marginal References; Matthew Henry's Commentary, Condensed, but Retaining Every Useful Thought; The Practical Observations of Rev. Thomas Scott, D.D., with Extensive Explanatory, Critical, and Philological Notes, Selected from Scott, Doddridge, Gill, Adam Clarke, Patrick, Poole, Lowth, Burder, Harmer, Calmet, Stuart, Robinson, Bush, Rosenmueller, Bloomfield, and Many Other Writers on the Scriptures; The Whole Designed to Be a Digest and Combination of the Advantages of the Best Bible Commentaries, and Embracing Nearly All That Is Valuable in Henry, Scott, and Doddridge; Conveniently Arranged for Family and Private Reading, and at the Same Time Particularly Adapted to the Wants of Sabbath School Teachers, and Bible Classes; With Numerous Useful Tables, and a Neatly Engraved Family Record; Embellished with Five Portraits, and Other Elegant Engravings, from Steel Plates; Several Maps, and Many Wood Cuts, Illustrative of Scripture Manners, Customs, Antiquities, etc.* Edited by Rev. William Jenks. 5 vols. Brattleboro: Fessenden, 1835. The first volume of Henry's original commentary was published in 1708.

BIBLIOGRAPHY

Jamieson, Robert, A. R. Fausset, and David Brown. *A Commentary, Critical, Experimental and Practical, on the Old and New Testaments*. 6 vols. Grand Rapids: Eerdmans, 1945. The first edition appeared 1864–1870.

Sarna, Nahum M. *Genesis: The Traditional Hebrew Text with New JPS Translation/Commentary*. The JPS Torah Commentary. Philadelphia: Jewish Publication Society, 1989.

Scofield, C. I. *The Scofield Reference Bible: The Holy Bible; Containing the Old and New Testaments; Authorized Version; With a New System of Connected Topical References to All the Greater Themes of Scripture, with Annotations, Revised Marginal Renderings, Summaries, Definitions, Chronology and Index. To Which Are Added, Helps at Hard Places, Explanations of Seeming Discrepancies, and a New System of Paragraphs*. New and improved edition. London: Oxford UP, 1945. Reprinted from the 1917 edition.

Viviano, Pauline A. Introduction and commentary on Genesis in *The Collegeville Bible Commentary: Based on the New American Bible with Revised New Testament*, 35–78. Edited by Dianne Bergant and Robert J. Karris. Collegeville: Liturgical Press, 1989.

Waltke, Bruce K., with Cathi J. Fredricks. *Genesis: A Commentary*. Grand Rapids: Zondervan, 2001.

Wesley, John. *Explanatory Notes upon the Old Testament*. 3 vols. Salem, Ohio: Schmul, 1975. Reprinted from the 1765–1766 edition. Script updated when quoted.

Whittingham, William, Miles Coverdale, Christopher Goodman, Anthony Gilby, Thomas Sampson, William Cole, John Knox, William Kethe, Rowland Hall, John Pullain, John Bodley, John Baron, and William Williams. Marginal annotations in *The Geneva Bible: A Facsimile of the 1560 Edition*. Facsimile introduction by Lloyd E. Berry. Madison: University of Wisconsin Press, 1969. Attribution uncertain, including the influence of John Calvin. Pagination by leafs, not pages; script updated when quoted.

Modern Christian Thought

Lewis, C. S. *Mere Christianity*. A revised and enlarged edition, with a new introduction, of the three books *The Case for Christianity*, *Christian Behavior*, and *Beyond Personality*. New York: Macmillan, 1984. The revised edition was first published in 1952.

Lewis, C. S. *The Screwtape Letters, with Screwtape Proposes a Toast*. Revised edition. New York: Macmillan, 1982. Lewis's preface dated 1960.

BIBLIOGRAPHY

CATECHISMS, ENCYCLOPEDIAS, DICTIONARIES

Aquinas, Thomas. *Summa theologica*. First complete American edition. Translated by Fathers of the English Dominican Province. 3 vols. New York: Benziger, 1947–1948. *Summa theologica* was originally written ca. 1265–1273.

Hopko, Thomas. *The Orthodox Faith*. Second edition. 4 vols. New York: Department of Religious Education, OCA, 1976–1981.

Luther, Martin. *The Large Catechism of Martin Luther*. Translated by Robert H. Fischer. Philadelphia: Fortress, 1959. Luther's *Large Catechism* was formulated in 1529.

Pace, Edward A., James J. Walsh, Peter Guilday, John J. Wynne, and Blanche M. Kelly, eds. *The Catholic Encyclopedia: A General Work of Reference for Art, Biography, Education, History, Law, Literature, Philosophy, the Sciences, Religion, and the Church*. Revised and enlarged edition. 16 vols. New York: Gilmary Society, ca. 1936.

Roman Catholic Church. *Catechism of the Catholic Church: With Modifications from the Editio typica*. Second edition. New York: Doubleday, 1997.

Singer, Isidore, ed., assisted by American and foreign boards of consulting editors. *The Jewish Encyclopedia: A Descriptive Record of the History, Religion, Literature, and Customs of the Jewish People from the Earliest Times*. 12 vols. New York: KTAV, 1916.

Unger, Merrill F. *The New Unger's Bible Dictionary*. Revised and updated edition. Edited by R. K. Harrison, Howard F. Vos, and Cyril J. Barber. Chicago: Moody Press, 1988. Original work copyrighted 1957.

APOLOGETICS

McDowell, Josh. *Evidence That Demands a Verdict: Historical Evidences for the Christian Faith*. San Bernardino: Campus Crusade for Christ International, 1972.

McDowell, Josh. *More Evidence That Demands a Verdict: Historical Evidences for the Christian Scriptures*. San Bernardino: Campus Crusade for Christ International, 1975.

BIBLIOGRAPHY

Hermeneutics

Alter, Robert, and Frank Kermode, eds. *The Literary Guide to the Bible*. Cambridge, Mass.: Belknap Press of Harvard UP, 1987.

Perrine, Laurence. *Literature: Structure, Sound, and Sense*. Second edition. New York: Harcourt Brace Jovanovich, 1974.

Ramm, Bernard. *Protestant Biblical Interpretation: A Textbook of Hermeneutics*. Third revised edition. Grand Rapids: Baker, 2004. Copyrighted 1970.

Historical Works

Darwin, Charles. *The Descent of Man, and Selection in Relation to Sex*. New edition, revised and augmented. New York: D. Appleton, 1876.

De Hamel, Christopher. *The Book: A History of the Bible*. London: Phaidon, 2001.

Nicolson, Adam. *God's Secretaries: The Making of the King James Bible*. New York: HarperCollins, 2003.

Norton, David. *A Textual History of the King James Bible*. Cambridge: Cambridge UP, 2005.

Shanks, Hershel. *The Mystery and Meaning of the Dead Sea Scrolls*. New York: Random House, 1998.

Ussher, James. *The Annals of the World*. Revised and updated by Larry and Marion Pierce. Green Forest: Master, 2003. The first English edition was published in 1658.

Prophecy

Haggith, David. *End-Time Prophecies of the Bible*. New York: Putnam's Sons, 1999.

Demonology

Martin, Malachi. *Hostage to the Devil: The Possession and Exorcism of Five Living Americans*. [San Francisco]: HarperSanFrancisco, 1992.

REX FROST was born in the late 1960s and was raised in the Midwestern United States. The religious backdrop of the author's youth was Separate Baptist and Southern Baptist, though he is now a nondenominational Bible Christian. The author holds bachelor's degrees in chemistry and chemical engineering and a doctor's degree in physical chemistry, and he has worked in the field of microprocessor fabrication research and development. The author's earliest publications are technical, comprising epitaxy modeling, atmospheric photochemistry, and molecular spectroscopy journal articles, as well as various semiconductor lithography patents.

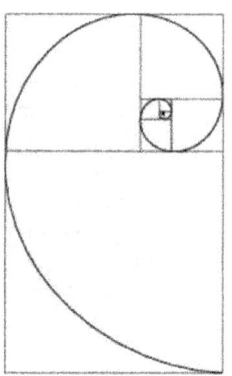

www.ingramcontent.com/pod-product-compliance
Lightning Source LLC
Chambersburg PA
CBHW051645040426
42446CB00009B/988